Interstate Compacts

A Question of Federalism

MARIAN E. RIDGEWAY

Southern Illinois University Press   Carbondale and Edwardsville

Feffer & Simons, Inc.   London and Amsterdam

CONTENTS

CONTENTS

PREFACE

INTERSTATE COMPACTS, in domestic United States political literature, have been inadequately examined. Possibly this results from a
condition which for many years of our national life characterized such
compacts: they were seldom utilized and, where they were, they were
applied in a traditional pattern, based on rather settled legal understandings and concerned with matters of limited controversy. They
were used as means to reach agreement between two or more states on
troublesome matters of a narrow, intimate kind, of vital importance
only to the states involved. They were never used to shape and administer complicated and intricate problems of far-reaching state social
and economic policy. Boundary disputes—the surveying and laying of
a proper and acceptable dividing line, or determination of respective
jurisdictions where a stream served as a boundary—were their most
common subjects.

In such uses the Compact Clause of the Constitution was applied according to its original intent. Modeling it on the long-held
principle of international law that sovereign states should have means
to resolve joint matters of mutual concern administratively, without
engaging the full government in its full operations if not absolutely
needed, the Founding Fathers included the Compact Clause almost
as a matter of course, with little discussion and almost no debate. It
is certain that none foresaw any such uses for interstate compacts as
are assigned to them today by more and more state and national
legislation. It is also certain that if such uses had been foreseen, there
would very likely have been extensive debate.

For many of the Constitution's authors were intensely concerned
with guaranteeing the continuity of the individual states, their shape,
powers, independence and sovereignty. They were keenly aware that
the state system itself was not altogether compatible with centralized

government and that some states might sometime make some kind of formal interstate agreement which would endanger the Union as a whole. Therefore, while conceding to the states a power they already held, they hedged it by requiring Congress's permission for any such proposed interstate treaty before it can take effect.

It is clear the expectation was that Congress would give full consideration to each compact coming before it, examining purposes and content and possibilities for state encroachment upon national powers. It is equally clear that the envisaged dangers lay in possibilities for interstate conspiracy by a few states against the remainder, or of entangling alliances which might imperil the national peace and safety. Assuredly not anticipated were interstate compacts which would provide means for semiprivate exercise of governmental policy-making power with few or no controls by any government whatsoever, such as today's Interstate Oil and Gas Compact appears to have encouraged. None foresaw possibilities in interstate compacts for bypassing state governments in order to augment the power of metropolitan areas — great concentrations of dense population, nonexistent in 1781, sprawling across municipal, county, and state lines — rendering them in many matters virtually independent of controls either by their states or by their electorates, and handing over policy and administration to small bodies of appointive and ex officio officials, unknown and often unaccountable in a regular way to the masses of inhabitants. Such are today's several "economic development compacts" — the Delaware River Commission, the New York Port Authority, the Bi-State Development Agency of Illinois and Missouri. (In some respects such are the "councils of government," encouraged for metropolitan areas in recent federal laws now in effect to supplant and circumvent the delays and obstructions of established state and local governments, and in which interstate compacts today frequently are involved.)

Our concern, however, is not altogether with the intent of the Constitution's authors but with interstate compacts that have actually occurred, what they do and what can be expected in the future from this inadequately defined but potentially quite useful legal mechanism. Is it a tool to subvert established government or is it a constitutional doorway to the modern federalism of an adaptable kind which so many have been seeking? What can a proliferation of many-purposed interstate compacts mean to the federal system over the long run? Is the current ubiquity of compacts indicative of an end to traditional views of state and local governments and the beginning of new concepts concerning them?

These are important questions. As noted, they have been inadequately examined. To be sure, the Council of State Governments has long kept an eye on all new activity in this field, gathering the surface facts, lending tacit and generally uncritical approval to new compacts, and occasionally designing them for state adoption. But the Council has not provided the probing, analytical examination of active compacts such as would seem demanded of so dynamic a constitutional development. Further, the seemingly routine handling of some compact renewals by Congress is a rather disturbing revelation to persons holding traditional academic views of the proper role of Congress in policy matters. As a regular practice, it appears, congressional committee recommendations on compacts in the past have been approved with little more than a flurry of attention from the whole Congress, and the committees themselves generally issue scanty, sterile reports, barren of any but the most innocuous statements of approval. Interstate compacts, once entered with consent granted, too frequently receive no more congressional attention. This picture is duplicated in state governments.

Enlightenment from state governments on the workings of particular interstate compacts is not easily or quickly obtained. Information can never be found in a single source, clear, detailed, and complete. With the exception of those who administer particular compacts, few state officials know anything about their operations, and those who do sometimes evince surprise that any questions should arise at all. This is, then, something of a "dark continent."

This study, therefore, seeks to cast a little light on this aspect of today's state governments. Prompted as it is by the uncomfortable knowledge that changes are being wrought in the constitutional system, and that these are coming about without wide public awareness or appreciation, it attempts to bring into focus and attention four of the more dynamic interstate compacts of a single state: Illinois (and by necessity also of the other states to which she is party in each of them). These have been examined from an Illinois interest. That is, where such a "treaty" has involved Illinois and Indiana as, for example, does the Wabash Valley Interstate Compact, it has been examined primarily from the Illinois point of view. Where a compact has involved Illinois and Missouri, it is Illinois's interest that has been chiefly considered. Physical, time, and energy limitations require this. To provide a full examination of each compact to which Illinois is party could require a researcher's traveling into as many as thirty or more states of the Union, as are involved in the Interstate Oil and Gas Compact. No matter how desirable this intensive examination might be, it is not necessary for the kind of survey that is attempted here. The present study, limited as it is, necessitated visits to five additional states.

What is sought is information as to the number, nature, kind, and potentialities of the interstate compacts Illinois has entered. What is partially probed is the background and history of a few of these efforts to discover why the compacts arose, how they have been applied, what they have accomplished, and where we are headed in continuing their use. The difficulties of delving deeply into all of Illinois's existing and anticipated interstate arrangements of a formal compact nature are so great as to require confining effort to a selected few. It is regrettable that this is so, for depth probes and close examination of all of them are needed.

The Illinois compacts which most impellingly engage attention are those which least resemble the interstate compacts of the Founding Fathers' acquaintance. Today's governmental economic and social welfare activities appear to be intimately interwoven with the future of this device. Certain ones of these compacts reveal much of the governmental policy-shaping process at the state level today, and show as well the built-in limitations of interstate operations of a cooperative nature and the difficulties encountered.

This, then, is a development in American government involving the nation, the states, the constitutional and organic political life of the American people. A macrocosmic view of a microcosmic segment of that life seems indicated, even at the risk of allowing a few open-ended and ill-defined ideas to creep into the fabric of the piece. The study is scientific in the sense that it has been written by one who has acquired some technical knowledge of the subject and who assumes also that those who read it will quite likely be only those who have a specialized interest in the workings of American government, and that reasonably accurate ideas can thus be handed from writer to reader without too much confusion, inaccuracy, or misdirection.

An active area of governmental concern always carries with it the likelihood that legislation will be enacted before the study appears which may change the factual picture presented. This study's review of data surrounding the four interstate compacts here examined was for the most part carried only through June 1969.

What results is of course uniquely the author's responsibility, as it is customary to observe. The writer was given a large boost toward accomplishing this work by the 1966 Commission on State Government—Illinois, which utilized her as a research consultant in its survey of existing executive branch organization and functioning. Subsequently a grant by Southern Illinois University of a full year's sabbatical leave made possible the completion of earlier research effort, superficially begun and only partially completed. Due gratitude and appreciation is here expressed. More universities should provide more of this kind of untrammeled freedom to those of their faculties who wish to examine important problems of human existence. It is a great help, and the writer is happy to be a part of an institution which not only recognizes the need, but is quick and generous in responding to it.

Marian E. Ridgeway

Carbondale, Illinois
January 1971

ACKNOWLEDGMENTS

THE ASSISTANCE, cooperation, and advice of numerous persons have gone into this study's preparation. It is hoped that recognition here of those most helpful will partially repay them for their courtesy, kindness, time, and toleration and adequately express the author's gratitude and appreciation.

A most special debt is owed to the author's colleagues, Professors Jack F. Isakoff and David Kenney of the Department of Government at Southern Illinois University. The former provided the initial opportunity to explore more thoroughly a field which first engaged the author's attention in the 1950s; the latter provided encouragement, reading, analysis and advice on parts of the manuscript in its early stages. No less a debt is owed Professor Orville Alexander, former chairman of the department, for his willingness to allow released time from teaching obligations. Last, special appreciation is here expressed for the financial assistance granted by Southern Illinois University's Office of Research and Projects.

Among the others who made it possible to bring something more than an academic approach to the study were Mr. B. K. Barton, Executive Director of the Wabash Valley Interstate Commission; Col. R. E. Smyser, Jr., Executive Director of the Bi-State Development Agency; Mr. Earl Foster, a former executive secretary of the Interstate Oil and Gas Compact Commission, and the late Mr. Lawrence Alley, also a former executive secretary of that agency; Mr. Leonard J. Goodsell, executive director of the Great Lakes Commission; Mr. Eugene Moody of the East-West Gateway Coordinating Council; Mr. Guy E. McGaughey, Illinois representative of the Interstate Oil Compact Commission; Mr. C. W. Klassen, technical secretary of the Illinois Sanitary Water Board; Mr. Bill Day, of the Illinois Legislative Research Council; and attorneys Randall Robertson and Leo H. Konzen of the law firm of Lueders, Robertson & Konzen, Granite City, Illinois. Not the least of all the helpful persons was Mrs. Mara Lou Hawse, whose services in the tedious work of typing the final manuscript the writer was fortunate to obtain.

I   The American federal system is the greatest invention of government in the world. It provides a dynamic balance between national unity and local autonomy. But federalism is under fire. If our several layers of government cannot be coordinated to meet the needs of our citizens, and cannot adopt priorities to reach the urban ghetto and the pockets of rural blight, then what is to become of our federal system? If government can't do the job, is the result to be anarchy? This is the serious concern of this subcommittee. We know the problems, and we want to find out what positive action must come from the governmental machinery best equipped to solve them.

·   ·   ·   ·   ·   ·   ·   ·   ·   ·   ·   ·

I don't want broad general answers to these questions for political science scholars to add to already overstocked libraries. I want the details of what hasn't been done—and what is being done.

Senator Edmund S. Muskie, Maine, to the United States Senate Committee on Government Operations Subcommittee on Intergovernmental Relations, February 6, 1967.

There is a fresh spirit in the State houses of the Nation—a spirit that is working to adapt State and local structures to the realities of our changing social and economic scene—a spirit that seeks to articulate broad national objectives while expanding public participation in their implementation.

It is the spirit of interstate compacts, regional cooperation for the conservation of our huge river basins and for economic development of depressed and deprived areas.

Governor Philip H. Hoff, Vermont, to the United States Senate Committee on Government Operations Subcommittee on Intergovernmental Relations, January 31, 1967.

Introduction: *Today's Federalism*

MUCH HAS BEEN SAID about the myriad problems of vast complexity which confront American governments and our citizens today. Threaded through most of this outpouring of literature and legislation is the question: What about the system of American government—is it capable of surviving, as well as meeting and resolving the demands which arise from the needs of the American people and the other peoples of the world who look to us for help?

It is a troubling question, unnerving to all who know our government intimately. All aspects of the system reveal trouble spots. Some would say that it is like an old machine which has reached the end of its endurance and can only be shored up here and there for a few more miles of use. And they would point to its foundations, all of which have been shaken and shifted: constitutional government, popular will, states' rights, free elections, separation of powers, representative policy-making, rule by law, civil rights, federalism. None has been immune, none has escaped, none has demonstrated imperviousness to pressure or to challenge, none has withstood the erosion and corrosion of change, for better or for worse.

For governmental authority, today in the United States, is undergoing more serious and far-reaching distress than it has encountered in more than a century. The scale and substance of the pressures upon it defy easy and simplistic explanations. The magnitude and momentum of social needs and social movements have greatly accelerated, inflated, and escalated the burdens of all levels of government, and the resultant impetus for change in governmental powers, functions, duties, processes has become apparent to even the most resistant "stand-pat" elements of the people.

An increasing population, at once more mobile and fluid while remaining in many ways static and lethargic, is confronted with the tightening constrictions of decreasing space, diminishing and frequently mismanaged natural resources, altered economic opportunities, a shattered yet persistent moral and ethical code, an excessively complex web of law, and the limited vision, information, understanding, and prejudices that are always the lot of ordinary men. While no level of American government is insulated from the effects of all of this, it is the state and local governments which are particularly vulnerable and least able to respond to the challenges. For, under the federal principle, it is these governments which hold fundamental constitutional authority over the lives of men, down at the grass roots where they are born and die and have their being. It is these governments which seem all too often incapable of rising above their circumscribed worlds of established activity to obtain new perspectives on themselves and the clamoring populations to whom they are responsible.

All students of American government know that around the turn of this century the relationships of states, national government, and people began to alter with a heightening role being played by the national government in matters formerly of scant concern to it, the offshoot of urbanism, industrialization, and the First World War. The Great Depression and the New Deal substantially augmented the forces of change, and the post–World War II decades provided the additional stimuli necessary to complete the trend. Today, our federal system, in its manifest image, is a centralized system consisting of a vast and powerful national government, subsidiary state governments, and increasingly autonomous municipal governments, and counties (except for a few notable exceptions) that have become relatively static—the sleepy, vestigial remains of a dying ruralism—agents of diminishing vitality and essentiality clinging tenaciously to powers long held. Added to the whole as a not very new but still largely ill-defined and bewildering variable are further jurisdictions: regional authorities, metropolitan districts and governmental arrangements of a multiple sort, special-purpose districts, and combination private-governmental agencies for combined private-governmental purposes.

These are the realities of our national life, yet the underpinnings of the system remain almost the same as they were originally constructed. Written constitutions and laws allocating powers and responsibilities read much as they have always read. The text, the common understandings and interpretations, the processes, have altered very little, and then in detail rather than in basic design. What the theory and the law say about American government is not altogether what American government has become.

It was inescapable that the many governmental elements of the system would sometime have to respond more effectively to the needs and demands of the population or the whole noble structure would long since have collapsed. The response to the need came primarily from the national government, powerless under the Constitution to deal directly with most of the vital human problems requiring resolution, but blessed with a kind of impersonality which the state and local governments can never have, which enabled it to escape much of the powerful resistances of local and special interests antagonistic to change. It was, as well, armed with financial resources drawn from rich areas and poor areas alike, with an almost unlimited constitutional power to spend, enabling it to redistribute those financial resources and spend them where the national government felt the needs required it. The federal "welfare" law came into being, and the federal grant-in-aid became canonized as the chief instrument for accomplishing that which was not being accomplished by the grass-roots governments and which the federal government could not itself do.

Today we are experiencing the cumulative effects of this evolution. The pattern, at best, was born of expediency and improvisation. As such it has demonstrated the unwieldiness, inconsistency, and inefficiencies of all practices which are not part of a well-conceived policy that has carefully evolved under watchful oversight and attentive review. At best it has enabled the system to keep pace with time and circumstance, bridging the gaps in the federal structure and removing some of the barriers obstructing the relatively unified nation we have become. It has, at once, corrected and created problems. It has been enormously expensive and wasteful. Laws have proliferated to a point where even the Congress does not know what it has enacted. State and local governments flounder in a morass of random, duplicating, overlapping, and conflicting possibilities. Whether any other design would have been less costly and complicated is a moot question. Generally speaking, with all of the obvious benefits it made possible, it has not resulted in a viable government that can continue much longer under present conditions.

Most recently, the objectives of the Great Society program of the Johnson administration, impelled by the widespread civil disorders attending the dissents of the Negro community and the anti–Vietnam war elements, stimulated intensive reexamination of the entire federal-state relationship. As one might expect, the main arena for this reexamination was the Congress of the United States, increasingly troubled by the seeming failure of domestic America to make advances on many fronts which the national government in both its legislative and executive branches urged as imperative and to which the Congress responded affirmatively through enactment of a host of new national laws oriented around state and local assistance.

The search for a "creative federalism" expanded Congressional and national concern for the condition of state and local affairs. Rather than attempt the impossible—that is, seek constitutional alterations in the federal concept itself—national leaders, administrators, and students of government have urged that new and imaginative methods be sought to improve the existing mechanisms of state and local government. While money is an ever-present problem, the prime focus has been upon management and politics. The question is how to get the states, counties, and cities to work effectively, thus relieving the national government of its inadequate, legally restricted, adopted role wherever possible and enabling it to return to its proper role as guardian of overall national interests. In this, the role of the federal government itself has been exposed to new and critical review.

It is perhaps folly to entertain any sensible hope, in a country as governmentally fragmented as the United States, ever to obtain coordinated, evenly energetic, and simultaneous attacks everywhere on any particular governmental problem at one stipulated time. Yet this appears to have been the naïve aspiration of the New Deal years, and it seems to have been the implicit hope of Congress in almost all of the Great Society legislation. A social or economic problem is seen as a pressing need in all the major urban centers, and part of the rural. Legislation is drafted containing a statement of congressional recognition of need and providing the broad outlines of a program of correction designed to induce the interest, participation, and compliance of states, cities, counties, and private persons. A formula is included for distribution of the usual grants-in-aid, providing a stipulated sum for the first stages of the program, with added provisions for subsequent years to an agreed-upon cutoff date, at which time congressional renewal or discontinuation of the program presumably is to be given; and it will suggest or direct arrangements for administration of the program. At an earlier stage in the evolutionary development of the grant-in-aid type of legislation, a fiercely jealous federal bureau or department would be established to push and police the program. Sufficient inducement to the states was seen in the federal offer to donate a part of the necessary money, and the elaboration of the details of administration was largely left up to the federal field staff, closely reporting to its Washington bureau. To a considerable extent, this traditional pattern continues to govern the minds of congressmen, but with time and experience and many national tribulations in effectuating the purposes of many programs, some legislators have acquired a more knowledgeable awareness that few if any of the welfare needs of the nation can be controlled and governed by Washington, from Washington, in Washington, and at Washington's desire, as long as there are literally thousands of smaller but enormously powerful little strongholds of political obtuseness and legally independent authority standing monumentally in the way of Washington's conceptions of progress, upholding their own legal rights, their entrenched and habitual political alignments, and preferred local ways of doing things.

Thus recognition has come to be accorded to disparities within areas, and the concept of the region has crept into the legislation, attending which is a chronic difficulty of ascertaining the proper boundaries of a particular region for particular purposes. Even smaller bailiwicks of narrower interests have been designated as districts for the administration of particular programs. But with both the region and the district, Congress is confronted with the sin of aiding and abetting governmental proliferation through superimposition by federal statute of new levels, strata, entities of government, unanticipated by the Constitution and in essence neither federal, state, or local, thus being proportionately fragmented in authority and power to compel respect while complicating greatly the already complex structure. Insistently, congressional committees have been beset with demands from governors, mayors, local officials, and lobbyists of special interest groups, for relief from the burgeoning, labyrinthian architecture, and for increased autonomy and independence in the handling of grants-in-aid programs.

Quite recently the no-strings-attached block grant to states has been urged, particularly by the Republican party in an effort to acquire a new and effective lure for that beleagured party and, no doubt, because it offers some obvious advantages to states and local governments if it can be worked out feasibly. To date the disadvantages have appeared greater than the possible benefits, and although congressional committees have repeatedly referred to the concept, little has been done to bring it about.

The Johnson administration itself promoted the idea of "councils of government"—alluded to by public administrators as COGs—to supplement and replace the unworkable and unworking arrangements of the past in local governmental affairs. Some of the more significant legislation of the Johnson years included a new clause in grants-in-aid laws: broadly worded provisions giving federal sanction and encouragement to states to create "regional arrangements, interstate compacts, districts, metropolitan economic and social planning agencies, and councils of government" to effectuate the purposes and goals of the laws.

Inevitably, the result has been monumental confusion. With the domestic, economic and social welfare laws of the Johnson and previous administrations multiplying in number, there was disorder approaching chaos as to knowledge of what was happening in the planning-and-getting activities of states, counties, villages, cities, special districts, interstate compact agencies, towns, metropolitan areas, and the federal government's bureaus and departments. Nowhere was the knowledge more confused than in Washington itself, yet the same kind of ignorance was acutely manifest in state capitols, city halls, and state and local bureaus. County and city jurisdictions, overlapping and operating side by side, did not know what each other was doing, and their special purpose districts' commissions moved untrammeled and alone, with minimal regard to any other governmental bodies except those to which they were linked by some kind of legal umbilical cord.

By September 1966, there were 173 federal aid programs administered by thirteen federal departments and agencies; 125 federal bureaus were involved, as well as hundreds of state and local offices. Within this imposing statistical morass, there were more than 92,000 units of local government, which in the words of Senator Edmund S. Muskie, were operating "each with its own degree of independent autonomy, taxing and financing power and operating capability." [1]

Belatedly, the federal government, through its executive branch, recognized the "obvious need for developing jurisdictional and planning coordination at state and local levels." The congressional response resulted from a Presidential Memorandum of September 2, 1966, in which the president requested the secretaries of Commerce, HEW, HUD, Interior, Agriculture; the director of OEO, the cochairmen of the Appalachian Regional Commission, and the director of the Bureau of the Budget, to work with the last-named official "to insure the fullest coordination in fixing the boundaries of multijurisdictional planning units assisted by the Federal Government." Pointing out that comprehensive planning offered promise as a means to resolve the critical state, metropolitan and regional problems confronting the nation, the memorandum urged cooperation and coordination through the use of common or consistent planning bases—defined as "statistical and economic estimates"—the sharing of facilities and resources, and the fixing of boundaries for planning and development districts which would be the same and consistent with established state planning districts and regions. Exceptions were to be made only where there was "clear justification." [2]

Actually, while emanating from the president's office, the memorandum was in part a response to a general proposal made by Senator Muskie earlier in 1966 for more effective federal handling of this gigantic problem. The proposal, as shaped into bills, consisted of S. 3408, S. 3509, and S. 561, to upgrade personnel operating in the intergovernmental field at all levels of government, to establish a new permanent operating unit in the Executive Office of the President to coordinate and enforce federal programs and policies in this area, and to provide more effectively for intergovernmental cooperation. All of these became the subject of the extensive "creative federalism" hearings held during 1967 by Senator Muskie's Subcommittee on Intergovernmental Relations, involving the 90th Congress's S. 671 and S. 698, bills containing the same proposals as those of 1966.[3]

As with almost all major constitutional developments in American government, improvements in ways of doing things nearly always result only after cataclysmic events. The present compulsive efforts being accorded the intergovernmental relations problem are evidence of the urgency of the need, now elevated to something more than the threshold level of public awareness. Attention has moved out of the halls of governmental and academic bodies and into the arena of popular journalism and man-in-the-streets thinking. But that it has not progressed very far into public consciousness is reflected by the 1968 annual meeting of the American Society for Public Administration which, for the first time in its history, gave over to its full program the intergovernmental question. And it can certainly be said that even with heightened attention and awareness of need for solutions, there has not yet been a corresponding response in workable answers.

Many governmental realities militate against immediate resolution of the tremendous difficulties. First in importance, of course, are the constitutions and laws of this nation, relatively unchanging and extraordinarily difficult to change once in effect, and daily acquiring more and more solidity and permanence as, like coral reefs, they gradually build up their encrustations of particularistic special interests with a stake in their perpetuation. It is a truism that, once created, American governmental agencies rarely are abolished. Their purposes and procedures quickly harden into lasting expectations and traditions, and only social revolution itself can finally blast them away or into obsolescence and decay by attrition. Second, and equally imperative, are legal boundary lines which delineate and delimit the exercise of authority. A city's outermost limits are more flexible and fluid than most governmental boundaries, but even they are all too frequently altered only after traumatic local effort. State lines are, to all intents and purposes, eternal. State authority, likewise, is as eternal as the United States Constitution. Third, and by no means less important than the others, are the agencies, offices, officeholders, property owners, political parties and party officials, businessmen, professionals who serve all the others, and rank-and-file Americans with permanent jobs and daily needs and habits which require round-the-clock regularity in public services for their yesterdays, todays, and tomorrows, if they are to function, to live in decency and reasonable public peace, and to pay the taxes which government cannot exist without. Fourth, and by no stretch of the imagination of lesser rank than all the rest, is human communication, understanding, knowledge, always lagging behind in social and economic affairs. The god-view is the privilege and gift of few men; yet ours is a democracy in which ordinary men of ordinary knowledge and intelligence are bequeathed the power to govern.

All of these realities and countless others operate to maintain that which exists and militate against that which might be. Yet change occurs. To date it has been occurring by superimposition of the new upon the foundations and superstructure of the old, and the edifice which is emerging is the one we have been describing.

Order Out of Chaos?

As surely as night follows day, governmental reform efforts spawn in their wake organizational accretions. Old established agencies, hardened into their bureaucratic moulds of self-service and special interest-service, are usually deemed incapable of grasping and absorbing policies which come upon them from outside rather than at their own behest. Policy-makers therefore anticipate bureaucratic resistances and incapacities when new policies are enacted and inevitably provide for creation of a new, untried agency, staffed as a rule with the zealots and proponents of the new idea, the new regime. The stratagem carries with it a certain built-in antagonism, a charge of tensions, and a momentum which instantly sparks to life and sets in motion the reactions of those elements of the established regime which most immediately relate to the new. The wave of shock travels outward, until an entire government, an entire community, an entire state, may be engulfed and embroiled in various of its influences. Depending upon the spirit pervading the community-at-large, the new agency will either triumph and supersede the old, will itself succumb under the opposition it encounters, or be gradually accomodated and, if so, take its place among the older members as a respectable and accepted bureau of tolerable status. In any eventuality, some portion of the new agency's purposes remain a part of the old, either in spirit or in substance, and this is the reason for governmental proliferation.

It is this process that characterizes today's widespread concern for the states and local governments, giving rise to a myriad criticisms like the following not surprising reaction of the National Association of Manufacturers, a cogent and all-too-true appraisal.

Four hundred sets of compliance requirements have led to federal interference with both state administration and policy. State and local officials have indicated that the results have been more coercive than stimulative. Planning, performance, and budgeting are all influenced, sometimes distorted—not only by the grants, but by the lure of them. Grants have acted as a wedge, or heightened the differences, between the state administrative and legislative branches, and between the states and their localities.

Instead of welding the federal system into a fully functional operation, the best intentions of a concerned Congress and an earnest Administration have resulted in doing the federal system the disservice of weakening its fulcrum—the states.[4]

It is this state of affairs, which carries within it the seeds of total breakdown for the American system through activities and policies arising out of urgencies and the best intentions in the world, but based on inadequate understanding and interpretation of the complexities of the system itself, that has stimulated a considerable number of scattered efforts to bring control and order into the picture before it is too late.

It was during the Truman administration that attention first was drawn by the first "Hoover Commission" to the intergovernmental question. During the Eisenhower administration, a President's Advisory Committee on Intergovernmental Relations (the "Kestnbaum Commission") was named to investigate the need for a federally-based agency to explore and inform the president on intergovernmental matters. In 1959, the Advisory Commission on Intergovernmental

Relations was created, a staff agency designed to study, gather data, and advise both executive and legislative of problems of the federal system.[5] In nearly a decade this agency has more than proved the wisdom of its creation, particularly in terms of its usefulness to the federal government. Today the question is whether it ought not to be placed upon a stronger and more purposeful basis.

Other moves have resulted. President Lyndon Johnson took the ground-breaking step in March 1965, of naming the vice-president as his liaison with local government. This use of the vice-presidential office was of course not to be construed as either a permanent role or creation of a permanent agency or division within the Office of the President, since it was founded entirely upon a particular president's requirements and upon his relationships to a particular vice-president who happened to have an interest in and an aptitude for the matter at hand. If, however, the duties can somehow become institutionalized in future administrations, the arrangement offers definite possibilities as an answer to the old and persistent American governmental question of what to do with the vice-president, how to involve him in top-level administration and make best use of his talents, and how to train him for takeover of the presidency if the need arises. If a president and a vice-president work well together, it can provide a powerful channel of information and advice for any president on state and local matters. Hopefully, it can improve the institutional needs of the presidential office as well. While Spiro Agnew's duties as of this writing have not yet been clearly defined, it is heartening to note President Richard Nixon's seeming approval of the Humphrey precedent, for his early announcements stressed a state-oriented liaison role for Agnew.

Concurrently, another move at the top of the federal government was the dynamic activation of the Subcommittee on Intergovernmental Relations of the Senate Committee on Governmental Operations, under Senator Edmund S. Muskie's chairmanship. This and its House equivalent have sponsored research, held hearings of a most comprehensive sort, and introduced legislation that has had the total effect of lifting to the surface of the murky morass the points where reform and constructive action are imperatively needed. The subcommittee has not only itself developed high expertise and accumulated knowledge of the world with which it is dealing, it has through its hearings and its relationships with governors, municipal officials, federal and other governmental figures, and the press, become an increasingly important fulcrum of public education, stimulating thought, interest, and action on the part of more and more persons intimately concerned and vitally motivated throughout the nation.

Within the states, at least twenty-two efforts have been made in the last several state governmental biennia to revise state constitutions comprehensively. Not all of these efforts have been successful in attaining the up-to-date charters that are so pressingly needed, but no such efforts are ever totally wasteful, for they bring to light the under-surface problems of state politics and provide the foundation for further action.

Another move of direct consequence to the states has been the establishment by the Governors' Conference of a national office in Washington. The exact value of this office is yet to be revealed, but its creation is evidence of heightening awareness by the states' chief executives that the intergovernmental problem requires close dealings on a bipartisan or nonpartisan basis with the sources of authority in the national capitol: more contacts with the Congress in the formulation of legislation; involvement in presidential policy moves; so that the flow of information comes from the states' top offices down to a state's administrators, rather than according to the prevalent process of information filtering up inadequately from state bureaus and city governments, after the fact, to a chief executive who is thus only informed as these lesser officials and politicians feel the need and to the extent they wish to reveal the facts.

Furthermore, by September 1967, sixteen states had created special agencies for local affairs within their state governments.[6] Ranging from California's Intergovernmental Council on Urban Growth, to Vermont's Office of Local Affairs, some are independent administrative departments, some are arms of the governor, placed within his office (or, like Tennessee, under its Comptroller of Treasury); but all are alike in being set up to provide coordinating and advisory functions to the states on the labyrinthian and exploding local governmental problem and its direct connection with federal welfare and grants-in-aid programs. They vary widely in the comprehensiveness of their powers and policy interests.[7] Perhaps the broadest are Pennsylvania's, New Jersey's, and Missouri's Departments of Community Affairs. The weakest of all are Tennessee's and Illinois's arrangements. Tennessee's Office of Local Government is confined to the legal aspects of intra-state relations, assisting and advising the governor in coordinating the state's relations with its local governments, and developing interlocal cooperation. Just as feeble was Illinois's Division of Local Government. Created in 1965 by an item in that year's appropriations act,[8] it was placed in the governor's office with a single employee, an assistant to the governor. His task was to gather facts to assist the governor in his coordinating efforts, with power to recommend programs and legislation. While a potentially influential office, its status without statutory action was dependent upon the wishes of the incumbent governor. In December 1968, newly elected Governor Richard B. Ogilvie announced his intention to request action by the legislature to create an office of local government. It is apparent the information gleaned under the previous arrangement was significant. Such an agency is imperatively needed by this great state with its 6,452 lesser units of government and its two great urban centers of metropolitan Chicago and metropolitan St. Louis.

Certain other moves arising from the work of the Advisory Commission on Intergovernmental Relations are indicative of the quickening responses in this field. For the first time in the nation's history, state legislative leaders were convened in Washington, October 13–14, 1967, to take a look at the need for reform of state legislatures and to spark awareness of the vital importance of a new approach to state legislative affairs. Significant appraisals of the results of this effort have not yet appeared, perhaps because of the obvious difficulties of measurement. It could not, however, have failed to have constructive effects on the thinking of the men who attended, opening minds to the crying need for intimate state legislative-congressional-federal involvement in the making of national laws and the carrying out of these laws for the assistance and improvement of state and local governments.

Additionally engaging recent congressional attention have been the newly enacted Intergovernmental Cooperation Act of 1968, and its fellow measure (not yet enacted), the proposed Act To Establish a National Intergovernmental Affairs Council.[9] Supplementing these two forward-looking proposals has been legislative action on the idea of creating a national "information bank" for the states and localities, investigation into which was authorized by the 89th Congress, Second Session, in S.J.Res. 187.

The proposed Intergovernmental Affairs Council would, if established, have an operating role within the Executive Office of the

President to coordinate federal aid policy, resolve agency conflicts, and provide a centralized office to which state and local governments might direct their problems. To date, senatorial opposition has deterred the idea's advancement.

The new Intergovernmental Cooperation Act of 1968, in Senator Muskie's words, is intended to

achieve the fullest cooperation and coordination of activities among the levels of government in order to improve the operation of our Federal system in an increasingly complex society to improve the administration of grants-in-aid; to provide technical services to State and local governments; to establish a coordinated intergovernmental policy and administration of grants and loans for urban development; to authorize the President to submit to the Congress for its consideration plans for the consolidation of individual categorical grants within broad functional areas; to provide for conformity in Federal acquisition, use, and development of urban land with local government programs; to provide for uniform relocation assistance to persons and businesses affected by federally assisted real property acquisition; and to provide for a uniform land acquisition policy in Federal and federally assisted programs.[10]

While it is too early to appraise the effectiveness of the new law, it is notable in that it was drafted after several sessions of Congress during which it received extensive attention from all levels of government. The Advisory Commission on Intergovernmental Relations played a prime role in drafting the law's various titles. Particularly admirable is the stipulation of the law that Federal granting agencies must favor existing general purpose governments in future, rather than bypass them for special purpose agencies as has been the practice in the past.

Other developments are emerging in the semipublic arena of the great nationwide special interest organizations. The National Association of Manufacturers, the Chamber of Commerce of the United States, the Committee for Economic Development, the American Assembly of Columbia University, the National Municipal League, the Association of American Cities, and the labor organizations have all recently adopted resolutions, written policy statements, and issued information materials voicing their attitudes and intentions to explore the intergovernmental relations problem.[11]

All of these cumulative activities suggest the nation can anticipate rapid developments in this area within the next several years. The problem is recognized, it exists, and concerned persons are exploring it. But constructive achievement is altogether another proposition, for we are dealing with the states; we are dealing with the local governments; we are dealing with the most stubborn, intractible, often unprogressive, ill-equipped, most constricted and—sadly—short-sighted areas of our national life, and improvement or change will not necessarily be achieved by issuing policy statements, writing additional laws, or creating new federal, state, or local agencies. Change and improvement must take place at the grass roots, in grass-roots attitudes and performances. At the present time, only the first inklings of the scope of the problem have filtered into the consciousness of the grass-roots populations and the elected or appointed officials of the nation's smaller cities and counties.

Interstate Compacts and Intergovernmental Relations

While the federal-state-local relationship is the prime concern of the national government, it is the interstate, the state-local, and the interregional relationships which engross the states and the grass-roots governments. These are of concern to the Congress as well, but that body until quite recently has given more attention to creating some of the complications now enjoyed in the lower levels of government than it has to finding methods to bring order and control into the overall picture. It is generous to a fault in giving blanket permission to the states, their counties and cities, to create regional arrangements to effectuate federally-desired policies and goals, but what kind of regional arrangements? What kind of interstate compacts? Districts? Metropolitan economic and social planning agencies? Councils of government? The Congress suggests but it does not altogether know; it stimulates creation and hopefully awaits something constructive to emerge as a result of its prodding.

Some guidelines exist for these regional designs. Some arrangements are in the experimental stage, some are merely hopeful aspirations. Most have not gotten beyond endless state and local planning sessions and the conference-committee-discussion-meeting-survey stage. Where the efforts of a state, a city, or a county in any of these devices for intergovernmental interaction have attained some shape and reality and a degree of success in action, they have become models which are eagerly seized and touted locally throughout the nation as examples of brilliant achievement, panaceas for emulation in any other local situation, without regard to the unresolved problems which may yet be confronting the original model on its own home ground. Thus borrowed methods and models have become local disasters, local headaches, local white elephants, and local failures. There is unfortunately no escape from this, for creativity in American government is not a universal talent and the pressure provided by the lure of a federal grant or the threat of a federal takeover in the absence of state or local response, to get something done as soon as possible and on the books requires men to look for patterns of action already existing. Today's expert professional groups and private consulting agencies add to the spread of the disease through their surveys and reports to governmental bodies which hire them, and their recommendations for action which are usually based upon what has demonstrated at least a surface degree of acceptance and workability in some other locality.

Thus, today, congressional inclusion of interstate compacts as acceptable interstate devices for effectuating interstate action, with the tacit and expressed permission of the Congress to the states to experiment widely and freely, is evidence of the universal acceptance by experts of the alleged merits of interstate compacts for doing anything which involves more than a single state. But this support is being given without regard to the deficiencies of the device, for there has been scant study accorded to the deficiencies except in isolated instances, and then the findings have not been widely disseminated.

But Congress is not alone. The highly respected Committee for Economic Development in 1967 issued its recommendations, *Modernizing State Governments*, and unqualifiedly included the following:

6. Interstate cooperation in solving mutual problems should be exploited actively through interstate compacts. Positive encouragement should be given to counties and other local units seeking collaboration with their counterparts both within the state and beyond its boundaries. Wider adoption of uniform state laws is needed. Active experimentation with new formulas for federal-multistate cooperation should be encouraged. All these measures can be taken without constitutional revision.

The Council of State Governments could play a more aggressive role in stimulating and coordinating action in each of these areas.

The committee rested its recommendations on its expressed fear of national governmental expansion, rather than on careful study of existing compacts and an increasing body of literature raising thought-provoking questions on the complexities of centralization, whether at the national or the local level.

According to the Council of State Governments, which has been a leading and uncritical proponent of interstate compacts for a widening range of activities, until 1920 only thirty-six compacts had been ratified by the creating states and the United States Congress. In 1921, however, the Port of New York Authority came into being, an experimental model which after a period of initial caution stimulated sixty-five additional compacts within a period of thirty-five years—nearly double the number on the books from the country's beginnings until New York's ground-breaking experiment. Even more dramatically, between 1956 and 1966, forty additional compacts made their appearance, with countless others proposed and in process of being legislated throughout the nation.

So unevaluated, in terms of their general worth as an adjunct of federalism, are these potentially revolutionary agreements, the *Book of the States* in its 1966–67 edition unwittingly reveals the poverty of technical knowledge about them as follows:

> To summarize recently emerging highlights is difficult because they [interstate compacts] are in various stages of development, with no certainty as yet as to their ultimate outcome. . . . By now enough compacts have come into operation, in enough different subject matter areas, that broad categories can be drawn within which virtually any new development can be placed.[12]

In brief, only after creation of more than one hundred and fifty interstate compacts and serious legislative proposal and consideration of countless others, can even a simple classification scheme now be attempted. Doubtless this is a step toward proper appraisal of what we may be doing to the federal system via the route of interstate compacts, but it tells us nothing of state performance under these agreements or of their general effects on American democracy and life.

The classification scheme suggested by the authors of the above identifies existing interstate compacts by general purposes: agreements for (1) mutual aid, (2) settlement of interstate disputes, (3) study and recommendation, (4) multijurisdictional regulations, and (5) provision of interstate services. They add, "But in at least several instances, the current example belonging to the category is sufficiently different from previous illustrations of it to merit the description 'new.' " [13]

A student of government needs only to glance at the above listing to grasp the tremendous implications of the terms mutual aid, multi-jurisdictional regulation, and interstate services. Regulation of economic life is of the very essence of government today: rule-making, rate-making, arbitration, and all the other techniques and processes which it embraces as the United States has developed the concept. A single state's practices herein are frequently deficient; the involvement of two or more states is infinitely more complicated and significant. Persons living within a single state may enjoy a singular degree of personal freedom, personal benefit, perhaps personal security—any condition which he regards as of value—because of his state's policies and laws. What, then, happens to his life condition when his state enters into a binding agreement with a sister state that intimately concerns his condition? What new obligations are placed upon him as a citizen and as a taxpayer which he did not have before? How was the agreement arrived at? Through full democratic processes? Through administrative negotiation? Through pressure politics? Through thorough investigation by the United States Congress of the merits of the agreement before it granted its consent?

Here we encounter the great and unexplored question of the new federalism that is coming into being with a speed that defies measure and under conditions of observation that are woefully deficient. Future research will no doubt provide us with solid understandings of the nature, character, performance, worth, predictable expectations and effects one may assume as possible and likely with any given kinds of interstate agreements. Such is not the case today, and such is not within the powers or scope of this present study. The best we propose to do, here, is to state the problem and to demonstrate the content of a particular state's efforts in a few of its actions along these lines.

2

No State shall, without the Consent of Congress, lay any Duty of Tonnage, keep Troops, or Ships of War in time of Peace, enter into any Agreement or Compact with another State, or with a foreign power, or engage in War, unless actually invaded, or in such imminent Danger as will not admit of delay.

U.S. CONSTITUTION, Article I, Section 10, Clause 3.

Interstate Compacts

A Device of Federalism

THERE IS NO MORE potentially beneficial clause of the United States Constitution than that of Article IV, section 10 which enables the states to enter interstate compacts with the consent of the United States Congress. Without it the Constitution would have to be implemented by such a provision, or extraconstitutional means would have to be found to provide for the interstate action and cooperation which the clause makes possible.

Cooperating American governments in their normal activities often make good use of various forms of intergovernmental aid, consultation, and cooperation of both a formal and an informal kind. Such are the concurrent action taken in crisis situations, the interchange of ideas and manpower in technical affairs, and many reciprocal agreements of a binding nature requiring regular commitments in money, personnel, and performance.

In practice, most of the interstate activities of a cooperative nature take place without a federally approved compact to govern them. States have power as sovereignties to enter contracts and reciprocal arrangements involving matters within their constitutional jurisdiction, without resort to Congress for permission. They are of course subject to judicial action if their actions infringe upon or abridge fundamental individual rights guaranteed by the United States or state constitutions, and in any event are bound by their own constitutions and statutes, and the laws, treaties, and judicial decisions of the United States.

The more formal interstate compact is required solely when

particular contemplated interstate activities hold the possibility of altering the fundamental nature of the federal system: that is, if they bestow powers without proper guarantees of protection for the national government, enhance the power of a particular state or a private agent, or create a potential for overthrow of the American system of government. In recent years, another condition requiring this kind of formal agreement is that in which two or more states propose to attack jointly some matter within the national government's power to govern but in which that government has not acted, or has acted in such a way as to allow the states a prior role or an important partnership role. Matters of this kind are frequently of a regulatory nature such as those involving navigable waters and their uses; mining and resources use; more recently, of air pollution and of broad economic developmental arrangements crossing state lines. Compacts generally relate to the states alone, but they may include the federal government as active or inactive partner, and they have been written to involve a foreign power.[1] The full definition is yet to be written in statute law, judicial action, and everyday practice. Until the last two decades few cases came before the courts involving compacts. As was inevitable with their increasing use, more adjudication is resulting.

Congressional Consent

The question of congressional consent has been one of the more litigated aspects of the interstate compact clause. Why is consent required? How is it to be given? When must it be given? What is consent?

In regard to the why of the matter, Chief Justice John Marshall in an early case, *Barron* v. *Baltimore* (1833), ruled that state agreements with a foreign country interfered with the national government's treaty-making power, and agreements with each other could "scarcely fail to interfere with the general purposes and intent of the Constitution." [2] Powerful support was given the Marshallian view in *Virginia* v. *Tennessee* (1893), a probing and leading case on compact definition. The Court here held that the prohibition was directed to formation of any "combination tending to the increase of political power in the states which may encroach upon or interfere with the just supremacy of the United States." [3] Subsequent cases continue to uphold this view. As recently as 1960 a United States district court ruled that a state in its sovereign capacity might contract with another or with the federal government through Congress if the "essence of statehood" is maintained without impairment.[4] And a 1964 Vermont case emphasized that the requirement of congressional consent was not based on constitutional prohibition against a state's delegating away its sovereignty, but upon preservation of the union.[5] The principle is firmly established. All such cases point clearly to a prime role for the Congress in allowing or forbidding interstate combinations; clearly, the responsibility for preserving constitutional relationships intact rests in its hands.

But the question of how consent is to be given is one of expanding definition. Is it required before or after compacting states sign an agreement? Is consent to be expressly stated, or may it be implied? Can the states enter a compact which has not been reviewed by Congress, establish practices under it, only to have Congress abolish it at a later time?

Again, an early case of the Marshall Court examined the clause and found the Constitution silent on the matter of timing or of the mode or form in which congressional consent is to be signified. In this case the State of Virginia had agreed with the people of the District of Kentucky by means of a compact to allow the latter to become a state. In granting statehood to Kentucky, Congress mentioned the compact as the basis for its approval. By this inference, the Court held, Congress "expressly consented to the compact between Virginia and Kentucky" even though the compact itself had not been subjected to prior congressional scrutiny.[6]

Congress can also fail to enumerate the stipulations of a compact in a special act and yet may give its consent. In *Virginia* v. *West Virginia* (1871), Congress's act of creating the State of West Virginia was itself endorsement of an agreement between the two states, even though it was not in the form of an express and formal statement of every proposition of the agreement.[7]

Furthermore, consent may be granted by Congress by either a formal legislative act or by a resolution,[8] and its consent may be given by such formal action after the enactment of such an agreement by two or more states.[9]

Congressional concern with interstate compacts has traditionally been permissive and to some extent casual. It is evident that standard procedures for enacting them have not resulted from congressional delineation of requirements but, rather, through improvisation on the part of the states and through court rulings. Yet, in recent years as important social and economic matters have been increasingly subject to compact legislation, observers have noted a tendency toward an increasing congressional concern with proposals and more caution in granting consent.[10] Probably this is as it should be, although such a judgment would be opposed or debated by many as a standing rule for all cases.

The troublesome question of regulation of petroleum production was resolved in 1934 and 1935 by the federal government and the states after many tribulations and great difficulties with passage of the Connally "Hot Oil" Act and adoption of the Interstate Oil Compact. Congressional and New Deal administration relief at finding a formula which would satisfy and quiet the contending factions of the oil industry was reflected in congressional willingness to renew the compact repeatedly in subsequent years with little more than the most cursory examination of matters as they stood in the producing side of the industry under the protections and purposes of the compact, particularly as that regulation seemed to be influenced and exercised primarily by the Texas Railroad Commission. It was not until 1955 that Congress at last probed more deeply into oil and gas production matters and the operations of state and private interests under the compact. Its investigations were far from involving the whole Congress or the entire industry, yet sufficient evidence of need prompted it to add to the compact a requirement for the United States attorney general to make an annual report to Congress as to whether or not the activities of the states thereunder were consistent with its purposes. Compliance with this stipulation was thereafter less than energetic, although the 1955 law made continuation of the oil compact contingent upon such an annual review and report. Three such reports were made, all of which were innocuous documents containing facts of general knowledge and providing no grounds for alarm. Then, in 1959 and 1960, and for two more years after the accession of Robert Kennedy to the office of attorney general, no reports at all were issued, until Senator William Proxmire of Wisconsin (a non-oil-producing state) inquired as to the reason for the omission and was informed it was a matter of oversight; no particular reason existed for failure to issue a report. Thereafter, one was promptly issued, even less informative than its predecessors. Virtually the only protest within the Congress was that of the Wisconsin senator, who had participated with Senator Paul Douglas of Illinois in the 1955 legislation which enacted the reporting requirement.[11]

But as the number and types of compacts have increased, a certain slowness to act has characterized congressional responses on compacts. The delays attending their enactment have been a source of frustration to interested state and special interest proponents, and there is developing an effort to seek escape from congressional delay by persuading Congress to enact legislation enabling the states in certain situations to proceed with congressional "consent in advance." Such a procedure is of course possible under the Constitution and judicial rulings, and Congress has given such consent in advance to a number of kinds of compacts. Blanket permission in the granting of consent in advance to interstate compacts created by planning agencies in those metropolitan areas crossing state lines, strongly recommended by the Advisory Commission on Intergovernmental Relations, was implemented in the Housing Act of 1961.[12] Developments under this permissive law should, and probably will, bear close watching.

As far as the courts have gone with their limited reasoning on limited cases, the core of all litigious consent questions seems to be whether or not a compact is essentially a political arrangement, as opposed to a commercial, procedural, economic, or some other kind of agreement. Social matters involving state action—that is, of a civil or criminal nature—may intimately affect or burden the exercise of political power, but these have not been the focus of much judicial attention to date.

Certain interstate agreements relating to the care of the poor, made pursuant to state statutes but without congressional consent, were held not to be compacts challenging the supremacy of the United States, and were therefore declared validly entered.[13] Such was the Missouri Uniform Support of Dependents Law, which contemplated no interstate compacts for the interstate agreements the state made under it[14] and, said the Court, even if the law actually could be construed as constituting a compact, it did not increase or decrease the participating states' political power. This ruling echoed an earlier case which held a similar Kentucky law as not constituting a compact.[15]

States have been prohibited from entering into negotiations with foreign governments for the extradition of fugitives from justice,[16] but a compact between two states for the reciprocal return of parolees was held to be in contemplation of advancing law enforcement generally, wholly in accord with federal legislation promoting it,[17] and therefore was constitutional even without specific congressional consent.

The Port of New York Authority Case

As mentioned above, Congress is tending to become more cautious in its granting of consent. This trend (in no way a settled practice as yet) has been accompanied with a related tendency to add qualifying amendments to previously granted compacts, usually provisions which assert Congress's right to withhold renewal of a compact, to review compact developments, and to amend compact laws. In the light of previous congressional unconcern with interstate compacts of some duration, such clauses seem to have been viewed as "more rhetorical than necessary," [18] particularly in consideration of the generally assumed constitutional supremacy of the federal government in such matters. However, a recent case of considerable significance which aroused widespread interest has demonstrated that simply because Congress writes permissive legislation and then attaches certain binding conditions to its consent is not in itself an answer to constitutional questions of congressional power. In *Tobin v. U.S.* (1962),[19] the United States Court of Appeals, District of Columbia, agreed that Congress can write laws to encourage interstate compacts and can attach binding conditions to its consent but such laws and conditions must be, themselves, constitutional.

The *Tobin* case arose in 1960 when the House Committee on the Judiciary under Representative Emanuel Celler's chairmanship initiated an investigation into the activities of the Port of New York Authority and, in pursuance of certain clearly stated objectives, demanded the general records of the authority for congressional scrutiny. According to committee and congressional records, the investigation was prompted by a request from all of New Jersey's House members, Republicans and Democrats, who had become concerned about the authority's plans for construction of a jet airport on a site at Morris County, New Jersey. In explaining to the Congress the unanimous request for a staff study, New Jersey Representative William T. Cahill observed,

We received through the newspapers in New Jersey an announcement that the New York Port Authority was going to erect a jet airport in one of the most desirable residential sections in the entire State of New Jersey. This was the first notice that any of us received of this proposed jet airport.

The [congressman] . . . from that district of New Jersey [Mr. Frelinghuysen] immediately called a meeting of the New Jersey delegation. It then became apparent to all of us, many of whom had served in the New Jersey Legislature, and I happened to be one of them, that none of us really knew what was going on with the New York Port Authority, because there had never been any investigation and none of us knew whether this port authority was exceeding its powers that had been granted to it under this compact or whether it was fulfilling its obligations under the compact. So we decided as Representatives that the intelligent thing to do was to request a study by the proper congressional committee.[20]

To this statement, Representative Peter Frelinghuysen added his own comments:

I should like to point out that the recommended site lies beyond the jurisdiction of the port authority in that it is some 30 miles west of Manhattan and therefore falls beyond the geographical limits of the authority's jurisdiction. This proposal has been very much opposed by the thousands of people who reside in this section of New Jersey.

However, inasmuch as there were no formal records, no minutes of the port authority regarding this Morris County site, there was nothing which could be vetoed by Governor Meyner or Governor Rockefeller. In other words, when this recommendation was made last December, and until the present there is still no way by which either State or both Governors could formally pass on what the port authority recommended. In other words, in this particular situation there has been no possibility of controlling the port authority by either or both of the States.[21]

This comprised the controversial background situation which stimulated congressional authorization of Mr. Celler's proposed probe of Port Authority activities. It should be noted that Congressman Frelinghuysen's observation about the inability of the two governors to veto the matter was more academic than otherwise; in due time both governors not only aligned themselves with the authority and its plans, but did so with great vigor.

All parties to the conflict, including Austin J. Tobin, executive director of the authority, initially seemed to believe that Congress under the Port Authority compact was within its rights in initiating the investigation. The compact provided,

That the consent of Congress is hereby given to the said Government [the Port of N.Y. Authority], and to each and every part and article thereof; *Provided,* That nothing herein contained shall be construed as impairing or in any manner affecting any right or jurisdiction of the United States in and over the region which forms the subject of said agreement.

SEC. 2. That the right to alter, amend, or repeal this resolution is hereby expressly reserved.[22]

In 1922, following the development by New York and New Jersey of a comprehensive plan for the Port Authority, the Sixty-Seventh Congress, Second Session, granted its consent to the plan, but in section 2 of the approving joint resolution also provided that "the right to alter, amend, or repeal this resolution is hereby expressly reserved." [23]

In reviewing these two sections, the District Court found,

An examination of the legislative history of the reservations, as well as interpretations of the Compact Clause itself, suggests the lengths to which Congress may go in exercising its power.

Floor discussion of the 1921 compact resolution in the House of Representatives included assent by Congressman Ansorge, the resolution's sponsor, to an assertion that "the port of New York is an asset of the entire Nation . . . [and] as the trustees of that asset, the people of New York and New Jersey owe it to themselves and to the country to properly develop it."

He also stated that "the joint resolution before the House fully protects the Federal Government by the [Federal jurisdiction reservation]." This reservation was suggested by Treasury Secretary Andrew Mellon.

In 1922 the same legislator, also sponsor of the second compact resolution, assured the House that the cities, states and nation are fully protected, and noted: "The cost of doing business at the port of New York is reflected throughout the entire country. The port of New York is not a local matter. It is distinctly national in scope and function."

These statements indicate that the reservations were not included in the compacts as an automatic, purposeless gesture; rather they reflect Executive awareness of the port of New York's unique status in the nation's commercial life, and appreciation that a compact provoding for comprehensive development of the port was charged with Federal interests.

A further recognition of these facts appears in contemporaneous statements made by Julius Henry Cohen, the Authority's first counsel. Their thrust is that since the comprehensive plan is "a regulation of interstate commerce . . . the port authority [is] the instrumentality in that sense of the Federal government for the purpose of effectuating the . . . plan." [24]

The District Court referred to another source of legal interpretation, Frankfurter and Landis, who in their study of the Constitution's compact clause [25] considered the clause to contain a number of objectives, among which was the enabling of Congress to "exercise national supervision through its power to grant or withhold consent, or to grant it under appropriate conditions." [26]

This view of a congressionally created agency, established by interstate agreement for development of a national port, conceived and begun by the two states involved but embracing navigable waters and interstate commerce—important federal jurisdictional matters which appeared to make it necessary for the United States Congress to hold a firm control over the compact's existence—seems superficially to be a reasonable interpretation of the laws' meanings and the understandings held by the laws' creators. However the United States Appeals Court did not so hold as will be shown, and the Supreme Court in denying certiorari seemed at least tacitly to agree.

Following the New Jersey Congressional delegation's request for an investigation of the Port Authority, Congressman Celler initiated committee action on an informal basis in February 1960, at which time the committee received its first refusal from Director Tobin to provide all records. Faced with the Port Authority's recalcitrance, Celler proposed a joint resolution for Congress's consideration, which, if adopted, would have amended the Port Authority compact to (1) require advance congressional approval of any legislation by the two states "amending or supplementing" the compact; (2) require submission to Congress of all periodic reports made by the authority to the two states; and (3) permit congressional committees to demand disclosure of any information deemed relevant; to inspect any books, records, and papers requested; and to inspect any authority facility. Celler then directed the staff of the Judiciary Committee to make a study of the authority's activities and operations under the 1921 and 1922 laws, including a review of the scope of its major operations.[27]

Following a rather long delay during which Tobin informed the committee that he was withholding the materials in accordance with a decision of the Port Authority's board of commissioners and after "consultation with . . . the Governors of New York [and] . . . New Jersey," on June 1, 1960, the House of Representatives unanimously granted the committee subpoena powers. On June 8, 1960, Subcommittee No. 5 of the Judiciary Committee instituted a formal inquiry into the authority. What followed is best told in the words of the District Court:

On June 10, Mr. Tobin replied. He detailed the material which the Authority had already furnished and stated that because the Authority was a "state agency" and because the subpoenaed documents related "solely to the internal administration" of the Authority, they never could assist in any valid purpose of the committee and were not pertinent to its stated purposes. He added that an investigation of the type proposed would inhibit use by the States of the interstate compact device, and closed with an expression of hope that the June 15 meeting between the Authority and committee staffs could result in agreement as to any future production of documents.[28]

This interesting point of view expressed the strategy apparently agreed upon by the Port Authority commissioners and their legal advisors: Congress had no right to make a sweeping investigation of the authority's "internal operations" for the authority was a "state agency" conducting "state business," and thus under the Constitution was outside the reach of the federal legislature. Tobin refused to provide the requested documents, he said, because he had been so "directed" by the Board of Commissioners who, in turn, had been "instructed" in identical letters by Governors Rockefeller of New York and Meyner of New Jersey to order Mr. Tobin not to comply with the subpoena. In the public and congressional squabble which developed, considerable evidence emerged that Tobin had acted on his own initiative in refusing the committee and had then sought support from the governors who, in turn, quickly sent their memoranda to the Board. This point was rather an important one, for Tobin's defense was built in part around the argument that he acted simply as a "state employee" in obedience to orders of his superiors and therefore ought not to be charged as in contempt of Congress. On June 29, 1960, the subcommittee met to receive the subpoenaed documents from Tobin, who failed to comply, citing all reasons he had previously given such as his assertion that the documents lacked pertinency and that the authority enjoyed the general immunity of a state agency from congressional power.

On August 23, 1960, the House voted to cite Tobin for criminal prosecution. In November 1960, the subcommittee held hearings in New York City in pursuance of its investigation. Tobin was thereafter brought to trial in the United States District Court, District of Columbia, which on June 15, 1961, found him guilty.*

The viewpoint of the two states, in all of this, emerged rather clearly during August 1960. At that time (August 22) a letter of Nelson Rockefeller's, bearing cosignatures of W. Averell Harriman, Thomas E. Dewey, and Herbert H. Lehman, was sent to New York Congressman John H. Ray, stating:

We join together in our respective capacities as Governor of the State of New York and as his immediate predecessors in that great State office to express our concern over the recommendation to be made to the House of Representatives tomorrow that the House cite three respected officers of this State and the State of New Jersey for contempt of Congress. . . .

To the best of our information and belief such precipitate and unhappy action would mark the first time in the history of the United States that the Congress ever voted to instigate criminal prosecution for contempt against State officers serving a State agency in a matter that concerns the proper exercise of their official State duties. What is more they will have been cited for carrying out the express and written instructions of the Governors of New York and New Jersey, based on the conclusion of the two Governors that "the furnishing of the internal records now requested, in the opinion of [the Governors'] legal advisers, would represent a serious infringement of the rights of the States under the Constitution and could constitute a dangerous precedent as recognition of Federal authority in an area of State responsibility." [29]

Herein the case became obscured. The important issue, as far as Celler and his committee were concerned, was whether the Compact Clause of the Constitution did or did not allow the Congress to retain a reviewing role over an interstate compact to which it had given consent. They believed that refusal by the agency's officers to cooperate with Congress in its legitimate search for information about the

---

* The complete historical account is recorded in detail in Justice Youngdahl's excellent analysis of the case, 195 F. Supp. 588 (1961).

agency's use of its powers, in order that Congress might review its own legislation to repeal or amend it (and thus to protect the interests of the federal system), constituted a contempt of the United States government. In order to reach the uncooperative agency officers, Congress had no recourse other than resort to the contempt process, an admittedly clumsy and unappealing device which had the effect of branding quite honorable and respected (even though stubborn and intractable) public officials as criminals. In addition to their desire conclusively to establish state jurisdiction over the Port Authority, the governors and Port Authority commissioners also sought to remove their highly respected director, Austin J. Tobin, from the disgraceful position in which he now found himself and, as is clear in the final decision as rendered by the United States Court of Appeals, they successfully accomplished this, but at the expense of a comprehensive court statement on the proper interpretation of the Compact Clause.

On August 14, 1960, Station WNEW-TV of New York City held a program, "Metropolitan Probe," at which New York Representative Alfred E. Santangelo, Governor Robert B. Meyner, City Councilman Stanley Isaacs, and William Peer, the moderator, participated. Some of the comments illuminate the issues. The following exchange is from the program's transcript:

ISAACS: Governor Meyner, I understand that in connection with this controversy . . . you wrote a letter to the various Governors of the States and Members of Congress asking their support in your dispute with Congressman Celler. Can you tell me why so few have responded?

MEYNER: Well I might say, Councilman Isaacs, that practically every Governor feels favorable to the proposition. I was out at Glacier National Park at the national Governors conference, and it was there that a resolution was presented which in essence opposes the very thing Congress is trying to do. This resolution was passed unanimously. Now to date I have probably had about six Governors answer me personally and not one has taken the side of the congressional leaders. . . . I know that practically all of the governors are opposed to the proposition of probing into the internal records. I want to make it clear that we are not trying to prevent Congress from looking into the areas Congress is expected to look into. What we are objecting to is that they look at the internal records. For instance, we might as a port authority look into the question of whether a contractor is fit to do business. Look into his financial responsibility. Get a lot of internal confidential information. I don't think that should be available. We might check the employment record of a person who is to be employed or promoted. We don't think that should be the subject of a record. . . . Even the Congressmen who might be favorable to a probe in the sense that they want some of these internal records, say that there ought to be some method by which we ought to determine this controversy without holding reputable citizens in criminal contempt.

ISAACS: You do feel that Congress of course has general power over interstate commerce and foreign commerce and is interested in the substance of what the port authority does. Is there anything in the original act which gave you and the Governor of . . . New York the power to organize this commission originally? And to continue to appoint its members? *Is there anything in that act that gives Congress continued supervision over its details?*

MEYNER: *Congress takes the attitude that they do have this continuing supervision. We say it is not supervision. We say that they have the power to give consent.* . . . Now I say if they—if the Government gives us money for airways or for airports they can come in and check our records to see that we use the money properly. If we are engaged in some type of enterprise by which commerce is affected they can come in and look into the internal administration of the port authority. The port authority is carrying on functions that a city or a State could be carrying on.

   ·   ·   ·   ·   ·   ·   ·   ·   ·   ·

SANTANGELO: Governor, I am glad to see that you feel that Congress has the power to investigate the port authority if the conditions warrant. Your position apparently is diametrically opposite to that taken by the attorney general of the State of New York who has sent letters and briefs to the Congressmen to the position, to the effect, that Congress does not have the power to investigate the port authority, and that it is a bistate agency. And so I am very happy to see that you feel that we have the right if conditions warrant.

MEYNER: I don't think I am in disagreement with the attorney general of New York.

   ·   ·   ·   ·   ·   ·   ·   ·   ·   ·

SANTANGELO: . . . But it is a fact, is it not, that since 1921 when the compact between the State of New York and the State of New Jersey was entered into with the consent of the Congress of the United States that no one investigation, or one inquiry, into the inner workings of the port authority has taken place.

MEYNER: I can't say that that is a fact.

SANTANGELO: I know that in 1954 when I was in the State Senate I introduced a resolution to the effect that we should investigate the exploitation of the motorists who were compelled to pay 50 cents for crossing the Port Authority bridges and tunnels when the original bonds which had constructed these had been paid off. And it was at that time the port authority approached me and said that this was a bistate investigation, or a congressional investigation and therefore should not be done by one particular State, or one particular legislature. Now the question is whether or not this investigation should take place. Not whether or not Congress has the power because in this compact of 1921 Congress reserved unto itself the right to repeal, alter or modify the compact.

MEYNER: It reserved the right to withdraw its consent. I fully believe that consent is a lot different from having power. It is my feeling that most of the activity in the port authority is in the area that can be normally done by a State or a municipality or authorized by a State. These are functions that are ordinarily done by . . . a port like Norfolk or Mobile or New Orleans. It happens that this port is in two States and because it is in two States we get together and do it by compact. And the Constitution only says "consent." It doesn't say a power. It doesn't say you run the thing. . . . I don't think Congress can go into the President's office and get his records, or into a Cabinet member's office and get his records. If conservation and economic developments are engaged in some program that affects navigable streams they can come in and look at it and we'll give them all the information. But to look any time at general records it seems to me is going a bit too far.[30] [*Italics added.*]

More important than this informal exchange via public broadcasting facility, however, are the official records of the case: congressional debates, committee reports and minority member views, legal briefs, and the court decisions. Congressman Celler's use of proper procedure and adherence to due process requirements was never questioned seriously. A rather tenuous charge of hastiness to act was made, but it never impressed the courts. The record indicates a wholly sincere belief held by Chairman Celler and his subcommittee that Congress was empowered to act as it did.

In presenting his case to the House of Representatives on August 23, 1960, Celler outlined the far-reaching scope of Port Authority operations:

The magnitude of the activities of the port authority is apparent from a simple recital of the facilities it operates.

It operates La Guardia Airport, New York International Airport, Newark Airport, Port Authority Heliport, Teterboro Airport, Brooklyn Port Authority piers, Hoboken Port Authority piers, a grain elevator, a grain pier, Columbia Street Pier, pits, public open storage areas, Elizabeth Port Authority piers, Port Newark.

Erie Basin Port Authority, Newark Union Motor Truck Terminal,

Port Authority Building which includes the Union Railroad Freight Terminal, Port Authority Bus Terminal.

It operates tunnels and bridges like the George Washington Bridge, Goethals Bridge and the Outerbridge Crossing.

Its activities include the operation of a hotel, office buildings, and factory and industrial sites, and other commercial undertakings in direct competition with private enterprise. *It will also be borne in mind that the port authority is exempt from all Federal and State taxes.*

The operations of the authority exercise a far-flung influence on interstate commerce. They yield tax-exempt revenues in excess of $100 million annually from interstate tunnels, interstate bridges, terminals, airports and shops valued at more than $900 million. *The port authority maintains offices in London, Zurich, Rio de Janeiro, San Juan, P.R., Chicago, Cleveland, Pittsburgh, and Washington, D.C.* Its representatives appear frequently before congressional committees and Federal regulatory agencies for purposes of improving the competitive position of the Port of New York Authority vis-a-vis other U.S. ports. They lobbied against the St. Lawrence Seaway. The States that border on the St. Lawrence Seaway should take heed in that regard. What right did they have to oppose the St. Lawrence Seaway? Yet they did just that.

The port authority's operations affect the economic lives of millions of Americans living outside as well as inside the port development area, and the States of New York and New Jersey. They intimately affect *the operation of Federal agencies responsible, among other things, for the national defense, navigable waterways, and air, rail, and highway traffic. In short, they profoundly affect Federal interests of many and various kinds.*

.   .   .   .

It is well also to recall that the port authority itself has told the Supreme Court of the United States that "there can be no doubt that Congress has made the port authority its agent for the effectuation of the comprehensive plan."

It is indisputable that Congress may enact legislation withdrawing its consent to any and all of the provisions of the port authority compacts. It may, as was proposed in 1952, enact legislation to repeal its consent to the compacts and thereby dissolve the port authority. It may enact legislation making its consent conditional upon the agreement of New York and New Jersey to delegate certain additional functions or withdraw certain functions from the port authority. Clearly, decisions of this kind have an enormous potential impact upon the Nation's greatest metropolitan area, its largest port, upon large segments of industry. *To even suggest that Congress, entrusted with such powers cannot inquire into the operation of the Port of New York Authority is to say that Congress must exercise its legislative responsibilities blindfolded.*[31] [*Italics added.*]

He concluded by noting that the general operations of the agency had at no time been subjected to a comprehensive or overall audit by any government agency. After questioning by Congressman William M. McCulloch (R., Ohio), Celler stated there had been audits by accountants of private firms, "but the accountants were compelled to accept the figures given to them by the port authority." [32]

The excerpts here given by no means cover the entire debate or all of the points at issue. They merely suggest the nature of the controversy and highlight the contentions of the opposing factions: the two states, and the United States Congress. Congressmen John V. Lindsay and John H. Ray of New York filed minority views with the Judiciary Committee. Lindsay's statement contained a strong legal argument very similar to that which later won the case for Tobin.[33] There is not much question that this argument was developed under the guidance of Thomas E. Dewey, who accepted the role of chief counsellor for Tobin when the case was appealed, and who on the successful termination of all legal proceedings accepted a fee of $85,000 for his work.[34]

Referring to various Supreme Court cases and quoting from statements by the National Association of Attorneys General and the Council of State Governments, Lindsay developed the stand taken by Governor Meyner in his TV interview. The committee's actions, he asserted, constituted "an unprecedented, unlawful, and unconstitutional exercise of Federal authority over a bistate agency." [35]

Congress [he averred] consented to the compact between New York and New Jersey creating the Port of New York Authority. It did not create the Authority. All the powers exercised by the authority are delegated to it by the legislatures of New York and New Jersey.

. . . .

The port authority was created by the States of New York and New Jersey. It is fully subject to their control. It is their agency, not a Federal agency. Authoritative decisions in both the State and Federal courts conclusively establish the port authority's status as an agency of the States which created it to serve as their local port development agency.

. . . .

Although Congress reserved the right to alter, amend, or repeal the resolution consenting to the port compact, this did not create power to amend the compact itself, which can only by altered by the contracting states.[36]

On June 15, 1961, the United States District Court handed down its decision upholding Congress's position and supporting its right to scrutinize interstate compacts to which it has given consent, its right to compel production of necessary documents and records, and declaring Mr. Tobin to be in criminal contempt of Congress for willfully withholding the evidence sought. It stated that the test of whether the subpoenaed documents were privileged from nondisclosure was made by the court by balancing the congressional need for them against the dangers to the Port Authority and to the interstate compact process in general, and found in the present case that the balance was required to be struck in favor of disclosure. In answer to defense's assertion that such congressional investigations imperiled use of interstate compacts by the states because they would in effect "supersede the States in their control of the internal management and policies of their agencies," and "would 'destroy' compacts and severely inhibit states from entering into them," the court responded,

The existence of a power to investigate does not, irrespective of the extent of that power, immutably lead to control by the investigating agency. Moreover, the fact that in several recent compacts the Federal Government has been included as a participant and that Congress has expressly reserved power to secure compact agency documents of the type here at issue strongly suggests that no serious inhibition to use of the compact device is presented. In two instances, the Tennessee River Basin Water Pollution Control Compact and the Wabash Valley Compact, provision is made for Presidential appointment of a "Federal representative." In two others, the New York–New Jersey Transportation Agency Compact and the Washington Metropolitan Area Transit Regulation Compact, Congress has reserved the right of "access to all books, records, and papers . . . as well as the right of inspection of any facility. . . ." Moreover, the recently signed compact to develop the water resources of the Delaware River Basin includes the Federal Government as a full partner with the States of Delaware, New Jersey, New York and Pennsylvania.[37]

The court did not rule upon the question of whether the Port Authority was or was not a "state agency" fulfilling "state functions," per se, although it did refer to the agency as a "hybrid" while skirting around any specific answer to this important question. It said "its very existence depended upon joint action by the States and Congress, and aspects of its continued operation remain subject to the legislative power of both." [38] A single footnote brushed aside the question, thus:

From time to time there has been argument as to whether the Port Authority is a "state" agency. Whatever value such conclusionary characterizations may have, it is clear that they must be limited to the context in which they are made, none having been made on Constitutional grounds. For purposes here relevant the Authority must be treated as a repository of both Federal and state interests, *sui generis* in the Federal system.[39]

With the addition of Thomas E. Dewey as chief counselor, the case was carried to the United States Court of Appeals, District of Columbia, which handed down a reversal of the District Court's decision on June 7, 1962.[40] In a brief and pointed decision, Justice Bastian made quite clear that the court had neither any desire nor any real sanction to pass judgment on "serious constitutional questions" such as had been raised by this case. Indeed, he said, it was his duty to obviate the need for passing on them. Citing two of the most important of Tobin's defense arguments—that Congress under the Compact Clause does not have power to alter, amend, or repeal its consent once given to an interstate compact, and that the subcommittee's subpoena was an unconstitutional invasion of the reserved powers of the states—Bastian wrote a revealing explanation of what the constitutional question would involve if the court attempted to pass upon it.

In granting its consent Congress can attach certain binding conditions, not only to its consent to the admission of a new state into the Union, but also to its consent to the formation of an interstate compact. However, the vital condition precedent to the validity of any such attached condition is that it be constitutional. If Congress does not have the power under the Constitution, then it cannot confer such power upon itself by way of a legislative fiat imposed as a condition to the granting of its consent.

. . . *The compact clause of the Constitution does not specifically confer such power upon Congress. No case has been cited to us, nor have we been able to find any case through our own research, holding that Congress has such constitutional power. Nor do we find any to the contrary. Since no such power appears expressly in the compact clause, any holding that it exists and that Congress possesses it must be predicated on the conclusion that it exists as an implied power.*

We have addressed ourselves at some length to this issue in order to show the gravity of passing upon even only one of the constitutional questions posed by this case. Moreover, in view of appellant's argument that the plenary powers specified in and by the Constitution [power over interstate and foreign commerce, national defense, etc.] are more than sufficient to enable Congress to protect, supervise and preserve all federal interests affected by the existence of interstate compacts, we are even less inclined to reach the constitutional issues involved here. We have no way of knowing what ramifications would result from a holding that Congress has the implied constitutional power "to alter, amend or repeal" its consent to an interstate compact. Certainly, in view of the number and variety of interstate compacts in effect today, such a holding would stir up an air of uncertainty in those areas of our national life presently affected by the existence of these compacts.[41] [*Italics added.*]

Justice Bastian was acutely concerned with the criminal nature of this case and emphasized that as presented to the court it contained both civil and criminal law questions. The court chose to set aside the civil law aspects and confine itself solely to the criminal law question of Tobin's guilt. Deploring the lack of any means established in law by Congress for reaching situations such as this, except via the path of contempt of Congress proceedings,* the court concentrated upon a showing of whether the House Judiciary Committee had the power to conduct such an investigation as it had initiated. It concluded that the committee did have the power to investigate interstate compact agencies, but that the documents which Tobin first placed at the committee's disposal were all that the committee was entitled to under its granted powers over interstate compacts. The withheld "intra-authority documents" were outside Congress's defined jurisdiction and, therefore, Tobin in withholding the documents was not in contempt of Congress.

Thus the case was left to stand. The Supreme Court denied certiorari on November 13, 1962,[42] and the issues raised stand as they did before the case began—undefined and undecided, except for the one legal principle that Congress, in attaching binding conditions to interstate compacts and in granting its consent must act constitutionally.

---

* During the earlier course of the controversy, Representative Lindsay and Governor Meyner had both suggested that declaratory judgment proceedings were a proper means at Congress' disposal to reach the issue of the propriety of Tobin's and Congress's respective actions. Congressional interests prepared a memorandum showing why declaratory judgment procedures were not an available means in the instant case, and inserted it in the *Congressional Record*. The Court observed, "Although this question is not before the Court, it does feel that if contempt is, indeed, the only existing method, Congress should consider creating a method of allowing these issues to be settled by declaratory judgment." Earlier Justice Bastian noted, "Appellant is no criminal and no one seriously considers him one. He stands before us convicted of crime merely because no method has been provided for testing the merits of his contentions save that of prosecution for contempt of Congress." *Tobin* v. *U.S.*, 306 F. 2d 270, 274, 276 (1962).

The Significance of the Tobin Case

Why detail so extensively a legal decision which, after all, left unresolved extremely important constitutional questions about interstate compacts?

First, the case has particular relevance to Illinois and its own interstate compact arrangements, for at least one of Illinois's existing compacts is a bistate arrangement admittedly modeled to some extent on the Port of New York Authority concept. The Bi-State Development Compact of 1949 (treated at length in Chapter 3 hereafter), involving the St. Louis metropolitan area of Missouri and Illinois, while at present in no sense as extended or as involved in a vast array of interstate enterprises as is the New York agency, yet holds in its law a potential for precisely the kinds of constitutional and statutory difficulties as arose in this case. Daily administration of the Bi-State Development Agency, as will be shown, certainly requires that Illinois and Missouri publics (and indeed all persons concerned) be aware of the Congress's, the Port Authority's, and the court's experiences and rulings in the Tobin litigation and the inherent difficulties and shortcomings of the compact device for handling great metropolitan area problems.

Second, the Tobin matter brought into the record a great deal of discussion of what interstate compacts of the developmental type portend in our system of federalism. No more telling illustration exists than is provided by this case of the complexities of the issue. No more pointed example can be shown of the inherent potentials for great and unregulated adjustments to creep into the United States constitutional system via the sanctions which may lie dormant, concealed, and unanticipated in any broadly conceived interstate compact involving extensive economic and social matters.

Third, the case makes unmistakeably clear why Congress today shows a tendency to fight shy of granting its quick and inadequately considered consent to compact proposals. It also illuminates the motives behind congressional inclusion of more and more restrictive provisions in the compacts it approves. To be sure, even before the Tobin case arose interstate compacts were being written with congressional reservations attached. Today, after the Port Authority litigation, there is doubt as to the protections such clauses have heretofore been deemed to provide. There is not much doubt that in future Congress will give more probing attention to interstate compact proposals which come before it, as it has with the Illinois–Indiana Interstate Air Pollution Compact and proposed air pollution agreements of other states.

Fourth, the case is revelatory in regard to one of the most important and heretofore attractive aspects of the interstate compact device: its promotion by constitutional lawyers and legislators, and its use by interests, whether public or private, as a means to circumvent or avoid federal control of interstate matters and retain authority over them within the states or the local governments, thus protecting and even encouraging a large area of private or state privilege which might and probably would be endangered under federal control. The quick oppositional responses of Tobin's supporters and their denial of a philosophy apparently formerly held by Port Authority proponents that the federal interests in the New York port were established and amply protected under the compact, indicates the scope of the threat which the Judiciary Committee's investigation held. That they were successful in staving off any final definition of relative federal-state powers on this issue was, as compact proponents (the National Association of Attorneys General, the Council of State Governments) saw it, of vital importance to the future of the interstate compact device. In brief, the case provided a red signal light, a heralding of the kind of problems which can and may arise in the future evolution of interstate compacts and their influences in the American federal system. To compact proponents the existing ground gained had to be protected at all costs. In this sense it is very much a landmark case.

And, fifth, although the various courts, debates, and defense counsel repeatedly characterized this as a controversy between state and federal governments, something was left unsaid in regard to the people generally of the United States. It is clear that an interstate compact agency takes orders only from all parent states acting in unison, not from an individual state party to the compact acting unilaterally. This means that if an agency such as the Port Authority takes independent action in a matter such as acquisition of land thirty miles outside its legal geographical boundaries for the location of an airport, the people of one state may strenuously object only to find that the people of the other state or states are delighted or are, more generally, indifferent to the matter. If such a situation were an ordinary decision of a county or a municipality, the people directly concerned would be able through established political channels to take action for or against the decision. Likewise, an objecting state could control its municipal corporation so acting. In interstate compact agencies, Congress (or the possibility of Congress) has provided the public with the image of a protector of interstate interests, a general supervisor, a guarantor that respective state and local rights and desires will not be overridden by a powerful agency independent of any single state's control. By removing Congress from this role, or emasculating its and the public's conceptions of its role, the courts in effect create a totally new governmental entity, independent and unrestrained by any government superior to it.

If, as happened in the Port Authority matter, both state governments choose to act in harmony but in defiance of the wishes of the people of one of the states (in this instance, the alarmed citizens of Morris County, New Jersey), the people are thus rendered impotent of any control over their own state government to which they ordinarily would turn for protection. Until the Tobin case, the people of Morris County, New Jersey had every reason to believe that if they carried their troubles to their congressmen, Congress would and could at least look into the matter. The *Tobin* case unfortunately casts some doubts as to Congress' future powers in such instances.

Compacts Without Consent?

In view of the lucid language of Article I, section 10, clause 3, it is difficult to accept an interpretation which in effect says that the states can enter into agreements or compacts with another state without the consent of Congress and, indeed, can thereafter operate for an indefinite time—even forever—without it. Yet this is a possibility of the "consent in advance" concept, and "no consent" compacts actually can and do exist. As indicated above, the "consent in advance" idea implies a certain assumption of faith in Congress's right to approve or repeal altogether, since it relies upon Congress's broad preliminary grant of permission. But the validity of a compact entered into by several cooperating states which Congress has refused to recognize is another matter altogether. On this point we have no court rulings whatsoever on which to rely.

Following World War II, a cooperative regional higher education program was entered into by fifteen of the Southern states involving considerable sums of money and administrative cooperation., In, February 1948 the Southern Regional Education Compact was submitted to Congress for its approval; the House gave its consent, but the resolution to approve was killed in the Senate on May 13, 1948, when it was referred back to committee. No further congressional action was ever taken on it.

Examining this legal puzzle in 1950, Leslie W. Dunbar scrutinized the law of interstate compacts and concluded that since the Supreme Court "has never held that the language of Article I, section 10, admits any exception . . . , such agreements are . . . voidable at the option of Congress." [43] His opinion, however, is that of a single scholar; until the courts finally rule on the issue the participating states will not only continue to operate under their agreement but, indeed, are operating daily more boldly and confidently.

Those originating fifteen states, functioning under their education compact, are no longer alone. Today, spawned in the wake of their precedent, there are also the Western Interstate Commission for Higher Education (created by interstate compact in 1951 and including Alaska, Arizona, California, Colorado, Hawaii, Idaho, Montana, Nevada, New Mexico, Oregon, Utah, Washington and Wyoming); and the New England Board of Higher Education (also created by compact in 1955 and embracing Connecticut, Maine, Massachusetts, New Hampshire, Rhode Island and Vermont). And a decade later, in 1965, a new "recommendatory compact" was born, the Compact on Education. [44]

The Compact on Education is largely the product of the zeal and energy of former governor Terry Sanford of North Carolina, acting on a suggestion of James B. Conant in his *Shaping Educational Policy* (1964). [45] Sanford, leaving office in 1965, and concerned with the future of the states and the federal system following his intimate brush with state problems in his four years as governor of North Carolina, obtained grants from the Ford Foundation and the Carnegie Corporation and set up an office at Duke University to conduct a research project which he termed, "A Study of American States." [46]

Although his purposes were broad-ranging, covering the entire spectrum of state powers and functions, "in quest of solutions and ideas for more effective government," a major achievement of his efforts was the promotion of the idea and the assembling of interested states and interested educational organizations of every conceivable kind in meetings at Washington and Kansas City during 1965 to organize and formulate the educational compact. A drafting committee, which included experts on education law and Mitchell Wendell of the Council of State Governments as chief draftsman, came up with specific proposals which were acted upon in the Kansas City conference of September. Every state in the Union, plus Puerto Rico and the territories, were represented at this meeting. Nineteen governors were there in person. The group further explored and debated the proposed compact, and organized an Education Commission of the States headquartered at Denver. By May 1967 thirty-seven states had become members, fifteen of which were by legislative action, and twenty-three others by executive order.[47] Illinois was among the latter.

The compact provided that a state could become a member by executive action, but only until the end of 1967. For permanent membership, legislative action is required. Identical bills to give Illinois permanent membership were introduced in the Seventy-fifth General Assembly in 1967 (H.B. 908 and S.B. 690). The compact was ratified and approved on July 26, 1967 on the recommendation of former governor Otto Kerner and the endorsement of the Illinois Commission on Intergovernmental Cooperation.[48] But interestingly enough, a move to repeal the law has been made by the Seventy-sixth General Assembly.[49]

What is the meaning of the Council of State Government's term, "recommendatory compacts"? Apparently it refers to the pooling by member states of advice, joint research, study, and recommendations for improved state performance, including proposals for model laws and model administrative procedures. It includes interstate agencies created to effectuate such purposes but holding no delegated authority to act in a regulatory manner. Such supposedly are the Interstate Oil Compact Commission, and the Vehicle Equipment Safety Compact Commission.

Of the newly proposed Interstate Mining Compact creating a similar agency, The Council of State Governments has this to say:

Like the successful Interstate Oil Compact of the Thirties, the new agreement, in addition to creating a study body, *would impose a moral obligation on a party state "that within a reasonable time it will formulate and establish an effective program for the conservation and use of mined land, by the establishment of standards, enactment of laws, or the continuing of the same force."*[50] [*Italics added.*]

And its interpretation of the Compact on Education is as follows:

It would establish an interstate commission whose functions would be to provide a forum for the development of public educational policy on all levels from primary school to graduate education. The compact's proponents believe that its integral connection with and support by state governments would give the proposed "Educational Commission for the States" an opportunity to unite the best in educational leadership and research with the policy making levels of state and local government. . . . The Commission would not be able to enforce acceptance of any of its recommendations by state and local authorities, but it would be organically responsible to the states and could furnish them with information which may not now be readily available to them.[51]

While these descriptive comments suggest a strictly service role for the new interstate educational agency, unrelated to regulation and control of education and without power to "impose a moral obligation on a party state" to enact legislation in conformity with the compact agency's recommendations, the scope of its interests—comprising the entire range of American public education—would give to it an authority which would be well-nigh irresistible to state legislators and congressmen. Further, the Illinois law created an "Illinois Educational Council" composed of the Illinois member of the compact's educational Commission of the States and six other persons to be appointed by the governor. The council was empowered to "consider any matter related to the recommendations of the Educational Commission of the States or to the activities of the Commission members representing" Illinois.[52] The Illinois Commission on Intergovernmental Cooperation emphasized in its report to the General Assembly, that "The commission does not . . . have any authority to impose any of its recommendations on the member States." [53] It did not comment on its possible effects and influences on Illinois's own educational policies, practices, and educational machinery.

Any sanguine expectation that such an agency would be without a power greatly to influence law and policy completely denies any reason for the widespread interest the compact has evoked, and the extensive time, energies, and talents which have gone into its creation. Quite to the contrary, it is expected to influence law and policy. That is its reason for existence.

But, again, the major question here confronting us is the long-range status of both the interstate educational agency and the interstate compact creating it, while it is without Congress's specific consent. Are the member states, with confidence, warranted in appropriating even minimal sums of money to the uses of such an agency? Although the Compact on Education gives to its interstate education commission power to represent member states before the Congress on legislation in which it is interested (that is, the power to lobby for its interests), need the Congress give heed to such lobbying activity if it has never officially approved the compact? It seems obvious that whether it is required to do so by law, or not, that it will have no other alternative. Thirty-seven states add up to seventy-four Senators. An agency of such specialized scope, supported so widely with top level talent and extensive public and private funds to which it will have access, cannot be other than a fount of power and information which Congress can do little other than to heed.

At the time the earlier Southern Regional Education Compact was considered in Congress, Senators Cooper of Kentucky and Morse of Oregon opposed the granting of congressional consent, but on grounds that education, a nonfederal function, was involved and therefore did not need congressional approval. Such an argument had the effect of granting approval while withholding consent, but it was a questionable interpretation of the law in the light of the Constitution's wording, especially when the proposed interstate operation would involve fifteen states in extensive exchanges on educational policy matters which could have run counter to federal decrees and utterances on that policy (desegregation rulings, especially), and certainly did involve many educational institutions which were drawing a considerable portion of their operating funds from federal grants-in-aid.

All such considerations must, as well, be regarded as part and parcel of the new Compact on Education. Congress's inaction, in either declaring the entire compact illegitimate or in granting its consent, enables the compact to put down roots which may very well strip Congress of any future power to abolish it or to amend it. In effect, this is enactment of interstate compact under "no consent" at all, an interesting and somewhat formidable development in interstate compact practice.

Conclusions

Among the more enthusiastic supporters of the interstate compact device are governors, who almost universally acclaim the merits of this tool of executive action. Not enough research has been done into the reasons for this phenomenon, but it may be speculated that it arises from the governors' limited power over state government generally. An interstate compact today frequently enables a governor to tap federal grants-in-aid and resources of sister states which would not otherwise be available to him in promoting his own state's program and internal improvements. It removes some of the legal barriers of regional interstate problems: poverty in the Appalachian area, for example, can only feebly be attacked by each of the Appalachian states operating alone; together, with the assistance of the federal government's massive resources, constructive improvements can be obtained. Since most interstate compacts provide a governing board or commission for their administration, almost always comprised of gubernatorial appointees and by law required to report to him, his control over his state's bureaucracy is somewhat enhanced. This latter point, however, is a double-edged matter. His control over his state's functioning may become more complicated, less flexible, more burdened with interstate obligations which must be met if the compact is to succeed. But, probably, the feature that has always been attractive to states' rights proponents—namely, the assumption of state authority by compact in a realm which may easily be preempted under federal control—is that which especially pleases the governors. Whatever the reasons, they have shown repeatedly that they like this method of handling interstate problems.

Another strong advocate of interstate compacts is the Council of State Governments which in many years has yet to deny the merits of any of those already on the books and which has repeatedly utilized as exemplary models such powerful interstate arrangements as the Port of New York Authority, the Delaware River Commission, the Interstate Oil and Gas Compact, and the like. No other agency has maintained as close watch over developments in this field. Two of its writers, Wendell Mitchell and Richard H. Leach, have done most of the research and writing that have been done in exploring interstate compacts. Professor Leach has given attention to the question of congressional consent and has made a number of recommendations in regard to it. On the whole, he urges relaxation and diminution of Congress's role in compact activity generally. Among his recommendations are the following: [54]

1) Congress should define, once and for all, which compacts require its attention for consent and which do not.

2) In general, Congress should take care that compacts do not threaten or burden federal Supremacy or the interests of states not parties to a given compact.

3) Internally, Congress should adopt some formula, such as that proposed by Senator Alan Bible of Nevada to the Eighty-fifth Congress,[55] which would grant consent within ninety days of a compact's submission to Congress unless Congress specifically denies its consent within that period.

4) Congress should reexamine the meaning of its "consent in advance" legislation, now in effect.

5) Where Congress has granted only limited consent (as in the Interstate Oil and Gas Compact, which must be renewed each four years), it should provide for permanent consent.

6) Congress should review its practice of referring compacts automatically to executive agencies for comments and suggestions; there is evidence of an "anti-compact bias" in "many departments and agencies," and such referrals "may invite opposition."

It is difficult to see how Congress can arrive at any fixed policy or formula which it can apply automatically to every interstate compact it is asked to examine. Each new compact proposal is, inevitably, substantively different from all others that have preceded it. The great obligation placed upon Congress by the Constitution cannot be bypassed. Already at this stage of interstate compact evolution there are obscurities in the concept's meanings and effects. Not enough is known about them; not enough critical research is being done. It may very well be that the states, which now so eagerly embrace interstate compact arrangements, may yet come to rue the complications they are introducing into the federal system. It may very well be that not only congressmen, but representatives of the states also, should sit down together in a conference called for the purpose of looking seriously and penetratingly into the implications of present and future compact activity. This is a task for high officials of the states and the national government and ought not merely to rest on the recommendations of special interest organizations such as the Council of State Governments, the National Association of Attorneys General, the American Bar Association, and the desires of other special interests which from time to time place before the Congress and the legislatures their own special interest compact proposals.

3

There is no let-up in the pressure to shift responsibility for governmental activities from the general city or county government to special authorities and independent boards. Throughout the country parking authorities, traffic authorities, airport authorities, and redevelopment agencies are being added to the large number of existing police and fire commissions, sewerage commissions, soil conservation districts, school boards, recreation boards, health boards, hospital boards, library boards, museum boards, housing agencies, public works boards, cemetery boards and other boards.

It does not follow, however, that each function of government should be separately organized over a distinctive area.

Victor Jones. Metropolitan Authorities. In The Future of Cities and Urban Redevelopment, edited by Coleman Woodbury. *(Chicago: University of Chicago Press, 1953.)*

The Missouri-Illinois
Bi-State Development Compact

PART 1—THE BI-STATE DEVELOPMENT AGENCY

CONSIDERING THE SWEEPING TERMS of its assignment and the two decades of its existence, the Bi-State Development Agency of Illinois and Missouri can hardly be classified as a sensational success in experimental metropolitan area designs for government. Neither can it be called a failure, for it has persisted in the face of difficulties which, a decade ago, seemed to portend an early but lingering demise, and it has accomplished some of its goals to the apparent satisfaction of the knowledgeable population which it serves. Its exact status in the St. Louis metropolitan area is impossible of measurement, but it can be safely stated that it is neither as important in St. Louis area development as its creators in 1947–49 hoped, nor as unimportant as its somewhat inconspicuous image in St. Louis events conveys. It is established, probably accepted by the powers that matter, and must be taken into account in any serious appraisement made of this important metropolitan community of the United States. If the general population of the area has only the vaguest knowledge of the agency and its activities, this is not unusual for agencies of this type, which prefer to avoid the white light of publicity except when it is useful to their designs, and which are removed from the direct—and educational— operation of the electoral processes.

Modeled in the image of the New York Port Authority, the Bi-State Development Agency is one of the newer semiautonomous public agencies created by state governments for local governmental purposes which appeared first with the Authority in the 1920s, received only occasional attention throughout the '30s, but sparked numerous copies nationwide in the decades following World War II. Created a "body corporate and politic" by an interstate compact of the two states in 1949, with consent granted by Congress in 1950,[1] the agency was established to carry out the states' mutual pledge of "faithful cooperation in the future planning and development" of the greater St. Louis metropolitan area, officially designated by the law as the Bi-State Metropolitan District.* While, legally, the two states are credited with having created the compact, in actuality it resulted from the efforts of a relatively small number of concerned persons. It has remained the special interest of less than the full population of the area it is designed to serve.

The district is not a flexible entity. Its boundaries do not necessarily frame precisely the population which it embraces. Rather, the two states have arbitrarily utilized existing counties and county lines to bound the metropolitan area, encompassing rural and urban areas alike, including the City of St. Louis, its suburban satellite towns, Illinois cities across the Mississippi River, and all other local governmental jurisdictions lying within the surrounding counties of St. Louis, St. Charles, and Jefferson of Missouri, and Madison, St. Clair, and Monroe of Illinois. The region thus encompassed contains 3,567 square miles and, in 1960, a population of 2,075,610. It holds 225 municipalities and an estimated 750 local taxing units.† By far, the

---

* Compact, Art. I. Other multistate arrangements of a similar nature, for similar purposes, are the Tri-State New York Region and its Regional Plan Association, involving New York, New Jersey, and Connecticut; the Philadelphia Metropolitan Region, embracing Pennsylvania, New Jersey, and Delaware; the Kansas City Metropolitan Area of Missouri and Kansas. Most of the other similar arrangements existing nationwide do not involve interstate compacts.

† Compact, Art. II. Cities of over 10,000 population (1969 estimates) within the district are: In *Illinois*— Alton, 48,500; Wood River, 13,100; Cahokia, 19,100; Centreville, 14,300;

greater political and economic power of the area rests in Missouri's cities and counties. Problems exist on both sides of the river, but they are not necessarily of the same kind or of the same degree. The district as created recognizes no distinctions, for the compact's purposes were designed to consider the district as a whole, to regard its problems as homogeneous and pervasive, with unified solutions to be sought for universal application. This is, of course, an artificial view. As such it is the source of the compact's serious limitations. But it also provides whatever strength the Bi-State Development Agency enjoys. It has been consistent with recent municipal governmental theory which holds that great metropolitan areas are actually single populations in the sense of having common needs, purposes, ultimate goals and objectives. That their needs and purposes are not held in common is obvious, since in an interstate metropolitan region the different laws of the separate states shape both needs and purposes and, no doubt, ultimate goals and objectives. This can also be said of the differing resources available to the populations of the separate states.

While the compact places no more emphasis on one than on the other of its two defined purposes of "planning" and "development," agency practice gives the accent to development, with planning generally confined to limited developmental objectives. Thus it must be classified as one of the nation's leading examples of an economic developmental interstate compact. Its creation was also evidence of postwar effort to find new and effective means and mechanisms for implementing the government of great metropolitan centers of dense population living within a multiplicity of jurisdictions and requiring area-wide services. Again, in practice, these objectives have been only meagerly attained, and the tangible accomplishments of the Bi-State Development Agency have not been impressive. It credits itself with a considerable creative role, however, in stimulating the few area-wide planning efforts which have been made, particularly on matters in which Bi-State is interested, and it has perhaps provided an element

---

Edwardsville, 10,000; Granite City, 40,000; Collinsville, 17,000; East St. Louis, 74,500; Belleville, 41,500. In *Missouri*—St. Louis, 688,000; St. Charles, 31,000; Clayton, 16,000; University City, 51,700; Florissant, 63,300; Webster Groves, 30,000; Kirkwood, 36,300; Ferguson, 30,100; Berkeley, 21,900; Brentwood, 13,300; Bellefontaine Neighbors, 15,600; Jennings, 22,900; St. Ann, 21,000; Overland, 27,600; Richmond Heights, 16,100; Maplewood, 16,000; Crestwood, 15,000; Affton, 34,000; Lemay, 22,000. Nearly all of the Missouri cities are today an integral part of metropolitan St. Louis.

of coordination of diverse interests in a few important instances where without it coordination, even the assembling, of such interests would have been impossible. But it has not been the creative force the compact suggests it was meant to be. No doubt this results from the difficulties inherent in the area itself, one which sprawls across state lines and one of the nation's greatest rivers, creating the kind of jurisdictional mare's nest that makes for the utter confusion and defeat of meaningful government along traditional lines and frustrates the best efforts of a congested population for a sensible, orderly life.

The compact and its agency can no longer be regarded as in their experimental stage. After twenty years of existence certain roots have been put down and some reckoning can be taken of performance. It is remarkable that an agency of government affecting such a large population has had so little attention from impartial and objective analysts; with a single exception, critical literature is nonexistent.

The Terms of the Compact

Since the adoption of the creative legislation in 1949, the Bi-State Development Compact has been amended with significant augmentation of its original powers. The two states in 1953, 1958, and 1959 enacted laws extending the agency's financial powers, granting it the same tax-free or tax-exempt status of municipalities of the two states, a limited power of condemnation, and contractual powers. These additional provisions were approved by Congress in 1959.[2]

As originally drawn, the compact created the Bi-State Metropolitan District and the Bi-State Development Agency to plan, establish, and operate projects and services deemed essential to the purposes of the district, enabling it to finance itself through revenue bonds, fees, and user charges from such facilities as it might subsequently establish. The compact's focus, as has been repeatedly stressed by agency officials, has concentrated heavily on transportation facilities, although the broad terms of the law command a considerably more diverse and comprehensive role in area functions, development, and planning. In its beginning years the agency reflected its commissioners' apparent belief that it held this broader planning role, with issuance of several important studies, surveys, and reports on matters within its general powers, but after its financing capacities were strengthened in

1959, it has devoted itself to transportation matters and, indeed, retreats from suggestions that it might play a different role.

As conceived, the agency through its tax-free status was intended to construct greatly needed public improvements, particularly those which might not be attractive to private developers or which might be beyond the capabilities of the various involved governmental units to provide. But it was also anticipated that it would perform a coordinative role through its community-wide planning which would serve to eliminate inefficiencies and costly duplication of efforts among the area's numerous taxing jurisdictions. Much, therefore, depended upon the vision and interests of the first commissioners appointed by the two states, upon the breadth of their understanding of the compact's potentials and their willingness to provide the dynamic action to accomplish such ends. Not less depended upon the two states' willingness to support the agency financially in its formative stages, and upon proper initial organization of the agency. The compact's terms anticipated the hiring of officers and employees, but a salaried executive director and proper headquarters were not established by the commission until 1960, shortly after obtaining its additional financial authority, and eleven years after its creation.

The agency's first decade of increasing incapacity resulted from the recalcitrance of the Missouri Legislature, which, after appropriating in 1949–50 its initial $50,000 share of the agency's requested funds, refused for two successive biennia to support the agency. Illinois appropriated its share regularly, but the funds were conditional upon Missouri's grant of equal sums and were thus rendered inoperable when Missouri failed to come through. Without funds, an adequate headquarters establishment was out of the question, and the commissioners were forced to seek financing for their work in other ways, sufficient to allow them to accomplish a number of necessary studies and surveys, but inadequate to the larger purposes of comprehensive planning, purchasing, building, and operating substantial revenue-producing facilities. Funds came from grants for particular studies from federal and state agencies (both states participating) and from St. Louis County. For its first major project, the Granite City Wharf and Docks, the agency acceded to the dubious expedient of financing itself with a loan from a highly interested private corporation, the Granite City Steel Company, which wanted the wharf and dock facilities built and did not want to build its own, and which subsequently has been the chief beneficiary of the improvements.

Most of the first commissioners appointed by Illinois and Missouri apparently cannot be faulted in their quality, their zeal or enthusiasm. In subsequent years, however, the two states' practices in appointing members offer possible explanations for some of the agency's first decade difficulties, as will be shown hereafter.

The Agency's Powers

As a "body corporate and politic," the agency enjoys the same general status in law as any public or municipal corporation, with all the rights, powers, and privileges of such status. Its specific powers are:

1. *Planning,* extended to (a) bridges, tunnels, airports, and terminal facilities; (b) harbors, wharves and docks, warehouses, grain elevators, commodity and other storage facilities, sewage disposal plants, passenger transportation facilities, and "air, water, rail, motor vehicle and other" terminal facilities [Added, 1953]; (c) policies for sewage and drainage facilities; (d) coordination of streets, highways, parkways, parking areas, terminals, water supply and sewage and disposal works, recreational and conservation facilities and projects, land use patterns, and "other matters" in which joint action of the area's communities will be beneficial; (e) the general development of the district. Plans of this nature become binding when approved by the legislatures of the two states.

2. *Construction, maintenance, ownership, and operation,* applicable to all of the facilities named above.

3. *Power to acquire title by gift, purchase, or lease,* to any and all of the named facilities.

4. *Self-financing power,* through fees (which it may set) for the facilities it owns or operates, through issuance of revenue bonds, through gifts or grants from other governmental bodies, through borrowing, and through issuance of negotiable bonds, notes, and other instruments for handling its valid indebtedness.

5. *Spending power,* of funds lawfully obtained.

6. *Power over its debt repayment,* but its notes, bonds, and other paper have a maximum life of thirty years, can bear interest not exceeding 6 percent per annum, and can be sold at no less than 85 percent of par value.

7. *Contractual power* on matters under its general authority.

8. *Power to petition regulatory agencies* or other administrative, judicial, or legislative authority operating within the metropolitan district, for changes in methods, adoption of physical improvements, changes in transportation rates, systems of handling freight, etc.

9. *Power to sue and be sued.*

10. *Power to appoint and remove* its own employees, and to designate their number and duties.

11. *Recommendatory power* over improvements in any matters under its general mandate, to the two states' legislatures and the United States Congress.

12. *Rule-making power,* for the Agency's governance and for the facilities under its jurisdiction (limited only as described below.)

13. *A power of condemnation* (limited only as described below.) [3]

While the specific powers granted to the agency are in themselves limitations, due to their specificity and enumeration, the agency is more positively limited in the following ways:

1. All powers and functions are subject to prior authorization through enacted law, concurred in by both states and by Congress.

2. Property held by political jurisdictions within the Bi-State Metropolitan District (states, counties, cities, towns, special districts)

is not subject to eminent domain. Consent to the agency's acquisitions must be obtained from the jurisdiction concerned.

Property owned, leased, controlled, operated or used by common carriers engaged in interstate commerce, or by any grain elevator, cannot be taken or condemned by the agency without written consent and approval of the common carrier and the owner or operator of the grain elevator. Property located in Illinois is subject to Illinois laws on eminent domain; in Missouri, to Missouri laws.

3. Existing bonded indebtedness of such political jurisdictions can in no way be impaired or invalidated by the compact's terms; neither can existing legal provisions regulating payment of public revenues into sinking funds, or dedication of such revenues to "earmarked" funds.

4. The agency has no power to levy taxes or assessments.

5. In its internal operations, the agency must file a detailed annual report with both states' governors. Its actions must be approved by majority vote of each state's delegation, with at least three members from each state present and voting in order to do business. It must render advice and assistance to municipal officials, to enable municipal improvements to fit in with the overall plans of development which the agency may make; and its rules and regulations for the improvement of the district must be consistent with the constitutions and laws of the United States, both of the states and their political subdivisions, and Congress may exercise its power over them. Once approved, such rules and regulations are binding on all persons and corporations affected.

6. It is required to create an advisory council of an undesignated number of representatives of district business, labor, and other civic bodies, the duties, meeting dates, and general authority of which are undefined in the law, but its objectives must be concerned with compact matters.[4]

One additional potential limitation is the compact's art. V, sec. 2, which reserves to each state the right to vest its governor with veto power over the actions of that state's appointed commissioners. As noted hereafter, this is an important omission on the part of Illinois and Missouri, since neither state has yet seen fit to extend such authority to its governors, thus leaving the central administration of each state with only such control as may be involved in the governors' appointments of commissioners, and such appointments are of course always subject to senatorial approval, thus allowing metropolitan area legislators a no doubt considerable influence in gubernatorial choices in both states.

Reservations by Congress

According to its slowly developing practices on consent to interstate compacts, Congress specifically reserved to the federal government the right to review any additional powers which might be conferred on the agency by the two states' legislatures and, as noted above, a right to review the rules and regulations made by the agency.[5] It also added four provisos in its consent resolution, one of which made the agency's income and financial obligations subject to the tax laws of the United States. This provision was subsequently amended in 1959. The other three follow:

And provided further, That nothing herein contained shall be construed to affect, impair, or diminish any right, power, or jurisdiction of the United States or of any court, department, board, bureau, officer, or official of the United States, in, over, or in regard to the territory which is embraced in the district created by the . . . compact . . . or any navigable waters, or any commerce between the States or with foreign countries, or any bridge, railroad, highway, pier, wharf, or other facility or improvement, or any other person, matter, or thing, forming the subject matter of the . . . compact . . . ; or otherwise affected by the terms thereof; *And provided further,* That no power or powers shall be exercised by the Bi-State Agency under that certain portion of Article III of such compact which reads:

"8. To exercise such additional powers as shall be conferred on it by the legislature of either state concurred in by the legislature of the other or by act of Congress."

unless and until such power or powers shall have been conferred upon the Bi-State Agency by the legislature of one of the States to the Compact and concurred in by the legislature of the other and shall have been approved by an Act of Congress; *And provided further,* That the right to alter, amend, or repeal this resolution is hereby expressly reserved.[6]

By Public Law 86–303,[7] enacted by Congress on September 21, 1959, to approve certain additional powers granted to the agency by the two states, an additional reservation was attached:

SEC. 4. The right is hereby reserved to the Congress and to its standing committees to require the disclosure and furnishing of such information or data by the Bi-State Development Agency as is deemed appropriate by the Congress or any such committee.[8]

As described in chapter 2 of this study, the Supreme Court's decision in *Tobin* v. *U.S.* (1962) casts considerable doubt upon congressional power to "alter, amend, or repeal" even though these basic and fundamental constitutional questions were certainly not answered in that case. In any event, no litigation has arisen to test the Bi-State Development Compact's clause, which is identical to that written into the New York Port Authority's law in 1921 and 1922, and may very well be regarded by the courts in some future case which may arise as having established a somewhat different congressional power than was involved in the Port Authority case. At best, the meanings of these clauses are rendered somewhat moot as matters presently stand.

Public Law 86–303 also approved amendment of the agency's tax status from taxable to tax-exempt, in accordance with Illinois's and Missouri's grant to the agency of municipal corporation status.[9] The agency thus enjoys a rather favorable position and has entered into extensive acquisitions of real and personal property since. The agency notes, "As stated, the Agency has no taxing powers, and neither the states, the counties, the cities or any other tax supported body makes any guarantee, or assumes any responsibility with respect to Agency securities. Thus all projects must be revenue producing, and show sufficient revenue to pay both the interest and the principal, together with some margin of safety." [10] As will be shown, not all projects have been revenue producing sufficient to meet this requirement. The agency has had to turn in recent years to Missouri and Illinois for two important bailing-out operations involving considerable sums.

Political and Other Limitations

Such other checks or limitations on agency activity as exist are derived from the compact's relationships to the two states' general laws, or are political, arising from the multiplicity of public bodies, areas, and private groups or interests embraced by the District. The latter are of formidable proportions.

The Bi-State Compact, in accord with other interstate arrangements of its kind, clearly establishes no single parent government having sole power over the agency and the district it is to serve. Illinois and Missouri have deliberately delegated to the agency a considerable realm of freedom in which to act, with certain powers making it to a high degree independent of traditional governmental controls at all levels of government. The United States, while reserving to itself an ultimate total authority through its asserted right to review, alter, or abolish, has not only been placed in a position of doubtful authority in all of these possible controls, but has also in fact acted in relation to the agency only permissively, extending and greatly broadening its original powers through endorsement of state-granted permissive financial arrangements. The major curbs on agency activities, to date, have come from the local governmental bodies (the City of St. Louis, St. Louis County, the City of Venice, Illinois; Cahokia, Illinois; and Madison County.) To the chagrin of the Bi-State Agency, the federal government was found to have partial authority through the Interstate Commerce Commission over the Bi-State Transit System (the St. Louis metropolitan area-wide system recently acquired by the agency) through its power over rates of transit lines operating outside the jurisdiction of particular municipalities. These are county coach lines and lines crossing state boundaries, such as the Belleville–St. Louis Coach Company, one of those acquired by Bi-State. Also, the United States Army Corps of Engineers continues to hold its traditional functions in relation to the Mississippi and Missouri Rivers' usages (flood control, navigation, construction, diversion, and the like). The Federal Water Pollution Control Administration now has an important interest in the area's industrial and governmental life, with ramifications which reach into the Bi-State Agency's planning and operational activities. The private businesses and interests of both sides of the river have both a legal and a political interest in the agency's acts, and these have been a restraint of incalculable proportions. Some specific instances of their actions both in support and opposition are described hereafter.

But another and most important type of check has developed in Illinois through the state's creation of additional governmental bodies with powers similar or identical to those held by the Bi-State Development Agency, most of which have been created since Bi-State's financial powers were enlarged, which duplicate or overlap the Bi–State Development District on the Illinois side of the Mississippi for much of the jurisdictional and geographical area under Illinois' sole control. These are the Tri-City Regional Port District,[11] (involving Granite City, Venice, and Nameoki, Illinois, and the townships of the same names, all in Madison County; a part of Chouteau Township, and all of Chouteau and Gaboret Islands); the Southwest Regional Port District [12] (comprising the St. Clair County townships of Canteen, Centreville, East St. Louis, Stites, and Sugar Loaf); the Little Egypt Regional Port District [13] (embracing all of Monroe and Randolph Counties, and Freeburg, Millstadt, Smithton, Prairie-DuLong, New Athens and Lenzburg Townships of St. Clair County); the South-western Illinois Metropolitan Area Planning Commission,[14] (generally vested with overall planning and developmental authority for the entire area of Madison, St. Clair, and Monroe Counties); and the Illinois–Missouri Bridge Commission, another interstate compact agency concerned with an area adjacent to but outside the defined boundaries of the Bi-State Agency, involving construction of a Mississippi River bridge in the vicinity of Ste. Genevieve, Missouri.[15] The Bridge Commission is not lacking in interest to Bi-State, for one of the latter's early anticipated developments was the proposed extension of Bi-State's jurisdiction southward to embrace Ste. Genevieve County, Missouri and Randolph County, Illinois. A meeting of Bi-State Commissioners with the Chester Bridge Commission on January 14, 1952, was the earliest evidence of agency ambitions, postponed at that time but ultimately resulting in a plan for con-structing a toll bridge at Crystal City, Missouri which was proposed and considered by Bi-State commissioners at their May 16, 1961, meeting. In response to questions on the agency's power to construct such a bridge outside its geographical jurisdiction, the plan's supporters asserted there was no need to create an additional authority; Bi-State already had the necessary power to act. Specific legal authority was not cited.[16] With the subsequent adoption of an additional interstate compact by Illinois and Missouri, rather than an enlargement of Bi-State's own jurisdictional area, it is clear that Bi-State was adjudged not to have the necessary power to build or acquire such a bridge and unidentified interests were opposed to granting it such an extensive addition to its territory just to enable it to do so.

Following adoption by the federal government of the Housing and Urban Development Act of 1965, which made organizations of local elected officials in metropolitan areas eligible to receive federal grants for the preparation of comprehensive metropolitan plans, the East–West Gateway Coordinating Council was created on December 8, 1965. Its establishment culminated months of effort and various attempts to create some kind of area-wide planning arrangement. Once established, it has tended to displace the Bi-State Development Agency as the Metropolitan District's overall planning agent, although "displace" is more of an academic term than otherwise, since Bi-State actually never engaged in area-wide planning to any significant extent, and it does continue to plan within the range of its interest. Further, the East–West Council has not yet become the sole planning agent for the district, nor is it likely to become such in the foreseeable future.

All of the above agencies have been created in at least partial oppositional response to certain real or proposed actions of the Bi-State Agency, or as a result of its inaction on matters of interest to Illinois. The East–West Gateway Coordinating Council was spurred into existence by the area's desire to catch a piece of the federal action in metropolitan area grants; distaste for Bi-State on the Illinois side of the river forced creation of the new body, but it is safe to assert that without the lure of such federal money, the Illinois intransigence would have continued to block creation of any such planning agency indefinitely. That the council and all of the other agencies here described have served to limit and confine the Bi-State Agency, effectively harnessing most of its expansionist efforts, is clearly evident over a period of time in the gradual diminution of Bi-State's range of interests. But the overall effect has not been to shift action or effort to these Illinois agencies for consummation of area-wide proposals and projects, for they have produced little in tangible accomplishments and have served primarily as mechanisms for special interest expression and manipulation of power.

The result is that Bi-State has virtually ceased any efforts in overall planning, and has become only one of several possible agencies for overall development of a coordinated system of area-wide transit services and facilities, overall development of an area-wide land use pattern, and the like. Instead, the agency has concentrated its efforts on what it can do—placing emphasis on a very few activities, not always easily defensible as beneficial to the entire area's range of interests. Rather, it seems to have most benefitted the City and County of St. Louis, private industry, and a few particular interests in Illinois.

Agency Organization: The Board of Commissioners

The Bi-State Development Agency consists of ten commissioners, five of whom are appointed by the governor of Missouri with senatorial consent from voting residents of the Missouri portion of the Metropolitan District, and five by the governor of Illinois under the same conditions. Their five-year terms are staggered on an annual basis. Vacancies may be filled only by the respective governors with senatorial consent. Commissioners serve without pay, but receive their necessary expenses.[17] A number of commissioners have served several successive terms. The commissioners elect a chairman and a vice-chairman from their own number, and one commissioner is designated by the governor of his state as chairman of that state's five-member delegation.[18]

The board thus constituted has the power to appoint and remove all other officers and employees of the agency, fixing duties, qualifications, and compensation.[19] It also elects from its own number a secretary and a treasurer (which offices may be held by one person), and these officers have appointive power, with board consent, over subordinate personnel.[20]

The agency's bylaws were specific in requiring that the regular meetings be held each month on the second Monday,[21] but meetings during the agency's life were not regular, with some being held on the fourth Thursday and, today, the fourth Wednesday adopted as the official meeting day. The agency's near-demise from 1955 through 1959 is clearly reflected in its record of meetings: [22]

1949—	2 meetings	1958—	1 meeting(s)
1950—	11 "	1959—	2 "
1951—	6 "	1960—	4 "
1952—	8 "	1961—	9 "
1953—	7 "	1962—	11 "
1954—	4 "	1963—	10 "
1955—	2 "	1964—	9 "
1956—	3 "	1965—	6 "
1957—	1 "		

A quorum at any meeting of the board is three commissioners from each state, and actions become official by favorable vote of a majority from each state's delegation present and voting.[23] The agency's minutes indicate most important board actions taken during the agency's lifetime (such as the decision to acquire the metropolitan area transit systems) have been by unanimous vote of those present and voting. In a very few instances, individual commissioners have left a meeting before an official vote was taken. Important agency decisions have usually been made by a substantial majority of the entire board present. However, the 1950 decision to sign an agreement with the Granite City Steel Company for construction of wharf and terminal facilities at Granite City harbor was made by unanimous vote of only seven members present and voting,[24] and subsequent action in agreeing to certain purchases and contracts in connection with the same project was approved in 1951 by the required quorum of six members only.[25] A quorum only also returned a favorable but divided (five-to-one) vote on the agency's Executive Committee activities in their efforts to acquire the McKinley Bridge in 1951,[26] and it was also a quorum of six which acted at a special meeting in 1954 called by Chairman L. J. Sverdrup to approve the $1,500,000 bond issue and lease for the Granite City wharf and dock facilities.[27] While under the established quorum rule it is possible for only five members of the board to make major policy decisions (as illustrated in the McKinley Bridge matter), only this one incident is recorded in the minutes.

Nothing in the agency's laws or bylaws stipulates that board meetings must be open to the public. The records indicate that guests, interested officials, and representatives of the press have frequently been present. The board, however, at a 1959 meeting (after the agency received its broadened financial power), adopted a policy of barring news representatives from the meetings on the grounds that their presence created an atmosphere of tension and reticence that was incompatible with the deliberative nature of the board's duties.[28] Whether this policy has been consistently followed since is impossible to determine from the agency's records. It is true that the press has been present by invitation at several meetings since that time and, on at least one or two special occasions, has been accompanied by both radio and television broadcasting representatives. The latter, however, were occasions when the agency sought special publicity for its activities.

Although each commissioner is named to a five-year term, the record of board appointees from each state shows considerable difference in practices between the two states in their delegations' tenure and deligence in attending, as indicated in table 1, containing the names and terms of all commissioners from the agency's beginnings through 1966. Missouri has had much greater turnover and variety among her appointees, they have generally served for briefer periods (often for less than the full term), and have attended meetings with less regularity than have the Illinois commissioners. Board members showing both long terms and regular attendance have generally been the agency's chief officers. It is not altogether clear in the existing records (those, at least, made available to the author; not all of the agency's records were placed at her disposal, as is indicated hereafter) what factors have played an influential part in the seemingly less concerned performance of most of Missouri's appointees as compared with those of Illinois. But in view of many factors of St. Louis's political life and the more favored position enjoyed by Missouri in the Metropolitan District, the Illinois commissioners seem to assume something of a "watchdog" role, while one is moved to guess the Missourians are confident their full attention to Bi-State matters is not quite so vital to the general developmental policies of St. Louis. A St. Louis appointee held the agency's chairmanship for the first ten years of its existence, during which time the agency made scant progress. Further, considering Illinois's general faithfulness in appropriating its share of agency moneys when requested, the Illinois concern for the agency and its purposes emerges as more substantial than Missouri's.

Indicative of the business and industrial affiliations of the agency's past and present board members are the following: Chester C. Davis, president, Federal Reserve Bank of St. Louis (which has been represented by a commissioner from the agency's beginnings); William G. Marbury, president, Mississippi River Fuel Corporation; Aloys P. Kaufmann, attorney and former mayor of St. Louis; Gale F. Johnston, president, Mercantile–Commerce Bank & Trust Company, St. Louis; C. M. Roos, civil engineer and retired superintendent of the East St. Louis and Interurban Water Company; Roy S. Rauschkolb, the Tri-Cities Chamber of Commerce; Delos C. Johns, president, Federal Reserve Bank of St. Louis; Sidney W. Souers, board chairman, General American Life Insurance Company; Charles F. Ford, a partner in A. G. Edwards & Sons, stock brokers of St. Louis; Frederick L. Deming,

1. COMMISSIONERS OF THE BI-STATE DEVELOPMENT AGENCY—*by state, showing tenure, and meetings attended*

ILLINOIS

Term	Name	Meetings attended
1949–63	C. M. Roos	74
1949–50	Albert L. Wegener	10
1949–53	H. E. Jackson	29*
1949–58	Roy S. Rauschkolb	42**
1949–61	John F. Schlafly, Jr.	45
1952–53	J. D. Gray	5*
1954–66	Herbert S. Wilhelm	52
1954–63	J. F. Schmidt	30
1959–66	C. E. Townsend	53
1961–66	Edward J. Delmore, Jr.	45
1963–64	R. H. Richards	1
1964–65	W. B. Bergfeld, Sr.	11
1964–66	Roy J. May	13
1966–	Terryl W. Francis	1

MISSOURI

Term	Name	Meetings attended
1949–51	Chester C. Davis	10
1949–58	Gen. L. J. Sverdrup	42
1949–53	William G. Marbury	18
1949–55	Aloys P. Kaufmann	29
1950–62	Gale F. Johnston	52
1951–52	Delos C. Johns	6
1953–56	Charles F. Ford	7
1954–56	Frederick L. Deming	6
1955–61	Morton R. Bearman	21 (two terms)
1965–66	" " "	
1957–63	Harry Harrington	23
1957–59	E. E. Pershall	2
1959–61	Preston Estep	14
1962–64	Leo A. Fisher	17
1963–64	Edwin J. Spiegel	12
1964–65	Donald V. Fraser	5
1965–66	Joseph Cousin	1
1965–66	Robert S. Knapp	6
1966–	Guy Roper	2

* Died before end of term
** Moved before end of term

vice president, Federal Reserve Bank, St. Louis; J. F. Schmidt, executive vice president, State Bank of Waterloo, Illinois; Herbert S. Wilhelm, executive secretary of an AF of L local; Harry Harrington, president, Boatmen's Bank, St. Louis; E. E. Pershall, chairman of the board, Moss Tie Company, St. Louis; Morton M. Bearman, investment broker and real estate, St. Louis; Preston Estep, president and board chairman, Transit Casualty Company, and Bank of St. Louis; D. Richard Adams, labor leader in Illinois; C. E. Townsend, editor, *Granite City Press Record*; and Donald V. Fraser, retired chairman, Missouri-Kansas-Texas Railroad.

The strong position of the St. Louis business community in the Bi-State Agency's activities is reflected in these selected affiliations. Particularly strong representation is given to financial and transit-using interests. Labor has been represented in the delegations from both states by at least one commissioner from each. Agriculture (which, as has emerged on questions of St. Louis County charter revision,[29] has a definite although negative interest in metropolitan area development), retail and wholesale business, the professions, householders, and the Negro community (which represents a great part of St. Louis City's population and a major part of that of E. St. Louis, Illinois and is certainly one of the chief elements served by the Bi-State Transit System), have had no direct representation.

While Gale F. Johnston served the agency as its treasurer, its checking accounts were deposited with the Mercantile-Commerce Bank and Trust Company. The Transit Casualty Company, of which Preston Estep is president, was the insurance company servicing most of the fifteen acquired transit lines. And, until the agency acquired offices and equipment of its own to accommodate its meetings, it met in the board of directors' room of the St. Louis Federal Reserve Bank.

Those familiar with St. Louis's civic life probably will not find this representational pattern surprising. The city's economic progress has for most of the two decades since World War II been the focus of considerable concern by the city's leading business interests, and a relatively small group of such men has taken the initiative in studying, planning, and promoting developmental activities. Until the creation of the Bi-State Development Agency and, much later, the East-West Gateway Coordinating Council, St. Louis County and Illinois-side business and industrial interests had scant opportunity to play a direct role in policy-making decisions affecting the entire metropolitan area.* It is noteworthy that only one newspaper editor has served on the agency's board, and he is from Granite City, Illinois. Yet even here the paramount nature of industrial concern and interest in metropolitan development is reflected, for Granite City is dominated by the Granite City Steel Company, and, presumably, C. E. Townsend's interest in his city's well-being includes an interest in the welfare of its chief industry.

The agency carries on most of its activities through standing or temporary committees invested with such powers as the board thinks fit to grant. The bylaws specifically designate an executive committee to be appointed by resolution and majority vote of the whole board, holding such powers as the board determines. The records suggest that most of the agency's important decisions are formulated and to a considerable extent determined within the executive committee, with the whole board generally amenable to its proposals.† All such committees are required to keep regular minutes of their meetings and transactions, available at the agency's headquarters.[30]

The present roster of committees and their membership is as shown in table 2 (as of June 30, 1968). This committee structure, with only a very few alterations, is virtually the same as the arrangement adopted in 1959 at the time of the agency's "rebirth" with

---

* Washington University political scientist Robert H. Salisbury sees the St. Louis situation in this regard as characteristic of most of the nation's large cities. Describing what he sees as new alignments of urban political power, he states, "The most active business firms in the new convergence, however, are those with major investments in the community, which are dependent on the growth of a particular community. . . . They include the major banks, utilities, railroads, department stores, large real estate firms, and metropolitan newspapers. Functionally, the list is remarkably similar from city to city. Also similar is the fact that active concern with community affairs is relatively recent, largely post–World War II, and coincides with the perception of threat to tangible 'downtown' economic values. Finally, the re-entry of these groups into the active quest for power coincides with the weakening of the party-political dominance of the governmental arena.

. . . Much of the lay leadership [in all such cities] of public campaigns for bonds, for example; much of the stimulus to action itself; and much of the private portion of new investment necessary to redevelopment came from this newly organized group. . . .

"Cities vary with respect not only to energy and skill of leadership but in tangible resources, public and private that may be mobilized for reallocation. In Pittsburgh, for example, there was probably no available substitute for the Mellon cash. In St. Louis the scarcity or stodginess or both of local private capital has made the redevelopment task more difficult."

See Robert H. Salisbury, "Urban Politics: The New Convergence of Power," *Journal of Politics*, Vol. 26, Nov. 1964, pp. 785 and 793.

† A positive statement in this regard is impossible to make, for the Minutes of the Executive Committee were not made available to the author.

2. COMMITTEES OF THE BI–STATE DEVELOPMENT AGENCY, AND MEMBERSHIP, AS OF 1968

Executive Committee:	Charles E. Hamilton, *Chmn.* (ILL.)**
	Sidney W. Souers (MO.) †
	Robert S. Knapp (MO.)*
	Edward J. Delmore, Jr. (ILL.)
Finance Committee:	Sidney W. Souers, *Chmn.*
	Ralph B. Jackson (ILL.)
	Roy J. May (ILL.)
	Guy Roper (MO.)
Legislative Liaison:	Guy Roper, *Chmn.*
	Morton R. Bearman (MO.)
	Terryl W. Francis (ILL.)
	Charles E. Hamilton
Transit Operations:	Edward J. Delmore, Jr., *Chmn.*
	Charles E. Hamilton
	Morton R. Bearman
	Guy Roper
Airport, Arch & Harbor:	Morton R. Bearman, *Chmn.*
	Joseph Cousin (MO.)
	Ralph B. Jackson
	Terryl W. Francis
Pension & Insurance:	Roy J. May, *Chmn.*
	Morton R. Bearman

* Chairman, Bi-State Agency
** Vice Chairman, Bi-State Agency
† Treasurer, Bi-State Agency

stronger financial powers. As thus constituted, the agency's chairman, vice-chairman, and treasurer are always members of the important executive committee, and the agency's treasurer is the finance committee's chairman. A degree of balance between the two states' delegations is established through equal distribution of committee assignments.

The considerations which enter into the commissioners' choice of their chairman are not revealed in agency records. Dissatisfaction on the part of Illinois's delegation erupted in a controversy over the chairmanship shortly after General L. J. Sverdrup's resignation in 1958. At the April 10, 1959, meeting, efforts by Illinoisans to elect one of their delegation were temporarily blocked. Strong objection to Missouri's domination of the agency was voiced by Illinois member John F. Schlafly, Jr., of Alton, as reported in the minutes:

For ten years the majority of the officers of the Agency had been from Missouri, that Illinois had been more liberal in appropriating funds for the Agency than Missouri and also had been more cooperative in providing proper legislation. He said further that there is certain opposition to the Agency in Illinois because the Agency is completely Missouri dominated, and he felt that there would be further serious criticism if the Chairman were elected from Missouri.[31]

The *East St. Louis Journal* recorded his remarks more specifically:

"I simply do not think we are a bi-state agency," Schlafly said. "We have a Missouri chairman, a Missouri majority on the executive committee [apparently true in 1959, before present committee organizational practices were established], a Missouri chief engineer, a Missouri office, and a Missouri secretariat.

"I feel we would be subject to serious criticism if we elect another Missouri chairman, regardless of qualifications. It is time for Illinois to be represented." [32]

To this Herbert S. Wilhelm, executive secretary of the Central Labor Council of Greater East St. Louis, agreed and thereupon nominated C. M. Roos of Belleville, who declined the nomination "for personal reasons" [33] and, in turn, nominated Preston Estep of Missouri, a newly appointed member, and further moved that Schlafly be named vice-chairman and Wilhelm be appointed as a fourth member of the executive committee. The *Journal* observed,

Roos had attempted to forestall the move by reporting the Agency was nearing a milestone after 10 years of effort. He said it appeared legislative problems in Missouri have been resolved and asked for a continuance of harmonious relations between the commissioners from the two states.

He reported all of the money the Agency has spent has gone to the east side of the river, citing the development of the Granite City Harbor which he said had increased payrolls in the Granite City area by $6 million per year. He also credited the Agency with much of the planning for the extensive highway improvement now under way on the Illinois side.

"We haven't as yet spent a penny on the Missouri side but the Missouri commissioners have raised no objections," he said.[34]

Upon withdrawal of Roos's and Wilhelm's nominations, Schlafly; J. F. Schmidt, executive vice-president of the State Bank of Waterloo;

Morton R. Bearman, St. Louis investment broker; and Harry F. Harrington, president of the Boatmen's Bank of St. Louis, were appointed to work out a compromise.

This committee's efforts resulted in adoption at the June 22, 1959, meeting of the agency's present system of balancing the two states in committee assignments; a decision to hold two simultaneous meetings of mayors, other municipal authorities, executives of chambers of commerce, and representatives of labor, in East St. Louis and St. Louis, upon adoption of certain legislation pending in the Illinois legislature; and nomination and election of Roos as chairman, Preston Estep as vice-chairman, Schlafly as chairman of the executive committee, Wilhelm as secretary, and Gale F. Johnston of St. Louis as treasurer. Milton Kinsey of St. Louis was continued as chief engineer.[35]

The two proposed meetings were to explore the wishes of Illinois's and Missouri's area interests in regard to projects which Bi-State might undertake. To this end the agency planned to solicit recommendations from the approximately two hundred municipalities of the area for proposals, and for suggestions on appointments to an agency advisory council. The latter, required by law but never established, resulted in further interstate controversy, as discussed hereafter.[36]

Chairman Roos served only briefly, resigning at the September 7, 1960, meeting, when Preston Estep was elected to replace him. Estep subsequently served as chairman until November 1961, when he resigned on grounds of a possible conflict of interest should Bi-State establish its anticipated metropolitan area-wide transit system. Estep, board chairman of the Bank of St. Louis, was also president of the Transit Casualty Company, which for many years had been the insurance agency for metropolitan area transit lines, with contracts written on a long-term basis.[37]

The Bi-State Board's relationships with the two states' governments had not, through 1966, been placed on a systematized basis. The agency in its earliest days functioned in its dealings with the state capitols through occasional visits to Springfield and Jefferson City by selected members of the board. But the record indicates that legislative and administrative relationships with Illinois, at least, were maintained on less than a satisfactory basis as the agency's organization matured.

Board discussion of this problem appears in the minutes of the March 31, 1965, meeting:

Chairman Townsend speaking from the Illinois point of view stated he deemed it desirable to obtain an audience with Governor Kerner to better acquaint him with Bi-State's activities and basic established policies. It was the view of Chairman Townsend, which view was shared by the other Illinois Commissioners, that relations between Bi-State and the Governor's office would be greatly improved following a frank and free exchange of ideas and factual information.

.   .   .   .

Commissioner Knapp questioned whether Bi-State had a Committee charged with the duty of maintaining a liaison between Bi-State and the legislative heads of the two states. Chairman Townsend replied that a legislative committee as such had never been established. However, he stated that this function would belong to the Executive Committee.[38]

This exchange occurred shortly before the agency began intensive efforts to obtain financial assistance from the two states; initially, with feelers for state support for development of a rapid transit system, which resulted in a 1965 Missouri appropriation of $150,000 to St. Louis for a St. Louis metropolitan area study of rapid transit needs and possibilities; and later, for much more substantial sums from both states for improvements of the existing transit system, described hereafter. The board did not agree that the Executive Committee should assume the suggested role posed for it by Chairman Townsend, but during the following fiscal year (1966–67) created the Legislative Liaison Committee, with the same membership it holds today. The committee's name stresses its prime function: legislation. It is not a liaison agency to work with the governors or the executive branches of the two states. The latter will undoubtedly continue on a personal, informal basis, as far as agency operations are concerned.

Further underscoring the agency's abandonment of its developmental planning role is the abolition of its Regional Planning Committee in 1966–67, following establishment of the East-West Gateway Coordinating Council on a relatively firm basis. The Bi-State Agency is a member of the council and works closely with it, but its own regional planning emphasis is confined to comprehensive transportation planning and it is quite content to leave the general planning problem to the council.

The Secretary

The board elects from its own membership a secretary and a treasurer. The secretary is required to issue notice of meetings, keep minutes of the meetings, have custody of the agency's books and seal, and perform such other secretarial duties as may arise. Special meetings may be called by the chairman, or by two commissioners, but one of the latter must be from Missouri and one from Illinois.[39]

The Treasurer

The Board's treasurer is custodian of Agency moneys and such of its securities as are not required by the laws of either state to be deposited with the respective state treasurers. He is charged with keeping accounts and is chief disbursing officer, with no authority to act without board permission.[40] Since the Agency's creation in 1949, only two commissioners have served as treasurer: Mr. Gale F. Johnston, president of the Mercantile-Commerce Bank & Trust Company, from 1950 through 1962; and from 1963 to the present, Admiral Sidney W. Souers, the first head of the United States government's Central Intelligence Agency, who joined the Bi-State Agency in 1961.

Other Agency Officers and Organization

Of the remainder of the agency's personnel, the most significant in terms of administrative organizational problems of an interstate compact agency are the executive director, the advisory council, and the operative personnel attached to each of the Agency's several enterprises.

The Executive Director

Following final adoption in 1959 by the two states and the United States Congress of certain Compact amendments broadening the agency's powers,[41] a permanent staff and office facilities were made possible. An executive director was appointed for the first time on September 7, 1960; he is Colonel R. E. Smyser, Jr., retired officer of the United States Army Corps of Engineers. Colonel Smyser had a long and extensive career with the corps in the St. Louis area of its Mississippi River operations prior to his retirement.

The executive director's duties are the customary ones for any chief administrative officer of a public agency. Like all such officers, he is in an excellent position to shape agency policy decisions through his advisory role and his firsthand, continuing role of general manager of agency affairs. His appointments to staff positions, recommendations for compensation of employees, appropriations for office expenses, purchases, audits, facilities, and the like, are subject to final board approval. Smyser was given general administrative supervision of the agency, with authority to sign or countersign certificates, contracts, and other agency instruments of value less than $50,000, on April 28, 1965.[42] He represents the agency at public functions, and is its spokesman in its day-by-day dealings with the mayors, business interests, and other public officials of the Metropolitan District.

Project and Enterprise Personnel

The Bi-State Agency operates its projects and facilities through service contracts with certain "service corporations" organized and chartered as "not-for-profit corporations" for the specific purpose of serving the Bi-State Agency's various enterprises while removing the agency from actual operation of them. The agency, therefore, has no employees on most of its operational projects. The estimated number of employees in 1966 working for these "not-for-profit corporations" was: Bi-State Transit System—2,235; Granite City Wharf & Terminal —6; Bi-State Parks Airport—4; Gateway Arch Transportation System —6 employees per shift.[43]

The Bi-State headquarters office at that time had seven employees: five professional and two clerical; one of the professional employees was the manager of the Gateway Arch Transportation System.

Advisory Council

The Illinois General Assembly in 1947 created a "Bi-State Commission,"[44] subsequently appointed, to explore the need for an interstate governmental arrangement of some kind in the St. Louis metropolitan area. The 1949 act which created the Bi-State Development

Agency charged its commissioners with the task of studying the recommendations made by the earlier Bi-State Commission, requiring public hearings and conferences to be held with federal, state, and municipal bodies within the district. The law was explicit in requiring the new board to create an advisory council of representatives of business, labor, and other civic interests to obtain their advice and information, and to enlist their active support of the agency and its purposes.[45]

Admittedly, the law is not too clear as to the expected permanence of this advisory council, since it links such a body with the earlier Bi-State Commission's recommendations. Nonetheless, the implication is reasonably clear that there shall be an advisory council, presumably at all times, "whose objectives include consideration of the matters embraced in the Compact," not further defined.

But such an advisory body was not created by the commissioners for the first ten years of the agency's existence. The first agency record of any attention given to the question is at the March 7, 1960, meeting. Noting that the compact required an advisory council, Preston Estep told the assembled commissioners that the presidents of Southern Illinois, St. Louis, and Washington Universities had formed a "Bi-State Pilot Committee," representing the same geographical area as that of the Bi-State Development Agency. Estep asked the board to approve this body as its advisory group, observing that Bi-State had no money for staff, while the heads of these universities could draw on personnel and facilities of great scope and value for research and planning purposes. The board approved the suggestion.[46]

News releases of the previous year indicate that the "pilot committee" was established by Presidents Delyte W. Morris of Southern Illinois University; the Very Reverend Paul C. Reinert, S.J., of St. Louis University; and Chancellor Ethan A. H. Shepley of Washington University, on the "recommendation of civic leaders on both sides of the Mississippi"[47] (unnamed) to "study means of better coordination and communication among agencies working toward the development of the Missouri-Illinois Bi-State area." W. Victor Weir, of Creve Coeur, Missouri, was named temporary chairman of the sixteen-member group. The temporary vice-chairman was C. E. Townsend, of the Bi-State Development Agency's board.

The appointment of such a pilot committee had been a major recommendation of the *Metropolitan Development Guide*, published in the fall of 1958 by the Metropolitan Plan Association, which had seen a pilot committee as "the most effective way to study the recommendations of a group of local specialists on land use, transportation, sanitation, water supply, parks, recreation, and economic development." The announcement of the appointments carefully explained that the new committee would be concerned solely with "voluntary coordination" and would not propose any changes in governmental organization. It noted that a survey of civic leaders had revealed "virtually unanimous agreement on the need for increased coordination among agencies concerned with improvement programs." [48]

Following this 1959 "outside" effort to promote the kind of activities the Bi-State Agency was empowered by law to perform but on which it had been less than active, the agency (as noted above in discussion of the 1959 board chairmanship controversy) was moved to call an "exploratory meeting" of some kind to get the sense of the area's community leaders on its problems, to acquaint them with Bi-State's powers and responsibilities, and to determine in what way the agency could be of service to the various municipalities. Simultaneous meetings were subsequently held in East St. Louis and St. Louis for leaders of the three Illinois counties on the one hand, and the three Missouri counties on the other.

At the St. Louis meeting, the Bi-State Agency presented a major program of public works needed by the district for its improvement and development, and stressed that Bi-State should play an important role in it. Girard C. Varnum, president of the St. Louis County Chamber of Commerce, suggested that a regional advisory council representing business, labor, and civic groups be appointed to help in selecting projects under the program.[49]

At the East St. Louis meeting, however, considerable dissatisfaction with existing metropolitan area affairs was voiced. Most of the objections centered around possibilities for promoting and developing an airport, and industrial site developments, on the Illinois side of the river, which seemingly had not received the support desired by the Illinoisans from St. Louis interests, including Bi-State.

A month later, on February 28, 1960, the pilot committee—now calling itself the "Bi-State Pilot Committee for Metropolitan Development," and enlarged to twenty-two members (eleven from Missouri and eleven from Illinois)—held a conference in St. Louis which was attended by some 125 civic leaders of the area, with the three university presidents prominently featured. President Morris stressed that the universities should offer more help in an advisory capacity to the Bi-State Agency; Chancellor Shepley emphasized that true bi-state collaboration could be accomplished only if the area realized its interdependence; and the Reverend Paul C. Reinert urged "voluntary action" to correct metropolitan ills. The program sought to explore means by which problems might be defined and priorities established, and consider how governmental agencies and organizations could work together, and how nongovernmental agencies and organizations might work together.[50]

Shortly thereafter, the Bi-State Agency voted to accept the "pilot committee" as its advisory group. C. E. Townsend thereupon resigned his chairmanship of the pilot committee because he was also a member of the Bi-State Agency's board. Fred B. Hunt, vice-president of the Southwestern Bell Telephone Company, St. Louis, was appointed to Townsend's position.

At the first meeting thereafter of the advisory council, on April 10, 1960, the group determined to appoint "appraisal committees" for six major developmental problems: economic development; transportation; land use; planning; water, sewage and draining; and neighborhood organizations. Each committee was to attempt determination of the present status of each of these six problem areas in the bistate district and assess the adequacy of coordination among agencies concerned with the problems. Preliminary work on these questions for the St. Louis side of the district had already been done by the Metropolitan St. Louis Survey conducted in 1957. That survey recommended a multi-government district for the St. Louis side of the river which would have had jurisdiction over metropolitan area-wide problems such as economic development. The proposal as made by the survey was later incorporated in a proposal placed by the St. Louis Board of Freeholders before the voters which was defeated in a 1959 election.[51]

But, despite all of this effort, the Bi-State Agency and the new "advisory council" seemingly did not function together thereafter, or, for that matter, at any time. In November 1961, the council, again calling itself the "Bi-State Pilot Committee," called for the formation of a new agency, Regional Progress, Inc., to promote orderly growth in the metropolitan area. This proposal was not concurred in by Bi-State. In fact, the agency pointedly referred to itself as an agency separate from the Pilot Committee, acknowledged receipt of a copy of the committee's report, and announced that it had invited representatives of the pilot group to meet with the agency on November 30th to discuss the plan further.

As proposed, Regional Progress, Inc., would have had a full-time executive director and be charged with the development of a sound land-use plan for the area. Additional functions would deal in fields already under the Bi-State Agency's legal jurisdiction: economic development, transportation, water and drainage, sewerage, parks and recreation, and neighborhood development. It was not intended that it be a governmental or regulatory agency, but that it would provide recommendations supported by a full-time professional staff. Governor Otto Kerner was reported as favorably inclined to the proposal, expecting regional solutions to bistate problems to be greatly improved as a result of the new agency.[52] Missouri Governor John Dalton was silent on the matter.

With two of the Bi-State Agency commissioners opposing formation of Regional Progress, Inc., on the grounds of conflict of purposes, the suggestion was not implemented. Further, simultaneously with the above, the Bi-State Agency announced its approval of a $100,000 appraisal study to be made of the area's mass transit facilities, and thus diverted public attention away from the Regional Progress, Inc. proposal, with a tabling of the issue, apparently for good.

The unresolved matter continued, however. On May 13, 1964, seven governmental officials of the area [53] announced they had agreed to take to their respective communities a proposal calling for a regional council to foster industrial development in the metropolitan area. Spokesman for the group was Lawrence K. Roos, St. Louis County supervisor from Clayton, Missouri. Roos stated that no determination had been reached as to what committee or agency would be in charge of the newly proposed regional council, but that the organization would in no way interfere with the pending Bi-State Development Agency's land-use and transportation plans, if any. Shortly after this, Bi-State announced to the press the creation of a "Regional Planning Coordinating Committee." This group, then, appears to have been prompted by Bi-State to counter the activities of the former elements, as well as to hasten into being an organization which might meet the federal government's qualifications for a metropolitan-area organization suitable to receive Housing Act and transportation grants. The agency credits itself with "serving as a catalyst in bringing together regional officials and civic leaders, culminating in 1965 in the creation of an East-West Gateway Coordinating Committee for overall metropolitan planning." [Bi-State's version of itself in the 1964–65 activities just described includes not only its claim or inference that it initiated action in the above; it also uses such phrases as the following: "Bi-State was ideally equipped to handle this task," and "it was happy to render the service." "Bi-State is . . . proud to have initiated the move for regional planning." "This Agency stands ready to proceed further."] "The predecessor of this Committee was the Regional Planning Coordinating Committee, established voluntarily in June 1964, also under the leadership of Bi-State." [54]

Since establishment of the East-West Gateway Coordinating Council (described in the next chapter) with its wide representation of Missouri-Illinois governmental officials and agencies, among which is the Bi-State Development Agency, Bi-State apparently assumes an advisory council is no longer imperative (if it ever did), for none has yet been activated. But the East-West Council has objectives and goals other than mere advisement and observation of Bi-State and its activities. Furthermore, its composition is essentially governmental. Important as that is, it does not provide the broad representational mechanism anticipated by the Bi-State Compact for grass-roots citizenry and interests to participate in the Metropolitan District's development as it may be charted by the Bi-State Agency's activities or inactivity. This can be regarded as an important omission in interstate compact performance, not only from the view that the participating states have allowed the law to be ignored, but also considering the obvious need for dispassionate, disinterested citizen representation in such an interstate arrangement. At the very least, closer state supervision appears demanded, to guarantee letter-of-the-law performance, if for no other reason.

PART 2—FUNCTIONS AND POLITICS

THE BI-STATE DEVELOPMENT AGENCY'S accomplishments must be considered as of two periods: that from 1949 to 1959, the year of the adoption by Illinois and Missouri with congressional approval of broadened financial powers for the agency; and from 1959 to the present, a period of stepped-up activity and function.

The First Decade

John C. Bollens, in his *Exploring the Metropolitan Community*, an account of the work of the Metropolitan St. Louis Survey of 1956–57, observes:

Although in organization and powers the bi-state agency was modeled after the Port of New York Authority, the resemblance stops there. When established, the local agency was endowed with a broad grant of authority, including constructing and operating bridges, tunnels, airports, and terminal facilities, and making plans for the coordination of highways, parking areas, and sewage disposal. It has done little, however, in part because of financial restrictions and legal disputes concerning its powers. Its revenue bonds, for example, have not been made legal for investment by trusts, estates, and similar funds. The necessary legislation to accomplish this purpose passed in the Illinois legislature, but has not been approved by the state legislature of Missouri.

. . . .

The Bi-State Development Agency is like a sleeping giant who lacks the means to arise from the lethargy that had enveloped him since birth.[55]

While the survey was intended to appraise the entire metropolitan area, the research group decided to concentrate attention on St. Louis City and St. Louis County rather than on the total Missouri-Illinois metropolitan district. The decision was in part due to the Bi-State Agency's recognized shortcomings, as noted by Bollens:

The interstate character of the metropolitan area meant that any governmental reform involving both the Missouri and Illinois sections could be accomplished only by compact between the two states or by enlargement of the powers of the already existing Bi-State Development Agency. The experiences of this agency demonstrated the difficulty of securing any action on an interstate basis under existing legal and political circumstances. . . . The Illinois legislature has been rather favorably disposed [to it], but the Missouri General Assembly has consistently refused to appropriate any funds for the operation of the agency or even to grant sufficient powers to make its bonds more marketable.[56]

Because of these differences in the two states' attitudes toward the agency, by 1957 it was virtually defunct. Bollens noted:

The existence of a governmental unit covering the City and County and two other Missouri and three Illinois counties appeared at the time of its establishment to offer an excellent opportunity for handling metropolitan problems that crossed the state line. However, . . . the activities of this . . . agency have been most disappointing. Its inability to generate widespread support, its lack of initiative, and its meager accomplishments have virtually stripped this governmental unit of all public prestige. These facts militated against the possibility of revitalizing the agency and endowing it with sufficient power to serve as an effective instrumentality for metropolitan coordination and planning. The Survey was convinced that any recommendations closely linked to the reactivation of the bi-state agency would be doomed to failure. It also felt that if strong emphasis were placed on extending the functional powers of the agency, such emphasis might detract from the proposals for the creation of a metropolitan government in the City-County area. Logically, certain powers, such as overall planning and control of mass transportation, should be vested in an agency with jurisdiction over the entire metropolitan area. From a practical standpoint, any recommendation for endowing the bi-state agency with such authority would be wholly unrealistic under existing circumstances.

In view of these various factors, the Survey decided to underplay the potential role of the bi-state agency in the plan for governmental reorganization. Recommendations pertaining to the agency were consequently limited in scope and objective. The Survey proposed the removal of certain legal impediments so the Bi-State Development Agency could acquire the Mississippi River bridges and coordinate traffic between the two sides of the river. The agency would then be in a position to develop a unified scheme of traffic control that could be integrated with the arterial and major street pattern of the recommended metropolitan government for St. Louis City-St. Louis County and with the federal and state highway system in the area. . . .

The Survey's policy toward the bi-state organization was adopted with considerable regret, but no realistic alternative was available. Ideally, the agency might be converted into a true metropolitan government with limited jurisdiction over the entire area. To accomplish this result, action by the legislatures of the two states would be required.[57]

The last two sentences express the oft-repeated hope that has from the beginning animated the Bi-State Compact's conception and its agency's existence, but which for the entire twenty years of its life has eluded its makers and the eternally hopeful and optimistic community boosters and planners who have observed the agency or sought to utilize it.

The St. Louis Survey was conducted in 1956–57. As previously noted, the Bi-State Agency's meetings were more and more infrequent until 1954, and thereafter became merely a gesture to keep the agency alive, especially during 1957 and 1958 when only one meeting each year was held. It is therefore not surprising that the agency's accomplishments during the first ten years of life were few. Some, however, were of considerable importance.

Completed Surveys

During the agency's first year it approved and by 1954 had completed four major studies of key metropolitan area matters:

FIRST, a survey and comprehensive "plan for development" of the Missouri-Illinois Metropolitan District. Agency funds came from appropriations made to it by the two states. (Required by the law creating the agency, this survey was made by Harlan Bartholomew and Associates, St. Louis.) Entitled *"Development of the Missouri-Illinois District,"* it provided detailed observations on major deficiencies and needs of the area. Completed by 1950 and handed to the two governors in January 1951, the survey and plan have never been "effectively implemented," according to the agency.[58]

It notes, "in the field of comprehensive planning, positive action by the agency was indicated, but the financial resources required were not available." (Bi-State has persistently taken the view that it has been handicapped in its comprehensive planning duties because of inadequate financial resources. There is more to the matter, as recounted hereafter.)

SECOND, at the request of the United States Public Health Service, the Missouri State Board of Health, and the Illinois Sanitary Water Board, the agency in its first year sponsored a major survey, *Mississippi River Water Pollution Investigation,* for the entire St. Louis Metropolitan area.

This study, completed in 1954, provided the basic information which in 1962 aided materially in bringing about the successful adoption by St. Louis of a $95,000,000 bond issue for a clean-up of Mississippi River water conditions. The Bi-State Agency cannot take credit for the referendum, however, for the United States government forced action on the matter through threats to withhold federal funds if the city failed in its efforts to raise money. But Bi-State credits itself with follow-up influences. It says it "then inaugurated a program securing voluntary cooperation of industries in the abatement of pollution through treatment of wastes before discharge into the river. The program met with success and most cities in the Bi-State area set about planning corrective measures." [59] The agency probably colors its rôle, here, as somewhat more brilliant than it was. Most certainly the "voluntary cooperation" received from industry on the Illinois side of the river was obtained in part from the efforts of the Illinois Sanitary Water Board, and most assuredly was stimulated by the threat of ultimate federal coercion under the strengthened federal water pollution control laws.

THIRD, with additional financial assistance from St. Louis County, the agency also undertook in 1950 a thorough-going study of St. Louis County sewer problems. Completed in 1954, the study was instrumental in securing the successful adoption by St. Louis and St. Louis County of the Metropolitan St. Louis Sewer District, a major accomplishment.

FOURTH, the agency was requested in 1950 to sponsor an area-wide study of the highway and expressway network of that portion of the two states adjacent to the Metropolitan District. The Highway and Expressway Survey presented a master plan which was coordinated with a similar study made for St. Louis City itself, and some of the main recommendations were subsequently adopted by local authorities. Some were not, and comprised difficult controversies which have not yet been wholly resolved.

The agency notes, "This involved one of the first instances of coordinating interstate highway planning, representing action that had been sadly lacking before the advent of the agency." [60]

FIFTH, because of the limited nature of its original financial powers, the agency sought in its beginning years to find improvement projects of a limited nature which could be financially self-supporting and which it might develop or cause to be developed. The only successful one was a study of the need for and feasibility of wharf and dock facilities on the Illinois side of the river. The result, as described hereafter, was the construction of the Wharf and Public Terminal, Granite City Harbor.

The other studies dealt with exploring means for acquiring the McKinley Bridge from its private owners, and possible acquisition of the Chester Bridge or of construction of another Mississippi River bridge below St. Louis.

These limited accomplishments of the agency's first decade, while far short of the aspirations of those backing Bi-State or of the role outlined for it in law, nonetheless revealed to agency commissioners and the area's interested public the scope, depth, and nature of some of the district's most pressing problems. They also laid bare the centers of economic, social, and political resistance which, in turn, made plain the agency's impotence to secure action without holding the financial powers it so desperately wanted and later obtained. But the years of inactivity and impotence served as well to fix a not-undeserved image of weakness, incapacity, suspicion and distrust on the public mind — especially in Illinois — from which the agency has never wholly rid itself. The only concrete project undertaken and brought to completion by the Bi-State Agency between 1949 and 1959 was its harbor project at Granite City, Illinois, the least defensible of all of the agency's enterprises, made possible only by the doubtful expedient of forming an alliance with a highly interested private company.

The Wharf and Public Terminal, Granite City, Illinois

An engineering study prepared for the agency in 1950 with financial assistance from the Granite City Steel Company showed a "river-rail harbor and wharf project" to be feasible and "necessary to continued economic growth of the area." [61] According to the study, Mississippi River traffic in the St. Louis area had increased tremendously since World War II. The site selected by the agency for development was one which it claimed would be beneficial not only to the steel company but also to the general area. Located on the Chain of Rocks Canal north of St. Louis, the site provided an accessible link with major United States highways and the main rail, river, and freight transportation arteries of the Midwest. It held the possibility of a reliable twelve-foot year-around channel for all major barge requirements.

An agreement was signed by the agency with Granite City Steel Company on July 10, 1950, and purchases and contracts for construction were consummated on February 23, 1951. [62] Actual construction began in February 1951, on land leased from the federal government. Dedication of the completed facilities came in January 1953, and at a special meeting of the Bi-State board of commissioners called later in the year by Chairman Sverdrup, approval was given to the lease and to issuance of $1,500,000 in revenue bonds carrying 4¾ percent interest.[63] (As noted in the previous chapter, the commissioners approved all of these important actions with less than the full membership of the board present and, in fact, by vote of seven members in one action and only six in two others.)

Operation of the terminal and wharf was placed in the hands of the St. Louis Terminal Distribution Corporation, a private concern created for the purpose which, in 1967, employed six persons at the facility. The device of contracting with ad hoc private, not-for-profit corporations to operate its enterprises has been followed by Bi-State ever since in all of its other operations.

The agency extolled this initial construction effort as successful. Success, in the agency's view, was measured in terms of financial capacity to meet agency obligations and not necessarily by the broader standard of whether the priorities of the area's needs were met by this first project, or whether the project has subsequently engendered the desired economic expansion agency projects are supposed to stimulate. Actually it has not, for in the harbor's lifetime the agency's efforts to keep it "public" with user contracts have generally failed. But it has provided sufficient revenues to meet all of its obligations and a little more. Small surpluses were obtained for the agency's own operating requirements.[64]

The chief user of the facilities has of course been the Granite City Steel Company. However, the St. Louis Terminal Distributing Corporation in 1956 requested the agency to reduce all dockage rates so that it might obtain bagged oyster shell coming from South America via New Orleans to St. Louis. This move required a reduction in the minimum payments on the wharf obligations, but in order to get the trade a special rate of ten cents per ton was granted by the board.[65]

By 1960 the Granite City Steel Company found it desirable to approach Bi-State for expansion of the harbor facilities. Bi-State responded that it had insufficient funds at its disposal for such expansion. After continued negotiations on the matter, the steel company in 1962 agreed to provide $356,000 to construct the facilities it desired. Of this amount, $202,000 would be added to the agency's Post Bond

Retirement Credit of the previous construction arrangements, to be paid off by the company's dock fees; by 1973, $90,000 would be refunded to the Granite City Steel Company through savings in the rental payments occasioned by the retirement of all debt from the bond issue; and $64,000 was a "lump sum contribution for betterments" and "payment in lieu of rent" for the increased facilities. Bi-State, of the $202,000 remaining construction loan, agreed to pay interest "at prime rate" to the Granite City Steel Company on $100,000, or whatever lesser amount in excess of $102,000 was required to complete construction. The agency's minutes record the following:

The Executive Director [Colonel Smyser] reported that Mr. W. R. Bascom, Vice-President, Granite City Steel Company, had advised him that he would submit to his Board of Directors a recommendation to proceed with the expansion of the dock under the general plan as previously discussed. . . . Granite City Steel will provide all funds needed for this expansion, part as an interest-free construction loan to be repaid through early retirement of those outstanding Wharf and Terminal Bonds. As a simple summary of the situation, Colonel Smyser stated that if no expansion were to take place, after retirement of the Wharf and Terminal Bonds in 1974 Bi-State would owe Granite City Steel Company $47,000 and would have a net income from the wharf and terminal of $37,000 annually. If the expansion takes place as planned, in 1974 the debt owed the Granite City Steel Company will be $92,000 but the net income will be $50,000 annually, based on guaranteed minimum payments. In addition to the fact that Bi-State will obtain ownership of capital improvements worth $256,000.[66]

It should be noted that Smyser's estimates do not altogether agree with previous comments appearing in the minutes:

In response to questions of various Commissioners the Executive Director explained that at the current time the dock operated at an annual cash deficit of about $9,000, which is made good by Granite City Steel Company as a charge against the Post Bond Retirement Credit. If there is no expansion of the wharf, we will probably retire the last bond in 1973, at which time we will owe Granite City Steel in excess of $200,000. [May 16, 1961, p. 309.] *

* The Financial Statement appearing in the Annual Reports of the Bi-State Agency through 1968, as issued by the accounting firm of Peat, Marwick, Mitchell & Company, St. Louis, carries this notation: "Note 3—The lease between Bi-State Development Agency and Granite City Steel Company provides for a Post Bond Retirement Credit which is a credit due Granite City Steel Company for certain payments made by that Company in excess of the $125,000 annual rental. Any funds received by the agency from operation of the terminal which are free of limitations or restrictions as to use or application are subject to a first lien for repayment of the Post Bond Retirement Credit. In

The expansion of the harbor proceeded apace and went into full operation in December 1963. It provided the wharf and terminal with overall dock facilities comprising 900 feet of space (nearly two-thirds of which is used solely by the steel company under long-term lease). The remainder is operated on a public utility basis with equal service and rates to all users.

It should be apparent that the advantages enjoyed by Granite City Steel under the arrangements here described are extensive. The company receives the benefits of properties in which it has all the freedom and conveniences of private ownership without the disadvantages of property taxes, labor costs, and maintenance. Bi-State, being tax exempt, can charge lower fees for the wharf's use than could a private company. No doubt there are also United States income tax advantages for the company. The State of Illinois and Illinois local governments lose property taxes, but these may be offset somewhat by heightened business and employment activity of the steel company and its servicing industries in the Granite City area. The major benefits, in any event, probably are private rather than governmental.

In addition to the above dock facilities, 700 feet of mooring clusters are now available at the wharf; a warehouse of 14,400 square feet; and a bulk-unloading facility with a maximum capacity of 200 tons per hour. Direct loading of railroad cars is now possible with two tracks built at the warehouse's rear. The agency holds additional acreage to allow for any further expansion it may desire.

The site has been consistently maintained by the United States Army Corps of Engineers as an eighteen-foot channel, dockside. During the period of December 1963 through March 1964, the river suffered from extremely low flow. At that time some of the St. Louis area barge traffic was diverted to the Granite City harbor facilities, which were able to handle all barges, including the largest, coming to it from the Missouri terminals.

The Bi-State Agency has not been free of difficulties in its opera-

the event that such funds are not available, the credit may be applied to the reduction of rentals after the revenue bond has been retired. In accordance with Sec. 3.3 of the depositary agreement, as amended, the Post Bond Retirement Credit is now an obligation of the general fund." It should also be noted that at the Nov. 10, 1960, meeting of the Bi-State commissioners, Col. Smyser called attention to the agency's financial condition, noting that no audit of the Post Bond Retirement Credit had ever been previously made, and that the agency was then operating at about a $16,000 deficit. Minutes, November 10, 1960.

tion of the wharf and terminal. In late 1961 the agency sued the Federal Barge Lines for damages done to its docks in April 1960, in a massive breakaway of barges from their moorings. The suit was lost, thus requiring out-of-pocket expenses of $7,500 by Bi-State, another expense spared the Granite City Steel Company through Bi-State ownership.

Furthermore, the expected additional custom from other users has failed to materialize to any extent and the oyster-shell contract was soon discontinued. In 1965 the agency reported that tonnage of fertilizer and other dry bulk products handled over the wharf increased, but the total tonnage handled had dropped due to the "almost complete loss of the oyster-shell business," caused by railroad tariffs put into effect early in 1964 which gave a favorable economic position to the oyster-shell dealers to ship by rail rather than by the more expensive operation of bargeline with transshipment to rail. The agency noted, "Efforts are being continued to find other cargoes which can be handled in sufficient volume to offset the lost oyster-shell tonnage." [67] Through June 1968, the agency had failed to regain either the oyster-shell operations or any substitute cargoes sufficient to offset the lost tonnage, although during 1967–68 it reported "material increases" in the shipment of newsprint.

More important, however, are the agency's relations in its operation of the river terminal facilities with other governmental bodies of the Metropolitan District. As noted, Illinois in 1959 created a Tri-City Port District, vested with powers similar to those of the Bi-State Development Agency and covering the same territory as that of the agency's Illinois jurisdiction. Bi-State did not oppose the Illinois General Assembly's creation of the Port District, but it did obtain some amendments to the enacting measure. According to the *East St. Louis Journal,* the Port District was created because the Tri-Cities area wanted "full development of the Chain of Rocks Canal Harbor and they grew weary of waiting for the handcuffed Bi-State Agency to do the job." *

Indicative of the kinds of difficulties the duplication of agencies

* Editorial, April 12, 1959, "The Logical View." This editorial also commented on observations of C. E. Townsend, new Illinois appointee of the Bi-State Board, that the agency and the port authority could work side by side if not together for area development. The *Journal* commented that Mayors Davis of Granite City and Macras of Madison, Illinois had called for outright abolition of Bi-State, as a "tool of St. Louis interests."

has provided are the following, gleaned from Bi-State's minutes, by no means a complete statement of happenings:

1) The records show the Bi-State Board held a closed session on September 7, 1960 at which it considered "some elaborate plans" (not explicated) of the Tri-Cities Port Authority for use of the Granite City Harbor. The board took no action.

2) On June 28, 1962, the minutes note that the Tri-City Port District had asked for switching rights without compensation. The St. Louis Terminal Distribution Company objected on grounds that this would be a breach of faith to permit the new unloading dock to be operated without compensation. The board appointed a committee to look into the matter.

3) By September 27, 1962, the Tri-Cities Port District requested a full meeting of both agencies' boards to discuss cooperative measures. One Bi-State commissioner observed that the Tri-Cities commissioners apparently felt that Bi-State had treated the Tri-Cities Authority adversely; no further explanation of the difficulties is made.

4) At the October 25, 1962 meeting of the board, note is taken of a meeting with Tri-Cities officials at which the latter asked Bi-State to agree that it would not interfere "if it began competing facilities and issued revenue bonds for them." Bi-State responded that it could not give a blanket nonintervention agreement since it might have to go to court to prove existence or nonexistence of agency conflict in what might be a dual or duplicating project in the harbor area. The difficulties of the two agencies have not subsequently been wholly resolved.

As a final note to the Bi-State Agency's efforts to establish river terminal operations under its mandate, it should be added that in late 1952 at the request of three grain companies, the agency considered construction of a grain elevator at the Granite City Harbor, but its legal authority to engage in such an operation was questioned and it went no further with the matter. The requesting companies were the Illinois Grain Corporation, Hart-Bartlett-Sturtevant Grain Company, and the Bunge Company.

Other Efforts, 1949–1959

One of the earliest agency efforts to develop projects was directed toward acquiring McKinley Bridge, the first of several such actions, all of which proved abortive. The original Harlan Bartholomew report envisaged Bi-State as the agency for an ultimately unified, area-wide system of transit facilities, including bridges. Bi-State's powers as detailed in the law also pointed in this direction. Therefore, preliminary negotiations of the agency's Executive Committee led to the board's favorable (five to one) vote on December 27, 1951, to purchase the McKinley Bridge. Without complete agreement among the commissioners on this matter and with numerous obstructions to final consummation, the matter dragged. At one point, August 2, 1954, consideration was given to the possible purchase of the Illinois Terminal Railroad in order to acquire the bridge.[68]

In October 1954 the Madison County (Illinois) state's attorney filed a suit challenging Bi-State's authority to acquire the bridge. Two additional suits were filed to enjoin the agency from further proceedings. The suits were dismissed on November 19, 1954, by the Madison County Circuit Court, which action cleared the way for sale of Bi-State's Granite City Harbor construction bond issue. The plaintiffs, however, appealed the suits to the Illinois Supreme Court with a brief from the City of Venice, Illinois. The court transferred the cases to the Illinois Appellate Court on grounds that constitutional questions were not involved.[69]

The suits successfully interfered with Bi-State's acquisition of the bridge, and in early 1956 the ICC approved its sale by the Illinois Terminal Railroad to the Illinois-Missouri Terminal Railway Company.[70] In June, Bi-State asked the railway company for a contract which would permit the agency to operate the bridge but failed in its bid.[71] The Terminal Railway Company finally sold the bridge to the City of Venice in 1958 and Bi-State got dismissal of the suits against it.[72]

Mention has been made of an early meeting (January 14, 1952) of the Bi-State commissioners with the Chester Bridge Commission to appraise bridge needs in that area of the Mississippi south of the metropolitan area. It also was at this time that further consideration was given to seek expansion of the Metropolitan District's territory to include Ste. Genevieve and Randolph Counties, apparently to make it possible for Bi-State to acquire the Chester Bridge. This inquiry came to nothing.

But in June 1956, while the suits were still pending in connection with the McKinley Bridge, the agency began efforts to acquire the Clark Bridge. This, too, proved abortive. All of these failures led to the recommendation by the Metropolitan St. Louis Survey in 1957 that the agency should be granted specific authority to buy bridges,[73] which recommendation was implemented by the grant of power to do so in the expanded 1959 Compact amendments and state laws. Although Bi-State has not yet acquired any bridges, there have been developments, as described below.

Agency Activities From 1959 to the Present

Until 1959, then, the Bi-State Agency in ten years of life was able to engage, in a limited single instance, in only one of the major activities originally projected for it: The Granite City Wharf and Terminal, a less-than-convincing enterprise brought to fruition only through the wishes and involvement of a private company which would be the principal beneficiary of the facilities. The story since 1960 has been considerably different. With broadened powers the agency has taken on some of the life it might have had in the previous ten years. Yet, even today, its accomplishments are quite limited and great deficiencies exist.

The agency's enterprises today consist not only of the wharf and terminal, but also of the Bi-State area-wide Transit System, the Bi-State Parks Airport, and operation of the Gateway Arch Passenger Transportation Service under a contract with the United States Department of the Interior. It has also assisted and participated in the Missouri-Illinois Interstate Air Pollution Study. Most recently it has been seeking the role of operational agency for a proposed St. Louis area airport authority. This study does not attempt a detailed history of each of these enterprises, but attention is given to the more important aspects of each as they reveal operations of this interstate compact agency.

The Bi-State Metropolitan Area Transit System

The establishment of unified, area-wide transit facilities was undoubtedly a part of the original conceptions which led to the Bi-State Compact's creation and its implementation. Without funds of its own, the Bi-State Agency had to depend upon cooperation from outside agencies to initiate action. Its efforts to acquire the privately operated transit lines of the metropolitan area were sponsored by the City of St. Louis and St. Louis County, which issued a report in 1959 recommending consolidation of all transit facilities on the Missouri side of the river. This report followed one that had been made without a preliminary survey of need by the St. Louis Board of Freeholders in 1955, which when submitted to the voters met defeat at the polls.*

The 1959 effort was attributed to fears of St. Louis County residents of "serious consequences" if the city's major transit facilities were permitted to fall into the hands of a municipally-controlled transit commission. St. Louis County Supervisor James H. J. McNary was spokesman for the advance promotional efforts in St. Louis County, pointing out that consolidation would implement recommendations of the Metropolitan St. Louis Survey. The Bi-State Agency at his "suggestion" sponsored a 1961 supplementary study of the area's Illinois-side transit needs. The W. C. Gilman and Company engineering firm, Cleveland, were engaged in June 1960 at a cost of $100,000 to make an economic feasibility study of the proposed consolidated system linking the two halves of the Metropolitan District. Funds for this costly promotional action were provided by the six major govern-

---

* There is strong evidence to suggest that it is Bi-State which now initiates its own plans through an established procedure that it has found to be successful: (1) contracting a "survey of need" and economic feasibility, which always recommends what Bi-State wants it to recommend; (2) obtaining public sponsorship of the idea by influential governmental officials or agencies; (3) a simultaneous "unveiling" of the study's recommendations by the press and an attention-getting meeting featuring prominent civic figures; and (4) quiet acceptance of recommendations that Bi-State be the operating agency, without seeming to press for the role.

Confirmation of this judgment is amply set forth in Seymour Z. Mann, "Across the Wide Missouri," in Rocco J. Tresolini and Richard T. Frost, *Cases in American National Government and Politics* (Englewood Cliffs, N.J.: Prentice-Hall, 1965), pp. 19–34. Mann's discussion treats in detail the efforts by Bi-State and other interested St. Louis elements to create a metropolitan area planning agency (which later became the East-West Gateway Coordinating Committee), discussed only briefly in the present study.

ments of the area: St. Louis, $40,000; St. Louis County, $40,000; East St. Louis, $5,000; Alton, $5,000; Belleville, $5,000; and Granite City, $5,000.[74]

Not surprisingly, the Gilman appraisal was favorable. Bi-State's tax-exempt status was stressed as a leading consideration, offering management possibilities in keeping fares low through tax savings. As additional advantages of consolidation, Bi-State could act immediately in acquiring the competing lines; if, also, Bi-State could acquire the several bridges linking the two states, they could be made toll-free; and the hope was expressed that Bi-State could establish a central bus terminal, lacking under the existing multiple ownership arrangements. Supervisor McNary observed that no elections and no "time-consuming Freeholders Board's deliberations" would be required.[75]

Bi-State's minutes cast further light on the matter:

Commissioner Clark pointed out that the negotiating committee felt constrained to take note of the fact that the St. Louis Public Service Company was a "going-concern" which had a record of successful operation for a period of years. It was apparent that the earnings record was not bright, especially in recent years but, as a public utility, the Company could charge for its services only the rates which the regulatory body authorized. In the case of the St. Louis Public Service Company, the negotiating committee noted the extraordinarily high tax burden, which had forced fares upward to the point of diminishing returns. With the same tax burden, based upon its capitalized earnings, the St. Louis Public Service Company would not be an attractive investment for another public utility. However, for a tax-exempt operator, the capitalized earnings would justify a substantially greater investment.[76]

The transit system as consolidated is not regulated by either the Public Service Commission of Missouri or the Illinois Commerce Commission. Further, the system receives its only regulation from the United States Interstate Commerce Commission through its control over rates charged in those parts of the system operating outside the boundaries of municipalities (formerly county coach lines). This United States control had not been expected by the Bi-State Agency, as indicated in numerous negative comments contained in its records.

Funds to purchase the physical assets of the fifteen operating companies[77] were provided by a revenue bond issue of $26,500,000, sold on March 12, 1963. The total cost of acquisition came to $23,194,740. Final control of the properties was obtained on April 1, 1963.

Operation of the consolidated system was given to the Transit Services Corporation, a Missouri company formed of key officials of the former St. Louis Public Service Company. Bi-State says this arrangement was determined upon after soliciting proposals from the entire transit industry of the area.[78]

The consolidation effort, according to the agency, "the first venture of this magnitude in the history of American transit operations," was complex and not without difficulties. It required combining the fifteen operating lines, their routes, fares, equipment, labor unions, and wage rates. It involved negotiation of a master labor contract, retraining of drivers for system-wide operation, reassignment and standardization of equipment, unification of business management procedures and records, unification of maintenance facilities, and centralized controls. Fifty new streamlined air-conditioned buses were purchased and placed in operation in November 1963, at a cost of $1,500,000,[79] and by 1968 the fleet of new fifty-passenger buses acquired since Bi-State's takeover had been increased to 270, while many of the older buses had been air conditioned. A "demonstration grant" from the United States Housing and Home Finance Agency in May 1964, partially underwrote a one-year experiment in offering high-speed, direct transit service into areas not formerly receiving such service. This was deemed "generally successful" with most of the new routes permanently incorporated into the existing transit system at the end of the experimental period. Service was extended to several new communities, and many routes were altered, combined, eliminated, and adjusted.[80]

How successful has Bi-State operation of the system actually been? The agency's records indicate that at no time since it assumed operation and control have actual revenues reached budgetary anticipations and, indeed, the system has shown only marginal ability to maintain itself—less, if the full terms of its Trust Agreement are to be met. This condition exists in the face of Commissioner Clark's 1960 claim that the acquired St. Louis Public Service Company line was a "going concern with a record of successful operation over a number of years," and despite Bi-State's tax-exempt status, an advantage not held by the former private owners.

The agency's annual reports until 1967 conveyed a generally optimistic and even glowing record of accomplishment. Closer analysis reveals that while transit services for the metropolitan area generally have improved, particularly in providing stability to a few local transit situations, there is considerable and widespread public dissatisfaction with fares, with services in many areas, and with Bi-State's efforts to obtain state funds for partial support of its operations. It has never yet met the full obligations of the financial agreements it entered at the time of the take over.

The agency began a practice almost immediately in 1963 which it has subsequently followed: budgeting in such a way as to meet its annual requirements in operating, debt service, and capital improvements, but neglecting its depreciation reserve fund which, under the system's Trust Agreement, requires an annual allocation equal to 7 percent of revenues. By February 1968, the fund was deficient by $755,897 [81] despite some sizeable payments into it in the years since 1966. Until 1967–68, the agency annually purchased new buses, continued its modernization of old ones, and constructed new shelters for its clients at selected bus stops scattered around the city. All such improvements were instrumental in providing the public with the "new face" of the transit system, lending an air of prosperity and efficiency and quieting some complaints of services rendered. But it was done at the expense of the depreciation reserve fund, which began accumulating a slow but steady deficit.

In 1966 the agency's consulting engineering firm, the W. C. Gilman Company (retained by the agency at an annual fee of $12,000 with special fees for special services which, since 1963, have been frequent), warned that the Trust Agreement's terms for the depreciation fund would have to be met for the coming year. To do this, it was necessary to divert funds from the capital improvements allocation and also to raise fares. In April 1966, the agency at the request of the mayor of St. Louis and the supervisor of St. Louis County held public hearings on the proposed fare increases in the city and county. None were held in Illinois. The agency stated that the question of holding such hearings was "discussed with officials [unnamed] in the Illinois area" but was advised "no public meetings would be required." The first major fare increases under Bi-State ownership were then put into effect. Shortly before (March 1966), the agency had negotiated a new wage contract which it expected would increase its annual operating expenses by approximately $500,000. By the fiscal year's end (February 1967), the depreciation reserve fund deficit had grown to $590,802.

The Bi-State Board issued in April 1967 a "revised forecast of revenues" which painted a gloomier future financial picture than it had shown in its announced budget in February, only six weeks before. While all of this was going on it was pursuing Illinois and Missouri legislative assistance with bills introduced in both Assemblies for a requested subsidy amounting to $400,000 from Illinois for the coming biennium, and $650,000 from Missouri. The pressure of its "revised forecast" apparently was sufficient to cause the Illinois legislature to appropriate the $400,000 subsidy. The Missouri effort was unsuccessful, largely through the opposition of a St. Louis area representative and the silence of Missouri's governor in support of the request.

Bi-State announced that it had hoped through these appropriations to apply for a federal grant under the Urban Mass Transportation Act, but Missouri's denial of funds would cause it to lose the Illinois appropriation and give up its grant application plans. In July 1967, it put into effect an additional bus fare increase, the second in thirteen months.

Despite the increased fares, the agency in February 1968 reported for the first time since its acquisition of the system a decline in operating revenues of 1½ percent. This report happened to coincide with the meeting of the Missouri legislature in a special budgetary session called by Governor Warren Hearnes. At this time, Hearnes included in his budget the Bi-State request for $300,000 for one year.* Negative reports were made by the appropriations committees of both houses of the Assembly, but both the Senate and the House of Representatives ultimately approved the $300,000 subsidy, thus making possible Illinois's payment of half of its $400,000 subsidy. Bi-State announced the $500,-000 thus obtained from the two states would be used for "purchase of motor vehicle transportation equipment." But in the meantime it awaited results from its $1,000,000 federal grant application. It expressed disappointment when it was awarded only $500,000 in June 1968.

According to Bi-State Board Chairman Robert S. Knapp, all of this financial maneuvering was done, first, to qualify Bi-State for the federal grant, and second, to "wipe out the existing and expected

* Hearnes was being threatened in this election year with the announced candidacy of Republican St. Louis County Supervisor Lawrence K. Roos for the governorship. Newspapers hinted that Hearnes was influenced to support the appropriation to satisfy St. Louis area constituencies.

deficit in the depreciation reserve." Knapp stressed that the state moneys and the federal grant were to be spent for new equipment and could not be spent for operating purposes.[82]

Nonetheless, with two fare increases in effect since 1966 and with $1,000,000 in additional funds from Illinois, Missouri, and the federal government, the agency issued a proposed budget in March 1969, which was reported as follows:

Bi-State Transit System revenues continued to slip in January and deficits incurred by the utility continue to mount, the commissioners of the Bi-State Development Agency were told yesterday.

Passenger revenue in January was $1,692,181, or $114,000 less than earlier projections. Total revenues of $1,874,709 were $65,000 below estimates, the commission was told.

At the same time, operating expenses rose $34,000 over what was expected, resulting in net operating revenue of only $55,164. This balance was insufficient to meet even the agency's $82,258 interest payment on revenue bonds.

John C. Baine, president of Transit Services Corp., the contract operator of the bus system, said the cumulative cash deficiency in the depreciation reserve fund in the 11-month period that ended Jan. 31 was $1,662,324.[83] [The February 1968 reported deficit was $755,897; Baines' figures show an increase of $906,427 in an 11-month period.]

While close analysis of the agency's financial management picture of the transit system is impossible in this study, seeming conflicts in the cumulative image are difficult to interpret. First, until 1966, the agency's major reported deficiency was that of the depreciation reserve fund. In three years of operations the agency annually reported small net profits and it annually improved its capital equipment. In 1965 it was additionally able to eliminate by purchase certain service car operations within the city which had competed with the transit system. The largest of these operations was that of the Consolidated Service Car Company, of which newly elected St. Louis Mayor A. J. Cervantes was one of the chief owners. Since conflict-of-interest criticisms of the mayor's business connections had arisen, it was necessary to sell, and since Bi-State wanted the service cars eliminated anyway, Bi-State purchased the Service Car Company in November 1965, for $625,000 payable in monthly installments over a five-year period (not necessarily to favor the sellers in their tax obligations). It also purchased a smaller operation, the United Service Car Company, for $20,000.

Second, the St. Louis Model City Agency announced in December 1967 that it had received a grant of $1,147,500 from the Department of Housing and Urban Development to develop and promote over an eighteen-month period "government-subsidized bus lines" "to link low-income sections of the city with industrial complexes in the suburbs." Bi-State Transit System was given operation of the lines. The grant's approved budget contained the somewhat puzzling allocations of only $650,000 for actual operations of the proposed lines, but $190,750 for research, analysis and evaluation (to be performed by the St. Louis Human Development Corporation); $36,000 to the transit system for the bus company's supervisory personnel; and $117,600 for advertising and promotional purposes, an item that was much questioned.[84]

Thus, with apparent financial solvency sufficient to warrant purchase of the service car operations, and with all of these increases in its income and income expectations, the agency's 1969 prognosis of its financial condition is difficult to understand. Operating problems the agency has had, without question. Beginning in late 1966 the system suffered an increase in night robberies of bus operators which required corrective protectionary measures, and which by December 1967 had contributed to a reported 20 percent decline in night usage of the buses. At the same time the transit system in December discontinued "a number" of night bus services in twenty-one of its bus lines. This move prompted a public protest in the form of a "ride-in," surprisingly, in the affluent suburbs of Kirkwood and Webster Groves rather than in the central city where the protest moves might have been expected. Organized groups of riders made use of unlimited ride passes to keep buses busy without earning additional revenues for the system.[85]

The earlier fare increase and other discontinued night services aroused strong negative response in the Belleville area, one that has not been happy with Bi-State Transit System operations throughout. Under the heading, "Typical 'Bi-State Service,'" an editorial in the *Belleville News-Democrat* commented abrasively:

The Bi-State Transit System has rated front page headlines again. Last month it put into effect some whopping fare increases. This week it has whacked off more of our tottering local bus service.

After it entered the picture, Bi-State arbitrarily demoted Belleville to a nine o'clock town. But now 7:30 P.M. is the last daily departure from the Public Square on one bus run and 7, 6:30 and 6 P.M., respectively, on three other routes.

This bad news comes as a stunning shock to the local business community. The majority of our downtown retail stores remain open for the convenience of shoppers until 8:30 o'clock two nights a week—a full hour after the last bus leaves the Square to call it a day.

. . . Maybe Bi-State is telling the truth when it claims it hasn't any more riders. But that wouldn't be surprising; the St. Louis operators have been systematically alienating the public. . . .

Bi-State this week also virtually eliminated bus service to Scott Air Force Base—and that cruel cut came on the very eve of Scott's big golden jubilee birthday party day after tomorrow!

Bi-State spokesmen are still harping and carping about the lush subsidy they expected but didn't get from the joint Illinois-Missouri legislative action. They suckered Illinois assemblymen but fell down in Missouri with the result that the anticipated melon rotted on the vine.

Now Bi-State is taking out its pique on the public, jacking up rates and ruthlessly slashing service . . . if the scheme is to stimulate public pressure on legislators for kindlier treatment toward Bi-State we predict it won't work. . . .

The smartest thing the Illinois General Assembly could do would be to get out from under the monstrous Bi-State Compact. . . .

The public, bless 'em, has just about got its belly full of Bi-State.[86]

In acquiring the various private lines which previously serviced Illinois areas, Bi-State had to assume certain school district contracts held by those lines in Madison, St. Clair, and Monroe Counties for transporting school children at reduced rates of fare.[87] [See Appendix A for 1967 contract terms.] Bi-State has maintained that it consistently lost money on these contracts and used this argument to obtain Illinois support of its requested subsidy in 1967. It has used it again in 1969 when additional subsidies from the two states (at the time of this writing, still in process) are being sought:

Two bills were introduced in the Illinois House of Representatives yesterday for the assistance of the Bi-State Transit System's operations in the Illinois part of its service area. . . .

One measure would appropriate $425,000 for the improvement of the service, facilities and equipment of the system in Illinois. The money would be released by the Governor at his sole discretion as may "from time to time be necessary and upon request of the Bi-State Development Agency."

House Speaker Ralph T. Smith, Alton, said he had been told the money would be used for capital improvements and as such could be used to generate federal grants on the basis of $2 federal to $1 state. . . .

Smith said the bill was similar to legislation passed in 1967 and signed by then Gov. Otto Kerner that provided $400,000 over a two-year period for the transit system's Illinois operations. It was passed over the bitter objections of some legislators that it was special-interest legislation on behalf of the East Side.

The second Lehman bill would provide $250,000 for the payment of transportation of school children to and from school in Madison and St. Clair counties. The purpose of the subsidy would be to make up the difference between adult fares and those paid by school children.

Smith said the bill was roughly parallel to a 1967 appropriation of $7,300,000 to the Chicago Transit Authority to help defray the cost of carrying school children to and from school.[88]

While bills of this type had not been introduced in the Missouri Assembly by Easter, expectations were that they shortly would be but that prospects for appropriation of the requested moneys appeared "slim." Governor Warren E. Hearnes was quoted as saying he was "personally opposed to the subsidizing of Bi-State or any other transit authority so long as the employee-employer relationship remains as it is at present.

"The bus operators," he said, "who won a 60-cent hourly increase over a 30-month period after a 19-day strike last month, are employed by Transit Services Corp., which operates the system under contract with Bi-State Development Agency, its owner.

"They (the employes) use this subterfuge to keep from being public employes," Hearnes said. "If they are not public employes, there is a question of the constitutionality of appropriating public money for non-public employes.

"But I think the transit systems will have to be subsidized either locally, as is done here in Jefferson City, or at the state level if they are going to survive."

Hearnes said subsidization would have to be done on a state-wide basis rather than by individual systems if the state was to be "fair" toward all publicly owned systems.

. . . .

An increase in the bus fare schedule was approved yesterday by the commissioners of the Bi-State Development Agency. It will go into effect in about two weeks.

The increases, expected to produce about $2,800,000 a year, were recommended by the W. C. Gilman Company. [This was the third fare increase in less than three years.] [89]

On May 20, 1969 Bi-State announced further discontinuance of "8 or 9 percent" of miles traveled, to be effective June 16, 1969. The decision appeared nicely timed and planned to bring the full impact of an annoyed public to bear on the two state assemblies before their adjournment on June 30, 1969. The new labor contract signed earlier in the spring was attributed as the cause. Bi-State announced it also intended to lay off about fifty employees of the transit system.

All of the Bi-State Agency's difficulties with its transit system are perhaps characteristic of most public transit systems in today's United States. But the agency's operations demand more convincing evidence that the fullest possible efforts are being made by all the agencies and governments now involved to meet the transit needs of the Metropolitan District and, indeed, that operations, costs, and revenues are reasonably well managed. No appraisals of managerial efficiency have been made by either state to date, and it would probably be advantageous for the system to be periodically exposed to such a searching examination, initiated by some agency other than the Bi-State Development Agency itself through its hireling engineering consultant. Without any public service commission except the United States Interstate Commerce Commission to police operations, a gap between plans, promises, and actual performance may exist which the public of the area cannot reach under the terms of the interstate compact. Either or both states might make such an appraisal through state budgetary or auditing machinery, now that Bi-State is receiving state appropriations. But without some organized or centralized effort to push it, it is extremely unlikely that either state will venture into St. Louis politics to this extent. As matters now stand only the legislatures of the two states provide any means for review, a feeble and most unreliable policing operation as state assemblies function today or, indeed, as they have always functioned.

There is considerable indication that Bi-State in its political activities of the past three years has an axe to grind which can be most effectively honed by regular revelations of distress. Such appears to be its effort to focus attention upon a goal which, if achieved, would make for great expansion of its transit operations: the authorization by the two states of a tax-supported rapid transit system for the area, entailing a massive remaking of existing arrangements and extensive financing by the two states and the national government, but with retention of control and operations by the Bi-State Agency—if legally left as it stands now, a managerial and financial independency which under the proposed plans would be without a great many of its managerial and financial headaches and demands to demonstrate self-support. Bond purchasers under such a system would be assured of repayment of their bonds at "prime" interest; local populations could shift a great part of the system's costs to the general taxpayers of each state. Such arrangements have of course been set up in states like California and New York where populations are densely urbanized. Illinois and Missouri are still to a considerable extent rural or small-town states, and the plan is certain to encounter extensive legislative opposition. Bi-State's approach to the matter has been skillful.

In 1965 it first began to look ahead, preparing the ground for such expansion:

By far the most important consideration for the future . . . is the proposed "new look" study of *rapid transit possibilities* for this area, which the Bi-State Board of Commissioners authorized earlier this year. The need for a high-speed, grade-separated rapid transit system, which would be operated in coordination with the existing surface system, becomes more evident almost daily. Also, public recognition has been given to the fact that *funds for the engineering, constructing and equipping of such a system must receive support from tax revenues of the municipalities, counties, or states affected.* This is the case in all cities and urban areas where rapid transit now exists and where, interestingly enough, improvement and expansion progress are under way or in the planning stage, including Boston, Chicago, Cleveland, Montreal, New York City, Philadelphia, South Jersey and Toronto. [Italics added.] [90]

In 1966 the agency undertook the direct sponsorship of such a rapid transit study, utilizing a Missouri state appropriation of $150,000 as a prop for a technical study grant application to the United States Department of Housing and Urban Development under section 9 of the Urban Mass Transportation Act. While Bi-State was doing this its sister planning agency (of which Bi-State is one of the original thirteen members), the East-West Gateway Coordinating Council, was undertaking the first phases of an overall Land Use and Transportation study. HUD therefore decided that "federal funding [for Bi-State] would more appropriately be obtained from the funds allotted through the Council." [91] In early 1967 HUD approved a $30,000 work program which was given to Bi-State's chosen consultants, the engineering firms of Parsons-Brinckerhoff-Tudor-Bechtel and Sverdrup & Parcel & Associates, Inc.*

Additional funds were requested of HUD for continuation of the study but it was not until mid-1968 that the Department released $105,000 for the beginnings of Phase II. These delays required Bi-State to obtain reappropriation by Missouri in 1967 of its original $150,000 appropriation. In the meantime, HUD granted $170,000 for Phases III and IV in February 1968.

Promotion of the idea was probably given something of an initial boost by the issuance in July 1967 of a report by the Missouri Office of State and Regional Planning which recommended construction by the state of a high-speed mass transportation system to serve Missouri's major metropolitan areas, estimated to cost about $300,000,000 under revenue bond financing. The proposal was linked to another recommending construction of toll roads in Missouri, an idea that has heretofore not received warm reception from the Missouri Assembly. It also stressed that the system would regularly require partial state subsidization.[92] It is doubtful whether this report, coming as it did from the state and focusing on state rather than a particular metropolitan area's needs, helped Bi-State and the East-West Gateway Council in their designs for a system of their own, but it doubtless had the effect of impressing Missouri legislators with urban transit realities everywhere. The Missouri Assembly, however, reflects the frequently conflicting demands of the two great cities on its eastern and western borders and such conflicts have often rendered neutral proposals of benefit to either, with the wishes of the southern, central, and northern rural belts of the state tending to prevail in matters of huge expenditure.

But in April 1968 the Engineers' Club of St. Louis held a symposium to which it invited John C. Baine, chief executive officer of the Bi-State Transit System, and John W. Dameron, executive director of the Port Authority of Allegheny County, Pennsylvania. Baine outlined a seven-point proposal of a $30,000,000 plan to improve the existing St. Louis metropolitan area transit services. Dameron revealed how Pittsburgh was able to obtain $25,260,000 in capital grants from

---

* The Sverdrup of Sverdrup & Parcel & Associates, Inc., is the former chairman of the Bi-State Board of Commissioners, Gen. L. J. Sverdrup. This firm is a leading bridge-building engineering group.

county, state, and federal sources since its Port Authority's inception in March 1963.

Dameron told the symposium that the key to this generosity toward an industry that is notoriously short of capital funds is cooperation. The cooperation is between the transit operator on the one hand and community planners, elective governmental agencies, the financial-business-industrial sector and the civic leadership and news media on the other.

. . . .

"Shortly after I arrived in Pittsburgh I was invited to lunch by a top executive of one of the largest private foundations," Dameron told the symposium. "He quickly got down to cases and I will sum it up by repeating his question: 'John, what can we do to help transit?' " [93]

No reference was made by either man to the wishes of taxpayers of local areas or of the states generally, nor the wishes and needs of users of metropolitan area transportation facilities of whatever kind. It can also be said that the Bi-State Agency is no stranger to the Dameron formula for obtaining subsidies and approval of its plans.

While all plans theretofore made provision for subsidies, the East-West Gateway Council made public on May 8, 1969, some standards it had adopted for a "fixed rapid transit system" for metropolitan St. Louis that would permit it to operate without a subsidy. (The "fixed" system refers to subways, monorail, and commuter lines.) Such a system would be regional in nature. The more "flexible" bus line system would operate in specific localities. Fares would be based, the council said, on distance traveled. The arrangement as projected plans for a subway system in downtown St. Louis, East St. Louis, and Clayton, Missouri. Clyde E. Sweet, director of the council's transit planning, was quoted:

"We would like an operating subsidy, but don't foresee any government giving the system one."

The lack of an operating subsidy rules out a single fare for all rides, Sweet said. Under a single fare and no subsidy, the short distance rider would too heavily subsidize the long-distance one, he said. Because more low-income people would be short rather than long-distance riders, a single fare would work against the poor.

. . . .

The standards were written by a transportation planning task force including representatives from the Bi-State Development Agency, the Bi-State Transit System, other bus companies, highway departments and railroad unions. The task force was headed by William P. Hamilton III, a planner with the Bi-State Development Agency.[94]

While the standards thus adopted emphasize user interests and the avoidance of state subsidization, it should be noted that if federal grants-in-aid policies continue as they have heretofore operated, the lure of a federal grant for some kind of real or desired expansion will probably require state subsidies no matter what kind of prearrangements designed to obtain public approval have been made.

Thus the affairs of the Bi-State Transit System now stand. Comments and conclusions about some of these matters under the Bi-State Development Compact are made hereafter in this chapter and elsewhere in this study.

Parks Metropolitan Airport

While the compact creating the Bi-State Agency anticipated airports as one of the agency's permissible facilities, Bi-State evinced little interest in this area until after 1960. The Harlan Bartholomew plan noted the lack of an area-wide airport system and recommended development of one, based upon the FAA national airport plan. Bi-State asserts approaches were made to it from time to time, but the controversial question of a suitable site was hopelessly interwoven with all other of its troublesome considerations to the end of stalemate and inaction on any proposals. For many years certain private St. Louis interests had promoted the Columbia Bottoms area in north St. Louis County as a possible airport site (later, as an industrial park site), but costs of improvement and the existence of large amounts of more immediately useable land on the Illinois side of the river blocked this effort. Further, the Metropolitan St. Louis Survey rejected serious consideration of additional city-county airport facilities, as described by Bollens:

The question of airports was also considered. The city of St. Louis operates the only major airport in the area and, according to traffic projections, it will not reach the saturation point for ten to fifteen years. Since the airport is a revenue-producing facility for the City, any attempt to transfer it to a metropolitan agency would be vigorously resisted by City officials. The Survey realized that the question of future airport facilities for the metropolitan area could not be postponed indefinitely. At the same time, it considered inadvisable the inclusion of this item in the list of functions that should be immediately transferred to a metropolitan agency.[95]

The airport question came up at last for public discussion at the East St. Louis meeting of Illinois-side metropolitan area interests when efforts were made by Bi-State to determine its goals and purposes in the January 1960 meeting described in part 1 of this chapter. Noting that "distrust of St. Louis interests dominated discussions" of industrial and airport development, the *East St. Louis Journal* of January 26, 1960, reported extensive criticisms of St. Louis for lack of cooperation in airport planning. As might be expected, the gist of this East Side discussion held that any anticipated airport properly should be located on the Illinois side of the Mississippi because of its accessibility to downtown St. Louis. St. Louis County plans for an airport on Howell Island in the Missouri River were also criticized, and support was voiced for the Illinois Tri-City Port Authority's studies for a projected metropolitan airport to be located within its jurisdictional area.

This meeting served only to introduce the airport issue as one of various metropolitan area needs. The St. Louis Chamber of Commerce, however, through its Air Board called a meeting in November to advance bistate cooperation of aviation and governmental interests in airport development.[96] The Bi-State Development Agency's prime interest in this meeting (and probably in bringing it about) is indicated in that its chief engineer, Milton M. Kinsey, presided. This first meeting confined itself to exploration of means to coordinate special interests and the various completed studies, plans, and ambitions, without considering any specific sites for an airport.

The chairman of the St. Louis Airport Commission, Walter T. Malloy, reported that Lambert Field improvements had given the St. Louis airport "a longer lease on life" and that the saturation point at Lambert might not be reached for several more years. But, he said, it was imperative to "reserve space for another airport" because of the impossibility of accurately determining future developmental needs in air traffic and the air industry.

The chairman of the St. Louis County Airport Committee, Kent Ravenscroft, while denying any personal opposition to a major airport to be located on the Illinois side, expressed the need for immediate action on "an airport for executive type and freight planes" in St. Louis County to relieve Lambert pressure.

Illinois interest was voiced by the president of the Southwestern Illinois Council of Mayors, Mayor Leonard Davis of Granite City, who favored a St. Clair-Madison County "airport commission" and stated he had proposed a special committee for this purpose. The general manager of the Tri-City Regional Port Authority, Commander John L. Barron, called attention to Tri-City's study of airport possibilities, but said no further action would be taken unless assurances were given to the Port Authority of support by the airlines and municipalities to be served. He noted that major airlines had shown no indication of willingness to share in the cost. Executive director Smyser of Bi-State suggested that the various interests and organizations should adopt a resolution specifying which agency should be designated to advance the airport.

East St. Louis had no official airport agency at this time, but Harold G. Baker, Jr., president of its Chamber of Commerce, sat as the city's representative. The agency with which Bi-State later cooperated in acquiring Parks Airport was the Southwest Civic Memorial Airport Association, of which Baker was president.

Between this November 1960 meeting and November 1962, a number of developments took place. At some time the above-named Southwest Civic Memorial Airport Association, "a not-for-profit Illinois corporation," [97] came into being and acquired a lease and option to purchase the Parks Metropolitan Airport site in Cahokia, Illinois, which had been closed since 1959. The property consisted of 520 acres of the airport site proper, and the option to purchase included adjoining tracts of 290 acres. Data was gathered during Southwest's "preliminary negotiations and investigations," real estate appraisals were made, FAA approval was obtained, and certain "permanent improvements and repairs" were made during an eighteen-month period. [98]

At an annual dinner meeting of the East St. Louis Chamber of Commerce in late October 1962, announcement was made by Leo A. Fisher, newly-elected chairman of the Bi-State Agency, and Harold G. Baker, Jr., president of the Southwest Civic Memorial Airport Association, that Bi-State had signed an agreement to "cooperate with" the association "in acquiring and operating" Parks Airport. Southwest, under the agreement, would assign to Bi-State its lease and option to purchase, make available all the information it had gathered, and assist Bi-State in "conducting further investigation and research to determine the 'economic feasibility' " of the project. In return, Bi-State agreed to reimburse Southwest "from proceeds of the revenue bond issue for funds previously spent by it in making such improvements and repairs and in preliminary redevelopment of the field." The reimbursement was not to exceed $47,654.55. Bi-State further agreed to conduct engineering and feasibility studies, secure necessary financing for acquisition of the airport and adjoining land, acquire additional adjoining land when necessary, obtain all permits, file applications for federal and state financial assistance and conduct promotional programs to encourage the fullest use of the facilities.[99]

Fundamental to the arrangements was Bi-State's agreement that the airport would be operated as an "executive-type port for twin-engine aircraft" (primarily the planes of industrial firms having business dealings in the St. Louis area). Harold G. Baker announced that his organization had previously signed an agreement with St. Louis University (owner and operator of Parks Air College in Cahokia) to transfer its flight and student training operations to Parks Metropolitan.

The project was to be financed by revenue bonds, with federal and State of Illinois assistance. It was anticipated that rental payments from St. Louis, if it became the operator of the field, would be sufficient to retire the bonds. Negotiations with the St. Louis City Airport Commission also included promises of an FAA grant of $1,037,475 to assist in the purchase and improvement of the field, and a possible Illinois contribution of an additional $275,000.

Subsequent Bi-State negotiations for the St. Louis Airport Commission to operate the field for Bi-State revealed a "major problem"—the possibility of Illinois taxation of St. Louis's leasehold interests. This, Bi-State reported, "was apparently resolved by action of the Illinois General Assembly in June 1963," with "legislation specifically exempting airport facilities owned or operated by the City." [100] Even so, Bi-State suspended discussions with the city in July "on the premise that its tax status in Illinois would be uncertain." Whereupon, the St. Louis Airport Commission, with St. Louis County, engaged a firm of engineering consultants to review the general aviation requirements of the metropolitan area and Bi-State explored possibilities of reopening Parks without assistance from St. Louis. The agency states:

A supplemental agreement was executed with the Southwest Civic Memorial Airport Association under which that organization. . . . would operate the airport for the Agency *under a fully reimbursable contract.*[101] [*Italics added.*]

By March 1964, the St. Louis-St. Louis County engineering study came up with the recommendation that Weiss Airport, in southwest St. Louis County, be acquired by the city at an estimated initial cost of $12,733,300. Bi-State interpreted this as resulting from St. Louis efforts to get the airport on the Missouri side of the river, for estimates indicated Weiss would cost about four times that of Parks. Public support from the area press gave preference to Parks on grounds of economics and Parks's proximity to downtown St. Louis. In June the city negotiated a contract with Bi-State, in which it agreed to advance $100,000 a year for three years, and $50,000 a year over a four-year period thereafter, in return for Bi-State's agreement that it would operate Parks as a public airport to which Lambert Field traffic might be diverted.

This contract was signed in July 1964, the FAA grant was concluded, and the governor of Illinois released the $275,000 contribution the state had promised.[102] Illinois agreed to serve as the contracting agency for work on the port.[103]

Bi-State finally sold $1,700,000 in revenue bonds, acquiring title to the Parks properties from Indiana-National Homes, Inc., in March 1965, and commenced operations in April 1965. The $500,000 grant from St. Louis was made conditional upon repayment—but only if the airport's revenues proved adequate during the thirty-year life of its revenue bonds. Total cost of the 539.49 acres was $2,107,781, a sum which reflected sufficient compensation to Indiana-National Homes for the loss of the residential subdivision it had expected to build; total construction costs were estimated at $593,346, and other necessary expenditures came to an estimated $311,348. The agency reported:

In late June . . . agreement was reached with Southwest Regional Port District by which certain additional lands necessary for the future development of the airfield are to be purchased by the Port District, with funds made available by the State of Illinois, and then transferred to Bi-State to be incorporated in the airfield. These purchases will add an additional 81 acres to the 582 already purchased, thus essentially providing all the land required for the future development of the proposed 7000-foot instrument runway.[104]

This land, acquired in July, gave the airport a total of 664 acres. By June 1968, Bi-State was nearly ready to begin construction of the 7000-foot runway.

While during the first four years of Parks's new role under Bi-State ownership the field had a number of disappointments in anticipated usage of the facilities, it still was able to show small but annually increasing profits and by year's end, 1968, Bi-State could speak hopefully of a future holding "great promise." All necessary personnel and actual management of the airport are provided by Southwest Civic Memorial Airport Association under a reimbursable contract by Bi-State with the "not-for-profit" Illinois corporation, thus paralleling the procedure used in operating the Bi-State Transit System. The association's officers included Harold G. Baker, Jr., as president, and Oliver L. Parks as general manager, the airport's founder and former owner and, according to Bi-State, "whose efforts were so instrumental in making the project possible." [105] Mr. Parks stepped out of office in 1967 and was replaced by S. W. Sisk, operator of a smaller St. Louis-area airport.

Congestion at Lambert Field was only partially relieved with development of Parks Metropolitan. In spite of great improvements and expansions at Lambert, St. Louis aviation problems continue to strain local resources. A new phase of Bi-State Development Agency activity therefore began in 1967 which has not, as of this writing, been resolved. This is the issue of whether it is to become the owning and operating agency—a possible "St. Louis Metropolitan Aviation Authority"—of the entire system of airports in the two-state area, with taxing and bonding power.

The Proposed Regional Airport System

In 1967 two simultaneous moves were made. First, the East-West Gateway Coordinating Council authorized a feasibility study of a unified airport authority for the metropolitan area. The council, acting on a recommendation from executive director Eugene Moody, hired Governmental Research Institute, Inc., a private governmental research agency of St. Louis, to make a six-month study from November 1967 to April 30, 1968. Second, Alderman Raymond Leisure of St. Louis's seventh ward suggested that St. Louis should sell Lambert-St. Louis Municipal Airport for $200,000,000 and use the money to improve city services.[106] Funds for the airport authority study were provided by a federal grant from the Department of Housing and Urban Development under its Urban Planning Assistance Program.

Very soon thereafter, the St. Louis Municipal Airport Commission decided in October to proceed with development of a "secondary facility" to relieve crowded conditions at Lambert on a 500-acre section of the controversial Columbia Bottoms tract in north St. Louis County. In opposition to this move, the Missouri Pilots Association requested the Federal Aviation Agency to investigate the matter. FAA agreed to do so in January 1968. Lawrence L. Burian, secretary and spokesman for the pilots group, stated that "many general aviation pilots opposed Columbia Bottoms as an airport site because it would be too difficult to reach the ground," the site was too close to flight patterns at Lambert, it was too small for further expansion, and it had no protection against flooding. His observations were corroborated by a previous FAA report which had rejected a proposal for St. Louis to build a major airport there, but had given a tentative nod to creation of a small utility airport on the site, with a runway not to exceed 3200 feet. FAA's objections to the site had been based on its proximity to Lambert and to Alton Memorial Airport.[107]

This move was quickly followed by others. In a few days two bills were introduced in the St. Louis Board of Aldermen: one, a measure sponsored by Mayor Cervantes to create a St. Louis Airport Authority with a director appointed by the mayor; the other, introduced by Board President Donald Gunn, to create an airport division in the City Department of Public Utilities, to be headed by a merit system commissioner. Both would supplant the existing City Airport Commission, which was loosely attached to the Department of Public Utilities with the Lambert airport manager reporting directly to the department's director. The mayor's bill was adopted. This move was clearly in anticipation of the Research Institute's report which, sponsored as it was by the East-West Gateway Council, was expected to recommend some kind of regional arrangement for governing St. Louis aviation. By creation of an "authority," both the mayor's and St. Louis's positions in efforts to retain city control might be strengthened. The move provided only a change in title for the existing governing agency, since the Airport Commission was retained as the authority's planning, development, management, and operations body. A new director of airports was added, thus giving the mayor a direct voice in airport management matters through his appointee. Lambert Field's management was still handled by the city-employed professional airport manager.[108]

Creation of the authority was followed rapidly by adoption by certain East-West Gateway Council members of the proposal for St.

Louis to proceed with plans for a federal grant application to build a 3800-foot landing strip on the Columbia Bottoms site at an estimated cost of $350,000. This stratagem was achieved in the face of a unanimous negative recommendation of the council's executive advisory committee and was heatedly opposed by the St. Louis County supervisor, Lawrence K. Roos, who insisted the county was not opposed to development of such an airport, but that the council should await issuance in June of its own Research Institute report on airport development, and also because the county wanted clear knowledge of what its commitment in the Columbia Bottoms project would be. Support for the measure came from both sides of the river: Missouri council members favoring were Mayor Cervantes and Alderman Gunn; Illinois supporting members were Mayor Alvin Fields of East St. Louis, Raymond Rogers of the Southwestern Illinois Council of Mayors, and Francis J. Foley of the St. Clair County Board of Supervisors. In opposition were Missouri members Lawrence K. Roos and Norman Myers of the St. Louis County League of Municipalities; and Illinois members Alton May of the Southwestern Illinois Metropolitan Area Planning Commission, and Harold Landolt of the Madison County Board of Supervisors. Two Missouri members abstained.[109]

The State of Illinois entered the controversy in April when J. E. Wenzel, director of the Illinois Department of Aeronautics, called for a conference or series of meetings to begin as soon as possible among the St. Louis area governing officials to discuss the problems and formulate plans for "a regional authority to supervise development of an integrated aviation system in the area." Wenzel noted that he had been in contact with Colonel Smyser of the Bi-State Agency on the question. He urged strong consideration of Illinois as the site for a second major airport and pointed out that Illinois already had a functioning interstate airport at Lawrenceville (described in chapter 5, this study) which could provide an example on a small scale of the problems and legislative needs of a regional aviation system.[110]

Harold Landolt, who opposed the Gateway Council's January 31 adoption of the Columbia Bottoms strip proposal, introduced at the Council's April 24 meeting a Madison County Board resolution calling for creation of a metropolitan airport authority and emphasizing that comprehensive airport planning and site selection could properly be done only on a metropolitan basis, with consideration given in planning to the entire metropolitan area.[111]

The Governmental Research Institute report was finally presented to the East-West Council on June 26, 1968. As expected, it called for creation of an area-wide, regional airport authority, and recommended strongly that the Bi-State Development Agency be designated to do the job. It further recommended that Missouri and Illinois adopt legislation that would empower Bi-State to levy a special property tax to finance the purchase of Lambert–St. Louis Metropolitan Airport from the city, and propose bond issues for airport development.

The institute's recommendation of Bi-State as the proper agency for the task was based on several important considerations: the lack of jurisdiction by the City of St. Louis over the entire area and its probable inability or unwillingness to finance area-wide airport needs; the same weaknesses in the area's county governments; and the character of the East-West Gateway Council, which was not a government agency and whose composition of ex officio governmental officials made it unsuitable for business-type operations. Further, Bi-State had been created specifically to perform such interstate metropolitan services, it already held authority to handle airport matters, and its use in this instance would make unnecessary the creation of an additional agency of government in an area which already had too many local governments. "If," the report urged, "Bi-State Agency has limitations, it is better to correct them than to create a new government for airports." [112]

Anticipating that its recommendation for a grant of taxing power to Bi-State would meet with opposition, the report stressed that such taxing power be limited to initial purchase of Lambert Field from St. Louis. It stated:

To compensate the City of St. Louis, the Bi-State Development Agency should be authorized to levy for not more than 10 years, and for this purpose only, an annual District-wide property tax not to exceed 5 cents per $100 assessed valuation.

To levy this tax equitably, the total amount of property taxes required should be apportioned between the Missouri and Illinois portions of the Bi-State District on the basis of the percentage that each has of the total population of the District. After this apportionment has been made by the Bi-State Agency, it should compute for each of the two District portions, on the basis of the total assessed valuation within that portion, the tax rate required to produce the apportioned taxes. The Bi-State Agency should then certify the necessary tax rate to each county and the City of St. Louis, and the tax should be levied and collected in the same manner as other property taxes. These procedures are necessary, because Missouri and Illinois do not have identical property tax bases, and because property is not assessed at the same percentage of value in the two states. The Institute has received an opinion from its attorney that these procedures would be legal.[113]

The report recommended as a suitable price for Lambert Field, $17,750,559, of which only $12,183,097 would be paid the city by Bi-State; the remaining $5,567,462 would represent the city's tax-payers' proportionate share of the total cost. The Bi-State tax levy, it said, would produce over a period of six to ten years enough revenue to provide the recommended $12,183,097 plus $5,567,462, "which will enable the City to reduce its own tax rate by the amount of the Bi-State tax rate, so that City taxpayers will not be required to pay taxes to compensate themselves." [114]

In another part of the report, however, the Institute was less specific about a general grant of taxing authority to Bi-State, conveying an impression that additional tax funds might be needed:

The Agency also has suitable jurisdiction if tax funds are needed for airport purposes. If given the power to issue general obligation bonds, which would require voter approval, or if authorized to levy a tax for airports its area-wide jurisdiction would permit required tax funds to be equitably raised.[115]

This comment was not explained further.

Opposition to the report's recommendations came immediately in the form of an announcement by Mayor Cervantes that he would not allow Lambert Field to be sold for less than its estimated value of $100,000,000. The report's figure of $17,750,559 represented St. Louis City's original investment; the mayor's figure, current value. Cervantes was quoted as saying he had always supported the principle of a metropolitan airport system, but the fact that Lambert was developed largely through airport operating revenues "does not detract one iota from the fact that this is the property of the people of St. Louis." Even though it was pointed out that the city had in the past given away certain unprofitable facilities such as the St. Louis State Hospital, Malcolm Bliss Hospital, and the St. Louis State School and Hospital, he insisted that sale of Lambert for only $12,000,000 would make him subject to a taxpayers' suit, and would be a violation of his office's trust.[116]

Other officials, unnamed, were quoted as "privately questioning the wisdom of proposing that Bi-State act as an area-wide airport authority" since "the agency does not enjoy the highest public confidence because of its operation of the bus system." [117] Not at all private was the public comment of Howard F. Baer, member of the Municipal Airport Commission, who stated on July 3 that he believed it was "extremely doubtful" that voters would approve any bond issues for the Bi-State Agency "because in the people's minds—whether rightly so or not—the agency is in disrepute because of bus operations by Bi-State." [118]

Baer further objected to the Institute's organizational proposal, which would have created a Bi-State Aviation Commission composed of one representative from St. Louis, and one from each of the six counties of the Metropolitan District. "The city," he said, "which has spent years of effort and millions of dollars in establishing the facility, would be placed in the position of having its one representative outvoted 6 to 1 at any time. This I do not believe fair." He also took issue with the taxing proposal, noting that, "This is as bad as anything I can think of—it is entirely unfair and inequitable. Seventy-five percent of the people in this country never have flown in an airplane and never will. It is not right to put the tax load on the property owners. The people who use our airways should pay the costs. Our highway systems on both the federal and state levels are financed by the users and this also should be true of the aviation systems." [119]

Additional objection to the Institute's taxing proposal came from a St. Charles County member of the East-West Gateway Council, Joseph Bappert. A flat tax rate on real and personal property for support of the airport authority, he said, would penalize residents of counties that have achieved equalization in assessments. Not all counties in Illinois and Missouri had done this, and he urged additional study to make such an authority self-supporting from fees and rentals. [120]

It remained for the major opposition to come from the General Assembly and governor of Illinois, prompted into action by East Side Senator Paul Simon of Troy who on July 16 introduced S.B. 2175, an emergency measure authorizing the Illinois Department of Aeronautics to operate a major airport on the East Side, to be located somewhere in St. Clair, Madison, or Monroe Counties. [121] This bill proposed $100,000 to the Department of Aeronautics for engineering and feasibility studies. Simultaneously, Governor Samuel Shapiro appointed a group to seek an appropriate airport site.

The *St. Louis Post-Dispatch*, which editorially had been supporting the Research Institute's report, hailed these Illinois moves with applause:

Illinois' interest in demonstrating the feasibility of an East Side location for the St. Louis area's proposed new major airport is doubly welcome. Not only should this assure that the facts regarding the East Side will be brought to light; it also tends to point up the need for regional representation and control of the decision-making process in this field.

As things stand now the site of this major metropolitan facility will be selected not by a metropolitan agency serving the whole two-state metropolitan constituency. Rather it is in the hands of the St. Louis Municipal Airport Commission, accountable only to those who represent about a third of the people of the bi-state region. The city commission's deep-seated suspicions of involvement in Illinois, evident in the long battle to persuade it to use metropolitan aviation revenues generated at Lambert Field to help underwrite reopening of Parks Airport on the East Side, suggest Illinois is wise to run its own feasibility study.[122]

But Eugene G. Moody, executive director of the East-West Gateway Council, responded to the legislative move more cautiously. Development by Illinois of a second major airport, he said, would still appear to be contingent upon establishment of a metropolitan authority to operate all airports in the area. "In this case," Moody said, "the city could ruin Illinois plans, because I'm sure the Illinois authority would need the co-operation of all local agencies. Besides this, revenues from Lambert likely will help finance development of the second major airport. So, the city has a major decision role. Its policy must favor the Illinois plans or that proposal could be doomed at the start."

Walter T. Malloy, chairman of the St. Louis Airport Commission, also asked to comment on the Illinois legislation, responded:

Just off the cuff, and without considering such things as noise factors, interference from high structures and so on, it looks like the second major airport should go on the East Side. At this time we have three sites on the East Side under consideration, in addition to several on the west side of the river.

We are doing somewhat of a hip pocket study of airport sites. I doubt that the total cost will be $10,000. Apparently Illinois plans to go into much greater depth on its initial studies. The things Illinois develops in its study will be valuable to the city.[123]

Simon's bill failed to pass on July 22, but another Senate Bill, No. 2051, for the same purpose but providing only $50,000 for the feasibility studies, passed both houses on July 25 and went to Governor Shapiro.[124] Shapiro signed the bill on August 20, 1968. New revised bills were introduced in 1969. Of these, an expanded version of the 1968 law, S.B. 263, would establish an Airport Study Commission composed of five House, five Senate, and six public members to analyze the need and potential location of major airports in northeastern and southwestern Illinois. An emergency measure, it provides $50,000 and requires a report to the Assembly and governor by February 1, 1971.[125]

The Bi-State Development Agency's role in all of this has been that of the "silent" but aiding and abetting partner to the work of the East-West Gateway Coordinating Council. The council's report, the agency's legal position, the logic of metropolitan decision-making, the press, are all on its side in the ultimate question of operation of whatever airport system the Metropolitan District develops. Prudence, and the knowledge that its reputation renders it somewhat vulnerable, demand a quiet and unobtrusive posture, particularly since the matter cannot be finally resolved before 1971 at the very earliest.

The Gateway Arch Passenger Transportation Facilities

An initially successful project of the Bi-State Agency is its Gateway Arch Passenger Transportation Service, the only enterprise operated directly by the agency. Once the long (thirty years) controversy surrounding the 630-foot Saarinen arch itself and the efforts to obtain federal development of the Jefferson National Expansion Memorial and waterfront were ended with actual construction begun, the need for transportation for sightseers when the completed arch should be ready was obvious.

Bi-State entered the National Park Service's construction efforts when bids to build the arch were finally let and the low bid turned out to be nearly $4,000,000 in excess of estimates. The Park Service then determined to proceed with construction, omitting the transportation system. On the basis of a favorable feasibility report, again by the W. C. Gilman Company, at this point Bi-State approached the Service with its bid to provide the transportation system through sale of revenue bonds and to operate it for the thirty-year life of the bonds, repaying the debt from fares collected. An agreement with the Park Service was signed on May 14, 1962, and shortly thereafter the agency sold $3,300,000 in revenue bonds. Herein (although the financial activities may have been in part unavoidable), the agency miscalculated, for it failed to anticipate that the scheduled deadlines for completion of the arch might not be met. For five years thereafter a series of difficulties plagued completion. The agency reported:

The continuing delay . . . has placed a serious financial burden on the Agency. The capitalized interest provided in the bond proceeds became exhausted with the interest payment made July 1, 1965. Contingency funds, supplemented by investment earnings and liquidated damages, were used to make an additional 12-months' interest payment through July 1, 1966.[126]

But omitted from the agency's annual report was the fact that it had sought to press the arch's contractors to speed up the work so that the opening date would be July 15, 1966, rather than October 1966, and to this end paid an additional $97,000 under an agreement with Hoel-Steffen as contractor. The contractor, in turn, was to pay Bi-State $750 per day in damages for late delivery. The penalty, it was believed, would partially insure Bi-State that it would be able to pay interest on its revenue bonds should the transportation system not be working by the time the interest was due.

The actual beginnings of operations took place more than a year later. In the meantime, Ralph Niehaus, manager for Bi-State of the arch transportation system, resigned on April 6, 1967, blaming the arch delays on "poor administration, inspection, and supervision on the part of the National Park Service and the indifferent performance of the general contractor.

"We never got one red cent of those liquidated damages," Niehaus told the St. Louis Post-Dispatch. "One charge order after another was granted to Hoel-Steffen until finally, on December 21, 1966, their portion of the work was accepted.

"Don't ask me how it was accepted. It certainly wasn't finished at that time. But acceptance got them off the liquidated damages hook.

. . . .

"It is inconceivable that the National Park Service would even infer that a contract which provided liquidated damages of $750 a day was completed without penalty to the contractor, and then indicate that standby charges of $6672 per week would be payable for standby personnel because the job was really not yet finished." [127]

The "stand-by" charges resulted from Bi-State's desire to begin testing of its equipment and the contractor's denial that the system was ready for testing, with the further objection that if Bi-State sought to use the area during regular working hours, the workmen on the project would have to use it from 4 P.M. to 8 A.M. at double time. The costs, the contractor implied, would have to be borne by Bi-State. Another troublesome matter was the question of who should pay for keeping the heat on in the winter of 1966–67.

The contractor was granted $1619 for installing a temporary plywood floor in the north leg loading area. "This was high for a lot of plywood," Niehaus said, "but that was nothing compared to the $5163 charge approved by the Park Service for installation of four ticket dispensers and two changemakers in the Visitor Center. We provided the machines. The only thing Hoel-Steffen had to do was punch six holes in the wall and set up wooden supports for them. We felt that $5163 for this job was exhorbitant."

All of the equipment installed by the Park Service was fully automated, included money changers and ticket dispensers. The public proved incapable of serving itself adequately, some of the equipment proved unreliable, and the agency was compelled to hire full-time attendants to assist visitors.

The transportation system in both legs of the arch went into full operation on March 19, 1968. The agency describes it as a "passenger transporter which is completely unique. It combines the elements of an elevator, a mine hoist and a ferris wheel and, because the eight capsules are operated as a unit, it is sometimes referred to as a capsule-train." [128] Under Bi-State's agreement with the National Park Service, maintenance of the system is the Service's responsibility. The firm of Sverdrup & Parcel & Associates, Inc., provided Bi-State with the inspectional services it needed for certification of the system's safety and operational efficiency.

By September 1, 1967, the system had transported its 100,000th passenger, and steady usage has marked its subsequent operations. An optimistic estimate that Bi-State would "get out of the financial hole caused by the delay in opening the Arch and have money left over in about three or four years" was made by Colonel Smyser in an interview with William H. Kester of the *Post-Dispatch* in July 1968. This included an additional loan of $180,000 the agency had to borrow from the Mercantile Trust Company of St. Louis to pay the interest on the bonds due in January and July 1967. The unexpected popularity of the system provided Bi-State's financial position an additional rosier hue.

Its arch bonds, which had sold at a low of 75 percent of par value in late 1967, sold in mid-1968 at 85 percent of par, according to Stifel Nicolaus & Company, brokers for the bonds.[129]

Thus, once operating, the arch transportation system has proved to be the one enterprise of the agency that has been popular, wholly profitable, generally successful in functioning, and a source of growing and continuing satisfaction to the agency. As of the present writing, the federal government has not yet completed the visitors' center or constructed all outside walks, bridges, and landscaping.

The Interstate Air Pollution Study

Following United States adoption of the Clean Air Act of 1963, the Bi-State Agency was made a member of the executive committee of the Missouri and Illinois Interstate Air Pollution Study and signed a project agreement on January 17, 1963, to participate in the investigation of the two-state metropolitan area's air pollution problems. The committee consisted of eleven cooperating organizations which, while not joined by the East-West Gateway Coordinating Council, was strengthened by the council's broadening of its program in June 1966, to include air pollution, thus enlisting the chief officials of the Metropolitan District's governments and giving promise of future cooperative possibilities in air pollution regulation. Bi-State, as a member of the council, will thus continue its participation in whatever program emerges.

During the three-year period from 1963 to June 1966, Bi-State participated in the study's investigations. Work was conducted in two states: Phase I made odor and contaminant surveys and sought definition of the area's problems and development of methodology for handling them; Phase II augmented knowledge of the source and nature of air pollution, investigated factors affecting prevention and control, and delineated an air resource management program. In the meantime, the Executive Committee pressed for adoption of the Missouri Clean Air Bill, passed in 1965, which established the Missouri Air Conservation Commission, thus providing both states with compatible authority in their respective portions of the Metropolitan District.

This study does not attempt an analysis of the air pollution difficulties which have attended both states' efforts. The Illinois-

Indiana Air Pollution Control Compact, passed by both states in 1965,[130] languished in Congress until it became apparent in 1968 that the compact's terms were inadequate for the broadened task of regulation and that amendatory legislation by both states would probably be demanded before congressional consent would be granted. A similar fate befell the Missouri-Kansas Interstate Clean Air Compact. Efforts to pass a Missouri-Illinois air pollution control compact resulted in three proposals before the 1967 Missouri Assembly, all of which failed of passage. Efforts to revive these measures in the 1969 Assembly have not been attempted as of this writing. The 1967 failure was attributed to the inability of officers of the Missouri Air Conservation Commission and the Illinois Air Pollution Control Board to reach agreement on terms of a compact. The Missouri commission charged that Illinois officials were opposed to stringent regulations for the metropolitan St. Louis area, a claim that was not without substance. The inaction of 1969, it was said, was due to the same reasons and the lack of any prospect for agreement to be reached by the two agencies.[131]

An interesting legal question may well be asked in connection with any future Illinois-Missouri interstate air pollution control compact. Should one be adopted, with a regulatory agency for its administration, will it be permissible for the Bi-State Agency as a member of the East-West Gateway Council to participate in planning decisions which will affect and involve a sister interstate compact regulatory agency? To the writer's knowledge, no exploration of the legal intricacies, if any, which may surround the regulatory interactions of interstate compact agencies has yet been made. This study attempts no speculation on the matter.

Further Bi-State Efforts to Acquire Bridges

Still seeking to acquire a Mississippi River bridge, a potentially lucrative enterprise, the lure of which strongly attracts the ever-financially pressed Bi-State Agency, the agency in 1962 sought enactment by Missouri and Illinois of legislation creating a special commission to construct a bridge between Monroe County, Illinois, and Jefferson County, Missouri, both within the agency's metropolitan area jurisdiction. The agency "offered to assist local sponsoring groups," and again negotiated its usual engineering feasibility study with funds raised by the usual interested groups, unnamed. The study, issued in

February 1963, was given to the sponsors but no further action was taken.[132]

As mentioned earlier in this chapter, Illinois thereafter adopted another interstate compact with Missouri, this one establishing an Illinois-Missouri-Jefferson-Monroe Bridge Commission which creates a public corporation to construct, maintain, and operate a bridge across the Mississippi "at or near Ste. Genevieve, Missouri." [133] Bi-State under this compact was again frustrated in its bridge-owning ambitions.

Missouri, in 1968, appropriated $15,000 to generate federal grants to pay for engineering surveys prior to construction of a bridge which would span the Mississippi from a point near Harrisonville in Monroe County to Herculaneum in Jefferson County, presumably the same area for which the Bi-State study was made in 1963.

The Bi-State Agency's Financial Methods

As sketched in numerous instances throughout this study, the Bi-State Agency, at present without taxing powers, draws its financial resources from numerous sources—grants from the United States government, the States of Illinois and Missouri, cities, counties and, in some instances, from private sources. It issues revenue bonds for financing particular projects which must be revenue-producing sufficient to amortize loans in an agreed-upon period. It may receive appropriations from the two parent states and did rely on such initially, but it received no appropriations from either state for approximately twelve years, until both states appropriated the subsidies described in the discussion of the Bi-State Transit System. It also receives the revenues from its various projects.

To date, grants from the various agencies of the United States government have come from the Federal Aviation Agency, the United States Public Health Service, the Housing and Home Finance Agency, the Urban Transportation Administration, and the Department of Housing and Urban Development. It has also received the services of the East-West Gateway Coordinating Council, which has been the beneficiary of federal grants.

Its fiscal year, for all of its operations except the transit system, is July 1 through June 30. Under the provisions of its trust indenture, the transit system was required to adopt a fiscal year beginning March 1 and ending on the last day of February.

No audit and no procedural report by the State of Illinois was made of the agency for more than a decade, dating from the appropriations of the 1950s until the 1967 appropriations were legislated. No thoroughgoing state audit has ever been made by either state. The operations of Bi-State's various enterprises, with the exception of the Gateway Arch Transportation System, have been placed in the hands of the not-for-profit "service corporations" created on an ad hoc basis, and the private auditing firm of Peat, Marwick, Mitchell & Company of St. Louis handles the agency's annual auditing for these and the agency's general operations. (The service corporations are the Transit Services Corporation of Metropolitan St. Louis, the St. Louis Terminal Distribution Company, and the Southwest Civic Memorial Airport Association.) Limited financial data concerning these enterprises is contained in the overall annual agency financial statements.

The public financial reporting of the agency leaves much to be desired. Until the 1967–68 annual report, it was not possible to ascertain from the summarized financial statements even the general status of the several enterprises other than the transit system. Until that year, no means were provided (short of direct examination of the agency's headquarters records) for determining the exact amounts of federal grants received and of their disposition. With the exception of the transit system it is still not wholly possible to obtain a full view of each individual service corporation's financial operations.*

Mention has been made of the neglect of the Depreciation Reserve Fund in the management of the Bi-State Transit System. Other obscurities in the financial management picture exist. As illustrative, the Transit Services Corporation has assumed certain pension obligations under collective bargaining and other agreements. As reported in the agency's annual reports, the system's financial statement showed, "Pensions are unfunded with the exception of the plan

---

* This study does not attempt to give intensive attention to agency financial methods. That, it would appear, would be a worthwhile exploration for those expert in public financial management. This study does, however, conclude that the States of Missouri and Illinois have been derelict in providing, and need to provide, close financial scrutiny for public corporations of this type, for which both states are directly responsible and others of which both states can be expected in the years to come to create from time to time.

for salaried employees, which is partially covered by insurance plans. The system follows the practice of charging pension costs to expenses as paid. For the eleven months ended February 29, 1964, these costs amounted to $895,836." [134] This statement was carried as "Note 6" of that year's financial report, but no equivalent notation was to be found under the itemized statements of earnings or summarization of funds. It was also unclear as to which item the note referred. The same comment can be made of the 1965 fiscal year's statement in regard to Note 7, which pointed out that costs (in which pension moneys were presumably included) for that year amounted to $982,619. Such ambiguities made it difficult, if not impossible, to determine whether the Transit Services Corporation could legitimately claim to be a "not-for-profit" agency. If so or if not, more intelligible financial reporting and accounting were indicated as clearly needed.

The auditing processes followed by the agency in the past appear to have been deficient. Shortly after assuming the duties of executive director, Colonel Smyser called the attention of the board of commissioners to the agency's financial condition at that time, November 10, 1960. He pointed out that no audit of the Post Bond Retirement Credit had ever been made and that the agency was then operating at about a $16,000 deficit. [135]

While some improvement in financial reporting is evident in the 1967–68 annual report, there are problems attending agency operations which indicate a strong and compelling need for better reporting methods. The financial pulling and hauling which attended the Gateway Arch; the suggested evidence that in order to show "need," to obtain federal grants and state subsidies, the transit system may not be putting the highest premium on good service and good management; the struggles with the transit system's Depreciation Reserve Fund; are all indicative of the expanding nature of the agency's financial picture. The sums of money now involved in agency operations are great and growing greater, its obligations are varied and extensive and obscured by the structure of service corporations plus Bi-State ownership divorced from operation. Such a pattern carries an ever-present potential of careless or mismanaged financial activities, not readily identifiable even to the individual commissioners of the agency's board, whose experience and tenure may not allow full knowledge to be brought to bear on particular agency practices for questioning. An overextension of the agency's capacities at any given time is possible in view of such unforeseen crises as accompanied the construction of the arch. Should the Bi-State Agency become the owner of vast and varied metropolitan area airport operations, it will become one of the nation's "big businesses," and the public will be acutely affected by the agency's practices, financial and operational. At present, the compact and the statutes governing the agency are ill-defined and inadequately structured for proper accounting, examining, and auditing for both states and the various subdivisional governments served by the agency.

Metropolitan Area Planning

Special attention must be given to one of the Bi-State Agency's major functions, obligatory under law but most superficially handled during the agency's life, and at all times with reluctance on the agency's part. That function is metropolitan area planning.

From this study's brief account of activities surrounding the agency's failure to establish an advisory council, some suggestion of the problems involved in this function can be gained. Although the agency in some of its recent annual reports has applauded itself for its accomplishments in and contributions to regional planning, the records and annual reports prior to 1965 take an entirely different tone. Further, an interview with the agency's executive director elicited ready agreement that the planning function was unsatisfactory as practiced by the agency, and it is possible to state that Bi-State probably welcomes such relief from this obligation as it has obtained through creation of the East-West Gateway Coordinating Council.

The original Harlan Bartholomew report for the agency placed emphasis on inadequacies in Metropolitan District planning and on the need for various physical improvements. Blame for the deficiencies was placed on "an obsolete governmental organization" and lack of clear understanding of metropolitan area needs. It touched upon land use, zoning, housing, highways, bridges, parks, recreation, water, sewers, flood control, as well as transportation, and recommended that Bi-State undertake preparation of a comprehensive area developmental plan as soon as possible. With the exception of the transportation facilities which have been developed by Bi-State, the remainder of the report's recommendations—in the agency's own words—has "never been effectively implemented. In particular, . . . positive action by the Agency" in comprehensive planning "was indicated, but the financial resources required were not available." [136] This is certainly true, but it does not explain why Bi-State has been able to find financial backing for the things it most wishes to do but none for metropolitan area planning. Furthermore, even the transportation functions have not been undertaken in accordance with a definite plan for overall transit development.

The answers are not hard to find: they are political, and the result of Bi-State's own heel-dragging which is in part the result of area politics, in part due to the agency's organizational limitations and interest orientation. It remained for the Federal Aid Highway Act of 1962, which requires urban areas of over 50,000 population to base their highway projects on a cooperative "continuing comprehensive planning process" if they are to receive federal highway funds, to trigger more constructive action by the various area interests on metropolitan area planning. The Urban Mass Transportation Act, the Demonstration Cities and Metropolitan Development Act of 1966, and certain changes in the Housing Act of 1954, also provided the additional necessary impetus for the metropolitan area to find an effective mechanism for area-wide planning on a broader basis than transportation alone.

From the time the agency received its broadened financial powers in 1959 to activation of the Federal Highway Act in 1965, the efforts of St. Louis-area persons and agencies interested in planning appear to have had few results.* There was no Bi-State effort to assume the initiative in realizing the planning goals expressed by the "pilot committee" and its resulting committees and groups. But during the spring of 1963 two developments occurred: the State of Illinois created the Southwestern Illinois Metropolitan Area Planning Commission, and Bi-State again received "several inquiries" as to its willingness and ability to initiate or assist in coordinated metropolitan planning.

The agency's attitude toward its planning function needs to be made very clear. The records are studded with references to it, but the

* A complete and detailed account of the entire story of the East-West Gateway Coordinating Council's creation is excellently handled in Seymour Z. Mann's "Across the Wide Missouri," in Rocco J. Tresolini and Richard T. Frost, *Cases in American National Government and Politics* (Englewood Cliffs, N.J.: Prentice-Hall, 1965). The present study attempts only to state the general direction and final results of this effort.

annual reports give a somewhat different public image of its planning role and attitude toward it from that which it privately holds. The following quotations, taken from the reports, agency minutes, area newspapers, provide their own emphasis.

For example, in response to the "several inquiries" referred to above, the agency says:

After careful consideration, the Agency agreed to undertake the role as a catalyst and as a coordinator of comprehensive planning in the Missouri-Illinois Metropolitan District, but emphasized that it would neither be a super-planning agency nor would it interfere with the functions of planning agencies already in existence on both sides of the Mississippi River.

and,

The Agency stands ready to assist in this vital development, not in the role of a super-planning agency, but by acting as a coordinator and secretariat for those agencies which comprise the Regional Planning Coordinating Committee.[137]

The agency's board in regular meeting on July 30, 1963, discussed "approaches" made to it and noted that the federal government was now providing substantial funds in matching grants to stimulate regional planning. The board recorded,

This matter was discussed at the recent meeting of the Executive Committee, which felt that Bi-State should not attempt to set itself up as a planning agency, nor to assume a major financial burden. . . . Ultimately, if a satisfactory program can be worked out that is of interest to other agencies, Bi-State should be prepared to act as a coordinator and as a sponsor in seeking necessary grants of Federal funds. However, we should make our position clear, that we will not interfere with the functions of existing planning agencies on either side of the River, and that we offer our services solely as a coordinating agency.[138]

The "East-West Gateway Planning Committee" meeting of October 14, 1963, set up a working committee which met on February 27, 1964, and agreed on a draft report, "East-West Gateway Land Use and Transportation Study," which would be the basis for aid under the Federal Highway Act of 1962. Bi-State's executive committee thereupon agreed Bi-State would participate, but it did not necessarily consent to or approve a specific course of action. The minutes note:

The Commission generally agreed that Bi-State would have to take the lead, as Bi-State was the only Agency whose geographical boundaries covered the whole area.[139]

This "Land Use and Transportation Study" recommended establishment of a Regional Planning Coordinating Committee. Bi-State's commissioners authorized agency participation in the committee on April 26, 1964. On June 18, 1964, representatives of fifteen governmental units met and agreed unanimously to participate in a permanent Regional Planning Coordinating Committee. The agency commented:

Unfortunately, even though this effort to coordinate planning was seemingly successful, there have been subsequent indications of a misunderstanding as to how the Regional Planning Coordinating Committee would function and as to the exact role of the Agency. This has resulted in some opposition to the proposed program.[140]

At the June 18, 1964, meeting, Colonel Smyser is quoted as saying that he felt that one of the major stumbling blocks in the establishing of the coordinated planning effort was the lack of a mechanism for coordinating the planning effort and for supervising the preparation of a detailed prospectus specifying the work to be undertaken, the data collection methods to be used and the responsibilities of the various cooperating parties. This appeared to him to be a work for professional planners and not something that could be accomplished by part time members of the committee.[141]

The Regional Planning Coordinating Committee met again on September 25, 1964, and agreed to continue under the name, "East-West Gateway Planning Committee." Bi-State reported that a Greenfelder Foundation grant was available to the committee and that there were also promises of aid from Mayor Tucker and Supervisor Roos of St. Louis and St. Louis County. Apparently the introduction of such a strong Missouri-side financial interest dismayed the Illinois members, for the record indicates

They had a feeling that if Bi-State was successful in getting a first Federal grant then all future grants for metropolitan planning might then be channeled through Bi-State and this they did not want.[142]

In response to the June developments, Bi-State gave an interview to the press in which it pointedly stated that several communities and organizations on the Illinois side "apparently are misinformed on the objectives of the recently formed Bi-State Regional Planning Coordinating Committee." C. E. Townsend of Granite City, the spokesman and a member of the Bi-State board as well as chairman of the

Coordinating Committee, stated that opposition to the committee had come from the Granite City city council and the Greater Alton Association of Commerce which objected to the committee as a "super-planning agency." Townsend said,

"The fact of the matter is that we're not a super-planning agency and we've gone to great pains to show this is not the case. . . . critics of the regional committee believe a 'super-planning agency' would be St. Louis dominated and not serve Illinois interests. Another fear is that a super-agency would take over the functions of the Southwestern Illinois Metropolitan Area Planning Commission, which is in the process of preparing a master plan for Metro-East." [143]

Additional evidence of the disturbed conditions and Illinois's wariness of metropolitan planning efforts is revealed in a memorandum from Gene Graves, director of the Illinois Board of Economic Development, to Governor Otto Kerner.[144] Graves applauded the Southwestern Illinois Metropolitan Area Planning Commission of the East Side, but stated that there was no similar enterprise on the Missouri side of the river and he thought it essential that Missouri create one for coordinated planning in the Missouri portion of the area. Herein he pointedly ignored the Bi-State Agency; his subsequent remarks reveal why.

In answer to the question, Is it possible to develop a metropolitan planning program over a two-state area without giving each state both the power to veto and to suggest new programs? he answered, "This veto power would be necessary so that each side of the river would feel confident that its interest would be protected as much as possible." In response to another question, Do we need a single planning organization to act as an umbrella over the St. Louis area's planning activities? he said "no," but added, "a single planning organization would almost have to serve the overwhelming influence of the City of St. Louis. On the other hand, there is little doubt that the products of such a program would be unacceptable to significant groups in the Illinois portion."

Why not Bi-State for the work? Graves observed:

The Bi-State Development Agency was originally conceived for the purpose of providing a mass transportation system, with buses, for the St. Louis area. It was given planning powers along with its authority to develop certain transportation facilities. Since the passage of its enabling legislation it has become thoroughly involved in investing funds in transportation facilities and equipment. It is completely committed to its present function as an operating agency, with a vested interest in its own profits.

Graves, strongly negative as he was toward the Bi-State Agency, sought an answer for the recommendation he had to make to Governor Kerner in the Southwestern Illinois Metropolitan Area Planning Commission (known locally as SWIMPAC), and a to-be-created similar Missouri commission. Coordination of the two would be the task of the governors through the Missouri State Division of Commerce and Industrial Development, and the Illinois Board of Economic Development. To this suggestion both governors appeared to agree, although their statements to the press were not altogether clear. On August 14, 1964, Governor Dalton sought to clarify his own viewpoint by issuing a statement that he would not bypass the role of Bi-State in any procedures that would be established at the state level. And late in August Governor Kerner addressed a letter to the chairman of SWIMPAC which suggested that his support would be given to Bi-State's efforts to create a new regional council of governments. Both governors took the view that planning funds should be held by the states and released to the planning organization, whatever it might be, only as requested. Both governors later abandoned this view when the federal government insisted that whatever agency was created had to be a genuinely coordinated, area-wide planning program for the total metropolitan area with power to receive federal grants directly for its programs.

In effect, then, it was the federal government's agencies which decided the form of the metropolitan area's planning structure. Possibly, had the Bureau of Public Roads and the Housing and Home Finance Agency been presented with a plan to give the Bi-State Agency a mandate and directive to perform the planning tasks, these federal agencies would not have objected. It was Illinois distrust for the agency that compelled creation of yet another governmental agency, the East-West Gateway Coordinating Council, which met the federal government's demands.

Bi-State's own version of the 1964–65 planning efforts is that it served to bring the interests together in 1964. It then obtained a $20,000 grant in July 1964, from the St. Louis Regional and Construction Foundation (the Greenfelder Foundation) to develop a prospectus on the scope and organizational structure required for bistate planning, subsequently prepared by Alan Voorhees and Associates.[145] The next step required implementation of the prospectus guide proposals with "memoranda agreements of cooperation" among the various governmental entities in the bistate area. To recount the opposition which developed following enactment of these "memoranda agreements" would require an additional chapter. Suffice it at this point simply to state that heavy objection arose from the Granite City area to the methods used by the Southwestern Illinois Council of Mayors in obtaining the agreements, with questions raised as to the legality of the arrangements.[146]

Bi-State's bland account of the results is a masterpiece of understatement:

As may be imagined, bringing together men of diverse ideas and opinions from widely separated communities in two different States to work toward a common cause, even when it was for their mutual benefit and that of their constituents, was not always easy. Representatives of at least two Illinois agencies expressed fear that a metropolitan planning organization, and Bi-State Development Agency in particular, would encroach on some of their powers and compete against them for federal funds. This fear was groundless, of course, and we hope it has since been allayed, as it should be, by word and action of the 10 Bi-State Development Agency Commissioners. . . .

Like other members of the East-West Gateway Coordinating Committee, Bi-State Agency is enthusiastic about the future potential of our metropolitan region. This Agency stands ready to proceed further with fulfillment of its obligation to areawide planning . . . to assume greater leadership and a major unifying role in this field.[147]

Even so, Colonel Smyser, in an interview connected with the present study, expressed his view that there was an excellent case to be made for leaving the planning function in the hands of the "elected officials" of the various governments, but did not elaborate on this idea. He thought that perhaps Bi-State might be better altered in some manner so that its role would be that of a transit agency or port authority only. If proper controls by both states, with some mechanism included to reflect the popular will and not merely the will of planners, experts, officials, industrialists and the like, can be established for such a new role for Bi-State, this study will then agree with Colonel Smyser. Sufficient suggestion has heretofore been made in this examination to point up the implications attendant upon further Bi-State expansion into the realm of monopoly of all transportation facilities in the

St. Louis area, including airports. The question of management and control is overriding.

The Bi-State Development Agency and Compact Conclusions

Certain conclusions concerning the Bi-State Development Agency and its interstate compact can be drawn, even though it is fair to say that the agency itself has been performing energetically for only a decade, not a long time for a final definitive appraisal to be made. But its character has crystallized, its aims and motives are now fairly clear, and the directions in which it tends no longer obscure.

Today, it is clear that it is not altogether the interstate compact agency which Congress approved in 1949, amended in 1959, and which its designers in the States of Illinois and Missouri wrote into law. Whether its existing character fulfills what its creators envisaged for it, as suggested by Gene Graves, is another matter. The law is one thing, plans are another, and fulfillment is yet something else. Besides, as emphasized early in this study, the exact character of such an agency as Bi-State is complex, defying exact description according to traditional concepts and definitions of government.

Certain major political factors have been instrumental in the shaping of the Bi-State Agency which perhaps have not operated so influentially in the case of its model, the recognizedly successful New York Port Authority. The authority, born in the 1920s, was confronted with little interference by the federal government. Since Bi-State's emergence, federal participation has become a constant factor, always to be taken into consideration in any facet of such a local governmental agency's activities. Planning, even for so limited a focus as transportation, can be today a major undertaking of long delays attended with more and more strategic involvement at strategic intervals and in strategic places. Thus, infinite amounts of time, energy, and public moneys go into the study phase which is, actually, the negotiating stage, the bargaining stage, the politicking stage. Literally years elapse before plans get out of the committee rooms and off the drawing boards and, too frequently, suffer from obsolescence by the time construction begins. With the effort to get federal funds comes federal bureaucracy, federal policies, federal plans. With federal funds likewise come state bureaucracy, state policies and politics, state plans. With federal funds come infinitely varied and multitudinous decision centers, little bailwicks of interest and obstruction, which make the autonomy, the power, the policy-making role of such an agency as Bi-State something of a fiction unless it develops protective devices and stratagems of its own. A premium therefore is placed on the agency's political ability rather than upon its operating or administrative talents. In the transition from operating agency to political actor, the local public interest will most certainly be assigned a secondary role as something to be attended to when the agency can and must get around to it.

The New York Port Authority was not without local opposition and local difficulties, but the nature of New York City and its harbor made a strong and independent transit agency, divorced from the political domination of Manhattan, a must. Success for the authority, while not necessarily assured, could be expected. The need for the Bi-State Agency in the St. Louis Metropolitan District has been not so clear, not so pressing. Area interests have had alternatives to which they can and do turn which weaken the concept the Bi-State Agency and its compact represent.

Intricately interwoven in St. Louis metropolitan area affairs today is the question of human welfare, a matter which did not concern the New York City port and transit interests in the 1920s. Across the river from St. Louis—indeed, under the very nose of the downtown business center—lies East St. Louis, a sick and disintegrating city whose white population has almost totally evacuated. Left behind are the thousands of blacks who today comprise most of its population. Unemployment, blight, crime, poverty, loss of industry, even terror, have become the leading characteristics of this once busy city. Any thought of or attempt to develop the East Side runs head-on into this almost insurmountable problem. The Bi-State Agency, frustrated in its early years by the inadequacies of the law under which it sought to operate, confined itself at that time to transportation as its first priority and most obtainable goal. The deterioration of the East Side has roughly paralleled the two decades of Bi-State's life. As the agency has grown in stature and potential competence, the East Side economic and welfare problem has grown. Bi-State's resources for dealing with social planning on the scale demanded are therefore no more adequate today than they were in 1949 and its officials have clearly perceived and been acutely aware that the agency's survival depends on avoidance of social planning embracing anything more than the narrow transportation focus it has chosen for its own.

These facts of St. Louis area political life are joined with many others easily identified and already mentioned: population distribution, two states, many local jurisdictions, the Mississippi River, Illinois-side hunger for more than the crumbs from the St. Louis table, Missouriside determination to keep what it has and relinquish nothing new, two state legislatures of decidedly different temperament, tradition, and influences. All such help to explain the seeming weakness and inadequacies of the Bi-State Agency.

As an operating agency, however, Bi-State cannot be so charitably viewed.

FIRST, as an interstate agency, created by two states and approved by Congress, it is one of several such unique developments of present-day United States. Interstate agencies of its type reflect the alteration in both kind and scope of activities deemed appropriate for interstate compacts, and their potential for great influence on existing governmental, economic, and social relationships is easier to appraise if not yet altogether certain.

As public bodies such interstate compact agencies are directed to fulfill certain policies set and defined by the parent governments, and they are deemed to be subject to the same governmental controls as any other agency of state or national government. That is, the supervision and oversight of the executive, legislative, and judicial branches of the nation and the involved states are considered to operate at all times. If, however, such an agency is created as a public corporation it immediately acquires a role of considerable liberty, holding nearly the same degree of freedom of action, individuality, and autonomy of decision in matters involving extensive and varied public services as does a private corporation operating in its own fields of private interest. The controls of both are much alike—designedly liberal, but the purposes of the one are public, the other private, and herein lies the problem and the difficulties.

As interstate agencies, these "authorities" are certainly unsupervised and relatively uncontrolled in their day-by-day activities by the governments which give them being. This results from the nature of the federal system, which provides no means or device for a "third level" of governmental control in the complex province which lies in federal-state, state-state, and federal-state-local relationships. Once created, neither the federal government nor the states have sole power of decision over the agency and its acts. The local governments it was created to serve likewise have no concentrated legal power to police and direct it, but—if the Bi-State Agency's experience can be used as illustrating a principle which seems to be emerging in this kind of intergovernmental operation—surprisingly enough, it is the local governments which exercise such controls and restraints as the agency receives. Unfortunately, they are political in nature rather than regular administrative processes of examination and review.

This, then, is the first conclusion: that interstate agencies of Bi-State's type occupy a position of potentially great freedom and independence of action, particularly if they also have the role of a public corporation. This role or position is ambiguous since it is not yet surrounded by sophisticated and refined developments in law, defining powers and providing effective restraints. The absence of such law encourages the development of practices and expedients which evolve from the agency's own actions and needs and as such are not necessarily the proper or best design for the general public interest. Yet, the agency's effectiveness depends in great degree upon the constant and wholehearted effort, active interest, and careful scrutiny of all participating governments, and the public expects and has a right to its expectation that this is being provided at all times.

SECOND, the Bi-State Agency is essentially a local government itself, but one which transcends the boundaries of individual cities, towns, counties, and most special districts. It is, indeed, the governing agent of a superspecial district. Unlike most special districts, however, it enjoys no taxing powers. Although municipal in nature, it holds some but not all of the powers of a true municipal corporation. As a public corporation, it does not fall under the curbs and restraints which delimit the quasi-corporate agencies of American government. It has, also, something of the nature and powers of a private holding company, but not all. A definition has yet to be drawn of its precise nature.

Because of its intimacy with local affairs, the milieu in which it functions is one of many and varied grass-roots interests of unequal strength, purpose, and resources. Effort is made by the parent governments to recognize this variety of interest by providing a multi-membered governing commission or board for the agency's administration, requiring representation on an equal basis between the two participating states and confining appointments to the local district's boundaries. Such a scheme cannot possibly reflect the inequalities and varied interests embraced within the basic division: private businesses, great and small municipalities, federal agencies, state agencies, suburban and urban, a lingering agriculturalism, all often operating at cross-purposes.

Yet such an agency is not a supergovernment, with power to lift its decision-making above the infighting and crosscurrents of the member interests. Therefore, its position of potential power which results from its freedom from state and local administrative controls can be and often is rendered a thing of impotence for many years on particular matters. Neither is it a local government, operating under the mandate and curbs of popular elections and referenda, clumsy but workable devices for resolving complex community questions.

To act at all, then, the agency must choose the open doors and courses of action which are available to it and which offer the least obstruction. Those channels may not always be the ones that are truly in the public interest, for the public interest is often that which is most tightly and inextricably bound in conflict and controversy. The agency's chosen course of action may thus result from the personal interests of the commissioners themselves which make it possible for them to find common areas of agreement so that a decision can be reached, without regard for urgency of need, priority, and the like.

In Bi-State's case, there appears to be a need for some means to make its governing board more truly responsive to its charge, while restraining proclivities toward self-interest. Two neglected aspects of the laws under which it operates could provide the means: activation of an advisory board of "lay" citizens, and a grant of veto power to the two governors.

At the present time there is scant means available for the governors to be currently abreast of Bi-State's plans, intentions, negotiations, and final commitments. The veto is needed now, but it will be imperative should the agency acquire the greatly expanded roles projected in plans for an airport authority and a rapid-transit system with a taxing power to support them.

The New York Port Authority has always operated under the

threat of veto. A New Jersey State Senate Investigating Committee's 1963 report on the authority stated:

The Port Authority has attempted to keep the Governors advised as to such of its proposals as it deems controversial before they are adopted so as to obtain the benefit of the thinking of the Governors . . . and avoid the necessity of veto and modification to meet . . . objection. The veto . . . continues as the most effective instrument of assuring that the policy of the Port Authority cannot depart from the policy of either State. We observe that the Governors have not hesitated to use the veto power when they deemed it appropriate.[148]

THIRD, close examination of the agency reveals matters on which changes in the two states' laws seem necessary and desirable. Today, a broadly outlined mandate of power is not so much needed as a definite mechanism of accountability. This should include not only the veto, but conflict-of-interest coverage for the board of commissioners and for the personnel of the service corporations which operate its enterprises. It should include regular, periodic state supervision and review through the auditing and budgeting processes. Such review ought to include annual scrutiny of managerial methods and procedures of the service corporations. Again, Bi-State's projected expansion demands that such changes in the laws need to be made before it receives the authority to expand.

As of the moment, the East-West Gateway Coordinating Council is serving as Bi-State's advisory committee. But Bi-State needs its own advisory committee to attend solely to its own activities. The Coordinating Council is the St. Louis area-wide planning mechanism, and it is not unfair to say that Bi-State is exceedingly influential in obtaining its own purposes through the council. It is no substitute for the kind of advisory committee suggested in the Bi-State Compact. But the compact needs to be more definitively worded if such an advisory committee is to exist at all and provide the review powers it probably ought to have.

Further revisions in the basic laws are indicated: Possible prohibitions against Bi-State's receiving any gifts, loans, lands, and the making of contracts contingent upon gifts, loans, lands with private business interests except on prior approval of the governors of the two states—and such approval ought to rest on proof that the contract with its contingent gifts gives full evidence of being in the public interest. Another possible revision might be the inclusion in the law of a broader requirement for representation of more varied interests. Bi-State's present board arrangements have placed heavy emphasis on financial and large business interests. No definitions appear in the law as to whether such a board is regulatory, policy-making, administrative, advisory, or something else. These need to be added.

Last—and this is not so much a task for the Bi-State Agency or the states and local governments as it is the task of all students and agencies of public administration: examination is strongly needed of the role played, today, by private survey companies, institutes, professional planning and engineering firms, in the use of feasibility studies which seem merely to lend the color of officialism to actions such developmental agencies wish to undertake. Some suspicion attaches to them in their possible solicitation of contracts, their fees, and their possible policy-making influences through gradual, subtle alterations of plans over a period of time when they are hired on a standing basis. This has been neglected.

Further comment on the Bi-State Agency will be made in this study's final chapter. It may be that in it and agencies like it we are witnessing the evolving shape of American federalism and government as they are to become. That chapter will seek to cast some light on the evolution.

The attempt to make an equitable apportionment of water among States within a given region has been sought through litigation as though it involved the riparian rights of neighboring individuals. The most informed professional opinion registers the failure of this attempt and the present movement towards solution by interstate treaties is a decisive recognition that the instrument of state-craft in this field is not court but compact. . . . Continuous and creative administration is needed; not litigation, necessarily a sporadic process.

. . . .

We are dealing with regions, like the Southwest clustering about the Colorado River, or the States dependent upon the Delaware for water. . . . The regions are less than the nation and are greater than any one State.
Felix Frankfurter and James M. Landis, "The Compact Clause of the Constitution—A Study in Interstate Adjustments," Yale Law Journal, May 1925, p. 707.

The Great Lakes Basin Compact

SEVERAL OF THE more successful interstate compacts of the nation have been those which concern water resources. One of the most recent, the Delaware River Commission, is at the same time one of the more mature efforts, having originally been developed by mutual agreement as a joint cooperative water regulatory commission by the States of Delaware, New Jersey, Pennsylvania, and New York. Proving through three decades its effectiveness as a means of dealing with problems of pollution and stream flow, the four states sought and obtained consent from Congress for the Delaware River Basin Compact, creating in 1961 a regional agency for the "planning, use and control of the water and related natural resources of the Delaware River Basin, including flood control, pollution," and other related matters.[1] Thus by interstate compact the former limited functions have been increased to embrace developmental concepts not originally anticipated.

Most of the nation's other early water resources compacts have concerned boundary disputes involving streams and their channel changes, water allocation (in compacts of the Western states), and flood control arrangements in a wide range of localities. The New York Port Authority Compact heralded a new era in interstate water matters which, as suggested by Frankfurter and Landis in 1925, seemed to practitioners in the water field to be highly suitable for interstate cooperation rather than for federal governmental control. Today Illinois is party to several such developmental water agreements: the Great Lakes Basin Compact, the Ohio River Valley Water Sanitation Compact, the Wabash Valley Interstate Compact, and the Bi-State Development Compact. (As demonstrated in chapter 3, the last named is not primarily a water compact, being more broadly conceived in its purposes, but having water and its problems as one of several economic developmental functions.)

Concomitantly with this trend on the part of the states to obtain first position in the realm of water control via the route of interstate compacts has been an even more extensive activity by the national government in broadening and extending its own authority over the nation's waters, waterways, navigable rivers, and river basins. The two parallel historical developments have underscored the imperative nature of the country's water questions, but complexities and head-on confrontations between all levels of government have inescapably occurred. Such legal and political tangles have pointed emphatically to the need for a settled nationwide water resources policy which will be accepted and adhered to. Such a comprehensive national policy could be attained were it not for infinitely complex political considerations, for the federal government's constitutional authority over the navigable waters of the nation, through a series of laws and Supreme Court cases, has been broadened and rendered more sophisticated over several decades until today ultimate federal authority is virtually total, even though actual control is not. Added to the federal government's sole power over international affairs, which includes international waters, its existing role and autonomy bring such a nationwide water policy within the realm of possibility.

Daily, however, the goal seems more remote. The deeply particularistic interests of the states, and the model of the New York Port Authority, the early scholarly influence of Frankfurter and Landis in placing such matters by legal theory in the hands of the states in a sincere belief that this is where they belong, have stimulated today's accumulation of interstate water compacts and interstate regulatory agencies holding broad economic developmental powers. Governmental difficulties today and in the foreseeable future are inevitable and ever present. As with almost all other American governmental developments, solutions are sought by superimposition of new agencies upon old foundations, with resultant overlapping, duplicating, and conflicting purposes.

Creation of the Great Lakes Basin Compact

There is no more litigated, conflict-ridden, fought-over water region in all of the United States than that of the Great Lakes. Embodying as it does the States of New York, Ohio, Pennsylvania, Illinois, Michigan, Indiana, Minnesota, and Wisconsin; and Lakes Erie, Huron, Michigan, Superior, and Ontario; it also involves for purposes of total inclusion, the St. Lawrence River, the Chicago Sanitary and Ship Canal, the Calumet and Sag Channel, the Detroit River, the Niagara River and Falls, and lesser streams and lakes of the United States. This includes an artificial link with the Illinois River and the Mississippi River. Furthermore, it embraces the Provinces of Ontario and Quebec, Lake Nipigon, Lake St. Clair, Long Lake, Georgian Bay, the Nipigon River, the Ogoki River, the Kenogami River, the Aguasabon River, Sault Ste. Marie and the St. Mary's River, the Welland Canal, the Ottawa River, and lesser streams and lakes in Canada. Common to both countries is the St. Lawrence Seaway.

Beyond all this the area includes some of the greatest agricultural and industrial development known to the world, involving some of the Midwestern "breadbasket" states and provinces and the great cities of Duluth, Port Arthur, Green Bay, Minneapolis–St. Paul, Milwaukee, Chicago, Gary and Hammond, Muskegon, Detroit, Hamilton, Toledo, Cleveland, Toronto, Buffalo, Rochester, Oswego, Quebec, and Montreal. As one of the world's outstanding centers of ports, harbors, and water carrying activities, it has made of the states and provinces which surround it one of the busiest, wealthiest, most populous areas of the North American continent and, indeed, of the globe itself.

This area of superlatives and tremendous pure water resources has another face. With industry and great population have come mismanagement and water pollution. With pollution has come disaster to the lakes' fishing resources, commercial and recreational. Heightened demands for more and more water for industry and population in all conceivable water uses have prompted diversions of water from this lake and that lake, with accompanying protests from hydroelectric power interests, shipping interests, and conservationists. Lake levels are said to have fallen and risen beyond their normal rise and fall. Accumulating pollution does not obligingly discharge into a beneficent ocean, but builds and builds within the lakes until some have envisaged them as ultimately becoming—if they are not already—great poisoned reservoirs, menacing wildlife and humanity alike. With certain natural climatological proclivities, such as violent summer winds and storms and hard winters which produce vast quantities of ice, the lakes' shores fall away, debris piles up, and private property is destroyed or greatly damaged. The needs, uses, demands, conflicts, and claims of nations, states, cities, peoples, and enterprises have produced laws, lawsuits, political struggles, treaties, animosities, and continuing need for intergovernmental negotiation, discussion, cooperation. A bevy of governmental agencies to cope with it all has resulted down through many years, most of which are the products of this century.

Technically, the geographical area designated as the Great Lakes–St. Lawrence Basin is described by the United States Army Corps of Engineers as follows:

[It] extends a distance of some 2,000 miles from the western end of the Lake Superior Basin in Minnesota, to the Gulf of St. Lawrence on the Atlantic Ocean. Thus, from east to west, the basin spans nearly one-half of the North American continent. The five Great Lakes, Superior, Michigan, Huron, Erie, and Ontario, with their connecting rivers and Lake St. Clair, have a water surface area of about 95,000 square miles above the head of the St. Lawrence River at the eastern end of Lake Ontario. The total area of the Great Lakes Basin, both land and water, above the head of the St. Lawrence River is approximately 295,000 square miles. The international boundary between Canada and the United States passes through all of the Great Lakes and their connecting channels, with the exception of Lake Michigan which is entirely within the United States, and through the St. Lawrence River to a point near Cornwall, Ontario, where the boundary turns eastward to continue along a line between the State of New York and the Province of Quebec. Downstream of this point, the St. Lawrence River is entirely within Canada.[2]

From the existing records, the one event most important in triggering several of the states of the Great Lakes Basin into seeking the formal interstate compact which they enacted in 1955 was creation of the St. Lawrence Seaway. The area's many problems and controversies for a great many years, however, had impressed persons most intimately related to the lakes that some medium for interstate communication and cooperation was needed—possibly not a regulatory mechanism, since one of importance already existed in the form of the International Joint Commission, an agency reflecting the national and international character of the Great Lakes—but a permanent agency of sufficiently authoritative nature that the Basin's states would and could unite as a working group holding common and interrelated interests rather than continue as separate sovereignties pulling and hauling against each other, acting independently on their problems or seeking favors unilaterally from the federal government and the International Joint Commission.

Several events of the early 1950s provided the impetus necessary for carrying to completion the formal agreement which the Great Lakes Basin Compact represents. These were the approval by President Eisenhower of the Canadian–New York State arrangements which created the St. Lawrence Seaway, certain activities concerning the Burns Ditch Harbor Project on Lake Michigan in the Chicago area (which began in Indiana in the 1930s but erupted in 1961 in the Indiana Dunes controversy), and another of a series of controversies concerning a proposed diversion of additional water at Chicago from Lake Michigan into the Chicago Sanitary and Ship Canal. Additional factors lay in certain other continuing problems and in future hopes and expectations: the anticipated expansion of ocean-carrying freight in Great Lakes harbors and port cities, possibly expanded industrial and real estate activity as a result, the heightening pollution of waters which serve as the water supply and recreational area of peoples and cities of two nations, the deteriorating lakes' fishing industries; and the unsolved problem of lake water levels which affect shore erosion and storm damages to the lakes' shore properties, the production of hydroelectric power, and the amount of cargo tonnage lakes' carriers can transport annually.

Prompted by all such matters, the Michigan legislature in 1954 enacted a law giving its governor authority to enter a compact with the other Great Lakes states and the Provinces of Quebec and Ontario.[3] Following this action certain of the interested Great Lakes states' governors, and officials of the existing state commissions of interstate cooperation, prevailed upon the Council of State Governments to organize the Great Lakes Seaway and Water Resources Conference of August 1954. In explaining this conference the Great Lakes Commission notes that, "In addition to focusing attention on State plans and programs pertaining to the recently approved St. Lawrence Seaway, the conference discussed the Michigan proposal for an interstate commission. A resolution unanimously approved by this conference set in motion the procedure and organization that led to the development of the Great Lakes Basin Compact." [4]

In the light of the many questions which subsequently have arisen concerning justification for the compact, inclusion at this point of portions of Michigan Governor G. Mennan Williams's 1958 explanatory letter to Senator Joseph C. O'Mahoney of the United States Senate Committee on the Judiciary is helpful:

The Great Lakes Basin constitutes the largest fresh-water area in the whole world. In it are immeasurable resources which belong either individually or collectively to these States bordering on the waters of the Great Lakes. These States are the owners of these resources and are charged by law with a solemn and inalienable public trust to administer them for the benefit of their people. In many cases decided by the United States Supreme Court as well as by the courts of each State, the existence of this trust has been affirmed and reaffirmed and consequently we have the obligation to utilize and administer the resources of the waters of this basin to the best advantage of all the people residing in our several Great Lakes States.

. . . .

Realizing that the time had arrived for the Great Lakes States to consult with one another and to engage in a continuing program of study and investigation with respect to the many problems that affected the interests of all or several of the States, we in Michigan took the lead several years ago in the promotion of a permanent organization among the Great Lakes States under the compact power of the Federal Constitution. Previous efforts of forming voluntary committees had failed. In addition, a legally constituted body had to be formed to which the legislature of each State could appropriate funds so that the work of the interstate organization could be carried on effectively. [5]

Michigan's motives in seeking such an organization are obvious. The state is virtually surrounded by the waters of the lakes, and until Hawaii was admitted to the Union, she was the only state having a substantial portion of her geographical area separated from her mainland by a large body of water, being at the same time physically attached to the mainland of another state. Michigan holds with Canada at Sault Ste. Marie a strategic position of potential control over inter-lake transportation from and to Lake Superior. At the Straits of Macki-nac she enjoys the same strategic position over the carrying routes to and from Lake Michigan. At Detroit, again with Canada, she holds such a position over the routes from and to the Atlantic. Tourism and recreation are of prime importance to Michigan, so that polluted lake waters and threatened water diversions are to her very real problems of large concern. Without individual representation in the various international governing bodies at work in the Great Lakes, she has had no more voice in the disposition of Great Lakes affairs by the United States and Canadian governments than any other state of the Union or province of the Dominion.

The proposed compact went into effect on July 1, 1955, following almost immediate ratification by five states: Illinois, Indiana, Michigan, Minnesota, and Wisconsin. Since the compact's terms required only four states' approval for its establishment, the Great Lakes Commission was promptly organized by December 1955. By 1956, Pennsylvania had ratified, but New York and Ohio encountered internal opposition which delayed ratification by these states until 1960 and 1963, respectively. A 1957 adoption of the compact by New York's legislature was vetoed by Governor Averill Harriman with objections ostensibly based on the treaty's provisions for appointing state representatives to the Great Lakes Commission, which he regarded as "an invasion of the responsibilities of the Governor with respect to appointments" under the New York constitution, and to the compact's language which seemingly compelled member states' officials to furnish information and aid to the Great Lakes Commission on command.[6] While he professed to hold "general support" of the agreement, regarding it as "a useful mechanism for the study and discussion of problems of common interest," it is possible that his objections were to some degree influenced by the strong opposition of the New York Power Authority, which steadily opposed the granting of congressional consent. As will be shown, the authority's rationale for opposition took a most interesting course of opposing while not opposing, and it had considerable influence upon Congress in that body's failure to grant consent.

Following ratification by the original five states, the compact and its commission functioned without a break for thirteen years before it obtained congressional consent to its existence in July 1968. In this regard the compact provides one of the more important illustrations of

Congress and the consent question, and the kinds of legal confusions and complications which can surround the interstate compact device. It is also an interstate compact that has received from Congress a larger than customary amount of congressional scrutiny.

Purposes and Provisions of the Compact

The Council of State Governments classifies the Great Lakes Basin Compact as "advisory and recommendatory." In view of the compact's long status of operating without Congress's consent, and its greatly limited status since 1968 with consent, this is probably wholly accurate. Yet the compact as enacted by its member states lists purposes which include promotional and planning activities in relation to "comprehensive development" and "conservation" of the Great Lakes Basin, and another somewhat unspecific and ill-defined clause (article I, sec. 3) charges the Great Lakes Commission with the task of making it "possible for the states of the Basin and their people to derive the maximum benefit from utilization of public works, in the form of navigational aids or otherwise, which may exist or which may be constructed from time to time." [7] While protestations have been made before congressional committees from the beginning that the Great Lakes Commission (the compact's executive agency) is not intended to be anything other than an advisory and recommendatory agency without regulatory power or, presumably, specific power to operate or build enterprises of various kinds, it nonetheless is granted power under the compact's article IV to sue and be sued, and to "acquire, hold and convey real and personal property and any interest therein." [8] It is immune to taxation by member states; [9] and it may accept monies from any state, any government, any governmental subdivision or agency, and any institution, person, firm or corporation. [10] These privileges and powers, combined with the several purposes of article I, would superficially appear to vest the commission with a considerable dormant or reserve power which to date has not been activated, attempted, or sought, and which probably will not be proposed for some time (if ever) in view of the difficulties it encountered in obtaining the 1968 grant of congressional consent, and as long as it is without specific power to issue revenue bonds or to construct or operate enterprises. This is not to say that at some future date such power could not easily be added without disturbing much of the compact's present structure and provisions, or that additional financial and operational powers might not be added as was the case in the Illinois-Missouri Bi-State Development Compact, but at present such additions appear not to be contemplated. The long years without congressional consent placed a certain constraint upon the commission and its activities that is quite evident in congressional records, a limitation which its strongest supporters (chiefly the Great Lakes Commission itself) would like to see removed.

Member states under article I agree to take cooperative action in promoting "orderly, integrated, and comprehensive" development and conservation of the Basin; to plan for the entire Basin's water resources, and for portions of it which have specialized problems; to advise as to the proper and most balanced uses of the Basin's water resources among competing economic and other interests and demands; to maintain an intergovernmental agency for these purposes; and to carry out the provisions of the previously mentioned article I, sec. 3. The commission's authority extends to as much of all the Great Lakes, the St. Lawrence River, and "any and all natural or man-made water interconnections" between and among them, as are within the party states, and all rivers, ponds, lakes, streams, and other watercourses which are tributary to the Great Lakes and Lake St. Clair, or which are part of any watershed draining into them.[11]

In general, the commission holds a research and fact-finding power, the power to plan, to deliberate, to consider and recommend, to report and publish its findings on development, use, and conservation of water resources; needed public works and improvements; improvement of navigation and port facilities; improvement and maintenance of Basin fisheries; institution and alteration of flood plain and other zoning laws, ordinances, and regulations; institution and alteration of uniform or other laws, ordinances, and regulations on Basin development to all related Basin governments of the United States; and an important anticipated international role which cannot be developed or matured with the Canadian Provinces of Quebec and Ontario until Congress removes the restraints it imposed when it granted consent. As originally drafted, the compact would have had an internationally involved commission, with power to recommend international agreements to the United States and Canada on the uses and disposition of the Basin's water resources, on mutual arrangements in connection with Article XIII of the treaty, *1909 Convention Relating to the Boundary Waters Between the United States and Canada*; and to assist on request of the two governments in negotiating and formulating any treaties or mutual arrangements having to do with future development of the Basin. The commission was empowered by the compact (as signed by the creating states) to cooperate with the Canadian and United States governments, with any other public agencies, and with any private agencies or bodies having Basin interests. Finally, it was intended that it could make recommendations for carrying out the compact itself, and draft and recommend proposed amendments to it (presumably using its influence to obtain state and congressional, as well as provincial and Dominion adoption), but the commission's actions in any or all of its powers were denied any force of law or binding effect upon any party state.[12] All of the original powers and duties still stand except that the compacting states have been denied the right to deal with Canada.

Although the commission's actions are denied any force of law, the compact's member states obligate themselves in article VII "to consider the action the Commission recommends" in respect to the following enumerated subjects: (1) stabilization of lake levels; (2) measures for combating pollution, beach erosion, floods, shore inundation; (3) uniformity in navigation regulations; (4) proposed navigation aids and improvements; (5) coordinating action in fishing laws and regulations, and cooperative action to eradicate destructive and parasitical forces endangering fisheries, wildlife, and other water resources; (6) suitable hydroelectric power developments; (7) cooperative programs for control of soil and bank erosion; (8) diversion of waters from and into the Great Lakes Basin; and (9) recreational use of water resources.[13]

Member states agree to implement the compact by statute to provide three to five designated or appointed commissioners from each state to serve without compensation except for expenses, and subject to each state's removal powers. Further, the commission prepares its own budget and recommends each member state's share. Such budgets need have only a majority of all commission votes cast, but cost allocations must be equitable among party states "in accordance with their respective interests." [14]

Once adopted the compact remains binding upon each member state until it is specifically renounced by a state's legislature. Such a withdrawal, however, cannot become effective until six months after notice of the repeal has been given to the other party states.[15] This provision aroused congressional questioning in 1958 as to whether acts of the commission could continue to obligate a member state even after its legislature had voiced its disapproval.

Congressman James G. Fulton (R.), of Pennsylvania, asked:

MR. FULTON. . . . Moving further . . . , I am from the State of Pennsylvania, and see that . . . Pennsylvania is a proposed member. . . . I question the constitutionality of the Sate of Pennsylvania under its present constitution being bound for 6 months after it decides to leave such a compact . . . by act of its legislature and approved by the Governor.

To me it would seem impossible to force a State . . . to be a member and subject to acts of this compact Commission for 6 months after it expressed its formal decision to withdraw from the commission.

. . . .

I am raising the constitutional point that I would like to have somebody answer some place. How can you have a member State, . . . or a Province of the Dominion of Canada bound for 6 months after they, by statute, decide they want to withdraw immediately.[16]

The commission responded by memorandum, as follows:

The validity of this particular provision would, of course, depend upon the constitutions of each of the member states. The legislatures in most States can commit the States to the term of 1 appropriation period, which is, generally, 2 years. Beyond that, it would appear that this provision is more an expression of good faith by the member States, rather than a provision which might be the subject of a lawsuit. Finally, insofar as this provision involves a constitutional issue, the question is a State rather than a Federal one, and a number of interstate compacts approved by the Congress in the past contain substantially similar provisions.[17]

Since such provisions have not, to this writer's knowledge, been the subject of any lawsuit in any state, the question seems to remain essentially unanswered.

The compact includes a "severability clause" which constitutionally maintains the remainder of the compact operable even though some part of it may be determined to be invalid by some member state, the United States government, or (as originally planned) the provinces or general government of Canada.[18]

The Illinois statutes which enact the compact contain the provision that, "The ratification and approval of said compact by this State shall not be binding or obligatory until it shall have been likewise approved . . . by the Congress of the United States." [19] In the light of Congress's failure to consent to the compact for thirteen years, it would appear that Illinois's participation during that time was purely voluntary and informal, although it regularly appropriated its share of the commission's budget and supported its efforts to obtain congressional consent.

As suggested above, the compact's general purposes and the specific powers granted to the Great Lakes Commission, seem to have been drafted with a forward view, looking to a time when the agency might be deemed to be ready for greater things. Very little alteration of the existing law would be required to broaden it into a regulatory and developmental agency of great authority, but it must be emphasized that this is a potential, or dormant power, not now functioning. It partially explains some of Congress's reluctance to grant consent and thus put a legal capstone to a union which would enable commission expansion efforts to proceed.

Executive Powers of the Great Lakes Commission

The compact provides for a commission to be composed of not less than three nor more than five commissioners from each state. Illinois, Michigan, Indiana, Minnesota, and Ohio have five commissioners each; New York and Wisconsin have four each; and Pennsylvania is represented by three. Each state delegation has three votes only, and to do business a quorum of commissioners from five states * must be present. Actions of the commission are approved by a majority of votes cast with one exception: recommendations of fact-finding, planning, advising, recommending, and the like, under the specific powers of the compact's article VI, require a majority of the votes cast from each of a majority of the states present and voting.[20] The New York Power Authority in its opposition to the compact emphasized to Congress:

This means that if there were 8 States present and voting and each had 5 commissioners, in order to make a recommendation, a majority

---

* With the present eight-state membership; it would have required commissioners from six, if Quebec and Ontario had joined, as originally planned.

of the commissioners in each of 5 States would have to vote affirmatively for the recommendation.

In other words, 15 affirmative votes of the commissioners could override 25 negative votes.[21]

By this reasoning, under present membership arrangements, fifteen affirmative votes from the five states with five members each can override twenty-one negative votes. Proxy voting with the written permission of an absent member is allowed within each state's delegation. Commissioners of any two or more member states may meet separately on matters of particular interest to them, although final full commission approval is required for any actions taken by such a minority group.

The commissioners annually elect from their membership a chairman and a vice-chairman and appoint an executive director who, in turn, has power to name the secretariat of the commission. The commission formulates its own bylaws, rules and regulations, and determines its committee structure. This, to date, appears to be somewhat fluid, although six substantive standing committees have heretofore existed to deal with the specialized interests of the commission: Seaway, Navigation and Commerce; Water Resources; Shoreline Use and Recreation; Fisheries and Wildlife; Pollution Control; and (until 1968, at least) International Relations. There is also an Executive Committee, and there have been in the recent past a Steering Committee, a Technical Advisory Committee, and various special committees such as the 1963 Special Committee on Financial Procedures, the 1964 Special Committee on Negotiations with Canada, and a "Consent Subcommittee" of the Executive Committee, which was very active in 1966 and 1967 when the Great Lakes Commission made its final major effort to obtain congressional sanction. The Executive Committee, consisting of the commission's chairman and vice-chairman and one representative from each member state, supervises the agency's activities between regular meetings. Individual state delegations maintain liaison relationships with their own governors and state agencies. The commission itself issues special reports to the governors from time to time.[22] The compact contains no provisions for gubernatorial veto of the acts of the commission, but such a power is not needed as the compact now stands since member states are not bound by the commission's acts.

Financing of the Commission

The broadly worded provisions of the compact on financing seem to envisage a considerable financial activity for the Great Lakes Commission which has certainly not materialized to date. The executive director is designated trustee for the commission, with power to borrow and contract for personnel services from any state or subdivisional government or agency, and to accept donations, gifts, grants, equipment, and supplies from them or from any other source including private corporations. The agency and its properties are exempted from state taxation, although employees are subject to withholding assessments for their retirement plan and must pay the usual state and national income taxes. While no provision is made for auditing, annual audits are conducted by Price, Waterhouse and Company,[23] and member states on an individual basis are granted free access to commission records at all times.

For the biennia of 1964–66 and 1966–68 the commission's sole sources of revenue were the annual appropriations made to it by member states, amounting to $9,000 apiece, providing total revenues of $72,000 annually. Additional income is from interest on invested surplus revenues.

As noted, the compact's wording seems to anticipate a considerably larger operation for the commission under its power to acquire, hold and dispose of real and personal property, and to establish "one or more offices" for the conduct of its activities. The headquarters offices today, however, are in space allocated to the commission by the University of Michigan at Ann Arbor. Each member state maintains offices for its own commission representatives. Illinois has an office in Chicago to which it makes nominal annual appropriations for the expenses of the state's delegation when attending commission or legislative meetings.[24] Thus the commission can hardly be termed a property owner.

But the compact's financial and property clauses troubled Congressman John M. Vorys (R.), Ohio, when the commission sought consent in 1958. In reply to his questions, Marvin Fast, representing the commission, submitted the following explanatory memorandum to the House Committee on Foreign Affairs:

Mr. Vorys . . . inquired into the power of the Great Lakes Commission to sue and be sued and to acquire, hold, and convey real and personal property. Legal counsel assures me that these powers are necessary but only of minor significance, and are the same powers which are commonly granted to other governmental agencies such as cities, towns, and villages, and in some States to State agencies such as public service commissions. . . . We could not contract validly in the name of the Commission even for office supplies, office equipment, airplane transportation, or similar matters unless the person with whom we are dealing realized that the Commission could be sued in the event of a default. Neither could the Commission protect itself against damage, destruction, or theft of any of the little personal property which it now has unless the Commission had the power to sue. . . . As to real property, we now have none, since the University of Michigan is kindly furnishing us office space free. . . . The time could well come when it might be necessary to move the office to some other location where we would have to rent space. . . . It is conceivable that some day we might desire and be able to own our own office building. . . . we could not do so without the power described.[25]

While there is no reason for concern for the commission's present property-holding activity, Mr. Fast's optimistic reference to a time when the commission might wish to own its own office building is important, for the compact provisions contain no limitations on property-owning powers in spite of legal counsel's opinion that the stated provisions are "necessary but of minor significance." They underscore the observation that with very little amendment—chiefly to the general statement of purposes and to the financial powers granted the commission—the compact could easily be converted to greater things, with its agency owning and operating its own enterprises as did occur with the Missouri-Illinois Bi-State Development Agency.

This speculation is not merely academic; certain interests have made quite clear a hope, and possibly a purpose, to create an agency for the Great Lakes area of considerably greater scope and power. The following is of interest:

But some of the officials around the lakes, weary of the interminable battles, are convinced that an even grander solution has to be found. One of these is the governor of Illinois, Otto H. Kerner. Kerner envisions a managerial agency to regulate all the conflicting demands and uses of Great Lakes water. All the states bordering on the Great

Lakes, as well as the provinces of Ontario and Quebec, would be represented on the agency—and, ideally, so would the governments of the United States and Canada.

Kerner believes fulfillment of this dream is a long way off.[26]

This prescription attributed to Governor Kerner, but also discussed and considered by others, would seem to have been specifically written with the Great Lakes Commission in mind—certainly with it as a model. Other comments can be taken into consideration. A 1968 Republican aspirant for the Illinois gubernatorial nomination, Peoria industrialist John Henry Alterfer, campaigned on a "Let's Build Illinois!" basis, including this proposed plank in his platform:

Port facilities on Lake Michigan and along the Illinois River must be expanded under a unified authority to accelerate shipping of Illinois products to foreign shores via the St. Lawrence Seaway.[27]

While Mr. Alterfer's vision of a Great Lakes agency is vague and not defined, suggesting an Illinois rather than an interstate agency, it is possible to suppose that the Great Lakes Commission if properly implemented might provide just the mechanism he had in mind, particularly in the light of the various concerns and controversies recounted hereafter in which Illinois is extensively involved. The Great Lakes Commission's persistent efforts to obtain congressional consent for the compacting states' agreement, and its willingness to accept the half loaf it received indicate more than a passing interest in the additional authority and expansion possibilities to which consent at least opens the door.

The Commissioners' Qualifications

Appointees to the Great Lakes Commission appear to be chosen by their respective states with special consideration given to representation of executive agencies, state legislatures, labor, industry, technically oriented professional groupings, and navigation interests. Municipalities and other local governments do not fare so well. Agriculture, a leading lakes user in shipment of grain and other products, has not had direct representation. All present commissioners have had close and active identification with Great Lakes matters and some have ties or interlocking relationships with various private special interest groups in the water field.

The chairman of the Illinois delegation in 1968 was Albert J.

Meserow, a Chicago attorney and former assistant attorney general of the state. Mr. Meserow has in the past been intimately associated as chief counsel with a private organization, the Association for the Protection of Great Lakes Property, Inc. In 1953 when an Illinois proposal was made to Congress for diversion of more Lake Michigan water into the Chicago Sanitary and Ship Canal to serve certain Chicago purposes, Mr. Meserow appeared before the United States Senate and House Committees on Public Works not only in behalf of the bill under consideration, but to urge even greater diversions of water than the bill called for. His association, he said, was a recently organized not-for-profit corporation, "an organization composed of lake-front property owners from the States of Michigan, Wisconsin, Indiana, and Illinois." [28] Certain of his comments follow:

We are in favor of this diversion bill, or all of these bills, not for the many worthy reasons you have heard yesterday and today, such as clean streams, fish life, navigation, and other reasons . . . . , but there is a primary reason as to why these bills should be passed immediately. That is to protect the property that has been damaged along the Great Lakes by the high-levels and the storms that ensue.

I think that that should be the primary consideration of this committee in the passage of this bill. We are not so much concerned with the Illinois Waterway as we are with lowering the levels of Lake Michigan.

You have heard several statements made that taking out an additional 2,000 cubic feet per second would lower the levels about 1⅜ inches. . . . If it is true we feel, and the property-owners feel, that an inch and a half or an inch and three-eighths lower is better than an inch and three-eighths higher.

We want to say that we are in favor of not only 3,500 cubic feet per second, but 10,000 cubic feet per second.

Congress can by immediately authorizing an increase of 10,000 cubic feet per second get those levels down about 6 inches, or maybe more. Six inches would mean an awful lot to these property owners, who have been clamoring for some relief. [29] [*Italics added.*]

Sketching the plight and sufferings of the lake-front property owners, he observed that they had had no relief of any kind from any agency of any government, and they were suffering from millions of dollars in damages. He said,

I will give you one instance in the city of Evanston. A man had a house there. He was an executive. He had a $60,000 home on the lake. He had a big, thick concrete seawall there. Last November in the storms the water came up so high that he had to employ 40 men to place sandbags around his house, and Congresswoman Church, who was the Congresswoman in his district, helped him move. He had to move his entire 8- to 10-room house out of there and live in a hotel because his whole house was surrounded like an island by water. Since that time he moved back and spent something like $10,000 to build jetties and take protective measures to protect his home.[30]

Under the questioning of Committee Chairman George Dondero (R.), Michigan, the United States Army Corps of Engineers testified as follows:

COLONEL W. D. MILNE. In our studies of what might be the effect of this increased diversion, we came to this conclusion: That if 1,000 additional second-feet were authorized to be diverted the water levels on Lake Michigan and Lake Huron would be lowered by 0.12 foot, or roughly just under 2 inches, and 0.08 foot on Lake Erie and Lake Ontario, or about 1 inch. . . .

MR. DONDERO. Does that amount of water in any way affect navigation adversely?

COLONEL MILNE. In periods of high water like we have now on the Great Lakes, the lowering of the water level by that much, let us say 2 inches, would have no effect on navigation. In periods of low flow on the Great Lakes 2 inches could be of considerable importance to navigation. I think for every inch that they have to lower their draft on the lake carriers they carry 100 tons of iron ore less than they could with a full draft. In really low stages 2 inches would be something to consider. . . .

MR. DONDERO. Does the committee understand even a difference of 1 inch of water makes a difference of 100 tons of cargo?

COLONEL MILNE. The channels on the Great Lakes, Mr. Chairman, have 25-foot downbound depth. With the new ore carriers that have been developed since the war they practically use every inch of draft that they can. When they have to lower their draft because of adverse channel conditions even 1 inch, each ship carries 100 tons of iron ore less than capacity.[31]

Attorney Meserow also served as secretary to a five-member committee appointed by Governor Dwight H. Green in January 1947, to study Lake Michigan water diversion through the Illinois Waterway. After four years of work and eighteen meetings and public hearings, the committee made a final report which recommended increased diversion to the extent of 3,500 cubic feet per second.[32] This report and Meserow's 1953 efforts were opposed not only by interests of other Great Lakes states, but also by Illinois communities such as Peoria and Beardstown on the Illinois River below Chicago, which feel the impact of Chicago's water diversions and have suffered from previous use of this waterway for sewage disposal purposes.

Of particular interest is the seeming conflict of interest which an Illinois delegation chairmanship in the Great Lakes Commission could impose on one holding the kinds of interests with which Meserow is identified. One of the major concerns of the commission has been the gradually lowering water levels of the lakes, a concern shared by most of the lakes' water users, by conservationists, water pollution regulationists, and United States and Canadian governments. It is certain that Mr. Meserow's special view of lake water usage is not representative of the people of Illinois generally.

Yet this seemingly irreconcilable problem in Great Lakes Commission appointments, of interests which point in opposing directions, is also reflected in various state project interests, as described below in discussion of the proposed Lake Erie–Ohio River Canal, the proposed Cross–Wabash Valley Waterway, the Burns Harbor development, the Indiana Dunes controversy, and the like. It would appear that Illinois is at times in conflict with itself in its various interstate relationships. Thus certain of the present effects of the Wabash Valley Interstate Commission (see chapter 5), of which Illinois is a member with Indiana, are not wholly compatible with the general interests of the Great Lakes Commission, which Illinois also supports.

To students of interstate compacts as devices to resolve federal problems of an interstate nature, the question is simply this: When a state belongs to two or more interstate compacts whose purposes are not altogether harmonious, who resolves the conflicts? The interstate compact agencies? If so, how? The governor? How? The legislature? The state's specialized bureaus and departments? The United States government? The question undoubtedly has a variety of answers, but examination of Illinois interstate compacts and compact relationships reveals little that is enlightening.

Congressional Consent and the International Question

A prime consideration of any proposed interstate compact which involves United States foreign relations and the interests of foreign states is: Can such a compact be enacted and, more importantly, be enforced? If so, under what circumstances? Some precedent exists to answer the question, but this—as with so many other aspects of interstate compacts—is neither settled nor well defined. Three such compacts have been enacted which involve the Canadian provinces and which obtained the consent of Congress. Only one concerns a natural resource of broad significance, the 1949 Northeast Interstate Forest Fire Protection Compact.[33] The others involving Canada are one for the building of a bridge, and another for construction of an international access highway: the Buffalo–Port Erie Public Bridge Authority,[34] and the Minnesota-Manitoba Highway Agreement.[35] Still another proposal concerning a bridge passed the United States Senate in 1966: an agreement between Maine and New Brunswick. As adopted by the several member states and submitted to Congress, the Northeast Interstate Forest Fire Protection Compact provides for membership by contiguous Canadian provinces. Congress, however, imposed the limitation that before such provinces could become parties to the agreement, the further review and consent of Congress had to be sought. This did occur in 1952, with Congress granting admission to contiguous provinces.[36] It is therefore clear that under rather limited circumstances an international agreement of the interstate compact type can be enacted and can function successfully. It is also probable that compacts on broader economic and social substantive matters involving international relations will not obtain support from the United States Department of State, unless (and this can by no means as yet be construed as applying to all cases) the international matters and actions which result shall be required to clear through the Department of State, which reserves the right to reject them.[37]

International Provisions of the Compact Prior to Consent

As adopted by the eight ratifying member states, the Great Lakes Basin Compact provides that

The Province of Ontario and the Province of Quebec, or either of them, may become states party to this compact by taking such action as their laws and the laws of the Government of Canada may prescribe for adherence thereto.[38]

As noted previously, the intent was to empower the Great Lakes Commission thereafter to "recommend agreements" and "mutual arrangements," to "cooperate," and "to assist in the negotiation and formulation of any treaty" (on the request of Canada or the United States government) with the two countries, party states, and private special interests and their agencies.*

The entire consent question was inextricably entangled with the international questions raised by the compact. Consent was most earnestly sought by the compact's proponents beginning in 1955; until 1968 it was just as regularly withheld on each occasion when the compact was brought to the Congress and seriously taken up for consideration. Since many other matters of an extraordinarily complex nature entered the consent picture, it must be emphasized that the international question was only one of the more important aspects of this compact which influenced Congress in its "no action" policy, but it was the most important.

It is clear that the original purposes of the compact's authors were to create an international agency to handle broad policy questions in which they wished to have a voice and which they specifically enumerated. This they undertook in the face of the preexisting boundary waters treaty of 1909 (see Appendix C for the text of the treaty) which concerned navigation on the waters of the Great Lakes; sanitary, irrigation, and other diversions; hydroelectric power production; and created the International Joint Commission which with its auxiliary international agencies has been and still is the official Great Lakes regulatory agency. This treaty, the Joint Commission, certain other international bodies, and certain long standing United States Supreme Court decisions have served to govern Great Lakes matters satisfactorily for nearly half a century. But contemporary water resources problems are infinitely more complex and varied than they were at the time the treaty was adopted in 1909, and the treaty as enacted certainly does not cover all water matters of great concern today. Further, the states contiguous to the Great Lakes were not given a place or a voice in the 1909 treaty's International Joint Commission. That body is solely an

---

* Great Lakes Basin Compact, Art. VI, Secs. J–M. It should be noted in connection with this power that Vernon W. Thompson, Governor of Wisconsin, in a letter to Senator Joseph O'Mahoney dated Aug. 9, 1957 disclaimed any empire-building role of the compact's authors: "I know from my participation in preparation of the original compact . . . that there never was any intention in any way to impinge upon the activities and prerogatives of any Federal agency such as the International Joint Commission or the Department of State." U.S., Congress, Senate, Committee on the Judiciary, *Great Lakes Basin Compact, Hearings*, 85th Cong., 2d Sess., 1958, p. 9.

agency of the United States and Dominion governments. One matter in which such interstate consultations might have been constructive—perhaps as important as any in stimulating the interests which combined to create the compact—was the approval of the New York–Canadian arrangements for the St. Lawrence Seaway and its control, a proposition which the International Joint Commission did not block and which appeared to others of the Great Lakes states as an unusually favored position to grant New York in Seaway and Great Lakes matters. Still another example of a state which would like to be heard with a voice of some influence is Illinois which, justifiably or not, has never been happy with the strictures placed upon it in water diversion matters, particularly since she regards Lake Michigan as a United States lake and heretofore has chosen to ignore the vital international effects of her existing and proposed water diversions on the remainder of the Great Lakes. In turn, other states and the Canadian governments view Illinois's ambitions with something less than enthusiasm. In all such questions the International Joint Commission has not altogether met the desires or needs of the states that promoted the Great Lakes Basin Compact.

The International Joint Commission does not regard itself as a creative or initiating regulatory agency. In testimony before the House Committee on Public Works on the proposed diversion of Lake Michigan water at Chicago, A. O. Stanley, chairman of the International Joint Commission, told House members that the commission had no objection "in the world" to the proposed diversion. "In fact," he said, *"in its present status,* it is not for the Commission to object or approve. We are an international tribunal and these matters are referred to us by the two Governments." [39] [*Italics added.*] The IJC does not, then, provide a mechanism for economic or other development of the lakes and their resources. Such matters when they come up at all must begin among private interests or in the states' governments.

The Great Lakes Compact was ratified by its eight member states in anticipation that it would become a state- and province-based and oriented international agency through the future membership of Quebec and Ontario. The compact failed to satisfy the Eighty-fourth Congress and the consent effort failed because of the international nature of the proposed agency. Thereupon the Great Lakes Commission drafted a new measure satisfactory to its member states which was designed to eliminate participation by the Canadian provinces. It is this measure and an amended version of it which subsequently have been before the Congress for consent.

The Measure Congress Approved

The proposal to which Congress finally gave consent provides two additional sections to the Compact's article IX (the "severability clause"), while retaining the original text with its clauses permitting provincial membership and certain stipulated international powers for the Great Lakes Commission. These "international" clauses, while retained, are rendered invalid by the new provisions—a legal problem which aroused some questions as to whether Congress could enact such a law or why it should, considering the ambiguity involved in the retained clauses, and also having the effect of repealing parts of a law duly enacted and approved by eight states. (The latter question appears to be somewhat academic, for these states were willing for the changes to be made, and seemingly would reenact the compact in some altered form if the need arises.) Furthermore, section 3 of the final draft, on the broader international question, specifically reserves the jurisdiction, powers, and prerogatives of the United States government in the Great Lakes Basin, which would in any event tend to restrain commission independence in acts of an international nature without United States consent.[40]

In addition to excluding the Canadian provinces, section 2 of the enacted version states, "In carrying out its functions under this Act the Commission shall be solely a consultative and recommendatory agency which will cooperate with the agencies of the United States." Section 3 adds, "nor shall anything contained herein be construed to establish an international agency or to limit or affect in any way the exercise of the treatymaking power or any other power or right of the United States." (See Appendix B for the text of the Act.)

The 1966–68 efforts of the Great Lakes Commission to obtain the consent Congress had persistently withheld arose primarily from the commission's wish to participate in the Great Lakes Basin Commission, the regional agency created under the Water Resources Planning Act of 1965, and the agency designated to receive federal funding under the act. No wholly convincing defense was ever made by the compact commission's supporters to justify its determination to continue in existence, shorn of its hoped-for international powers, and to an undefined degree displaced in its planning ambitions, but the Department of the Interior's April 30, 1968, memorandum to Senator Eastland of the Committee on the Judiciary, acquiescing in the revised version of the compact being offered for consent, clarifies that department's understanding of the matter:

The President, by Executive Order 11345 of April 20, 1967, established the Great Lakes Basin Commission pursuant to title II of the Water Resources Planning Act. This joint Federal-State Commission is composed of representatives of nine Federal agencies designated by the President as having an interest in the work of the Commission and the eight Great Lakes States. The Executive order provides, as required by section 202(d) of the Planning Act, that there may be added to the Commission a representative "from each interstate agency created by an interstate compact to which the consent of the Congress has been given and whose jurisdiction extends to the waters of the area." The enactment of S. 660 in accordance with the Committee print would qualify the Great Lakes Commission to appoint a member of the title II commission under this provision.

As provided by title II of the Water Resources Planning Act, *the Great Lakes Basin Commission established by Executive Order 11345 will serve as the principal agency for the coordination of Federal, State, and other plans within the Great Lakes area, will develop a comprehensive, coordinated, joint plan for the development of the water and related land resources of the area,* and will submit recommendations for implementing such plan. *The Great Lakes Commission established by the compact can be expected to serve as a useful mechanism for stimulating coordinated State thinking and participation* in the work of the title II commission. The committee print states in section 2, page 16, that the compact commission "shall be solely a consultative and recommendatory agency which will cooperate with the agencies of the United States." *We interpret this to mean that the work of the compact commission will not conflict with or duplicate the planning and coordinating responsibilities of the title II commission and that the granting of congressional consent to the compact at this time is not intended to limit the latter's freedom to consider various arrangements for implementing the comprehensive plan.*[41] [*Italics added.*]

In brief, the Great Lakes Commission will provide the states of the Basin a vehicle for state participation in the Great Lakes Basin Commission although they will occupy no such preeminent role in Basin planning activities as they originally sought through their compact. The confusion in agency titles disturbed the Department of the Army, which suggested that the Great Lakes Commission be called the "Great Lakes States Commission" to distinguish it from the Great Lakes Basin Commission created under the Water Resources Planning Act.[42]

In the commission's efforts to obtain consent a further question arose which troubled congressmen. This was whether any consent at all was necessary to a "recommendatory and advisory" agreement of this type, voluntarily entered by several cooperating states. An answer was sought from the Department of Justice, which replied with a long memorandum prepared by Nicholas Katzenbach in 1962, while deputy attorney general:

The Great Lakes Basin Compact . . . is a highly formal agreement, open to membership by eight states and two provinces of Canada. Its purposes include "to promote the orderly, integrated, and comprehensive development, use and conservation of the water resources of the Great Lakes Basin." The Great Lakes are a major navigable waterway; actions taken with respect to them are also matters of international concern, and various aspects of the Great Lakes have been the subject of international agreements with Canada. See e.g., the Treaty Relating to Boundary Waters, etc. of January 11, 1909, TS No. 548 and the Convention on Great Lakes Fisheries of September 10, 1954, TIAS 3326. *While the powers of the Commission appear to be primarily to collect and report on data and to make recommendations which the members agree merely to "consider," the formulation of such comprehensive recommendations is itself an important function which may significantly influence the legislative function of the member states and thus shape the future development of the Great Lakes Basin.* This appears to be recognized in the Compact itself by the formality of the provisions with respect to voting. *Moreover, serious question with respect to the proper conduct of international relations may be presented by the proposed establishment of an agency representing certain states and Canadian provinces to formulate recommendations on matters which may be regarded as a more appropriate subject for diplomatic negotiations conducted by the national governments of the two nations involved.*

Such an agreement, which could result in actions of great importance relating to a major navigable waterway over which Congress has broad legislative powers, and which may affect both the substance of and the proper channels for conducting our international relations with Canada, potentially affects "substantive federal interests." Hence, in my opinion, it requires Congressional consent under the compact clause . . . . I express no opinion with respect to the lawfulness of any particular action that may have been taken to date under the Compact.[43] [*Italics added.*]

Katzenbach's letter was a response to a question directed to him by Senator Clinton Anderson of New Mexico. Dated May 1962, it came after previous efforts of the Great Lakes Commission had failed to obtain consent and after it had been exposed to numerous questions on the actual need for formal consent. If the effect of the 1966–67 proposed amendments to the compact would be to eliminate the Canadian provinces from membership, and the compact itself provided only for a purely advisory and recommendatory agency, why was consent needed? An earlier exchange in 1958 points up the reasons for the commission's subsequent reliance upon the attorney general's opinion that consent, at least in this particular compact, was needed:

MR. SMITH [unidentified in text of hearings]: Is there any question at all about the right of the States to make this compact?

MR. RABAUT [Louis C., of Michigan]: No; I think the States ratified it by their legislatures, created it by their legislatures. . . .

MR. SMITH: Then my question is, why is it necessary to come to the Federal Government for this legislation?

MR. RABAUT: It deals with international waters and with programs in which the Federal Government has an interest.

MR. SMITH: This is dealing with a compact between the States?

MR. RABAUT: This is the compact between the States bordering upon the international waters, and the States can have no part of a contact with a foreign government, the government of Canada.

MR. SMITH: Don't we have treaties already, as a matter of fact, in these very problems?

MR. RABAUT: Yes; we do have treaties but these do not preclude the States from entering into a compact with each other such as this.

MR. SMITH: I wager you will find treaties which relate to some of these very activities that are mentioned in the compact.

MR. RABAUT: I used to deal with some of them when I was chairman of the State Department Appropriations Subcommittee.[44]

Such exchanges stud the pages of the hearings on the Great Lakes Basin Compact on all occasions and in both Houses of Congress. Katzenbach's opinion, which lent support to the commission's own very real desire for consent, thereafter was used by the commission to justify its efforts to obtain official United States sanction. In 1966, while questioning Edgar D. Whitcomb, Great Lakes Commission chairman, Congressman Thomas E. Morgan queried:

CHAIRMAN MORGAN: . . . Mr. Whitcomb, the Great Lakes compact apparently has been in business since 1955. Why is this legislation necessary now?

[Whitcomb yielded to Indiana state senator John W. Van Ness, a Commissioner of the Great Lakes Commission.]

MR. VAN NESS: First, I would like to say that this Commission has no desire to, or any right to infringe upon the activities or the prerogatives of any department of the Federal Government, and since its inception has cooperated with these various departments and I refer specifically to the State Department, because that question has been raised.

. . . *True, we have had relationships with Canada solely on an informal basis and after completely informing our State Department of what we were proposing to do.*

There is already a provision in Congressman Zablocki's bill, as well as the other bills which have been discussed here, which precludes the approval of Congress to the two Provinces of Canada entering into this compact. This is a matter that is strictly foreign affairs and over which we have no legal right to take action. *This does not mean that we have not been helpful and have not accomplished certain things through our activities with Canada, because we have. We have been able to stir up interest on both sides of the border through our informal contacts on the other side of the border and I think there is no doubt but what some of the interest stirred up by the Great Lakes Commission resulted in the two references which the Congress has made to the International Joint Commission,* one on the lake levels, and the other on pollution.

.   .   .   .

Now, why are we asking consent? True, in the past this matter has been up. It has never been pushed very hard until this time. *The main reason for this is the 1965 Water Resources Planning Act which says in effect that an interstate compact body may have membership on this if it is approved by Congress.* This is good and sufficient reason for this matter to be presented to the Congress.[45] [*Italics added.*]

The Illinois attitude toward consent was not clear despite Governor Kerner's support of the compact, earlier support by Governor William G. Stratton, and cosponsorship of the consent measure by Senators Douglas and Dirksen in the Senate. Congressman Barratt O'Hara of Illinois implied that there was considerable lack of unanimity within Illinois as to the merits of the agency. Certain of his 1966 comments follow:

MR. O'HARA: Why is this bill brought up at this time?

.   .   .   .

Is there any immediate need of its passage now?

MR. LATTA [Delbert L., Ohio]: My bill was introduced on January 25, 1966. I realize that this is a very busy committee and I welcome the opportunity even at this late date in the session to have it heard. . . .

MR. O'HARA: You know, do you not, that a bill of this nature has been before this committee for many years.

MR. LATTA: Yes; and I can remember when I was in the State Senate in Ohio back in 1952 they were toying with this idea then.

MR. O'HARA: And no one sought to push it over or dared to try during the lifetime of Tom O'Brien [6th Dist., Illinois]. You know that, don't you?

MR. LATTA: No; I do not.

MR. O'HARA: You would not expect this to have the approval of Illinois, would you?

MR. LATTA: It already has. Illinois is a party State to this compact already.

MR. O'HARA: I would have to be informed of that directly.[46]

Later, in an exchange with Great Lakes Commissioner John W. Van Ness, O'Hara continued:

MR. O'HARA: What we are doing in these compacts is more and more relegating the authority of the States to a second place to regional governments. Of course, there is a reason for it. Rivers that serve a number of States cause the States to get together in compacts, but despite the need in some cases, the wholesome trend toward compacts is whittling down the authority of State government. It may not happen in my lifetime, but we may someday have regional governments supplanting State governments, so I take these compacts very, very seriously.

.   .   .   .

MR. VAN NESS: The State of Illinois has been operating under this for several years, Congressman, and your own Governor has cooperated with the Great Lakes Commission to a great degree, to the extent of having his personal representative attend our meetings and he himself has addressed at least one or two of them and at one time he, along with Governor Welsh, of Indiana, attended two hearings held in Canada, one in Ontario, the other in Montreal, the idea being to survey some of these problems and to try to arrive at some solutions that would be beneficial to the Provinces as well as to the States.

MR. O'HARA: I know that you are making a truthful statement. I talked with the Governor of Illinois about a year ago on this, maybe longer than a year ago. I know that his sentiment was one of friendship and appreciation for what the Commission is doing. It may have been 2 years ago. I told him at that time that I should continue to confer with Tom O'Brien. You know, our people in Chicago had a very serious problem and twice the House of Representatives passed our Lake Michigan water diversion bill over to the Senate side. At that time Wisconsin didn't vote with us and Michigan didn't. I have always been a little bit leary about going to bed with the same States in the Great Lakes region that put a tiger on our back when we needed help in Lake Michigan water diversion.

Tom O'Brien is dead, but I have not forgotten. I told the Governor that I would lend my weight to delaying this until there was a more complete study of it.[47]

Still struggling with his own opposition to the compact while seeking to support Governor Kerner, O'Hara finally capitulated in the consent action of 1968, but reluctantly.

In November of this year, all the Great Lakes States will hold elections that will make changes in the gubernatorial and legislative offices. I would think it the part of wisdom to await the results of these elections instead of rushing to enactment a measure that has lain dormant for so many years and which . . . might not be acceptable to one or more of the new State administrations. . . .

Frankly, I have been opposed to the compact, because when Lake Michigan diversion was so vital to the health and welfare of Chicago and Illinois, the other Great Lakes States turned thumbs down. . . . While the matter of Lake Michigan water diversion may or may not be on its way to satisfactory adjustment, other questions of policy and interest will arise and I would feel easier if I knew to a certainty that always Illinois would not be outvoted as it was in the diversion matter; Illinois on one side, all the other Great Lakes States on the other.[48]

He placed in the *Record* a letter from Governor Kerner dated September 30, 1966, in which Kerner stated, "I have been most concerned and an active supporter of the work of the Great Lakes Commission. . . . I am in support of H.R. 937 . . . which grant[s] Congressional ratification. . . . Please bear in mind that these bills will not in any way affect Illinois's position with regard to the diversion problem." After receiving this letter, O'Hara said, he promised the governor his support, but the consent measure died in 1966 and had not been resurrected until now at the last moment in 1968. Now, with reservations, but keeping his pledge, he was "happy to keep my word to Governor Kerner in 1966 by voting in 1968 for the Great Lakes Basin compact." [49]

While this image of Illinois's compact affiliation is blurred by O'Hara's personal opposition to it, it still does not give a clear view of Governor Kerner's apparently strong support of it. In this compacting action the entire record suggests that Illinois became a member of the compact for (a) the possibility of defending in a forum of all the Great Lakes states her own particularistic concerns with the waters of Lake Michigan and influencing support for them; (b) the possibility of keeping a closer eye on the strivings and proposals of the other Great Lakes states on navigation, fishing, hydroelectric and diversion problems, and the amount of commerce passing into and through the St. Lawrence Seaway to Illinois's and other states' harbors; and (c) the strategic advantage of placing herself in a potentially stronger position in union with other Great Lakes states to oppose or to support federal and Dominion measures which might come up. In a compact of Great Lakes states, Illinois could hardly remain outside, no matter what her attitudes toward support and sanction might be. That she was one of the five original states to ratify indicates a strong interest of support. But it became even more imperative with the passage in 1965 of the Water Resources Planning Act with its promise of federal money for developmental projects, not available prior to recognition. A much clearer motive for support is thus provided.

Congressman O'Hara's views, while revealing a lack of Illinois unanimity, must be regarded in the light of all such considerations as well as of those of an aging statesman who finds in today's trends toward regionalism a threat to the states' rights concepts of the past. (It should be noted, however, that this study does not wholly disagree with some of Congressman O'Hara's more philosophical observations on interstate compacts, quoted in this study's final chapter.) A footnote to the whole is that O'Hara at age eighty-six was defeated in his bid for renomination to the House from his Chicago district in the June 1968 primary. He had sought renomination in the face of the Chicago–Cook County Democratic organization's opposition, but whether that opposition was in any way prompted or influenced by O'Hara's stand on the compact is impossible to conclude.

One final consideration of the international problem as it applied to congressional consent was the attitude toward the compact of the United States Department of State. Although the commission's amended draft of 1966 specifically eliminated the Canadian provinces from membership under the compact, the commission did not deny that it intended to continue its dealings with the provinces on an informal basis. The Department of State took particular note of other clauses in the 1966 version's article IX, section 2 which expressly provided for cooperation between the Great Lakes Commission and the government of Canada or its subdivisions. Under this section, such cooperation would have required the commission to obtain prior approval of the State Department on modes of cooperation and the kinds of endeavor intended to be pursued. Seeking clarification, Congressman James G. Fulton (R.), Pennsylvania, asked, "What technically does the word 'cooperation' mean? What actions can be taken under the word 'cooperation,' or is it simply a friendly touching of fingertips across the Great Lakes by various States in the Commission and the two Provinces of Canada?" [50] The Department of State in Douglas MacArthur II's reply made clear that it would probably oppose any provisions allowing the Canadian provinces to become members of the compact, and that it regarded the entire proposal with reservations for the following reasons:

Matters relating to the international waters of the Great Lakes are regarded in Canada as highly sensitive public issues. In the first place, they raise controversial constitutional questions regarding the authority of the national government vis-à-vis that of the provinces; secondly, widespread Canadian fears are being expressed concerning possible United States demands on Canadian water sources. As a consequence, these matters have a high degree of political sensitivity and are a fundamental part of our relations with the Government of Canada. Moreover, Canada and the United States have established intergovernmental mechanisms which have important functions in this area and which include extensive local as well as national participation. I have in mind the International Joint Commission and the Great Lakes Fisheries Commission, established by treaties in 1909 and 1954, respectively. For Canadian provinces to be permitted to become parties to the Great Lakes Basin Compact would turn the compact into an international body empowered to deal with these sensitive matters. We would be reluctant to see the establishment of additional state-provincial mechanisms which might either work at cross-purposes with the existing arrangements or needlessly duplicate them.

We would have further concern that studies, proposals and recommendations adopted by the states and provinces—acting under the compact—could very likely be misinterpreted in Canada as having the approbation of the United States Government. Such misunderstanding in these sensitive matters could cause serious difficulty with the conduct of our foreign relations.

While the Department would for these reasons oppose any provision permitting the Provinces of Quebec and Ontario to join formally the interstate compact as states party, the Department would not wish to hinder proper cooperation between the provinces and Great Lakes Commission on matters of common concern. Indeed, the proposed consent legislation provides for such cooperation with the Government of Canada or its political subdivisions with any international agency having the jurisdiction in the basin. . . . We believe it necessary that the authority of the Federal Government in this important area be thus safeguarded, but it is entirely possible that within this framework of policy control there could also be direct informal contact between the lesser authorities on specific common problems.

Although herein seemingly approving the proposed "informal cooperation" anticipated under the revised compact, the department added:

It is difficult for the Department to predict with any precision the nature and extent of the cooperation by the Great Lakes Commission. . . . This cooperation could, for example, take the following forms: assistance in the collection and correlation of data relating to the water resources of the basin; harmonization of conservation measures . . . [and the like]. *Of course, under the proposed legislation any such cooperation could be extended only through or with the approval of the Department of State* in the light of its effect on our relations with Canada. *Only as specific proposals for cooperation arise, . . . could the Department be in a position fully to consider their nature and extent as well as the proper method of execution.*[51] [*Italics added.*]

The department had not at this time sought the Canadian government's views of the compact and did not do so. At least a hint of the Canadian position on the international water question, however, is suggested in an exchange of aide-mémoires between the United States and Canada in 1959 on the proposed measure then before Congress to divert Lake Michigan waters at Chicago. Canada's February 20 reply made clear that it continued to oppose as it had in the past proposals envisaging increased diversion of water from Lake Michigan at Chicago. It stated:

While recognizing that the use of Lake Michigan water is a matter within the jurisdiction of the United States of America, it is the considered opinion of the Canadian Government that any authorization for an additional diversion would be incompatible with the arrangements for the St. Lawrence Seaway and power development, and with the Niagara Treaty of 1950, and would be prejudicial to navigation and power development which these mutual arrangements were designed to improve and facilitate.

The point has been made repeatedly by Canada, that every withdrawal of water from the basin means less depth available for shipping in harbors and in channels.[52]

In the light of this negative Canadian view, the Department of State made clear that on this matter at least it would be inclined to view the proposed diversion as having an adverse effect on the friendly relations of the United States and Canada and would, therefore, oppose the legislation.

It was clear that in all such matters which might come before the Great Lakes Commission it would encounter similar State Department reluctance to challenge the balance, the cooperation, and the means of exchange which exist between the two countries. With Ontario and Quebec as members of the commission, the United States and Canadian governments might find themselves inadvertently delegating away their foreign relations powers to their states and provinces. It was because of this overriding issue that the Compact Commission agreed to the final consent measure stripping it of even its power to "cooperate" with Canada on an informal basis.

Illinois and the Water Diversion Problem

Of the many influences which brought the compact into being, a few specific controversies are illustrative and of major importance. These are the water diversion question, with special emphasis on Illinois's unique involvement therein; the navigation problem in all of its aspects (the kinds and amounts of lake and ocean tonnage, the needs of carriers, the adequacy of ports and harbors, and the effects of these upon lake water levels); the pollution problem with its harmful attributes for humans, the fishing industry, and the lakes' wildlife situation; Canadian–United States relations; hydroelectric power production; and the uses and control of the St. Lawrence Seaway. This study cannot deal in depth with all of these matters in all of their ramifications, but at least three of them closely involve Illinois and attention should be given to these. Of first importance is the water diversion question.

Water diversions have been made at various points around the Great Lakes for many years. The purposes are varied: to augment hydroelectric power production, to operate a canal, for sanitary purposes, to irrigate dry land, to provide municipalities and industrial concerns with a water supply, and the like. Few diversions have much material effect on the water levels of a given lake, let alone upset the balance of all the other lake levels. Yet all of them together can have most harmful effects, particularly to shipping channels, which must be of a certain minimum depth for the freighters which have been built and are loaded to conform with the lakes' water carrying capacities. Further, a diversion at one spot without a compensatory diversion somewhere else on a proper lake, could upset the balance on a particular lake most adversely and this would ultimately have effects on all the others. Most diversions take water from one lake for special uses and then return it either to the same lake or to another, or to one of the Great Lakes' tributary waters. Some water is never returned: that which is consumed by human beings and animal life, that which is used for irrigation and which escapes either through evaporation or into subsurface reservoirs, and that which is diverted from one basin to an entirely different watershed. Students of hydrology have demonstrated that waters which are "lost" through evaporation and underground channels ultimately may be returned to use, through pumping in the latter case, and through evaporation via the natural cycle of the atmosphere and precipitation, although it may not return to its original source. It is the diversions of large quantities of water from one basin to another which are potentially most disruptive of the lakes' natural form and behavior. Without carefully designed engineering works and long-range plans involving measurement and planning for all of them, the lakes could ultimately be destroyed. No one wants this to happen. But many persons want to use more water for one thing and another and, as with other economic goods, the supply of the good often appears to be inexhaustible from the worm's eye view, even though the actual resource is neither inexhaustible nor immune to side effects if its delicate balance is upset.

The natural flow of the Great Lakes is as follows: from Lake Superior, water is discharged via the St. Mary's River into Lake Huron; Lake Michigan water also moves into Huron, slowly and in small quantities. The levels of both lakes are virtually the same and hydrologists tend to view the two lakes as one for hydrological purposes. Lake Huron discharges through the St. Clair River, Lake St. Clair, and the Detroit River into Lake Erie. Erie, in turn, discharges through the Niagara River into Lake Ontario, which discharges into the St. Lawrence River and, thence, to the Atlantic.

Major diversions are made at Sault Ste. Marie, at the metropolitan

Chicago area, at the Welland Canal and Niagara Falls, on Lake Ontario at the St. Lawrence Seaway, and on the St. Lawrence River at the International Rapids section. Most such diversions are under the close supervision of the International Joint Commission and the local international joint boards of control. The diversion at "The Soo" is totally under the International Joint Commission's control; that from Ontario into the St. Lawrence Seaway is regulated by the IJC and the International St. Lawrence River Board of Control.

The greatest diversion of all is that at Chicago from Lake Michigan into the Des Plaines River valley at the Illinois and Michigan Canal, the Chicago Sanitary and Ship Canal, and thence into the Des Plaines River, the Illinois River, and ultimately into the Mississippi. So controversial is it and has it been, that it has come to be referred to popularly and in places other than Illinois as the "Great Chicago Water Steal." Interstate and intergovernmental controversies began around the latter years of the last century. In the 1920s the Supreme Court settled some important litigation involving the federal government and the Sanitary District of Chicago by permanently fixing the amount of water which Chicago could divert and in its decree referred to United States obligations under the Boundary Waters Treaty of 1909 in justification of the decree. Therefore in the fullest sense that which is now being taken is not "stolen," except in the eyes of those who fear the great, sprawling Chicago area complex, seeing it as a potential menace whose every act in regard to the lakes must be closely watched. But another objector is Canada, which insists that although Lake Michigan legally belongs to the United States, it naturally belongs to the Great Lakes and she has never recognized the legitimacy of the Chicago diversion, regarding it as certainly not having been sanctioned by the Treaty of 1909.

That which is referred to in recent years as a "steal" is not the original diversion, controversial as it was, but various proposals which Chicago has made from time to time to take more water from Lake Michigan than the present law allows her to have. Since Lake Michigan is not an "international body" under the law, Chicago's efforts here have been wholly directed toward obtaining concessions from the United States, so it is primarily the other states of the Great Lakes area which have objected. The Canadian provinces, having never been indifferent to the matter, may be regarded today as altogether as interested and alert to proposed changes in the status quo as are the governments of the United States.

The Chicago Diversion

The Illinois Waterway is a series of rivers and canals extending from the Chicago River to the Mississippi. Beginning in 1836 the State of Illinois built the Illinois and Michigan Canal from the Chicago River's South Branch to La Salle, Illinois, and the Illinois River. It was completed in 1848. The Chicago Sanitary and Ship Canal was completed by the Sanitary District of Chicago in 1910, at which time part of the Illinois and Michigan Canal—that which lay between the Chicago River and the Des Plaines River at Joliet, Illinois—was abandoned, and in that portion diversion of Lake Michigan water into the summit level of the canal ceased. The new Chicago Sanitary and Ship Canal followed a course which lay between the Des Plaines River and the old Illinois and Michigan Canal. Lake Michigan waters which were diverted into the new Canal were (and are) controlled at Lockport, Illinois, where navigation locks were opened in July 1910. Additional locks were constructed at the mouth of the Chicago River at Chicago in 1938 and at Blue Island, Illinois, near the entrance of the Calumet-Sag Channel in 1922. Water diversions from Lake Michigan occur at three places: at Wilmette, Illinois, a suburb north of Chicago; at Chicago; and at South Chicago.

Originally the diversions into the Illinois and Michigan Canal were designed to maintain the canal's navigable depth, but additional diversions were soon made to help keep the polluted Chicago River clean. When the Chicago Sanitary District began work on the Sanitary and Ship Canal in 1890 it was with the intention of reversing the Chicago River's flow so that the city's polluted waters would be carried to the Mississippi River. Accordingly, the existing Sanitary and Ship Canal diversions dilute the Sanitary District's sewage and transport it into the Des Plaines and Illinois Rivers, and thence to the Mississippi. This was done to avoid discharging Chicago's sewage into Lake Michigan and thus polluting and endangering the city's water supply.

Since 1938, the Chicago diversions have averaged about 1,500 cubic feet per second which, in turn, has had the effect of lowering the levels of both Lake Michigan and Lake Huron about 0.11 feet. Pumpage at Chicago for domestic water uses during the same period has averaged about 1,600 cubic feet per second. The total of 3,100 cubic feet per second has tended to lower Lakes Michigan and Huron about 0.23 feet. Offsetting the effects of this lowering of the lake levels have been diversions at the Long Lake and Ogoki projects in Canada of waters back into Lake Superior, which ultimately raise Michigan and Huron by approximately 0.37 feet. These several diversions cause a net rise of 0.14 feet.[53]

It is to be noted that all of these diversions have the effect of raising the level of Lake Erie. In particular the Chicago diversion of 3,100 cubic feet per second causes Lake Erie's water level to lower about 0.14 feet, but the Canadian diversions raise it about 0.23 feet, making a net increase of 0.09 feet. But yet another major diversion from Lake Erie is that of the Welland Canal, which lowers the lake's level by about 0.32 feet, so that the toal effect on Lake Erie of all diversions is a lowered water level of about 0.23 feet.

A cubic foot of water is just short of 8 gallons. Thus, a diversion of 3,500 cubic feet per second amounts to about 2 and 2/5 billion gallons per day—a staggering amount to water-short cities of the Midwest and West, but not enough for a city like Chicago, according to Chicago's views.

By 1928 the total Chicago area diversions totaled more than 10,000 cubic feet per second, wholly unregulated and in disregard of the long-standing and increasing objections of neighboring states and the Canadian Dominion. In 1922, 1925, and 1926, Wisconsin, Michigan, and New York brought suits to enjoin Chicago and the State of Illinois from their unauthorized diversions of Lake Michigan water, and in 1926 the suits were consolidated and referred to Charles Evans Hughes as Special Master.[54] The Special Master and the United States Supreme Court rejected the complaining states' argument that Chicago should be required to return to Lake Michigan in the form of treated effluent the waters it diverted for sanitary purposes, but accepted the complainants' views that the city and the State of Illinois should cease and desist their unauthorized withdrawals of water. A gradual diminution of the amount diverted, to allow the Chicago Sanitary District opportunity to improve its sewage treatment and water purification facilities, was decreed according to the following formula: After July 1, 1930, no waters in excess of an annual average of 6,500 cubic feet per second, in addition to domestic pumpage, were to be diverted into the Illinois Waterway; after December 31, 1935, unless good cause could be shown to the contrary, none in excess of an annual average of 5,000 cubic feet per second, in addition to domestic pumpage; and after December 31, 1938, the defendants were limited to no more than 1,500 cubic feet per second in addition to domestic pumpage.[55]

Forced by the decree to improve Chicago area sanitation facilities, between 1930 and 1939 the Sanitary District built and put into operation the major part of its sewage treatment plants which existed until the massive improvements of the last decade, and by 1950 had achieved an operation which provided complete treatment for all sewage of the Sanitary District's area. Throughout most of this period, the district adhered to the Court's water diversion formula. In 1950 the Supreme Court authorized an additional diversion for a ten-day period in the interest of pollution abatement; again in 1942 and 1944 augmented diversions were permitted during the wartime emergency. Then came several dry years, and in 1956 the Mississippi River's waters reached so low a level normal navigation could not take place. On December 17, 1956, the Supreme Court authorized another major but temporary diversion of up to 8,500 cubic feet per second until January 31, 1957, to relieve this problem.[56] Under this order the actual diversion made by the Chicago Sanitary District averaged 7,500 cubic feet per second, with domestic pumpage averaging 1,660 cubic feet per second.

Although the city complied with the Supreme Court's 1930 ruling, it did so reluctantly. Between 1930 and 1953, numerous bills were introduced in Congress seeking to change the formula to give the city more of Lake Michigan, but none were passed. Applications were filed with Presidents Franklin Roosevelt and Harry Truman, and with United States boards and commissions, including the War Production Board and the Federal Power Commission. All were denied. As previously mentioned, by 1947 the interests seeking more water from Lake Michigan prevailed upon Governor Dwight Green to name an Illinois special committee to study the possibilities of increasing the allowed water diversion, which body recommended that it be raised to 3,500 cubic feet per second in addition to domestic pumpage. Subsequently, in 1952, 1953, 1956, 1957, 1958, and 1959 various bills were introduced in Congress by Illinois members which proposed additional diversions of varying amounts for Chicago, its Sanitary District, and the Illinois Waterway.

In 1952 and 1953, the bills proposed authorization of a three-year diversion of an additional 1,000 cubic feet per second, during which time the United States Army Corps of Engineers would conduct a study of the effects of this increased withdrawal upon the Great Lakes. The bills' stated purposes were "to regulate and promote commerce," "to protect, improve, and promote navigation and navigable waters in the Illinois waterway and Mississippi Valley," "to help control the lake level," and "to afford protection to property and shores" along the Great Lakes. The Corps of Engineers supported the measure, testifying that it believed a three-year study would reveal conclusively the effects on navigation and flood control so that it would be in a position confidently to report back to Congress on whether the increased diversion held any "bad effects" on either.[57] Nothing was said about fish and wildlife, losses in hydroelectric power production to plants on lakes other than Michigan, possible gains to some interests and losses to others in land matters, losses to lake carriers in decreased tonnage, or the like. H.R. 3300, passed by the Eighty-third Congress, was vetoed by President Eisenhower. H.R. 3210 passed the Eighty-fourth Congress in 1954 and was also vetoed. H.R. 2 and S. 1123 of the Eighty-fifth Congress did not pass.

Eisenhower's two earliest vetoes made the following points: (1) Existing diversions were adequate for navigation in the Illinois Waterway and the Mississippi River. (2) All methods of control of lake levels and protection of property on the Great Lakes should be considered before arbitrarily proceeding with the increased diversion. (3) The diversions are authorized without reference to negotiations with Canada. (4) Legitimate interests of other States affected by the diversion may be adversely affected.[58] His 1956 veto of H.R. 3210 added that he was requesting the Secretary of Defense to speed completion of a comprehensive report by the Corps of Engineers which was to include consideration of the best methods of obtaining improved control of the Great Lakes water levels, and which was to supplement other reports made by the Joint Lake Ontario Engineering Board to the International Joint Commission. He thought to proceed with diversion in the face of these pending reports would be "unwise," particularly in view of objections which had been raised by the Canadian government.[59]

The corps' report, issued on January 29, 1957, was based on information it had gathered for another report on Great Lakes water levels which the House Committee on Public Works requested in a 1952 resolution, and from a June, 1955, report in which the corps had participated for the International Lake Ontario Board of Engineers and the International Joint Commission. Presenting a thoroughgoing analysis of all pertinent facts, the corps concluded that the proposed three-year diversion of an additional 1,000 cubic feet per second would have beneficial effects in lessening possible damage to shore property during storms and high lake stages. It would have a generally adverse effect upon navigation during low lake stages and, if continued indefinitely, would have a permanently adverse effect on the Great Lakes carrying fleet as it was expected to be by 1985, to the extent of an estimated loss of $240,000 per annum (1957 computations). This estimate did not take into account the losses which might accrue to the Canadian carriers. Effects on Mississippi River navigation would be benefited, but the benefit would be too small for precise monetary measurement. The chief negative result, the corps believed, would be a generally adverse effect on hydroelectric energy generation— in monetary values and in theoretical dependable capacity resulting from a stable water supply.

Using a complex method of computation, the corps concluded that the additional 1,000 cubic feet per second from Lake Michigan into the Chicago Sanitary and Ship Canal would lower the levels of Lakes Michigan and Huron about ⅜ of an inch, the level of Lake Erie (over a thirty-nine month period) about ⅜ of an inch, and the level of Lake Ontario (over a forty-two-month period) about ⅜ of an inch. The ultimate effects of a permanent diversion of 1,000 cubic feet per second would, in about fifteen years, lower the levels of Michigan and Huron about one inch, Lake Erie about ⅝ of an inch, and Lake Ontario about ⅝ of an inch.

Several paragraphs from the report are worthy of repetition.

In general, an increase in the diversion from Lake Michigan at Chicago would affect the levels and outflows of Lakes Michigan, Huron, Erie, and Ontario and the St. Lawrence River, all of which are downstream, and would not affect the levels or outflows of Lake Superior, which is upstream from the diversion. A temporary increase in the diversion of 1,000 cubic feet per second for 3 years would have temporary effects that would reach a maximum in about 3 to 3½ years and then gradually diminish and disappear about 15 years after the temporary diversion was discontinued. The effects of a permanent diversion would increase progressively to a maximum in about 15 years and would then continue permanently at that amount.

. . . .

The foregoing reductions in outflows that would result from increasing the diversion at Chicago could not be compensated for except by increases in diversions into the Great Lakes system. The lowering of lake levels, however, could be compensated for in various ways. For Lakes Michigan and Huron the lowering could be offset by construction of a deeply submerged sill in the St. Clair River at an estimated cost of $1,530,000. The lowering effect in Lake Erie could be compensated for by operating the control gates of the Niagara River remedial works now nearing completion in such a way as to hold the level of the pool immediately above the works at a stage 0.22 of a foot higher than presently specified. For Lake Ontario, the approved plans for regulation that will be put into effect when the St. Lawrence power structures are completed can be readily adjusted within the prescribed 4-foot range of stage so that there would be no significant change in levels as a result of the increased diversions. All of the foregoing measures would require coordination with Canada.[60]

Even more important is the corps' assessment of the effects on hydroelectric power production:

The estimated reduction in generation of hydroelectric energy that would result from a 3-year increase in the diversion at Chicago would fall between a minimum of 188 million kilowatt-hours and a maximum of 443 million kilowatt-hours, depending on when the diversions were started and when proposed additional hydroelectric plants are put into operation.

Of this loss, 72 percent would be suffered by New York and Ontario, amounting to about $918,000 in 1957 values over the three-year period. But, pointed out the Engineers,

During this period the increased flow in the Illinois waterway would permit an increase in generation at the existing Lockport [Ill.] plant of 70,400,000 kilowatt-hours, an offset of about 16 percent of the estimated maximum reduction in generation on the Niagara and St. Lawrence. This increase would have a total value of about $202,000.[61]

If proposed additional generating installations were made, and the diversion of 1,000 cubic feet per second were made permanent, this would |

result in a reduction in generation of 123,400,000 kilowatt-hours annually at plants in New York, 123,400,000 kilowatt-hours in Ontario and 56,300,000 in Quebec. The monetary value of the New York and Ontario reductions, representing 81 percent of the total, would be $708,000 annually. The increase in possible generation at Lockport on the Illinois Waterway would be about 8 percent as much as the foregoing reductions of 23,500,000 kilowatt-hours annually, valued at $67,000 annually.[62]

The corps quickly noted that these monetary sums were small in relation to the total electricity output of the Great Lakes system, but the figures provide telling evidence of the reasons for New York's and Ontario's objections to Chicago's proposed diversion scheme.

Five years later another reporter appraised the situation in these terms:

The Great Lakes states battling Chicago claim they are paying in cold cash for what Chicago is currently "stealing." New York power engineers say that if Chicago is permitted to take still another 650,000,000 gallons a day, the Niagara and St. Lawrence power plants will be robbed of more than $1,000,000 a year. Shipowners, according to an estimate by the U.S. Army Engineers, would have to load their vessels more lightly to get through connecting channels and would lose more than $250,000 a year. These channels are now being deepened at a cost to the Government of $150,000,000. But what is the sense, ask Chicago's opponents, of spending huge amounts to scoop dirt from the bottom if Chicago is going to take water from the top? [63]

All interests who appeared in opposition to the bills were fearful that the "experimental" diversion would become permanent. The above reporter, Bernard Asbell, found the controversy at white-hot heat in 1962.

The ultimate argument against the "water steal" is, "Where will it end?" Already, three additional Chicago suburbs, Des Plaines, Arlington Heights and Mount Prospect, have organized a commission—called DAMP—with the goal of taking water from the Lake. If the courts rule that they may, by what rule will the courts say others may not? A group of Texas promoters recently proposed a pipeline from the Great Lakes to irrigate the wastelands of Texas. A Colorado state senator has said that the only long-range solution to his state's water problem is to tap the Great Lakes. If other places do what Chicago is doing—take lake water without returning it—the Great Lakes could indeed be severely depleted.[64]

Asbell, however, also pointed out that Chicago may have performed a service of incalculable merit for the Great Lakes states in diverting her wastes away from Lake Michigan, thus preserving the purity of waters which her neighboring states—Indiana and Wisconsin—have polluted without qualms for many years.

To date, although water diversion is very much an interest of Chicago, no diversion proposals have passed the Congress, and neither did the Congress consent to the Great Lakes Basin Compact as originally adopted by the compacting states—with Ontario and Quebec included. There is no question, Congress intends to keep its full control over the important international water diversion problem.

The Burns Waterway Harbor—Indiana Dunes Problem

Another highly significant controversy of the Lake Michigan area, illustrative of the kind of intense conflicts which can arise over questions of Great Lakes usages and influential in the formation of the Great Lakes Basin Compact, surrounds a matter which spans several decades but which only sensationally erupted on the national scene in the 1960s. This is the many-faceted Indiana Dunes issue, with its Burns Harbor-steel industry-land speculation-national park-conservation aspects, which occupied the attention of press and public for half a decade and embroiled the communities of Lake Michigan's south shore, land speculators, the steel industry, governors, state legislators, the United States Army Corps of Engineers, thousands of citizens, President John F. Kennedy, and more than thirty senators of the United States Congress.

Although the issue arose in Indiana, concerning Indiana property and Indiana ambitions, and was prompted and promoted by interests within Indiana who had links with certain interests outside of Indiana, it was and is of vital interest to Illinois as well, not only because the major burden of the "Save the Dunes" legislative efforts within the Congress was carried primarily by Senator Paul Douglas of Illinois, but also because the area lies within the reach of the Chicago metropolitan area. What happens to the steel and shipping industries in Gary-Hammond happens to Chicago; what affects the ports and port facilities of Lake Michigan affects the Chicago harbor facilities; what affects the uses of Lake Michigan and its beaches for much-needed recreation is an intimate concern of Chicago. And Chicago is interested in the St. Lawrence Seaway.

Shortly after the turn of the century the University of Chicago botanist, Professor Henry C. Cowles, the father of the science of plant ecology in America, first drew worldwide attention to the Indiana Dunes through his studies of the kinds and activities of plant life found there. A unique natural phenomenon which at that time covered about twenty-five miles of Lake Michigan's south shore, the Indiana Dunes proved over the years to be a scientific and botanical laboratory of tremendous significance in the development of geological knowledge of the Great Lakes' formation and evolution; in the growth of scientific research on plants and their environmental influences; and on oceanography, meteorology, and the like. The dunes were used by purposes, the dunes and their beaches provided a recreational area for study, research, and teaching. In addition to their value for scientific all the major institutions of higher learning in the Great Lakes area for the population of the Chicago and northern Indiana area. So prized by naturalists was the region, as early as 1916 the first director of the National Park Service, Stephen Mather, urged that the area be acquired by the federal government for a national park, something that was not done and which has frequently been regretted by dunes advocates in subsequent years.

Consisting of migrating dunes, the sands are formed by the winds and waves and shore action of the waters of Lake Michigan. Over many centuries they have created three major belts: just beyond the beach are the low-lying foredunes; next, caught by increasing plant life, are the older pine dunes; and further inland, with great amounts of long-standing plant life, is the beech-maple belt. Scientists say some of the vegetation of this area is thousands of years old. Between and among the dunes and several belts are ponds, bogs, marshes, and small lakes in which wildlife abounds. More than a thousand species of plants and trees are found here, including twenty-six members of the orchid family. The area is a meeting ground for northern and southern species of plants, containing both cactus and some of the flora of far northern climes.

As time has passed, gradual depredations and inroads upon the dunes by commercial developers of one kind and another reduced the undisturbed portion of the dunes to about seven miles of the original twenty-five. Of this, today something over two miles is embodied in the Indiana Dunes State Park, and a little more than four miles lies in the Burns Ditch area, west of the park and on either side of this small artificially constructed drainage channel that became the prized and fought-over focal point of numerous interests.

The entire dunes area lies between Gary, Indiana on the west, to Michigan City on the east. It is an easy automobile drive for millions of persons in the densely populated Chicago metropolitan area, a nonpareil potential recreational site of the type so recommended today for urban concentrations by planners and recreational experts. The trouble is that there is not much left of it for park purposes, and what is left is privately owned in residential development and by a very few large industries—chiefly three steel companies. Even more troublesome is the fact that the State of Indiana has never had a public harbor of its own on Lake Michigan and many years ago began activities to obtain one for itself in the dunes area, the only place available to it, for this and the immediate vicinity is all of the state that fronts upon Lake Michigan.

In 1919 the Inland Steel Company, which had established its only integrated steel mill at its Indiana Harbor section of East Chicago, Indiana, purchased its present holdings of dunes land, consisting today of 830 acres between Gary and the town of Ogden Dunes. Purchased in anticipation of future possible industrial use, the company had never developed it and, at the time of the dunes controversy, testified before Congress that it had no plans in view to do so.

In 1929 the Midwest Steel Company purchased 750 acres of dunes land which lay astride of Burns Ditch, which drains the Little Calumet River into Lake Michigan and which lies to the east of Inland Steel's holdings and of the town of Ogden Dunes. Beginning at that time, Midwest Steel sought public construction of a deepwater port near Burns Ditch and started the lengthy and necessarily involved maneuvers to obtain one. In 1931 the Army Corps of Engineers, at the behest of various private and Indiana state interests, made a preliminary examination of the site of the proposed harbor and gave a negative finding, based on the principle that the benefits of such a port would primarily accrue to one company only, Midwest Steel, and therefore could not be justified to the nation. A few years later the corps was again approached, and in 1935 it again refused to approve the matter. In 1935, however, Representative Charles A. Halleck of Indiana's Second Congressional District, Governor Paul V. McNutt, and Senators Sherman Minton and Frederick Van Nuys of Indiana, joined forces to obtain federal construction of the deepwater port, now being called "Indiana's port," and sought according to Halleck's 1965 testimony

To give the people of Indiana for the first time real access to the Great Lakes Waterway and to provide for the development there of an industrial complex which will not be just steelmills alone but will be so diversified that when steel goes down the whole area doesn't go down.[65]

The results of these efforts came to fruition in Congress's 1937 authorization to the corps to make preliminary examination of the entire Indiana shore to pick the best harbor site. But before the corps came up with a decision the Indiana State Planning Board issued its own report, unequivocally finding that the Burns Ditch area was the only possible, desirable, and available location—the exact area held by Midwest Steel.

Meanwhile World War II intervened, foreclosing any extensive advancement of the scheme, and it was not until 1944 that the Army engineers issued their report, again rejecting the proposal, but this time basing their recommendations on the proposition that Chicago, Calumet, and Michigan City harbor facilities were adequate for all of the area's industrial needs and uses. But pressure was strong, and in 1949 the Chicago district engineer of the corps finally issued a favorable "preliminary report" on the Burns Ditch site.

As recounted by William Peeples in *Atlantic Monthly*, in 1953 Republican Governor George Craig of Indiana took office and began to extend his influence to bring the Burns Ditch harbor project to realization. He first sought Indiana legislative appropriation of $3,500,000 to buy 1500 acres at Burns Ditch for the harbor, but the 1955 legislature killed the bill. Craig then turned to private sources for the financing he sought, resting his action on the favorable recommendations of a private engineering firm which had prepared a report financed by the National Steel Company, of which Midwest Steel is a subsidiary, and whose executive director was George Humphrey, Secretary of the Treasury under Eisenhower at this time; the New York Central Railroad, which has a right-of-way through the dunes; and the Texas Murchison family, owners of dunes land just east of Midwest Steel's Burns Ditch holdings, and also owners of the Consumers Company of Chicago. Consumers Company was then engaged in sand-mining on its dunes holdings. The Murchisons, in turn, had become interested in speculating in dunes land and, in 1954, in order to engage in such activity in Indiana, incorporated a land-buying agency, the Consumers Dunes Corporation, in Indianapolis just shortly before the time Governor Craig began action to obtain his appropriation and failed.

The tangled financial dealings which then ensued are ably recounted in Mr. Peeples's article and need not be recounted here. Enough to say that the Murchisons through their Consumers Dunes Corporation by 1955–56 acquired total holdings of some 1200 acres of the dunes which the corporation valued at $300 per acre, or $360,-000, and sold it a year later (1956) to Lake Shore Development Corporation (incorporated in Indianapolis in 1956), a land-buying agency of the Bethlehem Steel Company, for $3,326,500. Also involved in these financial manipulations was the board chairman of the Fletcher National Bank of Indianapolis, Frank McKinney, former national chairman of the Democratic Party. An associate of the Murchisons, McKinney was made a director of the New York Central Railroad, and his bank acted as transfer agent for the St. Lawrence Seaway Corporation, a firm headed by former Senator William Jenner of Indiana which had been created to engage in real estate activity in areas influenced by the St. Lawrence Seaway.

By 1957 the Indiana legislature capitulated and appropriated $2,000,000 to buy the land necessary for the harbor at Burns Ditch. In July 1959, Indiana's governor presented the corps with the state's proposed harbor plans which, subsequently, the corps approved with certain qualifications: (*a*) a north breakwater of steel sheet pile of cellular construction, 4,050 feet long; (*b*) a west breakwater of steel sheet pile of cellular construction, 1330 feet in length; (*c*) a west-shore connection of steel sheet pile, 2,500 feet in length; (*d*) an east rubble-mound breakwater, 1,340 feet in length; (*e*) an east-shore connection of steel sheet pile, 1,820 feet in length; (*f*) an approach channel 30 feet deep and 400 feet wide, extending from deep water in Lake Michigan to about the north end of the east breakwater; (*g*) an entrance channel 28 feet deep and 800 feet wide, from the end of the approach channel to the west breakwater; and (*h*) an outer harbor area of 225 acres, 27 feet deep.[66]

Added to this plan, under a Corps of Engineers' permit granted to the Midwest Steel Corporation in January 1961, would be a 225-acre plot of filled land, created between Burns Ditch and the west breakwater of the harbor, about four-fifths of a mile from the Ditch. Governor

Harold Handley at this time also named a North Indiana Lakefront Study Committee, to which he appointed John Van Ness, an employee of Midwest Steel, as its chairman. (Mr. Van Ness was in 1969 one of the commissioners of the Great Lakes basin compact commission from Indiana.) Van Ness was far from a disinterested appointee, through his Midwest Steel connection and his former activities as an Indiana senator, under which he had been one of the chief agents working in the Indiana legislature for the Burns Ditch harbor and for appropriations to finance Indiana's share in the scheme.

In 1959, also, Midwest Steel began construction of its $130,000,-000 rolling mill at the Burns Ditch harbor site, and at the same time the St. Lawrence Seaway opened. While these important events were occurring, other interesting developments were shaping. A few months earlier in 1957 a group of Indiana citizens, calling themselves the Save the Dunes Council, approached Senator Paul Douglas for help, for which they had been turned down by their senior United States senator, Homer Capehart. And thus began the final events of the dunes saga which brought the issue into public view and held national attention for five years.

The Indiana citizens who approached Senator Douglas were interested in rescuing what remained of the unspoiled dunes and, knowing that Douglas had for twelve years lived during summers in the dunes, hoped he would agree to lead a legislative effort to stop industrialization of the remainder of the dunes. Douglas, looking upon the matter as an important conservation issue, first approached Senator Capehart to enlist his assistance, but Capehart again refused to participate. Douglas then took up the matter, working with the Indiana group and ultimately enlisting the assistance and support of a great many other congressmen. He introduced his first bill to preserve outstanding sections of the Indiana Dunes as a national monument or park. Other bills were introduced by Congressmen Saylor of Pennsylvania, and O'Hara, Price, and Libonati of Illinois. By 1965 these early supporters had been joined by increasing numbers of congressmen, federal departments and bureaus, cities and towns, dozens of conservation groups throughout the country, and literally thousands of rank and file citizens. President Kennedy, in his March 1961 address on conservation, recommended that Congress create a national lakeshore of part of the Indiana Dunes.[67]

The measure upon which Douglas finally concentrated his efforts was actually an administration bill, having been formulated after extensive investigation and research by the Department of the Interior, the Bureau of the Budget, and the White House. The Kennedy administration took this step as a result of the Corps of Engineers' issuance of a favorable report in 1963 on the Burns Ditch harbor proposal, which Douglas viewed as having been "rushed through," and having "the effect of blocking action on the earlier bills to create an Indiana Dunes National Lakeshore." Certain of his comments follow:

In 1962, following hearings by this subcommittee on bills to create a lakeshore park, thousands of citizens, conservationists, members of Congress, and others appealed to President Kennedy that it would be wrong—indeed tragic—for the Federal Government to build an economically unjustified Federal harbor in the midst of the dunes and thereby approve the leveling and pollution of this irreplaceable gift of nature. The White House ordered a thorough review of the Corps of Engineers report on the harbor proposal. Numerous independent efforts were made to find a satisfactory solution which would preserve the unspoiled sections of the Indiana Dunes. All were . . . rejected out of hand by the steel companies.[68]

The corps' July 1963 favorable report, cleared through its District and Division Engineers and its Board of Engineers for Rivers and Harbors, recommended that Congress authorize construction of such a harbor if local interests—the State of Indiana and the steel companies—would obligate themselves to provide and maintain adequate public terminal and transfer facilities open to all; to construct shore connections; to provide necessary lands; to assume responsibility for damages; to provide and maintain adequate depths in access channels and berthing areas; and to reimburse the United States for any excess dredging costs. The corps also stipulated that the steel companies agree to build a fully integrated steel plant at the site in order to justify the project to the nation.[69]

Pointing out that industrial development by 1963 was well underway, with Midwest Steel Division of National Steel already operating a finishing plant which it had constructed immediately west of the selected harbor site, and under a January 1961 permit issued by the corps was empowered to build bulkheads and riparian fill extending 2,500 feet into Lake Michigan; and that Bethlehem Steel had recently initiated construction of a finishing plant with announced intentions of eventually developing an integrated steel plant on its acreage east of the harbor, the corps succinctly summarized the opposition as follows:

This industrial development is being strongly opposed by certain groups. The principal opposition comes from those who feel that the remaining dune lands should be preserved in their natural state. Others opposing industrialization believe that the area should become a great playground for the people of the nearby metropolitan area, through development for the most intensive types of public recreation. Still others wish to protect the fine residential areas that already exist in the dunes, and to have this type of development extended. As a result of the opposition to industrialization of the area, bills have been introduced in Congress which would authorize Federal acquisition of most of the potential industrial area and its inclusion in a national park.[70]

The corps noted that the opposing interests were denying that construction of a public harbor with federal funds would be economically justified, since it would be for the use of the two steel companies only. By 1963, Midwest Steel held 750 acres at the site and anticipated 225 more of filled land. Bethlehem Steel's holdings, through its purchases from the Murchisons, were about 4,000 acres.[71]

The Bureau of the Budget on September 24, 1963, took exception to the Army's cost estimates, methods of computing costs, and estimates of projected amounts of commerce which would pass through the harbor. It took particular issue with coal tonnage estimates which, while expected to increase with the added consumption of the two steel companies, would not in the bureau's view come anywhere near the corps' projected figures and could not reasonably be expected to expand greatly under the existing economic realities which surround coal usage. The bureau noted that the corps' report had failed to take into account possible nuclear power developments and their influence on energy consumption. But, the bureau said, in conformity with President Kennedy's expressed desire to see both a dunes park and an Indiana-based deepwater port materialize, the bureau granted qualified approval as indicated:

(1) The Army should first obtain more specific assurances from National Steel Corporation and Bethlehem Steel as to their plans to complete their fully integrated mills in the area.

(2) The Army should seek firm assurances from the State of Indiana that it could and would finance on a self-liquidating basis the

transfer and terminal facilities and other required items of local cooperation.

(3) The Army should restudy anticipated coal shipments, "in cooperation with other Federal agencies" concerned.

(4) The Army should obtain proof that water and air pollution by the steel operations would be maximally controlled.[72]

Approval was also reluctantly granted by the Department of the Interior, which pointed out,

Since [our letter of June 20, 1962] . . . , industrial and residential development have taken place and much of this natural scene has been destroyed. Recent inspection discloses that much of the area designated as unit 2 of the proposed national seashore is being prepared for the development of a steel mill and related industrial facilities, so that only about 674 acres of natural area are now left in the unit. . . . In the circumstances, we reluctantly conclude that it is no longer practicable to include this unit within the boundary of the proposed national lakeshore.[73]

The Public Health Service indicated that if water and air pollution were adequately controlled in the harbor area, these should not seriously interfere with public recreational use of the proposed dunes park area to the east. But, it observed,

If the anticipated development of an industrial complex is realized, problems of water pollution . . . will undoubtedly have to be met. These . . . are likely to include discharge of vessel wastes, sanitary conditions involving water supplies for vessels, disposal of sanitary and industrial wastes from industrial plant facilities, and protection from pollution of beaches and of public water supply intakes in the vicinity of the proposed development. . . . Adequate measure must be provided by the developers to prevent the discharge of such . . . wastes, raw or treated . . . in the vicinity of public water supply intakes or established bathing beaches.[74]

But 1963 Senator Vance Hartke, along with Senator Birch Bayh of Indiana, had joined Senator Douglas as cosponsor of the Kennedy administration's compromise measure, and subsequently worked energetically for its passage. Douglas's earliest bills had provided for a national park area of as much as 9,000 acres, which would have required purchase and inclusion of all of Inland Steel's land holdings in the Burns Ditch area. Hartke in 1961 countered these proposals with one of his own which embraced about 5,000 acres, including the 2,100 already embodied in the Indiana Dunes State Park, and omitting all of Inland Steel's acreage. With the 1963 administration compromise as reflected in the Corps of Engineers' report, the contending senatorial factions arrived at a compromise which acquiesced in the building of the harbor, exempted from the proposed national park all but 150 acres of the Bethlehem Steel lands and 227 acres of National Steel's, but included the entire 790 acres of Inland Steel. This action, regarded as discriminatory by Inland Steel, which had not until that time taken much part in the proceedings, brought it into open conflict with all of the park's supporters.

The final result of the controversy was enactment by the Eighty-ninth Congress of S. 360, which was approved by President Johnson on November 5, 1966. The act empowered the secretary of the interior to establish and administer the Indiana Dunes National Lakeshore, comprising an area delineated on a map filed with the director of the National Park Service, No. LNPNE 1003 ID, "A Proposed Indiana Dunes National Lakeshore," dated July 1964.[75] The secretary was authorized to begin purchasing land within the designated area and as soon as in his judgment an "administrable" amount has been acquired to designate it as the Indiana Dunes National Lakeshore, with publication of notice in the Federal Register.

The Great Lakes Basin Compact and the Burns Ditch Controversy

The Indiana Dunes–Burns Ditch controversy provides a particularly revealing illustration of the nature of Great Lakes Basin problems. Translated into the defined powers, objectives, and interests of the Great Lakes Commission, this controversy—if it had come before that interstate agency for resolution, as would be the case if the compact agency were the fully endowed regulatory authority its proponents appeared to want it to be—might very well have had an entirely different ending.

First, one result which can with almost absolute certainty be written off as a likely result of interstate rather than federal resolution of the issue is the creation of a national park of what remained of the Indiana Dunes. Although the Great Lakes Basin Compact speaks of the "conservation of water resources," it nowhere mentions the "conservation of unique natural phenomena," or for that matter, the "conservation of land." It is true that the compact empowers the commission to "advise" in "maintaining a proper balance" among possibly competing interests, including "recreational and other legitimate" uses of the water resources of the lakes, but the emphasis is upon water resources and not upon land. It is quite apparent that the compact's focus is on commercial, industrial, consumptive interests and uses of the Great Lakes' waters. Recreation is incidental.

Second, there is serious question as to whether the conflict could have been resolved at all by the states party to the compact. The system of voting within the commission might have made it possible for Indiana to obtain supporters of state delegations not connected with Lake Michigan, to counteract such opposition as Illinois, Wisconsin, and Michigan manifested. More probably, a kind of logrolling system of decision-making among the members would have been required: concessions negotiated with the delegations of states seeking support for controversial goals of their own. Yet the overriding facts of this case reveal only three major proponents of the Burns Ditch harbor: the steel companies, the State of Indiana, and certain land-speculating and land-financing special interests. There was no widespread, Basin-wide clamor for the harbor. There was a great deal of local opposition to the steel companies' activities, the Corps of Engineers' report, and to the destruction of the dunes. There was a negative nationwide reaction manifested by conservationists and water pollution control advocates. On a purely speculative basis it seems fair to say that without the federal hand on the helm, so to speak, the popular and local interests in this matter might very well have received even less shrift from an interstate compact agency. The nationwide conservation interests would have had no voice at all, for if the conflict had been confined to a specialized agency for resolution, the remainder of the nation would probably have known little or nothing about it until it was a fait accompli. While this cannot be said with finality, many factors suggest the judgment is not idle. Most of the state appointees to the Great Lakes Commission are men who have demonstrated strong economic experience, interests, and attachments in Great Lakes matters having to do with water, with navigation, with business development, with steel production, and the like. The compact itself has a strongly economic developmental coloration. Together, this does not add up to creation of a national or regional park out of what remains of a piece of extremely valuable industrial land. The decision to create a new deepwater port holding a potential for significant competition with existing Great Lakes port cities in the uses and benefits deriving from the St. Lawrence Seaway would have been an exceedingly difficult one for the Great Lakes Commission to make. This is why it is possible the agency could not have made such a decision at all.

Third, there is no conceivable way for the Great Lakes Basin states to govern or regulate Great Lakes matters in isolation from Canada or the United States. The waters, the shipping, the navigation channels are essentially international and national in their significance. This does not exclude the wholly "domestic" Lake Michigan. (See Appendix D, showing the United States Army Corps of Engineers' map of domestic freight tonnage movements through the lakes and St. Lawrence Seaway.) Great port cities like Chicago are great cities of the world. The federal government and the Canadian Dominion will neither stand idly by while particularistic state and economic interests seek to "divide the pie" and run things to suit themselves, nor will they relinquish their ultimate right of veto and decision over the area's waters. They cannot. It is therefore valid to assume that even if the Great Lakes Commission had been empowered to handle this matter it could not have done so without the active intervention of the national government. And this means, in the final sense, a final decision by that government, as did occur.

But the existing Great Lakes Commission seemingly had nothing to do with the Burns Ditch–Dunes controversy and, under its present powers, could have done little on the issue other than gather facts and advise. Then why introduce the matter in discussing the commission and its operations?

This controversy arose from and was stimulated by the establishment of the St. Lawrence Seaway, which opened the doors to realization of many industrial and commercial aspirations that had been only hopes and dreams for many years before the seaway was a reality. The economic developmental possibilities of the Great Lakes area were infinitely heightened everywhere by the seaway. The present controversy involving the south shore of Lake Michigan is only one of several such potential developmental conflicts which may arise and are arising around the lakes. There is not much doubt that the creation of the seaway and Indiana's long-sought harbor played their own significant roles in the creation and adoption of the Great Lakes Basin Compact which, with its underlying potential for future evolution into an interstate agency for regulating all such matters, provides developmental proponents with the nucleus, the foundation of the kind of agency that could someday make possible more specialized control over the lakes, with less national interference.

Impartial observers should be aware of some of the kinds of developmental possibilities which are now Great Lakes realities, not merely possibilities. One such reality is the increase in number of ocean-going carriers now entering the lakes—great ships of great size and tonnage, requiring deepwater channels and facilities for their handling. Note the Great Lakes Commission's enthusiastic comments:

April Brought Over 10 Miles of Salties into the Lakes—During the opening month of the 1968 season, 117 overseas ships passed through the U.S. Seaway locks into the Great Lakes. If placed end to end, the combined overall length of the ships (53,894 feet) would extend 10.2 miles. Their average length was 461 feet. Steel comprised the full cargo for 40 inbound ships, and many others carried partial cargoes of this commodity. In April 1967, overseas vessels entering the lakes totaled 143 and the average for their length was 448 feet. Eighteen of those ships had steel as their sole cargo. Preliminary cargo tonnage figures for April show general cargo traffic, handled largely by overseas ships, totaled 721,000 short tons compared to 563,000 tons in April, 1967.

1,000-Foot Lake Freighter Ordered—Bethlehem Steel at the end of April announced the order of a 1,000-foot ore carrier. The ship will be the longest in the American merchant marine and have the maximum length permitted to transit the new Poe Lock at Sault Ste. Marie. The vessel will be built by Litton Industries, the mid-section at the new yard at Erie, Pennsylvania and the bow and stern at the company's Gulf coast yard. Assembly will be carried out at the Erie facility. The new carrier, scheduled for delivery in 1970, will have a capacity of 51,500 gross tons, about twice as much as the largest boat on the lakes at present. A self-unloading system of new design is expected to permit discharge of iron ore pellets at a rate of up to 20,000 gross tons per hour.

The new ship will be engaged principally in carrying pellets from the upper lakes to Bethlehem's new integrated steel-making facility at Burns Harbor, Indiana which is scheduled to begin in 1970.

The first construction announcement of a Great Lakes super-carrier was made by U.S. Steel last fall . . . that ship to have an 858-foot overall length and a beam of 105 feet, the same as the Bethlehem vessel.[76]

It takes little imagination to grasp the developmental possibilities involved in this matter alone: expansion in steel production in all of its steps; expansion of United States Army Corps of Engineers (United States government) expenditures in port building, dredging, harbor maintenance, and port-planning activities; * expansion of shipbuilding facilities; expansion of Erie, Pennsylvania, as a port city; expansion in the businesses and industries which service lake carriers and the industries which consume the cargoes of lake carriers; crowding of existing ports and harbors, and developing need for more ports and harbors, etc. These are the immediate effects of the advent of super-carriers in the Great Lakes. The ramifying effects on wholesale and retail trade, real estate transactions, air services, trucking, pipelines, and rail facilities, financial activity, are incalculable. So are the probable effects on water pollution and air pollution.

Yet another kind of developmental matter is described by the commission:

Lake Erie Exploratory Drilling in Pennsylvania Waters Scheduled
Leasing of offshore areas in Lake Erie for exploratory gas and oil drilling is being consummated following dismissal of a suit in a Pennsylvania court to restrain such action. The City of Erie in early April filed a suit to stop the state's Department of Forests and Waters from leasing the lake lands for drilling activity which, it was contended, might contribute to water pollution and injury to the tourist trade.
A hearing on the suit was held and a Commonwealth Court judge on April 30 submitted a brief dismissing Erie's petition. A 1957 Pennsylvania Act vests offshore gas and oil leasing authority in the secretary of Forests and Waters.
Pending the outcome of the litigation, the Department of Forests and Waters had received drilling bids but had held in abeyance the awarding of leases. The area open for lease includes 37 blocks comprising 369,989 acres. Lying between the series of blocks nearest to the lakeshore is an open zone ranging from 2 to 8 miles in width. To date, bids have been received for four blocks totaling some 24,500 acres. The state agency has indicated that strict requirements virtually negate the chance of pollution resulting from drilling. In 1958–59, several wells were drilled in the Pennsylvania section of Lake Erie. Gas was discovered, but it was not in quantities sufficient to warrant commercial development.[77]

* In a report to Congress dated Sept. 1, 1967 (Doc. No. 1512, 90th Cong., 1st Sess.), *Great Lakes Harbor Study—Final Report*, the Corps of Engineers recommended "improvements" and deepening of thirty harbors and construction of one entirely new one (Burns Harbor). Many of the projects are underway or completed.

A question which may well be asked, is, what can the Great Lakes Commission do with all such problems now that it becomes, with congressional consent, only the "advisory" agency of the American states bordering the Lakes? The answer lies in the role the Great Lakes Basin Commission assigns to the Great Lakes Commission in future water planning activities, and this remains to be seen. It also lies in the compacting states, which may decide to give their commission the powers that will convert it into an operational agency, but this will require congressional consent and at this time the possibilities for this appear very dim.

The Lake Michigan–Wabash River–Ohio River Proposed Waterway

The third of the Great Lakes matters intimately involving Illinois also involves the State of Indiana, other Great Lakes Basin ports and shipping, and another Illinois interstate compact. Treated in detail in chapter 5, repetition is not called for here, save to call attention to the matter as an active and unresolved issue of considerable import. This is the Wabash Valley Interstate Commission with its projected plans and promotion of a very active kind for creation of a navigable waterway extending from the Burns Ditch or Chicago areas via many contemplated man-made cuts and channels, the tributaries of the Wabash River and that river itself, to juncture with the Ohio River. The project appears to have been actively taken up by the Wabash River agency around the time the Burns Ditch Waterway Harbor began to take realizable form. While Illinois has demonstrated much interest in this waterway it is Indiana, again, that is most concerned. Illinois was recognizably less than warm toward the proposed potential harbor complex at Burns Harbor, which as originally conceived held a threat to Chicago and its port enterprises. In the dual relationship involving the two aforementioned interstate compacts, Illinois appears to have some potential conflict in her own interstate compact purposes, although there may be no conflict at all if her reasons for entering such alliances are simply to place herself in a position to protect her own interests and to have an ear and a voice in proposed projects at the moment of their inception. Now that the Burns Harbor development is a reality, it is interesting to note that plans for the Cross-Wabash Valley Waterway now call for juncture with the Chicago River rather than with Burns Harbor, as earlier projected by the Wabash Valley Interstate Commission.

Present Activities of the Great Lakes Commission

Confined by law as it is to research, study, planning, and advice, the commission's activities have understandably been limited in scope. Its chief activities or contributions have been in keeping a close watch on industrial and legislative developments in the lakes, sponsoring conferences and interagency meetings on Great Lakes matters, and lobbying for measures in which it is interested in Congress and state legislatures. Its lobbying activity has been considerable in support of admirable laws such as the Federal Water Resources Planning Act and the Water Quality Act of 1965, as well as of the laws and proposed measures in which it has been interested but of which careful appraisal and evaluation are impossible in this study.

Its role as a possible lobbying agent was of concern to Congress in the commission's efforts to obtain congressional consent. A number of comments on the matter appear in the hearings. The exchange between Representative James G. Fulton of Pennsylvania, and Marvin Fast, executive director of the Great Lakes Commission in 1958 (while the commission sought approval for the original compact with its international clauses), is revealing:

MR. FULTON: *The question comes up as to what the real purpose of the compact Commission is. Is it to assist in the development of what is already there, or is it to be a lobbying activity to come up with the new projects which will then be pushed both through the Congress . . . and the various State legislatures, city councils, county organizations,* of which we have many in the United States, *which will then be the lobbyists for various new projects in the Great Lakes Basin?* This organization would then be used as a lobbying arm with the Congress and the various legislatures in the State and local governments. Is that the purpose, or what is it?

MR. FAST: I would answer that in the negative, and emphasize the fact that I certainly do not regard the Commission as a lobby. *I would prefer to put it this way, that we have been told by the States to serve . . . as the eyes and ears of the State governments on questions of lake development and to report with such recommendations to the States as the Commission deems proper for these developments.* The States retain such authority as always has been theirs to determine what programs, what projects, on the Great Lakes are desirable.

    .   .   .   .

MR. FULTON: *Then there is to be no personnel in this Commission which will lobby or promote specific projects or functions within the basin?* That will be left to the member States?
    MR. FAST: Under the terms of the compact, Mr. Fulton, the Commission—
    MR. FULTON: *Could you answer that yes or no, and then you can reply further.*

    .   .   .   .

    MR. FAST: *I would have to say "Yes," and then qualify it this way: If directed by the States to promote a particular objective, I would regard it my duty to promote that objective.* However, I regard my initial obligation to advise the States, the governors, the legislatures, and other appropriate State officials concerning developments on the Great Lakes, possibly with a recommendation as to a position the State might wish to take on that matter.
    MR. FULTON: I am sorry I can't see the function of such a compact commission lobbying with the various governments in Canada, the Dominion and Provinces, as well as the States . . . , and the legislatures as well as the Congress of the United States. I think that is clearly beyond the powers and functions of this Commission, and I wish that would be reconsidered.
    MR. RABAUT: Could I ask a question? I wanted to say, what is your definition of your idea in this instance of lobbying? Something for the betterment of the Great Lakes, somebody that is out for it; would that be lobbying? There is a connotation to this word "lobbying" which might not look good.
    MR. FULTON: I believe we in Congress all know what lobbying is and what is a lobbying organization. The question is, has this compact Commission as one of its functions, a function of lobbying in regard to either the Dominion of Canada or any of its provinces or any of the States or legislatures of the United States?
    MR. RABAUT: Doing something in concord for the betterment of the Great Lakes States in the compact and Canada, if done through the Department of State would not be lobbying in our opinion.[78] [*Italics added.*]

No doubt the rather substantial list of legislative efforts which the commission proudly presents in evidence of its contributions to date meets the commission's views of what is for the betterment of the Great Lakes states, but it is also evident that this is lobbying activity. Specific appearances before Congress have included such varied matters as water pollution control, control of the sea lamprey in lakes waters, flood control appropriations, construction of dual locks on the Illinois Waterway, federal extension of shore protection legislation to include projects in the Great Lakes, and the like. More important for future legislative activity, however, are a number of resolutions adopted, positions taken, which include "continuing" endorsement, urging, and "model legislation" drafting. These include a great many Great Lakes matters: efforts to effect "a more equitable share of military cargo movement through Great Lakes ports"; endorsement of action "by all states to acquire lake shore lands for recreational programs"; support of appropriation of federal funds for harbor and channel development and navigational aids; endorsement of federal subsidies for United States-flag vessels operating on Great Lakes trade routes; federal support for Great Lakes shipping companies which make capital investments on vessels, and many more. The commission has taken its causes not only into the legislative bodies, but also into the regulatory commissions and departments of the federal government. It maintains regular liaison with, and until consent was granted in 1968 had representation on, the following: the Great Lakes Study Group; the Association of State and Interstate Water Pollution Control Administrators; the International Association of Great Lakes Ports; the Council of Lake Erie Ports; the Sports Fishing Institute; various engineering societies; the Great Lakes Maritime Institute; the Great Lakes Historical Society; the American Association for the Advancement of Science; and the Lake Carriers' Association.

As for dealing with Canada prior to 1968 which troubled Congressman Fulton in 1958, the commission states that it had a number of engagements with the International Joint Commission; it endorsed implementation of the convention with Canada on Great Lakes fisheries; maintained relations with various Canadian agencies to effect international action on pollution in Lakes Ontario and Erie and their connecting channels, and to regulate water levels in the Great Lakes; presented its views to the Canadian Parliament on water resources matters, unnamed; and held an exploratory conference or two with Ontario and Quebec concerning augmentation of water supply in the Great Lakes.[79]

In keeping a close interest in the industrial developments of the lakes, the commission is acting within its lawful assignment and purposes. This appears to comprise by far the greater part of its activities and attention, as might be expected.

Opposition to the Compact

The chief opponent of the Great Lakes Commission's efforts to obtain congressional consent to the compact was the New York Power Authority. In both the 1958 and 1966 consent efforts, the authority waged unrelenting war against the legal validation and recognition of the interstate pact in its stated and implicit purposes. The final consent action was obtained only after a conference between the interested federal agencies, the compacting states, the commission, the Water Resources Council, and the New York Power Authority was held on February 7, 1968, when agreement was reached to make inclusion of Canada (to which both the Department of State and the Power Authority had objected) [80] and any direct relations between Canada and the Great Lakes Commission invalid.

The New York Power Authority is a New York State public corporation created to construct and operate that state's hydroelectric power developments in the International Rapids section of the St. Lawrence River and at Niagara Falls. Its St. Lawrence facilities were constructed through sale of $350,000,000 in bonds to private investors, with no supplemental state or federal assistance. The Niagara project in 1958 was financed by $700,000,000 from sale of bonds to private investors, again without governmental assistance. Under its charter and laws it is obligated to "uphold the right of the State of New York to the historic flow past its borders of the waters of the Niagara and St. Lawrence Rivers." This it must do in order to amortize the bonds sold to finance both projects, and to sell its generated power at such rates as will repay its indebtedness, maintain its capital operations, and cover its costs of transmission. Alarmed at the prospect of creation of some kind of superagency, empowered by the government of the United States through approval of the interstate compact to make decisions on Great Lakes matters which might bind the member states, the Power Authority protested to Congress that the compact and its commission were unnecessary. It voiced no objection to the commission as it stood without congressional consent. With consent, such a commission was quite another thing. The Power Authority believed consent would tend to elevate the Great Lakes Commission into stature approaching that of a federally-sanctioned, probably international, agency, and this it clearly did not want. John R. Davison, speaking for Robert Moses, chairman of the Power Authority, expressed the core of its opposition before Congress in 1958.

There has been functioning since 1955 a Great Lakes Commission such as would be established under [S. 1416]. The State of New York did not join in [creation of] that agreement or participate in the creation of that Commission.

In 1957 there was introduced in the New York legislature, a bill to ratify and make the State a party to that agreement. The Power Authority of the State of New York opposed the passage of that bill. One of the grounds of its opposition was that the bill provided that "all officers of this State are hereby authorized and directed to do all things falling within their respective jurisdictions necessary to or incidental to the carrying out of said compact in every particular." The legislature passed the bill but the Governor vetoed it. One of the grounds for his veto was the indefinite nature of this directive.

⋅   ⋅   ⋅   ⋅   ⋅   ⋅   ⋅   ⋅   ⋅   ⋅   ⋅   ⋅

In addition to urging the lack of any need for such a compact, power authority suggests to the committee that no congressional consent was or is necessary for the establishment by the Great Lakes States of such a consultative and recommendatory agency as is provided for in this bill.

As has been shown, a Commission has been functioning since 1955 without congressional sanction. Congressional consent and approval would add nothing to what the Commission has done, is doing and may do in the future. Furthermore, it should be noted that the agreement which the States adopted is not the compact they would now have the Congress approve. [Reference here is to the omission of the Canadian provinces from membership, agreed to by the adopting states.]

No one has questioned the validity, though it lacks congressional consent, of the present agreement among six of the Great Lakes States to cooperate to accomplish the hopes of that agreement which are the same as those expressed in the compact. Nor has any one shown that the Great Lakes Commission set up under that agreement needs congressional approval in order to function effectively as "solely a consultative and recommendatory agency."

No evidence has been or can be adduced showing that the United States Department of State, Department of Defense, Army Corps of Engineers, the International Joint Commission, Joint Board of Engineers, Joint Board of Control, the Governors and the Attorneys General of the Great Lakes States are not now properly performing their functions, or that these established responsible agencies and officers are not doing or would not continue to do everything which a Great Lakes Commission would do under the compact which this bill would approve.

The only thing such a Commission would do would be to debate what action should be taken by other agencies and officers responsible for action. This would only impede, if not prevent, responsible action.

Every one of the matters as to which the States would agree under the compact to consider the action recommended by the Commission, either relates to a subject of sole concern to the individual State or to a subject beyond the power of the Great Lakes States to deal with individually or collectively.

  .   .   .   .

The power authority, in carrying out the duties imposed on it, has to deal with all of these agencies and many others besides. In particular, the authority must work closely with its partners on the St. Lawrence, the Hydroelectric Power Commission of Ontario, with the St. Lawrence Seaway Development Corporation, and with its Canadian counterpart. It is possible to do this because each of these agencies has fairly well defined responsibilities, and there is a minimum of overlapping. But a congressionally approved Great Lakes Commission would have no clear purpose and would trespass on the responsibilities of others at every turn.[81]

The Power Authority was particularly concerned about Chicago's water diversion demands, calling Congress's attention to the fact that all of the Great Lakes states' "responsible officers" had joined in opposition to Illinois's legislative efforts in 1958. But it pointed out, "New York State cannot count on the continuance of such unity of purpose. It and the Power Authority have interests diverse from those of the other Great Lakes States."[82]

When questioned as to whether the Power Authority had ever had meetings or dealings with the Great Lakes Commission, Davison stated the authority had played no part in any meetings of the present commission and in fact had bypassed it to go directly to the attorneys general and governors of the states when responsible action had been called for. Certain members of the House Committee on Foreign Affairs, however, were not satisfied with the authority's views and wished to know why the Power Authority went to the trouble to oppose consent if it felt that consent would accomplish nothing additional in the compact's status or powers. Congresswoman Marguerite Stitt Church of Illinois asked:

MRS. CHURCH: Then why are you opposed to it?

MR. DAVISON: Well, we are opposed to it because if congressional consent is given to it, it will give it at least the semblance of some type of authority, as an instrument, which will be listened to in the formulation of policies.

MRS. CHURCH: Then, really, congressional consent would have some meaning rather than no meaning?

MR. DAVISON: It would have meaning—not legally—but it could have actual meaning in the sense that it would more or less strengthen the position of the body. . . . Legally, it wouldn't change the power or the authority of this body one bit from what it is today.

. . . .

MR. VORYS [Ohio]: Since consent is sought under the constitution of this thing, as a compact, then that consent will be assumed to create this as some sort of supergovernment because of its broad powers.

MR. DAVISON: That is right. The consent is only needed where you are going to use it as a political instrument.[83]

The New York Power Authority was joined in opposition by the Buffalo Chamber of Commerce, whose argument was almost identical. It is indeed difficult to disagree with these two agencies in their stand that the Great Lakes Commission "fills no need and performs no function not already more competently covered by other long-established agencies," except—and this is regarded by the compact's proponents as an extremely important exception—that none of the previously existing administrative and regulatory agencies provided a regular forum in which all of the Great Lakes states were represented at all times and in which any Great Lakes proposal or problem could have a hearing and consideration by all of the states at once. The commission as it now stands provides such a possible forum, even though it is powerless to take command of developmental and regulatory proposals which come before it. Whether the commission actually has heretofore had the opportunity to hear about and look at all Great Lakes plans and problems is quite another and most doubtful matter. There is no doubt it will now as a member of the Great Lakes Basin Commission have the opportunity to learn of and even be the initiator of significant plans. As the New York Power Authority suggested, on many matters the Great Lakes Commission was undoubtedly circumvented or ignored by the specialized agencies in taking their operating problems and planning proposals directly to those state and national officials most involved. It is exceedingly unlikely that state bureau and departmental officials ever referred their problems to the Great Lakes Commission, except in instances when wide dissemination of information might be advantageous or special technical assistance might be sought. Officials and bureaus jealously guard their powers. Only if the Great Lakes Commission were authorized to purchase, to build, to finance, to operate, and to regulate specific Great Lakes projects and enterprises would these officials have felt compelled to turn to the Great Lakes Commission. But it is also easy to agree with the Power Authority and the Buffalo Chamber of Commerce that consent provides the commission with one rung of the ladder leading to a status of authority which it may under the imponderable and unpredictable unrolling of future political actions yet attain as a full-fledged interstate regulatory agency and, indeed, even as an international agency. In the latter eventuality it is difficult to see how the agency could retain its status as a state and provincial agency. It would become something superior to and independent of its state creators, thus going beyond their original intent and purposes and making the child superior to the parent. But this is supposition and at the moment no such future seems likely for the Great Lakes Commission.

There is yet a further consideration of more than passing importance to take into account in appraising Congress's decision to acquiesce in creating this or some similar agency. This was well expressed by Senator William Proxmire of Wisconsin in testimony before the Senate subcommittee of the Committee on the Judiciary in 1958:

If the Congress permits the States to develop the means to solve their regional problems it will not be pure generosity on our part. The alternative is to solve them here. That means that committees will sit endless hours fretting with local details. I am sure that is not a prospect that appeals to anybody on this committee. So this is a bill of responsible and sensible decentralization.[84]

The statement expresses an admirable sentiment, but it omits an important additional thought: that Congress is not the only body handling important national and international problems and perhaps existing agencies might well have sufficed to do the tasks without creation of another agency.

Although as early as 1956 the compact's proponents presented Congress with a revised consent measure excluding the Canadian provinces, the original compact which included them was allowed to stand intact, retaining the clauses but with sections added barring the provinces from membership. This was criticized by Senator O'Mahoney in 1958 when he observed that it would be better for Congress to have before it a bill without conditions included, one that omitted any references whatsoever to Canada. This, however, would have entailed the adoption by the compacting states of a new compact, so the expedient of resubmitting the original document with qualifying sections was resorted to. Strong objection to this procedure was voiced by Attorney Murray Preston, counsel for the Great Lakes–St. Lawrence Association:

> The plain fact is that this legislation has been brought up for congressional action prematurely. The "compact" itself, effective since 1955, no longer expresses the present intentions and objectives of the parties signatory according to the testimony placed in the record by the proponents. Specifically, the admission of Ontario and Quebec to membership in the compact is no longer contemplated by any of the parties, although large portions of the compact as it now stands are devoted to this particular subject. Other parts of the legislation now under consideration have never been considered and approved by the legislatures of the parties signatory. . . .
>
> The need for a substantial and important change in the compact itself is evident on the face of the bill. The obvious remedy is to return it to the States and suggest they amend it to reflect all of the changes that are clearly necessary. . . .
>
> The proponents could then offer for congressional consent and approval what Senator O'Mahoney referred to as:
>
> ". . . a clean document, not subject to interpretation by reading this clause or that clause to find out what it meant." [85]

In the intervening years, after having failed to obtain congressional consent on a number of occasions, the compacting states still did not enact a revised compact as suggested and it is exceedingly difficult to understand why they did not. Why retain the old one unless its clauses hold some promise for future restoration of the states' original plan to include Canada? No one has satisfactorily answered this. Obviously there were also dangers in carrying the compact back into state assemblies with the need to rejustify the compact and to explain the reasons for its amendment. Dangers or not, it ought to have been done if for no other reason than to make the developing law of interstate compacts clear and consistent.

The records of congressional action and inaction on the compact reveal that congressional reluctance was based on two prime objections: the questionable international role of such an agency, and doubts as to the future expansion of the Great Lakes Commission. The arrangements as finally approved make of this interstate compact something less than an important development in American state and federal government, considerably short of the hopes of students of the system for new and experimental inventions to make federalism more workable. The international barrier was too great a one for Congress to ignore. Too much of the North American continent is involved for this area and its administration to be confined solely to the custody of the Great Lakes states in policy-determining matters. The interstate and interagency organization which the Water Resources Planning Act's Commission provides holds far more promise as machinery suitable for Stateside Great Lakes Basin planning. Yet even this arrangement lacks Canada as a participant, and it is difficult to see how any truly significant lakes planning can be done without Canada in the picture.

Obviously there is a yet-to-be-developed stage in the evolution of regional government for the Great Lakes Basin. The question is: Will there be a broadening by treaty with Canada of the powers and functions of the International Joint Commission, or will some new international agency be created? In the meantime, it will be worthwhile to watch what happens to the Great Lakes Commission and the interstate compact which created it.

5   *Although geographically compact, this Valley is a region of considerable contrast, exhibiting homogeneity only in the pattern of common drainage and showing little regionalism economically, physically, politically or socially. Within the area are millions of acres of some of the Nation's most productive farmlands, vast quantities of water, large acreages of potentially productive hardwood timberland, billions of tons of coal, large reserves of petroleum, bustling industrial centers, regions of population decline, counties with average income figures among the lowest in the Middle West and cities and towns with chronic problems of unemployment and underemployment.*

"The Wabash Valley: Problems and Opportunities," unpublished paper prepared for the Wabash Valley Interstate Commission, August 1968.

The Wabash Valley Interstate Compact: *A Bi-State Approach to Resource Development*

THE WABASH RIVER VALLEY is a subbasin of the Ohio River Basin. It is not inaccurate to call it Indiana's river, for most of the state is drained by it. Except during this country's earliest days, the streams and waterways of the Wabash have never served as major inland transportation routes. For most of Illinois's and Indiana's statehood the river and it tributaries served the needs of the farmers who until this century dominated the population, the economy, the society of this large segment of the Middle West.

Today, with agriculture of the small-farming type diminishing in national importance as a way of life, the Wabash Valley has been declining in population, productivity, and income. Yet the portion of the continent which it serves contains all of the natural characteristics and advantages deemed most desirable for human occupation, far more physically attractive than some parts more densely populated and blessed with wealth.

In a concerted effort to find the why and the how for reversing the decline of this potentially valuable area, Illinois and Indiana in 1959 entered into an interstate compact to develop jointly and in a coordinated manner the valley and its resources.[1] Identical laws were enacted by the two states, and final approval was given by Congress to Public Law 86–375 on September 23, 1959.[2] The two states' governors gave final approval at a ceremonial signing at Terre Haute, Indiana, on January 25, 1960. According to the Wabash Valley Interstate Commission, the interstate agency created by the compact, the agreement represents "the first attempt [by states] to obtain interstate cooperation for the purpose of developing all of the resources of a river basin."[3]

Purposes of the Compact

The compact's article I defines the framework of policy for the joint operation:

The party states find that the Wabash Valley has suffered from a lack of comprehensive planning for the optimal use of its human and natural resources and that under-utilization and inadequate benefits from its potential wealth are likely to continue until there is proper organization to encourage and facilitate coordinated development of the Wabash Valley as a region and to relate its agricultural, industrial, commercial, recreational, transportation, development and other problems to the opportunities in the Valley. To this end it is the purpose of the party states to recognize and provide for such development and coordination and to establish an agency of the party states with powers sufficient and appropriate to further regional planning for the Valley.

Those persons closest to the compact's operations, and some who were instrumental in securing its enactment, place heavy emphasis upon the phrase "for the optimal use of its human and natural resources" as the central purpose of the agreement. A broad reading of the compact, however, reveals that this is to be a planning operation primarily concentrated on economic planning and development of the area's natural resources rather than on social planning. Since economic development is essential to the improvement of employment and economic opportunity, social advancement of the valley's population is presumably the hoped-for ultimate goal, if not the central or immediate purpose.

While the compact officially underscores the two states' good intentions and mutuality of interest in developing the river basin, it grants no administrative role or authority to the Commission except that of planning, studying, and "coordinating" the plans and studies it makes of the Basin with those made by other agencies. The commission's experiences to date with "coordination" have elevated this activity to first place in commission activities, but with results that can hardly be called successful. Spheres of control and authority, compartmentalized under many other governmental agencies, remain for the actual performance of developmental work and the commission has no power to reach them except by persuasion. This, to date, has been virtually no power at all.

Area Embraced by the Compact

As defined in article II of the compact, the Wabash Valley includes the entire Wabash River watershed: that is, the Wabash River, its tributaries, and all the land area that is drained by these streams. The area involves all or parts of eighty-two counties of Illinois and Indiana, twenty-five of which are in Illinois.[4]

The United States Army Corps of Engineers divides the Wabash Basin into five major subbasins: (1) White River (excluding East Fork), (2) East Fork–White River, (3) Upper Wabash (Tippecanoe and above), (4) Middle Wabash (below Tippecanoe to mouth of the White), and (5) Lower Wabash (mouth of the White to mouth of the Wabash). The waterways of the area range from very small streams to major rivers.[5] Over many years much work has been done in the Basin by the Army Corps of Engineers in flood control and building of reservoirs. The corps' 1930s surveys of the Basin, the "308 Reports for the Wabash," provide the basis for its projects. Today some of the Basin's greatest assets are Army projects completed, under construction, or on the planning boards and approved for action.

Major corps projects include the Mississinewa Reservoir at Logansport, Indiana; Monroe Reservoir, at the confluence of the Ohio and the Wabash; and Lincoln Reservoir, on the Embarrass River in Illinois. Many other small reservoirs and projects have been built or are planned, such as Lake Lemon, at Bloomington, Indiana; Richland Creek, Bloomfield, Indiana; Morse Reservoir, Noblesville, Indiana;

lakes at Shafer, Sarah, and Mattoon, Illinois; Lafayette, Salamonie, Huntington, Mansfield, Cagles Mill, Monroe, Patoka, and Clifty Creek Reservoirs, and others. The traditional corps emphasis is, as always, on flood control and navigation, and overall development with coordinated planning of all natural and other resources is not undertaken by it. Many United States and state agencies are therefore necessarily involved in any developmental arrangements for such an extensive area.

The Wabash River itself starts in Ohio, diagonally crosses Indiana southwestward and turns south near Danville, Illinois, forming a portion of the boundary line between Indiana and Illinois beginning at Terre Haute and thereafter meandering southwestward until it finally empties into the Ohio River between Evansville, Indiana, and Shawneetown, Illinois. The total drainage area which it serves contains 33,100 square miles and approximately 3,250,000 population, an area comprising 68 percent of Indiana and 16 percent of Illinois. Proponents of valley development repeatedly assert that the Basin is economically static or losing ground as evidenced by continued loss of population in 30 of the 82 counties.*

From settlement until the present the area has been one devoted primarily to agricultural and exploitative activities. In all of its urban centers considerable industry, generally small and diversified, exists. But in keeping with steady trends over several decades industrial concentration has tended to seek the larger cities of the nation, and thus only Indianapolis within the valley can be regarded as a center of continuing growth in industrial development. This diminishing energy of the Basin has occurred despite obvious climatic, soil and water, location, natural resources, and population advantages which it holds in superior measure over many other river basins of the country. Such assets as adequate transportation facilities can also be counted as one of the valley's favorable attributes, for the area lies in the pathway of

* Cities of 10,000 population (1960 Census) and over in the Basin are: *Indiana*—Terre Haute, 70,500; Indianapolis, 510,000; Lafayette, 45,500; Logansport, 21,106; Kokomo, 47,197; Anderson, 48,000; Muncie, 69,500; Newcastle, 20,349; Vincennes, 18,046; Washington, 10,486; Bloomington, 31,357; Columbus, 24,782; Bedford, 13,024; Shelbyville, 14,317; Crawfords-ville, 14,231; Frankfort, 15,302; Marion, 37,854; Huntington, 16,185; Wabash, 12,621; Peru, 14,453. *Illinois*—Champaign, 52,000; Urbana, 29,000; Danville, 42,200; Charleston, 10,505. The commission notes: "1,750,000 are urban, 1,250,000 are rural non-farm, and 250,000 are farm persons," *Annual Report*, 1968, p. 3.

both the nation's East-West and North-South commercial movements and has been well equipped with highways and railroads in the past, and has not been neglected by pipelines, air lines, or trucking lines in more recent years. It also enjoys a certain amount of waterway service in the Great Lakes area and on the Ohio River, but greatly expanded development of navigation facilities across the Basin, north-south, is one of the current ambitions of valley promoters, high on the list of planning operations.

This compact seeks greater and more efficient use of the Basin's natural resources: water, soils, forests, wildlife, and minerals. None are regarded as having been altogether adequately or properly developed although all have had development, even overexploitation in some parts of the Basin, while in others very little has been done. Even less of a corrective nature has been accomplished to restore the wastes and losses of depleted resources and concentration on too narrow a range of economic activity. The commission summarizes it as follows:

Widespread flooding, nearly dry channels in late summer and fall, silt laden and polluted streams characterize our water resources; our forests contain poor quality scrub trees, weed trees and trees disfigured and damaged by grazing and fire; marginal and sub-marginal farms operated at a loss to the owner indicate a lack of adequate management of our soil and agricultural water resources.[6]

Aside from soil exhaustion and erosion, and water pollution and misuse, the greatest loss is in the gradual diminution of its petroleum resources which it had in abundant store only a few decades ago but today is losing, as reflected in lowered rates of production and increasing well abandonments.

The Basin area defies easy classification. While it is industralized, it has actually been so to a lesser extent than have some other adjacent areas of the great Middle West industrial complex. Although it is agricultural and potentially rich as such, the soils of the northern part of the Basin are generally far more productive than are those of the southern portions, making a considerable gap in agricultural and labor per capita wealth from north to south. Water resources also, while generally abundant throughout the valley, are found in far greater quantity in the glacially-created northern portion than in the claypan soil areas of the southern parts. Generally speaking it is the southern portion which draws the attention of economic development planners, for it is here that most of the Basin's economic problems can be found, and in higher degree.[7]

A recent study says,

The . . . Basin is best viewed as a region of contrasts—each activity with its own particular regional pattern. The fact that the Basin is so multi-regionalized makes the placement of a reservoir, or a factory, much more important than would otherwise be the case. If the Basin were a single *homogeneous* or *nodal* region, the location of such activities would make far less difference.[8]

Terms of the Compact

The compact's article I defines the law's purpose to be to create "an agency of the party states with powers sufficient and appropriate to further regional planning for the Valley." Article III of the compact thereafter creates an agency for this objective but whether its powers are sufficient and appropriate to accomplish the compact's purposes is by no means evident or certain.

The Wabash Valley Interstate Commission

Responsibility for the work of the interstate agreement rests in a fourteen-member commission, comprised of seven members from each party state chosen according to the laws of their individual states. Illinois law requires six-year terms on a staggered basis, with appointment by the governor without senatorial confirmation. Vacancies are also to be filled by the governor at his discretion for the unfulfilled terms of commissioners, and he holds complete power to remove an appointee before the end of his term.[9] The two states' delegations are therefore "arms of the governors" or, as is likely, independent of any state governmental control to a high degree.

The compact also provides for the appointment of a federal representative if the United States chooses to designate one, but such representatives serve without voting rights in the commission's work.[10] There has been a federal designee since 1961.

Quorum

The commission holds quarterly meetings on the third Thursday of January, April, July, and October. To do business a majority from each state's delegation must be present and binding decisions require concurrence by a majority of each state's delegation, although absent members by written proxy may have their votes cast by attending members of their choice. The commission's By-Laws stipulate, however, that official acts must be made by a majority of members present in person and not merely a proxy. Measures failing to receive the required majority may be ratified within thirty days by the required majority.[11]

Officers

The fourteen commissioners annually choose and elect from among their number a chairman, a vice-chairman, and a treasurer. They are required by law to appoint an executive director for the commission, who also serves as secretary. The executive director and the treasurer must be bonded in an amount determined by the commission.[12]

Duties of the Commission

The mandatory duties of the commission, and the pertinent sections of the compact and commission By-Laws, follow:

1. To report annually to each governor and state legislature the activities and adopted recommendations of the commission. (ART. III(k)). The annual report must also include an audit of the commission's accounts under procedures determined by the By-Laws, (ART. IV(e)), but always by a qualified public accountant (By-Laws, ART. II A(B)). All accounts must be open to public inspection. (Compact, ART. IV(f)).

2. To submit a budget to each state in accordance with applicable state law, recommending the amount or amounts to be appropriated by each of the party states. (ARTS. IV (a) and (b)).

3. To establish a technical advisory committee made up of representatives of the appropriate agencies of each state. Such repre-

sentatives may serve as commissioners if a state's laws allow it. (ART. V(a)). Citizen organization and activity are to be encouraged, and other advisory and technical citizens' committees may be established. These may be comprised of expert and law personnel and representatives of interested private groups and governmental bodies. (ART. V(b)).

4. To establish a seal of the commission. (ART. III(c)).

5. The commission may meet any of its obligations wholly or in part by funds acquired by gifts or donations, but it must specifically set aside any donated funds before incurring an obligation under them. It may incur no other financial obligations prior to state appropriation of funds with which to meet them. (ART. IV(c) and ART. III(h)).

Powers of the Commission

The permissive powers of the Commission, with the pertinent sections of the compact and commission By-Laws, follow:

1. The commission may enact, amend, and rescind By-Laws, Rules, and Regulations. These include auditing and accounting procedures, and procedures for payment of personal expenses and other costs incurred by commissioners. (ARTS. III(j); IV(d), and IV(e)).

2. Sue and be sued. (ART. IIIc).

3. Acquire, hold, and convey real and personal property and any interest therein. (ART. III(i)).

4. Establish and maintain such facilities as may be necessary for the transaction of its business. (ART. III(i)).

5. Accept gifts, donations, or grants (money, equipment, supplies, materials, services) from governments, private institutions, firms, corporations, and private parties, conditional or otherwise. (ART. III(h)).

6. Borrow, accept, or contract for the services of any governmental personnel or agencies, or private persons or companies. (Art. III(g)).

7. Hire and fire personnel without regard to either state's merit system or personnel laws. (Art. III(e)).

8. Establish an employee retirement system, participate in Social Security Old Age and Survivors Insurance, and establish or participate in any other programs of employee benefits appropriate to afford commission employees terms and conditions of employment similar to those of other state employees. (The State of Indiana has provided by law that the commission may by written agreement make its employees eligible to participate in the Public Employees Retirement Fund of that state, or any other program of employee benefits administered by a state agency.) (Art. II(f)).

Research and Advisory Functions of the Commission

Under the broad authority to "promote the balanced development of the Wabash Valley," the commission is vested with a comprehensive research and advisory role which includes but is not limited to the following:

1. Gathering, correlating, and reporting on data significant to each development undertaken.

2. Recommending coordination of state agency studies undertaken independently of the commission, to provide necessary data and information.

3. Publishing its studies and findings and distributing its materials and publications to encourage valley development.

4. Recommending standards to guide local and state zoning and taking such other action as will promote balanced development by encouraging: (a) establishment of industrial parks, (b) creation of reserved stream bank and lake shore areas for recreation and public access to water, (c) preservation of marshes and wildlife preserve areas, (d) afforestation and sustained yield forest management of

submarginal lands, (*e*) protection of scenic values and amenities, and (*f*) other appropriate measures.

5. Preparing in cooperation with appropriate governmental agencies a master plan for the valley, to identify and program the necessary public works.

6. Encouraging tourist traffic and developing facilities for it in cooperative action with governmental agencies.[13]

In its advisory and recommending role, the commission's integrated plans and programs for conservation, development and proper utilization of water, land, and related natural resources may include (but are not limited to):

1. Encouragement of valley land classification for appropriate uses.

2. Cooperation in developing appropriate flood protection plans and necessary construction of protective works and reservoirs.

3. Filling an educative role in developing public awareness of the need for flood plain zoning, and cooperating with member states' agencies and lesser governments in developing standards to implement and apply such zoning in the valley.

4. Gathering information and reviewing the water supply needs of the valley for all water uses, including appropriate sources of suitable water supplies.

5. Encouraging a pattern of land use and resource management which will increase the natural wealth of the valley and promote the welfare of its inhabitants.

6. Analyzing the valley's recreational needs and potentials in cooperation with appropriate agencies and developing a program for maximum use and development of recreational resources.[14]

In correlating its research and developmental activities, the commission is empowered to do independent original research or it can obtain the services of qualified public or private agencies to do it. This includes making contracts for such services and publishing and distributing the resulting reports.[15] It is also charged with making informed recommendations to the executive and legislative bodies of the party states and the federal government and all agencies of such bodies, and it may be assigned additional functions by formal state legislative action.[16]

Illinois has implemented all of the above compact requirements and provisions by authorizing the state's departments, agencies, and officers to cooperate with the commission. Within their own statutory powers they may make contracts with, lend, or furnish the commission with services, materials, and assistance on the matters under the commission's purview.[17]

Congressional Limitations Imposed on the Compact

While the compact as agreed to by Illinois and Indiana was permissive in allowing a federal representative to attend the commission (which, considering the broad spectrum of water planning activities projected, it would necessarily have had to be), the United States Congress expanded compact provisions as follows:

SEC. 2. A Federal representative to the Wabash Valley Interstate Commission shall be appointed by the President, and he shall report to the President either directly or through such agency or official as the President may specify. Such representative shall have no vote on the commission. His compensation shall be in such amount, not in excess of $100 per diem, as the President shall specify, but the total amount of compensation payable in any one calendar year shall not exceed $10,000; *Provided,* That if the Federal representative be an employee of the United States he shall serve without additional compensation; *Provided further,* That a retired military officer or a retired Federal civilian officer or employee may be appointed as such representative, without prejudice to his retired status, and he shall receive compensation as authorized herein in addition to his retired pay or annuity and such additional compensation as may be paid hereunder shall not exceed $12,000 in any one calendar year. The Federal representative shall be entitled to travel expenses, he shall also be provided with office space, stenographic service, and other necessary administrative services. The compensation of the Federal representative shall be paid from available appropriations for the White House Office or from funds available to the President in connection with special projects. Travel expenses, office space, stenographic, and administrative services shall be paid from any available appropriations selected by the head of such agency or agencies as may be designated by the President to provide such expenses.[18]

It is clear that this provision allows a much closer relationship of the Wabash Valley Interstate Commission with the United States government, its agencies, and the Congress than is provided in the Bi-State Development Compact of Illinois and Missouri. Much of course depends on the person appointed to this position. But the more involved role of the federal government emphasizes the basin-wide nature of the efforts being undertaken by Illinois and Indiana, concerned as they are with a navigable stream and its uses which under the United States Constitution are subject to federal control if the United States government chooses to assert its rights.*

Congress also requires the WVIC to make an annual report to it not later than sixty days after the beginning of each regular session.[19] And it has reserved its rights and jurisdiction over the waters and watersheds subject to the compact, requiring any additional concurrent legislation of Indiana and Illinois to be submitted to Congress for approval before it becomes effective. Specific mention is made of the United States government's interest in any activities which may impinge on antitrust and antimonopolistic laws, and congressional committees may require the commission to disclose and provide such information and data as the committees may require.[20] All such provisions definitely provide a considerable measure of public protection of the national interest that is not altogether afforded by the Illinois-Missouri Bi-State Development Compact.

---

* The Bi-State Development Agency of Missouri and Illinois has a narrower geographic sphere in which to operate and is, essentially, concerned with local governmental affairs. It, however, can by no means be regarded as immune to or independent of Federal oversight or control, for it also is engaged in developmental activities which involve a major navigable stream and interstate commerce. Yet no such administrative link between the federal and member state governments, and the Bi-State Agency, exists.

Organization and Conduct of Business of the Commission

The officers of the Wabash Valley Interstate Commission are elected annually with terms of office normally for one year, but service may be until an officer's successor has been elected and qualified. Only the chairmanship must be rotated annually between the two member states.[21]

The Chairman

The chairman presides at all commission meetings and at all Executive Committee meetings. He appoints members of all standing and special committees, with the exception of the Executive Committee.[22] *The Vice-Chairman* performs the duties of the chairman in his absence or disability, and succeeds automatically to the chairmanship for the unexpired term of a chairman who dies or resigns. With vacancies in both the chairmanship and the vice-chairmanship, the By-Laws provide that the immediate past chairman shall become the *Acting Chairman*, performing the regular duties of the chairman until the position has been filled by the commission at a special election.[23]

Treasurer

Before qualifying for his duties as treasurer, this official must be bonded in the amount of $50,000 (as also are the chairman and the executive director/secretary of the commission). He has custody of all commission funds, is under general commission supervision, and must perform any other duties the commission assigns to him. He can be required to give additional bonds with sufficient surety whenever the commission requires it by amendment of the By-Laws.[24]

Executive Director/Secretary

The compact requires the commission to appoint an executive director to head its administrative staff and specifically designates him to be secretary of the agency. The commission determines his qualifications, selects, appoints, and removes him, and sets his compensation.[25] At the first organizational meeting of the commission on January 25, 1960, the commission resolved to seek assistance of the six leading universities in the Wabash Basin to find a qualified man. A Committee on Budget and Staff was named for the task, and the present incumbent was chosen from a number of candidates. He is, to date, the only person to have held the office.[26]

Compensation for the position was originally set at $14,500, with "reasonable travel and expenses." Differences in Illinois and Indiana practices on such matters for their state employees required an early commission compromise.[27]

The director's duties are the usual ones of administrative officers of public agencies, with certain differences. Customary are the administration of the commission's general regular operations such as keeping custody of the commission's seal and affixing it to documents as directed by the chairman, recommending hiring and dismissal of employees, making interim appointments pending final commission approval, supervising the headquarters office, preparing annual reports for commission approval, preparing the commission's budget, and keeping financial records as directed by the treasurer. As commission secretary, his duties are the customary ones of such officers. If authorized by the commission he may name and appoint other officers, consultants, and employees as needed, designating duties, tenure, and compensation.[28]

The director's most important function, however, is that of maintaining liaison with the advisory or technical committees, if any, and the various governmental agencies, private associations, and universities in the coordinating activities of the commission. He may on his own initiative find and develop sources of information and make recommendations to the commission on all matters which he believes of significance to the commission's work. He may engage in research activities on projects approved by the commission, and a major part of his time has been spent in this throughout the present incumbent's tenure. His is a creative role, for the work of the commission rests chiefly on him alone between the quarterly meetings of the board. The commission's successes and achievements will to large extent be determined by the initiative, energy, interest, and responsibility of the man who holds the office. His general position is somewhat analagous to that of a lobbyist, with the exception of his research role.

Other Staff

At present writing the headquarters staff of the commission consists of the executive director, one secretary-stenographer, one stenographer-typist, and temporary or part-time research consultants on a contractual or informal agreement basis.

The Executive Committee conducts the commission's policy-making operations between its quarterly meetings. The committee is the executive director's chief source of advice, and works with him in preparing and coordinating the annual reports and budgetary requests. The committee's acts are not binding unless authorized by commission resolution and after approval by majority vote. If, however, there is unanimous agreement of the committee to act in some manner, it may do so without a resolution.[29] The committee consists of one commissioner from each member state designated by his state's full delegation, the chairman of the commission, the vice-chairman, and the immediate past chairman.[30]

The By-Laws require a *Committee on Audit* which consists of two members from each state delegation appointed by the chairman. It is charged with the audit of commission books and accounts.[31]

Under the compact the commission holds broad power to adopt its own internal organization, bylaws, rules and regulations. In addition to the two standing committees named above, various temporary committees have been named from time to time. Standing committees, with their membership indicated for particular dates, give some suggestion of commission efforts to provide bistate representation:

COMMITTEES OF THE WABASH VALLEY INTERSTATE
COMMISSION AND THEIR COMPOSITION

Finance (As of July 21, 1960):
Mrs. C. B. Baldwin, Montezuma, Ind., chairman
Mr. Charles Hedde, Lawrenceville, Ill., treasurer
Dr. C. J. Montgomery, Charleston, Ill.
Mr. Rabb Emison, Vincennes, Ind.

Audit (As of October 20, 1960):
Mr. E. Earl Allen, Palestine, Ill., chairman
Mr. Herschel S. Green, W. York, Ill.

Mr. Carlos A. Life, Peru, Ind.
Mr. John C. Siegesmund, Indianapolis, Ind.

Executive Committee (As of January 19, 1961):
Mr. Thomas Mumford, Griffin, Ind., chairman, WVIC
Mr. Rabb Emison, Vincennes, Ind.
Dr. D. W. Morris, Carbondale, Ill., vice-chairman, WVIC
Dr. C. J. Montgomery, Charleston, Ill.

The Technical Advisory Committee

As stated previously, the compact delineates for the commission a wide range of activities in the planning and developmental work of the Wabash Valley. The compact further requires the commission to establish a Technical Advisory Committee, to be composed of representatives from agencies and departments of the member states whose work is related to the work of the commission.[32] Through its By-Laws the commission has stipulated that this committee shall be composed of one representative from each of the member states' agencies and departments concerned with Wabash Valley matters, plus one representative from each of the federal agencies or departments likewise interested.[33] Thus, the original organization for the WVIC, which existed until 1962, consisted of the fourteen-member Board of Commissioners, the executive director, and the Technical Advisory Committee (whose 1966 composition follows):

WABASH VALLEY INTERSTATE COMMISSION
TECHNICAL ADVISORY COMMITTEE

Illinois Department of Conservation	William T. Lodge
Eastern Illinois University	Dr. Dalias Price
Dept. of Public Works & Buildings (Div. of Highways—Illinois)	R. H. Bartelsmeyer
Dept. of Registration & Education (Div. of Industrial Planning and Development—Illinois)	Victor de Grazia
Southern Illinois University	Dr. Robert A. Harper
Dept. of Public Health (Illinois)	Richard S. Nelle

University of Illinois	Harold W. Hannah
Dept. of Registration & Education (Water Survey Div.—Illinois)	William C. Ackermann
Dept. of Public Works & Buildings (Div. of Waterways—Illinois)	Thomas B. Casey
Dept. of Mines and Minerals (Illinois)	George R. Lane
Ball State Teachers College (Indiana)	J. C. Wagner
Indiana Dept. of Commerce	T. W. Schulenberg
Indiana Dept. of Conservation	Charles Bechert
Indiana State Board of Health	Robert W. Heider
State Highway Department (Indiana)	George M. Foster
Public Service Commission of Indiana	George G. Cline
Purdue University	Dr. Lowell S. Hardin
Indiana Stream Pollution Control Board	B. A. Poole
Indiana State Teachers College	R. W. Holmstedt
Indiana University	Dr. J. Edward Hedges
U.S. Dept. of Agriculture	C. E. Swain
U.S. Dept. of the Interior	Robert W. Burwell

This committee's composition clearly reveals the complexities involved in any efforts to obtain centralized coordination of planning and developmental efforts of such an area as an entire river basin. It was precisely for this multiple-agency situation that the Wabash Valley Interstate Commission was created: to provide a mechanism for coordinating the planning activities not only of state and federal agencies working alone on single projects and not always under a comprehensive program, but also the efforts of local agencies, both private and public, also in a limited way seeking development of the same resources.

It is apparent that the mere existence of such a Technical Advisory Committee required something more in definitive organization to clarify relationships and roles. By 1962, the commission approved the more elaborate organizational scheme (as shown in the organizational chart), created under the compact's mandate to establish

COMPREHENSIVE PLANNING—WABASH RIVER BASIN
ORGANIZATION

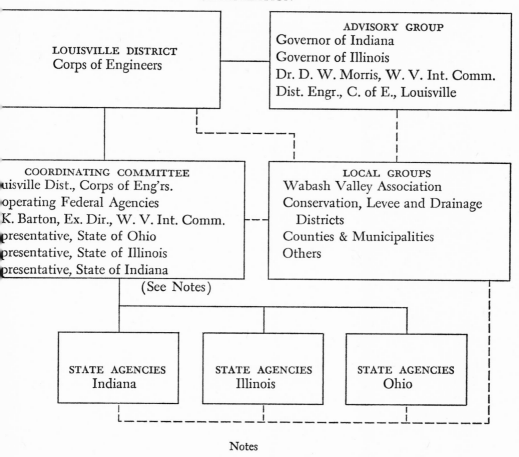

Notes

Each cooperating federal agency to work directly with counterpart state agencies, in its area of responsibility.

Louisville District, Corps of Engineers, to work directly with State agencies having general or overall responsibility for investigation and development of water resources.

Wabash Valley Interstate Commission to work directly with and assist in coordination of work and interests of all affected state agencies in Indiana and Illinois.

Ohio representative to work directly with and assist in coordination of work and interests of all affected agencies in that state, to extent of participation in the program.

"other advisory and technical committees composed of private citizens, expert and lay personnel, representatives of industry, labor, commerce, agriculture, civic associations, and officials of local, state and federal government." [34] It resulted specifically from 1961 and 1962 commission efforts to do a comprehensive survey of the Basin's water and related resources. After a number of meetings in which problems of organization emerged, Governor Welsh of Indiana suggested to Governor Kerner of Illinois the need for basic "policy and steering committees to effectively coordinate the various facets of a study of water and related land resources." He mentioned an "Advisory Committee to determine policy as it might arise in the development of the plan," and offered his suggestion that both governors sit on such a policy committee with the Corps of Engineers and the Wabash Valley Interstate Commission's representative. [35]

At a subsequent conference held in Springfield, Illinois, on May 22, 1962, the purposes of the new organization were explained, as recorded in commission minutes:

Colonel Lewis [Corps of Engineers] . . . indicated that the Advisory Group was proposed in accordance with prior exchange of views with the Governors. This group would provide overall direction and policy. The proposed Coordinating Committee would constitute the working, coordinating staff for the undertaking, patterned generally after a similar organization successfully employed on the Delaware Basin Survey. . . . [He] explained how the Federal Agencies of this committee would work directly with the state agencies in their respective fields of interest. He noted also the proposed direct lines of communications of all organizational elements with local groups, in the interest of optimum public information and local cooperation. . . .

In the ensuing general discussion, the Governors strongly endorsed the contemplated program and indicated general concurrence in the planning and procedures proposed. They suggested that consideration be given to making use of the talents and information available in the Universities of the States, particularly in such areas as economic base and population projections. . . . Mr. Ackermann [Illinois State Water Survey] suggested that favorable consideration be given to the addition of a single representative from each State, . . . to the Coordinating Committee, for more direct representation of State Agencies. Dr. Barton noted that . . . it was recognized that the procedures and results of this program, from the Commission standpoint, would therefore require coordination with planning by other agencies in fields outside of water and water-related resources.

The Governors, Dr. Barton and Colonel Lewis concurred in the proposed composition of the Advisory Group and agreed that it would be considered established as a result of this meeting.[36]

Thereafter a number of meetings were held with various combinations of agencies and personnel to discuss means to accomplish their joint purposes and planning.

The process sketched above has continued as the commission's mode of operations. Conferences of many persons, general meetings, committees, and individual contacts by the executive director with all agencies, states, governments and groups, comprise the machinery through which the commission seeks effectuation of its goals.

Other Committees

From time to time, other committees have been constituted for specialized tasks. A Land Use Committee and an Engineering Committee were authorized in 1961 before the above organization was adopted, with the executive director given discretion to choose the committee membership and time of appointment. Also while groping for a proper organization, the commission created at its April 26, 1962 meeting an Inter-University Committee of one representative from each college or university in the valley, plus Southern Illinois University (which is outside the Basin).

The problem of reaching and getting the fullest use of university research talent in the valley's developmental activities has been a continuing one with only a fair record of success. In late 1965 at a meeting held to consider the establishment of a "consortium" of the valley's universities and colleges, a committee was set up to explore possibilities. In January 1966, representatives from the University of Illinois, Purdue University, Indiana University, Indiana State University, Eastern Illinois University, Southern Illinois University, and Rose Polytechnical Institute met with Irving Fox of Resources for the Future, Inc., who presented his views of university research possibilities and commented on the need for developing new "decision-making structures." Thereafter, continued study was given to "consortium" plans, but it was not until more than a year later that the commission's Inter-University Council came into being with designated personnel from the faculties of each of the above schools under the chairmanship of Dr. Allen Agnew, Director of the Water Resources Research Center of Indiana University.[37] It was hoped that this council could "be extremely helpful in coordinating the research efforts of faculty and graduate students . . . which might be directed to consideration of specific aspects of resource management" in the valley.

While the services of the Water Resources Research Centers at Purdue, the University of Illinois, and Indiana University were available to the commission on all existing and contemplated water research activity of the Wabash Basin, some kind of additional "information bank" of general information and data on the Basin was indicated. Consequently, a River Basin Research Center was established in 1968 at Indiana State University, providing a half-time faculty member as director, and the full services of the University Computer Center for gathering and storing all pertinent information on counties, groups of counties, and subbasins of the Wabash Basin. Water resource data was to remain in the hands of the other research centers.

The problem of proliferation has, of course, not been solved with the creation of additional research centers of the Wabash River Basin Research Center's type. During 1966–67 Eastern Illinois University established an Illinois Regional Office of the Wabash Valley Interstate Commission under the supervision of a field director of the commission, Roger J. Barry. The commission explains,

The office was opened because of the variety of programs affecting the region; a major flood control reservoir, the Lincoln Reservoir; several watersheds; major interests in land stabilization; local interest in developing a national recreation area; extreme concern by the local people over sedimentation. . . . a growing university; increasing agricultural-industrial-municipal interest conflicts; planning commissions in three adjacent counties encompassing the upper reaches of the [Embarrass] river basin; and seven local planning commissions active within a three county area.

This portion of a sub-basin, . . . with its variety of interest groups, each proceeding with its own program, and, frequently, presenting to local governing bodies conflicting recommendations, appeared to be a prime area in which to attempt to weld a unified approach to local participation in the varied programs. . . .

. . . .

In the short period of time of operation of the office significant progress in this matter has been made but coordination of effort and mutual agreement on goals of the various planning groups has not yet been achieved.[38]

The commission's plight in performing its coordinating task is reflected in numerous and frequent comments in its Annual Reports on the need for more coordination—the very thing the commission is supposed to provide. Logic would suggest that creation of additional agencies, directorships, conferences, consortiums, et cetera, ad infinitum is perhaps not the best way to achieve coordination of an already proliferated condition, yet the process goes on.

Referral of all matters by the commission to its Technical Advisory Committee or any of its other committees, cooperating agencies, and the like must be by commission resolution. All reports or recommendations of the various agents and agencies are deemed to be advisory only.[39]

Commission Relations With Other Agencies

Since, apparently, the WVIC's sole reason for being is to provide a mechanism suitable for coordinating interstate and intergroup plans, aims, and actions having to do with the Wabash River Valley and its related areas, close relationships with governmental, research, agricultural, and industrial agencies and groups is therefore synonymous with the commission's purposes. As shown on the preceding early organization chart some of these more important agencies are so interrelated as to be integral parts of the commission's planning structure. Other than the two states involved (today with Ohio as a "party in interest" if not a compact member, three), these most important agents are the United States Army Corps of Engineers; the Wabash Valley Association; conservation, levee and drainage districts; and institutions of higher education. Without question, the two most important agencies in the life of the commission are the Corps of Engineers and the Wabash Valley Association. The latter agency credits itself with having been the medium through which the commission was conceived and brought into existence. No Board of Commissioners of the WVIC through 1967 has been without one or more members of the Wabash Valley Association on its roster.

The Wabash Valley Association

This private association claims attendance at its meetings of over one thousand interested persons. Its exact and active membership is probably somewhat less. It is composed of business, industrial, and professional persons who live in the Basin and are intimately affiliated with some of the Basin's leading enterprises, many of which concern natural resources and the goods and services needed in connection with their exploitation and use. Through certain members the association is also interlinked with the Interstate Oil and Gas Compact.

The association's founder, according to a Mt. Carmel, Illinois, president of that city's chamber of commerce,[40] was J. Roy Dee, an oilman and a member of the Wabash Valley Interstate Commission's board from its beginnings until his death in April 1966. According to the same observer and others, Mr. Dee and the Wabash Valley Association in turn led the drive to found the Wabash Valley Interstate Commission. The association, founded in 1957, was subsequently led by a small group of men whose names later could be found on one or another of all WVIC Boards of Commissioners.[41]

While focused generally on broad development of the Wabash Valley, early efforts of the association concentrated on the flood control and navigability studies made during the 1930s by the Corps of Engineers for the Wabash River. Its interests rapidly broadened. In testimony before a Corps of Engineers hearing on November 8, 1965, Henry J. Wallace of Crossville, Illinois, owner-operator of two oil field service companies and a member of the Wabash Valley Association's board of directors since 1960, testified that the association today has eighty-eight Indiana and Illinois counties in its "development program." He enumerated previous association efforts as including adoption of resolutions on water recreation, pollution, navigation, support for a one-cent Illinois tax on cigarettes for Wabash Valley development, support for a $450,000 United States appropriation for the Wabash Valley, an $80,000 survey for planning, and amendments of Public Law 566 for increasing the size of small watersheds eligible for federal funds, which change Congress made during 1965 (not alone as a result of Wabash Valley Association intervention).

In sketching the purposes of the association Mr. Wallace observed —possibly thus offering one of the paramount reasons for stepped-up interest in Basin developmental matters—"the oil is playing out. Unless new pools can be developed, at lower levels, fewer and fewer operators will remain here." It was the association's belief, he said, that water resources should replace oil as the chief source of economic promotion and development. He urged an all-out effort on all phases of water development. He added, "We [the association] will never cease working until we see the mighty Wabash and all its tributaries, including the Little Wabash, harnessed and put to worthwhile use."

Figures cited by Wallace claimed that the Wabash watershed, larger than 17 of the states, contained 100,000 farms, of which 31,000 are situated in flood plains. Of the 88 counties involved, 32 had fewer people than they had in 1900. None have shown an increase in population in 65 years comparable to the national growth rate of 3 to 5 percent per annum. The Valley contains approximately 3,500,000 persons but its effects, he said, extend to at least 16,000,000 residents of Illinois and Indiana. The area is one of chronic unemployment. In 1958 its farm products sold from 30 to 70 percent below the general average value of $11,708 per farming unit in the two states.

These, then, are the association's purposes: to cultivate within the valley an awareness of a shrinking economy which has rested heretofore on agriculture and petroleum, but which must give quickened attention to the deterioration of these resources and find substitutes for investment and employment, making better use of the Basin's existing resources which have had neglect and scant attention in the past. A "booster" agency similar to many other such groups, its chief purpose is legislative action and influence to obtain support for Corps of Engineers' projects and public financing for other river and watershed developmental works.

The Wabash Valley Compact which Russell Imbler, president of the Mt. Carmel Chamber of Commerce, stated was germinated in Mt. Carmel, came to fruition by the direct efforts of the association. The Terre Haute Chamber of Commerce asserted:

This Compact was conceived and initiated by a public spirited group of citizens from both states, the Wabash Valley Association, guided by J. Roy Dee, President; Hon. Ray Koehler, Vice President; Hon. Chas. H. Schenk, Vice President; Charles Hedde, Secretary; David I. Kay, Treasurer; and the following directors: Mrs. C. B. Baldwin, Hon. John Lewis, Thomas Mumford, Guy McGaughey, Rabb Emison, A. H. Lodge, Earl Allen, Joseph L. Quinn, Jr., George Gettinger, and Hon. Birch E. Bayh, Jr.[42]

The compact, the chamber continued, was drafted with the assistance of the Council of State Governments, a joint committee of the Illinois and Indiana legislatures, and certain others consisting of Herschel S. Green, John W. Lewis, Ray Koehler, Stillman J. Stanard, Latham Castle, Glen D. Palmer, E. A. Rosenstone, Roland R. Cross, Louis Wetmore, and Jerome Finkle, of Illinois; Wesley Malone, Leonard Conrad, W. O. Hughes, Charles Schenk, J. Edward Hedge, Lowell Hardin, B. A. Poole, Robert W. Kellum, Charles Bechert, Paul Brady and William A. Shipler, of Indiana,[43] most of them prominent business and political figures of southern Illinois and Indiana, members of the Wabash Valley Association, and with several intimately associated with the oil industry.

Relationships between the Wabash Valley Association and the compact commission have not only been interlocked through their respective boards of directors; much of the commission's early program was stimulated by the association. Early in 1958 the association invited Indiana University, Purdue University, and the University of Illinois to cooperate in offering guides to the development of the valley. This resulted in the formation of an Inter-University Research Planning Committee which studied the planning problem and submitted a plan for research to the directors of the association. Subsequently the Council on Community Development of the University of Illinois established a Wabash Valley Advisory Committee to aid in mobilizing effective cooperation with other educational institutions in both states, and to serve as a medium through which University of Illinois assistance in study and discussion of valley activities could be channeled. A report by Professor Louis B. Wetmore of the University of Illinois, "Program for Research and Planning," was accepted by the Wabash Valley Interstate Commission as its initial planning guide at one of its earliest meetings, June 17, 1960.

An additional link of the two agencies is maintained through a joint Association-Commission Committee. How satisfactory this has been is not apparent from official records. In fact, virtually no records of its work are contained in records of the WVIC. In 1964, however, the Wabash Valley Association formulated its own program of WVIC appropriation needs, which it expected to promote before federal and state legislative bodies. This program was deemed by some (those best acquainted with Corps of Engineers activities) as being totally out of line with reasonable federal expenditures and capabilities for the Wabash Valley. The program was prepared and used apparently without consultation with the commission's director or the full WVI Commission, and may have resulted in some negative reactions on the part of Congress to the commission's efforts.[44]

The two agencies' close ties are further emphasized by certain gifts of money to the commission by at least one association member. Almost from its beginnings, the commission has received occasional grants of varying size from Mrs. C. B. Baldwin, of Montezuma, Indiana. Her gift of $1,000 in December 1964, was accompanied with the following limitation on its use:

To be used to initiate an inter-institutional organization which may be of mutual benefit to the Commission and those colleges and universities which may participate in obtaining information needed to accomplish truly comprehensive planning in the Wabash Valley.[45]

Acceptance of such gifts is lawful under the compact's article III, and there is nothing in the law which would bar the commissioners themselves from making such donations on a continuing basis. The only obligation the commission must meet, as with all moneys it receives by grant, is that such funds must be set aside by specific action before any obligations may be incurred under them. Gifts or grants must also be for the commission's "purposes and functions," although this encompassing language provides little in the way of restraints and checks. But the commission has received few such gifts from individuals and, indeed, very little in the form of grants of any kind. It has been financed chiefly by appropriations from Illinois and Indiana, although benefits of considerable money value are received in the form of the services of technical and professional personnel who are on the payroll of other public agencies in the two states and who receive no additional compensation for the work they perform for the agency.

The relationships of the WVIC with the United States Army Corps of Engineers, one of the four most important groupings working with the commission, need not be elaborated here in detail for they will become apparent in the descriptions of the commission's actual achievements to date.

Relations With Other Private Groups

Through its intimate contacts with the Wabash Valley Association, the commission has frequent and necessarily close contacts with chambers of commerce, particularly those located in key cities of the area, such as Terre Haute, Indianapolis, Vincennes, Lawrenceville, and Mt. Carmel. The files of the commission contain considerable correspondence with such groups and, as in the case of the commission's efforts to establish George Field (recounted hereafter) as a joint Lawrenceville-Vincennes municipal airport, these groups have been essential to the accomplishment of the commission's purposes and, indeed, may be the chief means by which intercity disagreements may be reconciled, as was the case in the George Field matter.

The commission has ties with other groups in addition to chambers of commerce, although the extent of interaction is impossible to assess from records alone. Early in 1961 the board voted to take formal membership in the Ohio Valley Improvement Association, The Great Lakes States Industrial Development Council, the Wabash Valley Association, the American Forestry Association, and the Mississippi Valley Improvement Association.[46]

Relations With Conservation, Levee, and Drainage Districts

One of the more difficult problems of promotion and coordination for the commission has been with special district groups concerned with soil conservation, levees, drainage, and small watershed stabilization. The commission's first broad program of projects, adopted in 1960–61, emphasized the need for studies of land use, land classification, and conservation of land in the smaller watersheds of the Basin, and noted the need to encourage local groups to organize and actively promote local developments.[47] Studies were therefore launched in cooperation with the appropriate interested governmental agencies.

The effort to locate and describe all levees and drainage districts on which data was then available was undertaken in cooperation with the Indiana Flood Control and Water Resources Commission. Appraisal of soil resources capabilities and their classification was undertaken in cooperation with the Soil Conservation Service, the United States Department of Agriculture, and the University of Illinois's

College of Agriculture. The commission requested and was given the cooperation of the Soil Conservation Service and the Corps of Engineers in a survey of the entire Embarrass River watershed.

This area of the commission's work proved to be the least productive of its efforts in terms of concrete accomplishments, although a "pilot study" of the Embarrass River was successfully brought to fruition. But much of the future improvements of the Embarrass Basin, as well as of most of the other subbasins of the Wabash Valley, will need to be done by soil conservation districts and small watershed improvement groups, and formation of such groups has been very slow indeed.

The commission's 1962 Annual Report states,

Although Soil and Water Conservation Districts are organized in every county in the basin and have existed for 15 to 20 years, farm conservation practices have been applied on only a small percent of the total farm land. Few attempts have been made to develop conservation practices on other than an individual farm basis. Solutions to farm soil and water problems are still being sought with little or no consideration for the downstream effects and still less thought about the upstream causes. Only two watershed projects are proposed for development to control flooding and stabilize the land surface. One of these, the Upper Embarrass Watershed, has just been organized and the application for federal assistance under Public Law 566 was recently approved by Governor Kerner. . . . The other, Scattering Ford Watershed, also in the upper reaches of the basin has reached the final planning stage but it encompasses only 83,000 acres. Thus, only a small portion of this river basin is organized to obtain assistance in controlling water and stabilizing the land surface. Seven watersheds have been defined within the area drained by the Embarrass and each of these watersheds should be developed at the earliest possible date.

In addition to inadequate information on the effects of floods and flood control on municipal water supplies, farms, recreation areas, and industrial lands, the commission found the decision-making process to be handicapped by local apathy, indifference, and faulty or inadequate information. For example, the WVIC was interested in reforestation possibilities as a means of stabilizing land and providing possibilities for a future lumbering industry for the valley, but this encountered great indifference which the commission attributed to the "difficulty often experienced [by landowners in timber production] in marketing harvestable trees." This, the commission continued, arose from the small acreages of woodland under single ownership, the usually small number of harvestable trees in a single sales transaction, the lack of concentration of salable trees within the wooded area, and the relatively low quality of many mature trees. Likewise, exploitation of wildlife resources to develop new economic endeavors was not encouraged even though hunting and sportsmen pressures were strong. Little land for hunting game birds and mammals was available and landowners frequently viewed wildlife on their farms as nuisances because of the attraction of hunters. The commission noted, "most landowners in this basin are not as interested in obtaining income from the wildlife resources as they are in protecting their property from the ravages of a heavy hunting population."

Appraisal in 1960 of soil and water conservation projects revealed that the Wolf Creek Flood Control Reservoir Project on the Upper Embarrass River had been deauthorized; the commission sought to have it restored but was unsuccessful in its effort. Under Public Law 566 the Champaign County Soil Conservation District Board had to cosponsor all watershed projects in Champaign County, and it demonstrated lack of interest. "To date," the commission noted, "the Coles County Soil Conservation District Board has made little effort to promote watershed projects or to encourage further consideration of water development on the Embarrass River."

Attempts were also made during the 1961–62 period, through a conference of Illinois and Indiana Soil Conservation Service officers of the United States Soil Conservation Service, to define administrative procedures on small watersheds which lie across state boundaries. Nothing was accomplished. This abortive effort led Director Barton to recommend to the commission, "There is evidence of gross misunderstanding of the purpose and possible program of action of this Commission. It is apparent that a statement of policy and procedure is needed and should be published in a form which will permit wide distribution."

The successful efforts of the Coles County Soil and Water Conservation District to achieve effective stabilization of approximately 90 percent of the Rattlesnake Creek area through its Agricultural Conservation Program has been extensively publicized by the Wabash Valley Interstate Commission in its continuing efforts to stimulate more of this kind of work.[48] But essentially the task of promoting local interest in and development of such small watershed conservation projects lies with the United States Soil Conservation Service and not with the WVIC. The latter can only seek to provide a link between the Service and other specialized water agencies, as well as contribute its efforts to arouse local interest. It cannot decide, it cannot dictate, it cannot compel use of its services. Hence, accomplishments have been few and this area of its interests continues to be a frustrating one to the commission.

By 1965 the Corps of Engineers had developed a *Plan of Survey, Wabash River Basin,* which the commission both endorsed and criticized but thought fit to publish in its 1965 Annual Report. The following comments are worthy of inclusion:

Progress in land stabilization work in the Wabash Basin is being made but accomplishment in this work must be accelerated.

Both states . . . have appropriated funds to employ an additional watershed planning party in each state yet the work of initiating interest in watershed development is left entirely in the hands of local Soil and Water Conservation District Boards, comprised of five local farmers who have only meager funds available to them for operation of the District.

It is suggested that State Agencies, the Illinois Department of Agriculture and the State Soil Conservation Committee in Indiana, take a more active part in the local promotion of these much needed watershed projects.[49]

The negative nature of soil and water conservation districts in actually opposing developmental efforts is nowhere illustrated more clearly than in the commission's efforts to establish a land stabilization program throughout the valley. It chose to initiate its action in this field through the District Boards and Conservation Committees of the area adjacent to the Lincoln Reservoir of the Embarrass River in Illinois. Together with the boards and committees, the WVIC prepared a report showing the extent and need for stabilization, but the boards and committees revealed what the WVIC termed "a conflict of interest" that was well-nigh irreconcilable: the Lincoln Reservoir was wanted, seen as needed, but the soil and water boards feared loss of agricultural land use, loss of certain stabilization structures built by individual farmers, loss of ownership and control over certain drainage ditches and outlets, and the like. The commission noted, "Although progress is being made, acceleration of this program in this Valley is sorely needed if stabilization of the surface is to be accomplished." [50]

Only an entire reading of the 1965 corps' *Plan of Survey* can give an adequate and clear picture of the situation. The commission's many criticisms of the corps' *Plan* asserted that "under present programs both the opportunities for development and acceleration of project accomplishment depend upon increased nonfederal participation," [51] presumably an expression of the commission's own desire to play a larger part in federal programs which it finds are not moving either at the speed or to the extent that it would like to see.

Interests, Functions and Projects of the Commission

In searching for proper understanding of its assignment under the compact, the commission at its first official meeting, January 19, 1960, adopted this resolution or "statement of understanding:"

In reference to Article VI, functions of the Wabash Valley Compact, Public Law 86–375, 86th Congress, it is the stated policy of the Wabash Valley Commission that the use of the words *cooperating* and *cooperation* as contained therein is to be interpreted as authority for the Commission, and, specifically, its Executive Director, to approach and propose to appropriate agencies, public or private, projects, services, etc., and further to inform, contact and testify before related governmental legislative, administrative and judicial bodies or persons, or such other reasonable and proper activity as may assist the Commission to meet the responsibilities placed upon it by the Compact.[52]

This delineation of functions anticipates a promotional and lobbying role for the commission that is not altogether clear in the compact's mandate, and because of the public rather than private nature of the commission, stimulated the board to claim and clarify such a role for itself, as stated in the Resolution.

At its July 21, 1960 meeting, the commission again sought definition by approving the following statement as a preface to the commission's budget requests:

It is the unanimous opinion of the members of the Wabash Valley Interstate Commission that its major function is to coordinate the programs of all action groups engaged in solving the problems of control, management and development of all resources in the Wabash Valley and its tributaries; and furthermore, since the cost of coordination by the Wabash Valley Interstate Commission will be a relatively small percentage of the total cost of all the work which will be accomplished, the Commission members unanimously recommend that appropriations by the States of Illinois and Indiana to the Commission continue to be on an equal basis.[53]

Here the commission seems to view its role as essentially administrative. That is, its coordinative assignment is considered to be an "action function" of the entire process of administering problems of control, management, and development of Wabash Valley resources. This view, whether warranted or not by the commission, has not been held by all the other public special function agencies with which it has to work, for the commission has no authority in its hands to compel acquiescence to its coordinating efforts. It is not surprising that the commission has encountered suspicion and doubts, for coordination is a very broad and indefinite term in the language of management. Priorities inevitably must be established, roles assigned, modes of operation chosen, and subjects for action designated. All of this is the essence of top management and policy. It is bound to run head-on into the established agencies' power spheres. A liaison role, divorced from planning, might be successful, but liaison alone is not the role desired by the WVIC.

Further, the commission's 1961–63 budget request again expressed the commission's views of its functions as follows:

The Wabash Valley Interstate Commission is charged with the responsibility for formulating a regional plan under which uneconomical land use may be diverted to profitable usage and wasted resources efficiently and effectively utilized. Management of water through drainage, flood prevention and control, water storage for industrial and municipal use, pollution control; creation of new economic opportunity through additional forest products producers; diversion of submarginal and marginal cropland to profitable usage; these are some of the means through which the people of this area can acquire a healthy economic base.[54]

While the commission does not claim this sweeping catalog of activities as its own, the inference is there that these are powers in which it is extremely interested. This emphasis placed on planning, and the range of matters on which the commission implies it might act, convey an image of ultimate, authoritative action for Wabash River Basin economic and natural resources development, with the WVIC as central to the whole.

Yet another interpretation is that of the first chairman of the commission, Thomas Mumford, in a 1960 memorandum to the chiefs of the highway departments of Illinois and Indiana:

Under the provisions of a Compact entered into between the States of Indiana and Illinois, and ratified by the Congress . . . , the Wabash Valley Interstate Commission is charged with certain responsibilities relating to the coordination of various types of planning and development . . . in the Wabash River Valley. The legislative act creating the Commission is quite broad in its concept and will necessarily have to be quite broad in its application, but one of its primary functions is that of maintaining working relationships among corporations, individuals, governmental agencies and other parties which are active in the valley or contemplate activity therein.[55]

As seen by Mr. Mumford, the commission's role of coordination is conceived to be a kind of steering, expediting, liaison mission between and among private and public agencies and interests, implying both a policy-influencing and arbitrational role.

None of these statements reflect active expansionist desires of the commission, but are, rather, expressive of the difficulty of interpreting the compact's mandate of purpose. Presumably, the commission must do something; what it must do, and how it must do it, are not defined in the law with precision, and very little or no power is granted to carry through to completion whatever it undertakes — except in its research activities.

Much of the efforts of the commission and its executive director in the first few years of the commission's life were spent in trying to arrive at clear understandings of its mission. By 1965 a fairly condensed and digested view, if not altogether a definitive one, was detailed in the commission publication, *Regional Planning For The Wabash Valley*. This was compiled by a commission subcommittee as a result of the Corps of Engineers' initiation of the previously mentioned comprehensive survey of the Wabash Valley which was later contained in the WVIC's 1965 annual report. The commission's subcommittee stated,

The initiation of the comprehensive survey by the Corps of Engineers makes it imperative that the Wabash Valley Interstate Commission determine as quickly as possible   (a) in terms as definitive as possible, all those things which need to be studied and investigated to produce a comprehensive regional plan,   (b) those things which are being investigated under the current study,   (c) the means for research and investigation on those items not included in the present study,   (d) the mechanism for seeing that all investigations are coordinated in some fashion, (e) its own time-table and outline of procedure in producing a final comprehensive regional master plan into which will be fitted all the investigations it has been able to foster.[56]

Clearly evident in this statement of the commission's duty is the commission's own awareness of its limitations: the shortcomings of its definitions, the need to appraise its own knowledge of valley needs and accomplished activities, the need for a mechanism for coordination "in some fashion" yet to be discovered, and a procedure for producing a master plan which will include such of its own and others' contributions to the extent that "it has been able to foster" them.

The appraisal thus undertaken revealed the following federal agencies as currently working on valley natural resources matters and individually operating under some kind of programs of varying scope and interest: the Army Corps of Engineers, Louisville District; the Public Health Service; the Fish and Wildlife Service; the Bureau of Outdoor Recreation; the Department of Agriculture and its various bureaus holding water resources assignments; the Bureau of Mines; the Geological Survey; the Federal Power Commission; the Department of Commerce; the Department of the Interior; the Department of Labor; and the Atomic Energy Commission.

While specific statements from the two states' agencies on particular projects were not available, the Illinois agencies concerned were: the Department of Public Works and Buildings; the Department of Registration and Education; the Department of Conservation; Department of Agriculture; Department of Mines and Minerals; and the Department of Public Health. Indiana agencies included: the Flood Control and Water Resources Commission; Department of Conservation; Department of Commerce, Agriculture, Industry, and Public Relations; State Board of Health; State Highway Commission; Industrial Board; Legislative Advisory Commission; Public Service Commission; Real Estate Commission; Water Resources Study Commission. And although it is not a signatory to the compact, the State of Ohio was considered to be involved, with "several" of its departments interested through their work with and relations to the Corps of Engineers, Louisville District, and its projects.

The subcommittee thought the listed agencies were those having a direct and immediate interest in the master plan. However, the "human resources" mentioned in the compact are not a part of the Corps of Engineers' overall authority, even though they are presumably an important part of the compact commission's charge. The commission therefore noted:

> The Corps can undertake only these things which it is competent to undertake and which the law specifies it shall. As we have already pointed out, there are many other things that need to be surveyed to make the planning of the Wabash Basin really comprehensive. Many of these naturally fall outside the scope of the Corps of Engineers or of any other particular agency. For example, other Illinois departments which might be involved are Aeronautics, Labor, and Public Safety. Some of the other commissions or agencies which might be involved are the state Atomic Energy Commission, the American Heritage Commission, Illinois Nature Preserves Commission; the Cities, Villages, and Municipal Problems Commission; the Civil Defense Advisory Council, Community Services Advisory Board, Conservation Advisory Board, the Economic Development Board, Housing Board, Human Relations Commission, Intergovernmental Cooperation Commission, Illinois Legislative Council, Oil and Gas Board, Sanitary Water Board, School Problems Commission, and the Youth Commission. There are many others with responsibilities in the Wabash Valley. If one were to examine all the agencies in Indiana he would find perhaps even a higher proposition that would be involved because so much more of the state of Indiana is included in the Wabash Basin.[57]

The commission added that it was not overlooking many municipal and local agencies.

This is, of course, bureaucracy in the extreme. It is also nothing new to those who have worked with public regulation and control of natural resources in the United States. Excessive decentralization reflects the exaggerated caution and reluctance of American governments to do anything at all about matters so intimately involving private property and other rights of an economic nature, even though the public weal may demand it. The atomization of function results in narrowness of view, limited courses of action, spotty and piecemeal performance, futility and stalemate. The above listing is depressing enough, but one cannot omit mention that the Wabash Valley Interstate Commission itself is a bureaucratic creation to overcome bureaus' and bureaucratic shortcomings, as are many of the other agencies in the above roster.

Yet there is more. In answer to its question "What Coordinating Bodies Are Now Functioning?" (in Wabash Basin matters), it named the proposed United States Water Resources Council; the federal representative of the Wabash Valley Interstate Commission; the advisory group or committee of the Wabash Valley consisting of the governors of the two states, the district engineer of the corps, and a representative of the WVIC; the coordinating committee, consisting of "representatives from each cooperating federal agency, . . . and including the executive director of the Wabash Valley Interstate Commission"; and the WVIC itself.[58] With the exception of the federal Water Resources Council, these "coordinating bodies" are creations of the coordinating agency, the WVIC. Thus Parkinson's Law is again confirmed in all of its implications.

Notwithstanding all of this the commission persisted and sought to identify what it should do to meet its charge summarized in fourteen items which it indicated were "some of the responsibilities" facing it.[59] The summary projected an information-gathering task of monumental proportions for an agency which in 1965 had only one professional staff member and very little in funds for hiring professional assistance. Obviously it was intended for the WVIC to tap the universities for help and possibly stimulate a search for grants from any possible public or private sources. Some improvement in the commission's activities is reflected in the agency's 1968 Annual Report, but the general agency prospect is still one of search for a central purpose, attainable goals, concrete achievements.

The search led the Commission in 1967–68 to employ the firm of Marcou, O'Leary and Associates of Washington, D.C., for an evaluation of its work and aid in shaping its future directions. The result was not encouraging. A discussion of this report appears below in the section devoted to the present study's conclusions about the WVIC.

Promotion of the Lawrenceville-Vincennes Airport and Industrial Park

The Wabash Valley Interstate Commission has no taxing powers. Even though the compact expressly gives the commission power to acquire and convey property, the law does not grant the commission authority to acquire properties and enterprises by issuance of revenue bonds. Clearly, the intent is to establish an agency to encourage others to develop necessary enterprises when indicated by adopted plans.

George Field, a World War II air trainer base in Lawrence

County, Illinois, between Lawrenceville and Vincennes, Indiana, came to the commission's attention sometime during the first year of the commission's life. The agency's records are unclear as to the exact time discussions were begun but it was prior to the commission's October 18, 1961 meeting at which the matter was brought up, revealing that previous discussions had probably been held but not made of record:

> Mr. Emison reported on the proposal to develop the Lawrenceville Airport (George Field) as a Vincennes–Lawrenceville Airport. . . . Mr. Mumford moved and Mr. Allen seconded the motion to instruct the Executive Director to take all steps possible to assist the Vincennes-Lawrenceville group to enable the development of the airport at George Field as a cooperative project of the two cities for the purpose of providing a municipal airport jointly supported by the two cities.[60]

Although the origins of the proposal are unclear, the commission endorsed the proposed efforts and thereafter lent its support and services to establishment of this enterprise, which required adoption of suitable laws by both states before it could be accomplished.

George Field contained a tract of 3,067 acres; with four 5,200-foot runways, 13,400 feet of taxi strips, and over 2½ million square feet of concrete parking space, this Army air facility was one of the largest in Illinois. It was developed at a cost to the nation of $8,784,-940.14 during World War II, and provided physical facilities for a permanent installation of 10,000 persons, with a self-contained water and sewer system, and gas and electric transmission lines.

The entire property was acquired by the city of Lawrenceville from the War Assets Administration in 1948 under a quitclaim deed granted by the United States. The deed required that all of the property thus transferred to the city be used for improvement and maintenance of the facility as a municipal airport, but the record indicates this requirement was only casually observed, if at all. More than two thousand acres of the land comprising the total installation was cultivable and had been put into operation as farming property under the supervision of a farm manager.[61]

Those persons interested in developing the property for more suitable uses believed it represented a potential economic asset of great worth to the whole area, neglected by the city of Lawrenceville in its handling of the abandoned installation. First, they hoped to establish air accommodations for persons and industries in the lower Wabash Valley, an area served only by Terre Haute and Evansville, Indiana, air facilities through their regularly scheduled flights of commercial airlines. Second, the large acreage of the field, it was urged, warranted development not only of better agricultural use, but also of industry and industrial services. The substantial quantites of both ground and surface water in the George Field area, with small mineral content, was considered to be an attraction for industry, particularly in combination with the water resources of the Embarrass and Wabash Rivers. So, too, were the mineral resources—the coal reserves for possible steam-produced electric power; the petroleum and gas, both produced in exportable quantities, providing possibilities for new discovery and development; and unlimited supplies of sand, gravel, and limestone which could likewise be produced and enjoy "short haul" advantages to centers of both Illinois and Indiana. The area enjoyed good truck and rail transportation facilities, and it had long envisaged and aspired to the development of a navigable channel for the Wabash River (subsequently, the single most important project of the Wabash Valley Interstate Commission). Most encouraging of all, the promoters believed, was the large potential labor supply available to industry if the latter developed as anticipated.

One further factor influenced the promoters. Until the new airport was finally established the cities of Vincennes and Lawrenceville and their surrounding areas were served only by a small, privately owned and operated airport, O'Neill Field, which was not adequate for the operation of common air carriers and was "essentially impossible" to expand.

According to a publication authorized by the Lawrenceville Industrial Development Commission,[62] on July 19, 1961, "a group of Lawrenceville citizens organized the Lawrenceville Development Association Inc." to "broaden the economic base of the Lawrenceville area." It appears that the Wabash Valley Interstate Commission was enlisted in the airport project through the efforts of Commissioner Rabb Emison of Vincennes, and Charles Hedde, of Lawrenceville, who was at that time mayor of the city. Both were also members of the Wabash Valley Association.

In October 1961, Vincennes investigated, with the Indiana Aeronautics Commission, possibilities of developing its own municipal airport, but subsequent plans were not advanced.

On October 31, 1961, a meeting at Vincennes University was

attended by invited representatives of commercial and general aviation, the cities of Vincennes and Lawrenceville, and the States of Illinois and Indiana. Following this, the city of Vincennes established the Vincennes Airport Board, which met with and sought to interest the Knox County Commissioners and the Knox County Council in creating a county airport committee. The Knox County Council declined to respond.[63]

Even though the support of Governors Kerner of Illinois and Welsh of Indiana was enlisted for creation of a regional airport at George Field to be jointly controlled by the two cities, and numerous meetings of interested groups from both communities were held, meetings had to be discontinued during 1962 because of failure to reach agreement, chiefly in regard to ownership of the field. Thereafter acting on a suggestion of the executive director of the WVIC, Mayor Hedde of Lawrenceville appointed a new committee to represent Lawrenceville in negotiations, and on May 14, 1962, substantial agreement was reached. Lawrenceville retained ownership of the field, but agreed to its joint operation with Vincennes. Subsequently ordinances were adopted by the two cities which established George Field as the Lawrenceville-Vincennes Municipal Airport, an interstate operation but termed by its owners a "two-cities port."

Although the Wabash Valley Interstate Commission appears to have played a small part in all of this, it was actually a prime although indirect mover. Besides having two WVIC commissioners actively working in their private capacities for the airport, the WVIC Executive Director was instructed in 1961 by the Commission "to take all steps possible to assist the Vincennes-Lawrenceville group." In October 1962, the commission again instructed the executive director "to work with the appropriate federal, state, and local authorities and agencies in an effort to establish an authority or other managing agency under which George Field can be developed as an area airport, serving and being supported by a bistate region contiguous to George Field." [64]

Before creation of the above-mentioned bistate authority the commission issued its 1963 Annual Report which contained this recommendation:

It is the recommendation of this Commission . . . that: (1) A bi-state authority be created for the purpose of improving, rehabilitating, developing, managing and operating George Field as an airport facility, industrial park and such other economic developmental enterprises as may be found to provide for proper utilization of this tract of land subject to the conditions set forth in the transfer agreement with the War Assets Administration; (2) ownership of George Field be retained by the City of Lawrenceville and the proposed authority have control over the income from the 3,067 acres of land and the facilities thereupon both existing and to be established; (3) all buildings, facilities, improvements, etc., existing or to be constructed on and as a part of George Field, including cultivation of the farm land shall be constructed, improved, managed and operated by the proposed authority; (4) the proposed authority be granted the power to issue revenue bonds in anticipation of income to be received from the development and operation of George Field as an economic enterprise.[65]

To create this proposed bistate authority, it was necessary to obtain enabling legislation from the two states, accomplished in 1963 [66] by the commission's efforts.[67] In accordance with the permissive features of these laws, the two cities established the Lawrenceville-Vincennes Bi-State Airport Authority with an eight-member governing body consisting of four members from each state, six of whom represent the two cities, and two represent Indiana and Illinois.[68]

Anticipating development of the planned industrial park and the area adjacent to the airport, the chambers of commerce of Lawrenceville and Vincennes formed in 1963 the Lawrenceville-Vincennes Area Industrial Corporation, which leased an acreage from the airport authority for creation of the industrial park.[69] By April 1964, the authority had prepared and mailed out an advertising brochure entitled, *Land Yes! Over 500 Acres of Choice Industrial Sites*, which set forth the advantages to industry of locating at the airport's industrial park and suggested that financing assistance could be arranged.

The authority made major repairs to the facility, added new buildings and equipment to provide twenty-four-hour airport service, and persuaded the State of Illinois to open an interchange on United States Highway 50 connecting with the airport access road. By 1966 the Bi-State Authority was ready to petition the Civil Aeronautics Board to grant commercial air service to the airport by Ozark Airlines or Lake Central Airlines, Inc. The petition was prepared by the WVIC which attached to it an extensive analysis of the economic area to be served by the airport, persuasively arguing for recognition of economic need, and the commission subsequently appeared before the CAB's hearing examiner in support of the petition. While the examiner's decision was favorable to the petition, the airport had not been granted the desired services through December 1968.[70]

Development of the Wabash As A Navigable Waterway

The proposed development of the Wabash and some of its tributaries as a navigable waterway was not included as a part of the WVIC's earliest formally adopted program. The agency's headquarters records (other than its minutes) and its annual reports for 1961 and 1962 contain no mention of navigation as one of the commission's major studies. That the matter was one of prime interest to the commission from its very beginnings (or to particular commissioner) is evident in the early introduction in 1961 of the question at commission meetings. The first entry in the agency's minutes regarding this subject is

Consideration of the report on the development of navigation on the Wabash resulted in action by the Commission to refer to the engineering committee the study by Paul D. Cribbins entitled "A Proposed Navigable Waterway for the Wabash and Maumee Rivers." . . .

The Executive Director's report suggested three alternative navigation routes in the Wabash Valley to be considered in preparing an economic study of the impact of waterway development on the Wabash Valley. Commissioner Quinn suggested a fourth; namely, a route through the lower and middle Wabash River with an extension through the Tippecanoe Valley to Lake Michigan.[71]

The entry suggests previous WVIC discussion of the matter and authorization of the executive director to proceed with a report on possibilities.

The study referred to was a doctoral dissertation in civil engineering at Purdue University in May 1959. Its author investigated the engineering problem of constructing such a waterway and estimated its costs, analyzed economic need and probable use of the waterway, and concluded that construction of a Wabash-Maumee Waterway "would produce benefits considerably in excess of the costs." [72] He believed it would heighten the nation's use of coal through stimulation of mining by lowering of freight costs, which inland waterway transportation would make possible. A Wabash waterway, if developed in any of three proposed routes or all of them, would run through the heart of the great coal mining area of Illinois. It would also be accessible to the major petroleum-producing areas of both Indiana and Illinois, but the economic advantages of this were discounted, for, "The refineries at Wood River and East St. Louis, Illinois," he said, "which receive supplies from the Mid-Continent oil fields by pipeline, are not considered likely suppliers to the waterway market because of the strong competitive position of the nearby Chicago market." [73]

Based upon the assumptions of this study, with some modifications and additions of its own, the WVIC formulated a Wabash River navigation project on which it has concentrated great and growing effort without appreciable success to date in bringing it to fruition.

In anticipation of a comprehensive study of the water and related land resources of the Wabash Valley, the WVIC started working with the Corps of Engineers in January 1961. A number of meetings were held with the corps and other federal agencies in the Valley and in Washington, D.C., on the matter, and in March 1962, the corps announced its willingness to expand its flood control studies of the area's rivers into a comprehensive investigation of land and water resources. On May 22, 1962, a large number of interested persons met at a conference in the office of the Illinois governor for discussion of comprehensive planning for the Wabash River Basin, with both governors and representatives from the more important water agencies of the two states present. At this meeting the corps presented its proposed plan of survey. The minutes report the presentation of R. H. Hayes, chief of the Louisville district's engineering division:

Present Corps of Engineers survey investigations in the Wabash River Basin (including White River) have been proceeding for several years with primary objectives of developing a Main Control Plan, with emphasis on flood control but including other purposes where needed and feasible. The scope of investigation includes study of possible navigation development in the lower Wabash and local flood protection projects for urban and rural areas, as well as flood control and multiple-purpose reservoirs.[74]

The corps described "comprehensive planning" as "the determination of needs, the evaluation of resource capabilities and the formulation of a long-range plan of development for all water resources and water-related land resources in the basin." The minutes continued,

It includes consideration of all purposes related to these resources, such as flood control, navigation, water supply, water quality control, soil conservation, recreation, fish and wildlife, and hydro-electric power.[75]

The two governors endorsed the contemplated program of the corps and in the ensuing months the WVIC, working to establish George Field as a two-cities airport, found the proposal for navigation on the Wabash worthy of mention and use as a promotional argument in urging advantages of the hoped-for airport.[76] But with the corps assuming the planning and conduct of the water and land resources survey, the WVIC did little with the matter for the next two years while awaiting the corps' report.

As previously noted, the 1965 Annual Report of the commission was largely given over to a commentary on the Corps of Engineers' 1964 *Plan of Survey, Wabash River Basin,* with the WVIC's criticisms. The corps' study proposal outlined the navigation project as,

The navigation potential of the Wabash River from Terre Haute to the mouth will be studied initially to determine whether prospective economic justification is such as to warrant a survey scope investigation. . . . Possible furthur navigation investigations extending above Terre Haute will be dependent on the findings of other . . . studies.[77]

In commenting upon this proposal in the Annual Report the commission pointed to a study of freight flow patterns of the Lower Wabash Valley written by Dr. Armin K. Ludwig while a student at the University of Illinois,[78] and observed,

This study illustrates a freight flow through the Valley from the Ohio River to the Great Lakes; any study of a potential navigation channel must recognize this basic movement. There is little expectation that a study of a portion of such a freight lane could illustrate significantly the feasibility of a project extending the full distance of the existing freight flow.

The Commission has proposed an economic impact study to determine not only potential use of a competitive freight carrier but the total regional impact of a navigable waterway.[79]

The commission was not critical of the Army approach, but rather sought to outline the objectives of a study which would supplement the corps' findings. The objectives were included with its comments.

As envisaged by the Wabash Valley Interstate Commission, development of a navigable channel across the Basin could be obtained through five possible projects: (1) a navigation channel from Terre Haute, Indiana to the confluence with the Ohio River; (2) a navigation channel from Lafayette, Indiana to the confluence with the Ohio

River; (3) a navigable Wabash-Maumee waterway connecting Lake Erie at Toledo and the Ohio River; (4) a navigable Wabash River from the mouth to Lafayette, Indiana including an extension connecting with Lake Michigan; or (5) a navigation system combining the proposals in items 3 and 4.[80]

The commission's map of these various suggested routes indicates a total project of great length and potential costliness. The Wabash and the Maumee are excessively winding rivers which would require numerous cutoffs and canals. On the Maumee-Wabash, three canals of many miles in length are projected: (1) in the vicinity of Fort Wayne; (2) between Peru and Logansport, and to some distance west; and (3) between Logansport and beyond Lafayette. On the Tippecanoe–Big Monon Creek extension to Lake Michigan, the channel would be virtually all canal. Canals would be required on the Vermilion in Illinois, near Kankakee, and between the mouth of Sugar Creek and Danville; two rather long canals on the Wabash would be needed between Terre Haute and Vincennes, as well as two more below Mt. Carmel, one of which would be a new, man-made channel to join the Wabash and the Ohio near Mt. Vernon, Indiana. Such construction would, of course, not be all that would be required. Bridges, locks, dams, channel stabilization works, wharfs, and docks, and modifications of existing structures would be needed. (*See map on next page.*) The commission's estimate of certain other of these needs is quoted here:

> Navigation through the Wabash Valley, as proposed, will require large quantities of water or the installation of mechanical lifts at main channel dams. At least one study of a navigation system for this basin has indicated a sparsity of water for adequate operation. Design, construction and operation of those storage sites used for flood control should be analyzed as source areas for needed navigation water.[81]

Other costs would arise from provisions for fish and wildlife conservation, recreational uses, and flood control and drainage.

Following issuance of the corps' report, the WVIC determined its best course to be an economic impact study of the waterway on the Basin's economy. The commission emphasized that it was not making a feasibility study to appraise the waterway's cost, but rather seeking knowledge as to whether economic gains would warrant spending money for a feasibility study. With funds appropriated by the Illinois

Suggested routes for a cross-Wabash Valley waterway.—Courtesy of the Wabash Valley Interstate Commission

and Indiana legislatures, the impact study was placed in the hands of Dr. James E. Lane of Indiana State University, with various aspects of the survey conducted by Dr. Benjamin Moulton of Indiana State; Drs. Joseph Havlicek, Jr., Emerson M. Babb, and Richard C. Haidacker of Purdue University; and Dr. David Christensen of Southern Illinois University. Delays were encountered which included inability to utilize certain university faculty members expert in particular fields because of their previous commitments, delays in receiving responses from other agencies engaged in studies closely associated with the commission's study, and slow and inadequate returns from businesses and industries of the proposed waterway area which had never had the opportunity to use an inland waterway and had no way of knowing what it would do for them or whether it would be useful to them. The commission found that it had to limit the scope and degree of what it was seeking. The 1966 Annual Report observed,

Certain changes in economic and social trends apparently taking place in the Wabash Valley and affecting aspects of this study have raised some questions concerning the validity of some conclusions reached in parts of the study, thus necessitating time consuming reevaluations.[82]

When issued, the study [83] found economic benefits resulting from the proposed waterway by the year 2020 to be:

Agriculture	approximately	$70.0 million per year
Petroleum	approximately	12.5 million per year
Other Industry	approximately	3.0 million per year
Recreation	approximately	5.0 million per year
Total	approximately	90.5 million per year
		(by A.D. 2020)

Anticipating generation of both upbound and downbound volumes of traffic, the WVIC recommended some ambitious changes which would make the project costlier:

Considering the magnitude of the total benefits to the area, it is recommended that future study of the waterway be directed toward providing a facility comparable to the Ohio River lock capacities adequate to handle tows which now move through the modernized locks on that river.[84]

The suggested extension to Lake Michigan through eastern and northeastern Illinois, it urged, should be considered for improvement to meet the capacities projected above. Other recommendations were made.

Candor compelled recognition of certain potential disadvantages which the waterway might bring, stated as follows:

Among potential disadvantages to segments of the economy which may accrue to the development of water transportation in the Valley are the potential effects upon other freight carriers. Some railroads and exempt motor carriers may experience diminished growth in freight volume carried or, perhaps, an actual loss. This may result in some reduced service which could affect other than those shippers whose freight is diverted to water movement. Although the effect of the waterway probably will not force abandonment of railroad main lines, it may hasten discontinuance of service of some marginal branch line operations. This, of course, would affect employment and produce some reduction in the value of assessable property in those governmental units from which rail line property would be removed.[85]

It also found an appraisal of benefits to industry difficult, because

Industry does not exist in that area of the Wabash Valley which would be directly affected by the waterway. This statement may be somewhat exaggerated but only four counties in the study area have as much as 1% of the total manufacturing employees in the Basin, while four counties outside the study area, collectively, have 40% of the manufacturing employees.

Second, the industry which exists in this area . . . is not the kind of industry which can profit from barge movement.[86]

Nonetheless, the commission remained confident that the "relatively few millions of dollars in benefits to industry" represented only a small part of future potential valley benefits from such a waterway. And the commission's chairman, Frederic J. A. Beyer, in the WVIC's 1968 report to the governors, stressed,

Further attention must be given to the total impact of the Cross–Wabash Valley Waterway upon the economy of the Valley. An effort must be made to identify the potential for attracting new industries and expanding established industries.[87]

Since this is a long-term ambition of certain interests of the area, the project will continue to be pushed even in the face of indifference and negative factors, including a very negative report on a proposed Lake Erie–Ohio River Canal in the Mahoning River area which the Upper Ohio Valley Association prepared for the United States Board of Engineers for Rivers and Harbors in 1965.[88] As of this writing research continues apace by the WVIC for its own navigation routes to Lakes Michigan and Erie. The commission has not been wholly unsuccessful in its promotional efforts. It was able to obtain resolutions from both states' legislatures in 1967 memorializing Congress to authorize and appropriate funds for a study of a waterway along the lines desired by the WVIC. Congress subsequently authorized the Corps of Engineers to proceed with such a study.[89]

The Proposed Wabash National Wildlife Refuge

In 1963 the commission gave its qualified endorsement to a proposed wildlife refuge to be located in Clay and Vigo Counties, Indiana, on a site of 9,862 acres some five miles southeast of Riley, Indiana, near Splunge Reservoir. The commission desired assurance from the United States Fish and Wildlife Service that the selected site was the best in Indiana for such a refuge. Following a grant of tentative approval, studies were continued by other agencies of more than twenty additional Indiana areas. These were reported to the commission, which formally decided that the Clay-Vigo Counties site was the most satisfactory. Thereupon it began its promotion of the site, announcing that it would seek suitable procedures for land acquisition, project construction, and development.[90]

The proposal ran into considerable opposition, as might be expected from any project requiring purchase of a great amount of land in cultivation or serving other uses. Paul Haas, a landowner and farmer in the area near Riley touched off public controversy with letters to the *Terre Haute Star* and the *Terre Haute Tribune* on January 23, 1964, in which he attacked WVIC Executive Director Barton's right to speak for the United States Bureau of Sports Fisheries and Wildlife on the merits of the Clay-Vigo site, and also charged that Governor Welsh of Indiana had approved the wildlife refuge area without consultation with any of the eighty-six families who would be evicted from their homes by the decision. He stated,

Dr. Barton . . . has . . . used his time to try to promote this refuge throughout our state. . . . He has claimed that the refuge, as proposed, is to be on lowland farmland. The U.S. Government Geological Survey Map shows the lowest point in the refuge to be 533 feet above sea level. The elevation of Terre Haute, for comparison, is 498 feet, or 35 feet lower than is the proposed refuge area.

The site, he said, contained "some of the most valuable farmland in Indiana." [91]

The outcome of the commission's planning and promotional efforts in this project was that the United States Migratory Bird Conservation Commission approved on June 8, 1966, the purchase at a cost of $750,000 of 7,900 acres in Jennings and Jackson Counties, Indiana, for the wildlife refuge.[92] The chosen area is still within the Wabash River Basin, but directly opposite and southeast of the site approved by the WVIC, almost touching the Ohio River in the Wabash Valley's most southeastern portion.

The commission immediately took issue with the decision of the Bureau of Sport Fisheries and Wildlife. "The question," it declared, "where to locate a refuge for migratory waterfowl in the Wabash Valley, has been only partially answered." It pointed out that it had approved the Wabash National Wildlife Refuge project as proposed by the Fish and Wildlife Service, in April 1963, after having had assurances from the Service that the site in Clay and Vigo Counties was the best location for it. The WVIC and the Wildlife Service had considered the Muscatatuck site in Jackson and Jennings Counties, but had eliminated it on the grounds that it would not attract as many migratory ducks and geese as would the Wabash River site in Clay and Vigo.

The commission expressed its intention to pursue the matter further, as follows:

Our migratory waterfowl is an important regional and national resource. A resting and feeding area of the type proposed is required to protect this resource. There still is need for a refuge in Illinois and/or Indiana which will provide protection and feed for those species of waterfowl which semiannually migrate through the Wabash Valley. The Commission believes that the proposed site for development of the Wabash National Wildlife Refuge in Clay and Vigo Counties, Indiana is the best known natural site for this purpose.[93]

As of the present writing, the matter rests as decided in 1966.

Other Projects, Studies and Interests of the Commission

Since most of the developmental proposals of the Wabash Valley Interstate Commission must be obtained through the approval and cooperation of other agencies, and the commission itself has very little funds for independent study, requiring special grants for such studies as it has undertaken, most of the research work preliminary to approval of a plan or project is handled by these other agencies. Some of the current research has been stimulated by the commission's need for an overall survey of the Wabash Basin's water, land, and related resources.

By 1964 the following projects were reported by the commission:

1. The WVIC and the United States Soil Conservation Service: Establishment of a land classification system for the Wabash Valley.

2. The WVIC made a successful request of the United States Secretary of Health, Education and Welfare for a study of water pollution from mine wastes and oil field wastes in the Wabash Valley.

3. The United States Department of the Interior initiated, through several of its bureaus and offices, studies of the recreational needs and potentials of the Basin; it also launched studies of the Basin's mineral resources.

4. Cooperating with the Corps of Engineers in its overall survey of the land and water resources of the Basin were: the United States Department of Agriculture, the Public Health Service, the Fish and Wildlife Services, the Bureau of Mines, the Bureau of Outdoor Recreation, the Geological Survey, the Bureau of Labor Statistics, the United States Department of Commerce, the Coast and Geodetic Survey, the Weather Bureau, and the Bureau of Public Roads.[94]

In addition to its work with all of the above agencies, the commission in the years since its creation has served as a kind of lobby group in appearing before legislative committees of the two states' legislatures and the United States Congress in support of various projects of interest to it. Some of these legislative activities (by no means intended as a complete list, but only as indicative of the kinds of interests the commission has pursued), follow:

1960 Resolution adopted, March 17, 1960, on the location of certain federal and state highways in relation to certain specific highway plans of the commission.

1960 WVIC sought restoration of the Wolf Creek Flood Control Reservoir Project on the Embarrass River.

1961 B. K. Barton appeared before the United States Congress, Committees on Public Works, Appropriations Subcommittees, for approval of funds for Corps of Engineers's projects on the Upper Wabash, Mississinewa, Salamonie, and Huntington Reservoirs.

1961 Support of various budgetary requests of Illinois state agencies for projects of interest to WVIC.

1962 WVIC lent support to the Corps of Engineers for its $275,000 request for completion of its comprehensive flood control plan for the Wabash Basin.

1962 WVIC supported items of interest to it in United States appropriations bills for various federal agencies, especially, the Corps of Engineers:

Rochester-McCleary's Bluff Levee	$ 45,000
Tri-Pond Levee	48,000
Greenfield Bayou Levee	10,000
Levee Unit 5	350,000
Niblack Levee	700,000
West Terre Haute Levee	332,000
Mt. Carmel Flood Wall	75,000
Huntington Reservoir	1,000,000
Mississinewa Reservoir	1,690,000
Salamonie Reservoir	1,800,000
Monroe Reservoir	800,000
Funds for Survey of the Wabash River	200,000
Funds for Survey of the White River	60,000

1963 Promoted legislation in Illinois and Indiana to allow creation of interstate airport authorities.

1963 Action on Senator Hartke's (Ind.) Bill (S. 2280) to create a Wabash Basin Interagency Water Resources Commission (of state and federal agencies and the WVIC).

1964 Promotion of Clay-Vigo Counties Wildlife refuge site.

1965 Support for appropriation by Illinois General Assembly to continue investigation of Embarrass River Basin by Illinois Department of Public Works and Buildings.

1967 Support for the Cross-Wabash Valley Waterway study.

1967 Support before the CAB of Lawrenceville–Vincennes Airport petition for commercial airlines service.

No attempt is made in this study to appraise the effects of this lobbying activity, nor has a thorough investigation of all lobbying activity of the Wabash Valley Interstate Commission been made. Obviously some such activities are necessarily a part of the commission's work, for as a "coordinating" agency that is specifically charged with the advancement of the Basin it must present its case to the various legislative bodies which have to approve and finance projects. (Notable, however, is the fact that the commission thus becomes a support of some weight for certain existing bureaus and agencies of the federal and state governments which have on occasion been seriously attacked by demands for the agencies' abolition or curtailment of services. Such is the United States Army Corps of Engineers as one of the nation's chief water agencies. The corps was seriously criticized by the two Hoover Commissions in the 1940s and 1950s. It has not been without criticism from other students of American national government. When an interstate agency of a public nature such as the Wabash Valley Interstate Commission is enlisted in the corps' behalf, the corps' established and entrenched position becomes even more solidified. Through the years the corps has built itself into its enormously important water role through just such enlistment of "interests." In turn, the corps lends its own support to the interests and agencies which support it.)

Financing of the Wabash Valley Interstate Commission

The commission heretofore has been financed almost wholly by appropriations from Illinois and Indiana. The appropriations received from the two states, since the WVIC's creation are:

1959–61 $ 20,000   ($10,000 from each state)
1961–63   30,000   (15,000   ”   ”   ”)
1963–65   30,000   (15,000   ”   ”   ”)
1965–67   Recommended—$80,549   (Financial statement omitted from Annual Reports.)
1966–68   166,425

Auditing of the commission's accounts has been done to date by the private firm of Sackrider and Connelly, certified public accountants of Terre Haute, Indiana. As mentioned earlier in this study, the commission has received several small grants from a former commissioner, Mrs. C. B. Baldwin. One grant for $490 from an undesignated donor appears in the records for 1962–63, used to assist in payment of costs of publication of the Armin K. Ludwig study, *The*

Transportation Structure of the Lower Wabash Valley. Also, some $60,932.00 in grants and subsidies were recorded for 1965–66, most of which was transferred to the commission from other state funds and earmarked for the WVIC's special study of the water and land resources of the valley with particular attention to the navigational possibilities of the Wabash River system. As stated previously the financing of most of the matters of interest to the commission is done through the various state, federal, and private agencies with which it has to work.

Conclusions

A fair and accurate appraisal of the Wabash Valley Interstate Commission is difficult to make. In many ways it is a new kind of interstate agency and as such deserves the support and credit necessary for it to prove itself and thus make it possible for a firmer judgment of its experimental contributions to be made in the future. That is, as a coordinating agency serving two states in their mutual efforts to achieve common economic developmental goals in a particular geographical area, it is experimental. Even though there are some precedents to assist it in the experiences of previously established interstate agencies of the "inter-agency coordinating commission" type in the federal government which can lend some information and guidance, the WVIC must find its own paths and its own methods to fulfill the mandates of the law creating it. For it is unique.

Today the appeal for creativity in American state government is to be heard from all sides, from many sources, and from all persons who are intimately involved with national and state problems. The United States Congress manifests its own agreement with and willingness to contribute to this demand by its ready approval of interstate compacts designed to heighten and implement interstate cooperation in solving grass-roots problems. Private groups have long operated unofficially (and, thus, narrowly) to accomplish advantageous ends of a piecemeal sort, beneficial primarily to themselves, and requiring circumvention of interstate boundaries rather than seeking and obtaining interstate agreement and mutual assistance. Even the bureaus and agencies of state and national government have chafed under jurisdictional restraints and have wished for means to bridge legal and bureaucratic barriers which block effective action.

In this sense, the Wabash Valley Interstate Commission represents two states' creative efforts to find a suitable mechanism to fill the need. That the experiment to date seems to have accomplished little more than add another agency, to be consulted before any action is taken, to the growing pyramid of governmental bureaus, agencies, and offices of the nation and the two states which are concerned with the Wabash River, its tributaries, and the area it drains, is incontrovertible.

FIRST, the commission's purposes are made of tenuous and intangible stuff. That is, the two functions (possibly three) it has been created to perform—"coordination" and "planning" (and "fact-gathering")—are policy-making attributes, steps in a process, phases of a continuous operation which cannot constructively serve two or more masters or two or more disparate goals. It is a top-level function which cannot be performed properly or dynamically unless it is buttressed on the one hand with a position in the administrative structure which gives it an overview of the whole world it is designed to serve, and, on the other hand is accorded the recognition it needs for confidence to exist that the plans it makes will be carried through to at least some stage of completion. The Wabash Valley Interstate Commission has neither such a position nor any such recognition.

Even as a fact-gathering or research agency it must rely on the findings of other agents or agencies. It can only ask for the crumbs dropped from the planning tables of the various agencies with which it must deal or request a larger piece of the planning pie than it has been getting and hope that it will be forthcoming. It can persuade, it can "needle" and encourage, it can create by its own energy a form of activity by bringing together for meetings and conferences the representatives of all of the many agencies concerned with the same matters with which it is concerned, in the hope that physical contact and mutual interchange will stimulate ideas and the desire and effort to achieve jointly what they are unable to achieve separately. It can inform, if it is large enough, skillful enough, and strong enough to gather facts and information which are unobtainable to those it seeks to inform. If it is properly organized, and can remain uncaptured by special interests seeking to use it, it can express a point of view—hopefully, one that truly reflects the best interests and welfare of the people of the area with which it is involved. In none of this is the

WVIC quite large enough, quite powerful enough, quite purposeful enough to achieve its ends, and it can never on its own initiative carry through to fruition the plans that it makes.

SECOND, if the assumptions underlying the commission's creation are valid and logical, then some instrument of government is needed to develop the Wabash Basin in its entirety and in all of its ramifications. For proper accomplishment of such a vast task, an entirely new level of government would have to be created under the American constitutional system, supplanting the agency structure which now exists. This problem was seen in the congressional efforts which preceded creation of the Tennessee Valley Authority. In the long years of argument, debate, attempted legislation for that river's basin, Congress arrived at a solution. That solution has been a successful one in accomplishing the limited purposes assigned to the authority. No doubt part of its success can be attributed to the fact that it combines most of the elements needing reconciliation and furnishes the means to harness and utilize them. That is, state interests are given expression through the grass-roots organization of the TVA. National interest is recognized through the interstate character of the authority granted to it, and of the national financing which underwrites it. Local interests are enlisted, not opposed or compelled. And private industry has been given a share of the profits. The planning process, we are told, has involved all interests and agents. What has resulted with the TVA has not been a national agency but a regional one. Certainly it is not a state agency. As an agent of a region it accomplishes national, interstate, and local purposes, and to date it has also served private interests far better than they were serving themselves before the TVA came into being.

This study recognizes, however, that a WVA is not what is desired for the Wabash Basin by the states of Illinois and Indiana, and the private groups and persons who seek the Basin's development. Continuation of the present Wabash Valley Interstate Commission for retention of state control over what happens in and to the Basin is desired, and the present agency is the instrument created by the two states to do this. Since this is so, and whether or not it meets the best interests of the entire nation it is clearly apparent that the agency as constituted is an ineffective and limited mechanism imperatively needing the addition of certain strengthening elements: more money, more staff, more access to the sources of governmental power, more power to command.

Superficial examination by the Commission on State Government—Illinois (COSGI), a "Little Hoover Commission"-type group set up in 1966 to survey the state's executive branch activities, revealed WVIC shortcomings. In 1967, then, the WVIC sought an evaluation of its work and professional guidance in determining its future course of action by employing the consulting firm of Marcou, O'Leary and Associates of Washington, D.C. These consultants confirmed the limited COSGI findings and developed a more sophisticated analysis of WVIC limitations. Particularly noteworthy are their following conclusions.

1. The Wabash Valley is too large and has too little physical, social, economic, or political unity to be an appropriate region for comprehensive planning for the development of all human and natural resources.

2. The only unifying factor in the valley is the Wabash River itself; the Commission should devote its energies and resources to this.

3. The commission is inadequately staffed, inadequately financed, and inadequately empowered to perform its duties effectively.[95] With these three basic conclusions the present study emphatically agrees. The consultants noted in more detailed fashion,

The Wabash Valley Interstate Commission was originally organized in response to River-related problems, but its responsibilities were broadened to include other aspects of Valley development. To be susceptible to such a program, a region must have some sort of unity, be of a manageable size, and have some sort of governmental unit responsible for its total area and with powers related to the development program. But one of the clearest conclusions that emerges from analyses of the Wabash Valley is that it is a region only in terms of its surface drainage pattern. In economic terms, it has no particular unity as a focal or a homogeneous area. Indianapolis is by far the largest city but it does not dominate the whole region, which is surrounded by metropolitan centers—Chicago, St. Louis, Louisville, Cincinnati, Dayton, Fort Wayne, and South Bend—all of which include parts of it in their areas of metropolitan influence. The characteristics of agricultural, manufacturing, and other economic activities vary considerably through the area. In political, geological, and probably in social or cultural terms, the Region is similarly varied.

The Wabash River system is the only unifying factor in the Region. Yet the river appears at this time to have little economic or other impact on the Region: it is not an important transportation factor, or a source of electric power, or a substantial influence over land transportation or settlement patterns.

Thus, the only subject of planning for which the Wabash Valley is a logical region is the River itself, and the other aspects of natural and human resource development which are directly related to it.[96]

Logically from these premises it is possible only to arrive at an inevitable answer: expansion of the WVIC. The three alternatives— abolition of the agency as nonessential, continuation on its present inadequate and ineffectual basis, and expansion to bureaucratic standing with power and personnel—offer, actually, only the last choice for it is obvious its partisans will not allow it to be abolished. And herein the Wabash Valley Interstate Compact offers a case study of prime quality for understanding the nature of governmental growth in the American system of government.

The commission itself has not been unaware of the need. As is shown in its 1966 Annual Report in a discussion of reservoir and reservoir area development under the heading of "The Development Agency":

Repeated reference has been made to the state as a financing agent, a planning and development agent, a regulatory agent and as owner in project development. It is, and probably, it must be all of these. This does not, however, preclude assignment of these responsibilities and powers, to some authority which may be created for the specific purpose, having sufficient powers to accomplish efficient planning, development and management of the areas. Coordination of the efforts of various agencies and the different levels of government is not effective without an entity with powers for decision and action.

. . . .

This requires, not a modification of powers and responsibilities of a present entity, but rather a new concept in governmental organization with powers to fund developments of primary benefit to local citizens . . . and with authority to act as a profit making instrument capitalizing the investment of public funds. It must have power to initiate and obtain completion of projects entirely local in nature; to cooperate with federal and state agencies in cost-sharing programs, assuming local obligations as project sponsor when necessary. State and federal technical agencies must be advisory to it and governmental regulatory agencies must have authority within it. It must be governed by a local group; it must not be a part of any state or federal department, yet it must make decisions within a framework plan which insures desirable inter-regional benefits needed from regional development.[97]

Should the States of Illinois and Indiana agree, and should the consent of Congress be obtained to a revised interstate compact remaking the WVIC into the above image, the evolutionary process will have been completed. A new "independent, interstate economic and developmental regulatory agency" will have been born—adding to the "new level of American government" now being created by interstate compacts. No prescription, however, will have been provided for the most troublesome word of all in the above definition—independence.

6

I suggest greater communication between the people in the oil industry and the conservation regulatory agencies and the critics. We should get together and exchange views with the aim of not only eliminating some of our differences, but also developing practical, constructive ways to improve the conservation system, and there is room for improvement. . . .

We are entering an era in which the demands for energy are going to be colossal. Petroleum will be called upon to supply the bulk of these demands for many, many more years. It is imperative that our nation use present petroleum supplies wisely and prudently and discover sufficient additional supplies to meet the huge future demand.

Stanley Learned, vice-chairman of the board, Phillips Petroleum Company, in Petroleum Conservation—The Myths and Realities, (*New York: Matthew Bender & Co., 1968*), *pp. 28–29.*

The Interstate Oil Compact

ILLINOIS IS AN ORIGINAL MEMBER of the Interstate Oil Compact, one of the largest interstate compacts in its number of participating states.[1] Created in 1935 by representatives of the leading oil-producing states following a period of great economic and productive demoralization within the oil industry, it was submitted to the interested states' legislatures for ratification, and was approved by Illinois on July 10, 1935.[2] Congressional consent was granted on August 27, 1935, for a two-year period.[3] It was subsequently extended by Congress three times for such two-year periods; beginning in 1943, extensions were for four-year periods until in September 1967 Congress reverted to the two-year renewal interval, a move that was prompted by a controversial attorney general's report on the oil compact, described further hereafter. Continuation of the two-year practice seemed likely under the terms of the bill introduced by Senator Clinton P. Anderson in 1969.[4]

From the original six states in 1935 (New Mexico, Colorado, Illinois, Kansas, Oklahoma, and Texas), the compact has grown to include thirty member states and four associate states (Georgia, Idaho, Oregon, and Washington), either oil- and gas-producing themselves, conducting promising exploratory activities, or intimately concerned with the production and conservation of oil and gas. Saskatchewan and Alberta, Canada, and Colombia and Venezuela are "official observers," with membership held by the two Canadian provinces on a number of the commission's committees. The United States Departments of Defense and Interior, and the Federal Power Commission are also represented.

In adopting the compact Illinois gave the governor the power to decide when it is in the "best interests" of Illinois to withdraw from the compact, giving sixty days' notice and taking all steps necessary to effectuate the withdrawal.[5] The General Assembly reserved power to decide what laws it will enact, repeal, or amend.[6] In 1963 the governor was given the further power to agree with the compact's other member states to extend the compact each renewal period from September 1, 1963.[7]

Purposes of the Oil Compact

The law's terms closely define and limit the compact's scope as, "The purpose of this compact is to conserve oil and gas by the prevention of physical waste thereof from any cause."[8] This provision confines participating members to cooperative action only in regard to adoption of uniform, recommended conservation laws and practices, but the concepts of petroleum conservation for the avoidance of physical waste embrace an extensive variety of production and handling practices which, if adopted by member states and carried into full effect, result in a comprehensively and closely regulated and controlled producing and refining industry.

Member states agree to enact and enforce state legislation to prevent the waste of oil and gas. The compact contains no authority or power of compulsion. If participating states refuse to enact laws requiring commission-recommended practices there is no means under the compact to compel them to do so. Its sole and only purpose is to establish an advisory, research, and coordinating mechanism to assist the states, the oil industry, and the public in general in promoting the oil conservation program as follows:

The Commission [created by the Compact, as described below] shall have power to recommend the coordination of the exercise of the police powers of the several States within their several jurisdictions to promote the maximum ultimate recovery from the petroleum reserves of said States, and to recommend measures for the maximum ultimate recovery of oil and gas.[9]

The sole authority for carrying on the conservation program rests with the member states.

The compact creates for its proper effectuation an Interstate Oil Compact Commission, composed of the governors of the member states who, in turn, are entitled to appoint one representative to the commission. Some states (as Illinois) also have in addition one "associate" representative. All of the governors' appointed representatives comprise the commission, the duty of which is defined in the compact as,

To make inquiry and ascertain from time to time such methods, practices, circumstances, and conditions as may be disclosed for bringing about conservation and the prevention of physical waste of oil and gas, and at such intervals as said Commission deems beneficial it shall report its findings and recommendations to the several States for adoption or rejection.[10]

The commission maintains official headquarters in Oklahoma City with a full-time secretariat of six persons. It holds today two meetings a year of all participating states—an annual meeting in December and a midyear meeting in June at which information is exchanged on a wide variety of subjects of interest to the oil industry, but all, in the broadest sense, relating to some aspect of oil and gas conservation. The definition of conservation has been a somewhat troublesome one, as described hereafter, but its accepted meaning today is quite broadly construed and flexible to a considerable degree.

As for its financing, the commission reports of itself, "The Commission's activities are financed by voluntary contributions of the various member states. No money is accepted from any individual, oil or gas company, or trade association. There is full cooperation between the industry and the Commission, but its finances are absolutely controlled by the member state governments. No advertising is permitted in any of the publications of the Commission." [11] Although no member state is financially obligated by being a member of the compact, the commission's Executive Committee formulates an annual budget and determines each member state's portion of the necessary moneys, based on the proportion to total national production of the oil produced in each state. Since 1962 Illinois has appropriated $7,000 per annum for this purpose; all sums thus appropriated are allocated to the Oil and Gas Division of the Department of Mines and Minerals which pays the Illinois portion to the commission's headquarters office in Oklahoma City. The Illinois appropriation is audited annually by the state.

Administration of the Compact in Illinois

Illinois since 1935 has occupied a place as sixth- to ninth-largest oil-producing state in the nation, and fourth- or fifth-largest oil-refining state, and has been a party to the compact throughout this period. It has not, however, always acceded to compact recommendations on conservation laws, although the state's present statutes more closely conform than did those under which it operated prior to 1951. Its history of nonconformity is long and turbulent, carrying in its wake animosities which linger within the state as well as among some of the original compacting states. Today with the condition of its production advancing only slowly and manifesting many signs of diminution, there has been more willingness on the part of the producing elements who have dominated the Illinois legislative picture to accept commission-recommended conservation practices although they still remain adamant on some practices which fall short of the ideal.

Legally, the compact creates a "commission of governors of states." Actually, the active work of the compact is carried on by the governors' designated representatives, although the national commission chairmanship rotates among the member states' governors.

Representation on the Commission

Illinois has one official representative on the commission appointed by the governor, and one associate member. No qualifications for the representative are stipulated in the statutes. The present Illinois member is Lloyd A. Harris of Mattoon, a long-time independent operator in the oil industry. His immediate predecessor, Guy E. McGaughey, Sr., of Lawrenceville, is an oil attorney who served as compact commission representative under three governors, beginning in

1937 under Governor Horner, with reappointment subsequently by Governors Stevenson and Kerner.[12] As have the other originating states, Illinois has tended repeatedly to utilize men active in the compact's formative years in compact committee and other assignments. Over the thirty-year life of the compact this practice probably has contributed to the attitudes held by some of the compact's recent critics who charge it and the oil industry with imperviousness to change and obsolescence, a somewhat exaggerated accusation but one which has greatly disturbed the industry and roused strenuous action in denial and self-defense in the past several years.

Compensation

The Illinois Commission representative receives no pay or compensation from the state for his expenses and services on the commission. Neither does the associate member, although the present holder of the latter position is also the state's chief petroleum engineer and as such receives compensation for his expenses while traveling on official state business, which includes attendance at compact commission meetings. His salary as an employee of the state covers his services and time devoted to commission activities, whatever they may be.

Duties

As a member of the compact commission the Illinois representative is responsible for promoting and defending the purposes of the compact within the state; that is, in keeping informed on existing or proposed legislation concerning oil and gas, and on existing or proposed production methods which may not be in accord with the compact's expressed purposes or with recommended conservational activities; in expressing the policies of the compact commission to the governor and administrative agencies of the state; through informing and consulting with oil industry members on any matters having to do with oil and gas conservation practices; and in gathering and reporting pertinent information on Illinois production for transmittal to the compact commission and dissemination to the industry and compact member states. He represents the State and its oil industry at commission meetings, and at all times in connection with commission business. He occupies a position within the commission itself that is modified by the commission committees to which he may be appointed.

The Illinois associate representative (as chief of the State Oil and Gas Division) works closely with the director of the Department of Mines and Minerals which is charged by law with the enforcement of the state's oil and gas conservation laws. Under Illinois statutes, whoever serves as the compact representative may utilize the Oil and Gas Board and the Oil and Gas Division for "advice and consultation." [13] The other administrative agency most immediately concerned with regulation and enforcement of Illinois oil production laws is the State Geological Survey, which is charged with providing technical information to the State Mining Board and Oil and Gas Division at their request, and also fulfills certain other duties in connection with the regulation of oil and gas production,[14] such as mapping; filing and studying logs and core cuttings of wells drilled in the state; studying new technology in oil recovery, and the like.

The close relationship of the Illinois compact representative to the state's regulatory agencies is heightened by the presence on the compact commission's various committees of certain nonofficial Illinois members. Thus the State Geological Survey, the Oil and Gas Advisory Board, and the Department of Mines and Minerals are all represented on commission committees. One present member is also a member of the Wabash Valley Interstate Commission. The result is a substantial interlocking of official state agencies with the compact commission and its member oil-producing states and, in turn, through the other nonofficial Illinois members on commission committees with the oil industry itself. (See table 3 of 1969 Illinois membership on Compact Commission committees.)

Committees

The policies of the Interstate Oil Compact are determined within its various standing committees which for the most part have large memberships, frequently with more than one appointee representing each member state. Illinois, today, is represented on all committees and holds the vice-chairmanship of one (the 1969 Research Committee). Actions taken by these committees may be brought before the compact's full membership at its two regular annual meetings, but

3. ILLINOIS MEMBERS OF THE INTERSTATE OIL COMPACT COMMISSION'S COMMITTEES (1969)

Name	Role in Compact Commission	Official state position
* Lloyd A. Harris, Mattoon	1) Ill. representative, Compact Commission 2) Executive Committee 3) Finance & Publications Committee 4) Resolutions Committee	
George R. Lane, Springfield	1) Associate Ill. member, Compact Commission 2) Finance & Publications Committee 3) Regulatory Practices Committee 4) Resolutions Committee	Chief Engineer, Oil and Gas Division, Dept. of Mines & Minerals
C. E. Brehm, Mt. Vernon	Energy Resources Committee	
Harry C. Temple, Salem	Energy Resources Committee	Member, Oil and Gas Advisory Board
H. L. Murray, Salem	Energy Resources Committee	Member, Oil and Gas Advisory Board
R. W. Kuzmich, Mt. Carmel	Engineering Committee	
Richard F. Mast, Urbana	Engineering Committee	State Geological Survey
Joe McGuire, Mt. Carmel	Engineering Committee	
Jerry J. Wasicek, Olney	Engineering Committee	Member, Oil and Gas Advisory Board
C. Richard Turnbow, Robinson	Legal Committee	
Geo. W. Woodcock, Mt. Carmel	Legal Committee	

Name	Role in Compact Commission	Official state position
Clarence T. Smith, Flora	Legal Committee	Former IOCC official representative
Guy E. McGaughey, Lawrenceville	Legal Committee	Former IOCC official representative
C. Richard Collins, Mt. Vernon	Public Lands Committee	
Charles J. Pardee, Mt. Vernon	Public Lands Committee	
Walter B. Price, Mt. Vernon	Public Lands Committee	
Marion D. Oglesby, Springfield	Regulatory Practices Committee	Illinois Governor's Office
Donald C. Bond, Urbana	Research Committee	State Geological Survey
Bill G. Harmon, Carmi	Research Committee	
Bernard Podolsky, Fairfield	Research Committee	Member, Oil and Gas Advisory Board
N. A. Baldridge, Ashley	Secondary Recovery and Pressure Maintenance Committee	
T. W. George, Mt. Carmel	Secondary Recovery and Pressure Maintenance Committee	
Charles B. Rafferty, Mt. Carmel	Secondary Recovery and Pressure Maintenance Committee	
Joseph A. Dull, Mt. Vernon	Secondary Recovery and Pressure Maintenance Committee	

Name	Role in Compact Commission	Official state position
Thomas A. Lawry, Urbana	Secondary Recovery and Pressure Maintenance Committee	State Geological Survey
E. L. Manering, Carmi	Secondary Recovery and Pressure Maintenance Committee	
Paul M. Phillippi, Casey	Secondary Recovery and Pressure Maintenance Committee	
A. B. Vaughn, Zeigler	Secondary Recovery and Pressure Maintenance Committee	

* Mr. Harris was named by Governor Richard B. Ogilvie as Illinois representative on the IOCC to replace Guy McGaughey in 1969.

it is the commission itself which adopts or rejects committee proposals and decisions. Resolutions are adopted at the midyear and annual meetings.

The Oil Compact has been called an "industrial self-regulating" agreement. This results from its close ties with various of the industry's trade associations which give or withhold support of commission actions and recommendations and without which the IOCC would have little effectiveness if, indeed, it remained alive at all.

Within Illinois the commission's work is brought to the oil industry through the private Illinois Oil and Gas Association, and it is within this organization that the compact commission actually functions and obtains industry compliance, comment, and legislative proposals. In turn, the desires of association members are translated into the policies which Illinois Compact Commission members will support before the latter agency. It is through this rather complex set of relationships (not, actually, a formal structure) that the present Illinois oil conservation statutes have been screened and finally enacted into law. Thus, the state's failure to date to require prorationing is directly due to the opposition of the Oil and Gas Association.[15] Likewise, the association has opposed any serious consideration of a severance tax, although this matter is less intimately related to conservation practices than is prorationing, and less easy to defend as a proper subject for compact action. Compact commission members also keep a close eye on property taxation in the oil and gas producing counties, townships, and municipalities.

While in the strictest legal sense the state retains its full power to regulate this important minerals exploitative industry, it is also quite true that the compact has, with the Connally "Hot Oil" Act of 1935,[16] created a system of control that rests essentially within the industry in the states, with the federal government playing only a supporting role through its retention of authority over oil imports, its prohibition against interstate shipment of illegally produced petroleum, and its services through the Bureau of Mines of the Department of the Interior in preparing and publishing monthly demand forecasts. Statistical data on United States petroleum consumption is gathered and supplied to the industry and the states so that the latter can make their production quotas for each well, pool, and field of each state in accordance with market demand. In gathering this information the Bureau of Mines incorporates its own data with that gathered by the American Petroleum Institute and the Interstate Oil and Gas Compact Commission. The industry itself is thus placed in a position to determine its own regulatory operations. This becomes even more apparent when it is observed that the "big producing states"—Texas, Louisiana, Oklahoma—dominate industry production policy through their control over the nation's major oil resource areas. Some critics add that pricing policy is thus also determined, but this has consistently been denied by the industry and no antitrust or other litigation has revelaed it to be true. (California, the second largest producing state, has never joined the compact.) The industry itself recognizes the system as "industry self-regulating" and, in fact, strives to keep it so. The Oil Compact is an essential part of the system.

Illinois Conservation Background

A detailed history of Illinois struggles to adopt suitable oil production regulatory laws has been written by W. L. Summers, a professor of law at the University of Illinois and former legal consultant to Humble Oil and Refining Company, Texas Gulf Sulphur Company, and Shell Oil Company.[17] The full story needs not be recounted here, but its highlights provide understanding of the present Illinois regulatory pattern and the state's role in the compact and are therefore worthy of brief mention.

As noted by Professor Summers, at the time the oil industry was suffering from its near breakdown in the late twenties and early thirties, Illinois production was so small as to embroil few persons in the turmoil with which the States of Texas, Kansas, and Oklahoma were suffering at the time military rule had to be invoked to reestablish order. From 1889, when Illinois first discovered its oil resources, until 1935 when it joined the Interstate Oil Compact, the state's one oil field was that of Clark, Crawford, Lawrence, and adjoining counties. This old producing area had reached its peak between 1907 and 1915, at which time it averaged annual production of more than 27,500,000 barrels. By 1935 the field was generally given over to stripper wells whose total daily production was only 12,000 barrels. Since the state had adopted a number of such essential and customary regulatory laws as prevailed generally in oil-producing states during this early period, it regarded its situation as not pressingly in need of conservation legislation and its action in joining the compact was unopposed and without emotion. Certain drilling operations in the Illinois Basin began in 1936, however, and in the winter months of early 1937 the first exciting discovery near St. Elmo was made, opening up promising possibilities which were proved in short order. By the end of 1937, six new Illinois oil pools of rich proportions were discovered. The usual mad rush by "independents" and "majors" to lease land resulted, with approximately five million acres placed under lease by the year's end.

The first step in the subsequent drive to obtain regulatory legislation for "the prevention of physical waste" of petroleum was taken in October 1937 at an Illinois Mineral Industries Conference at the University of Illinois, where William Bell, president of the Illinois-Indiana Petroleum Association and Illinois member of the compact commission, urged that serious consideration be given to enactment of such laws. A "model" draft law was thereafter drawn up, based on what author Summers termed "the better features of the conservation laws of New Mexico, Texas, and Oklahoma"—actually, features being recommended and promoted by the Interstate Oil Compact Commission. As Summers describes it,

It defined and prohibited physical waste, created a commission with jurisdiction and authority over all persons and property necessary to administer and enforce the act and specific authority to make and enforce rules and regulations for certain purposes, including the limitation and proration of production, well spacing and the use of reservoir energy. With minor changes this statute was enacted in Arkansas in 1939, and in a number of other states. During the early months of 1938 while the Summers bill was being drafted, criticized and perfected through consultation with representatives of the Illinois–Indiana Petroleum Association, various drafts of it received wide circulation. Some persons, against conservation legislation of any sort, attacked it as a proration act, without regard for the fact that it was a comprehensive conservation measure for waste prevention, which gave the commission authority to limit and prorate production only after a hearing and finding that limitation of production in any pool was necessary for waste prevention.[18]

The opposition coalesced in succeeding months under the leadership of Clarence T. Smith, president of the Flora, Illinois, chamber of commerce, and Lieutenant Governor John Stelle, who also held oil interests in the Illinois Basin and was strongly opposed to any regulation of the prorationing type. (Clarence T. Smith later served as Illinois's representative on the Interstate Oil Compact Commission, is a 1969 member of the commission's Legal Committee, and was recently honored by the Illinois Oil and Gas Association with a merit citation for his twenty years of service as the association's general counsel and for his performance of "numerous assignments of importance to the Commission" while serving as Illinois representative.) [19]

An early resolution adopted by these opponents set the tone of political activity and legislative response in subsequent years. Echoing certain language of Clarence T. Smith, who was quoted as having told the meeting, "Let no one be fooled that under the guise of 'conservation talk' the budding industry in Illinois should be hampered and stopped by restrictive legislation at this early stage," [20] the resolution said,

Be it resolved by a group of citizens of the State of Illinois assembled in meeting at Flora, Ill., this 7th day of June, 1938, as representatives of the various present and future oil producing areas of this state that: "First—We are unalterably opposed to any legislation seeking to control or regulate the production of crude oil within this state until such time as our state production shall have attained a volume equal to at least the consumptive requirements of the state; Second—Be it further resolved that copies of this resolution be sent to the Honorable Henry M. Horner, Governor . . . and all members of the Legislature." [21]

Oil Weekly quoted Lieutenant Governor Stelle as having told a meeting of the Illinois Independent Oil Operators that the "motive of those urging proration under the guise of conservation was to make it impossible for smaller operators to continue, and that the enactment of conservation legislation would retard and destroy development, resulting in business depression and unemployment." [22] In 1939 a new organization of opponents was formed, the Petroleum Association of Illinois, which subsequently effectively blocked all conservation proposals. When a committee of the General Assembly held hearings in April 1939, the preponderance of witnesses giving testimony favored production restrictions, prorationing and well-spacing, yet the committee reported to the legislature, "there is no necessity at this time of enacting laws regulating proration, economic conservation and ratable taking. It is the belief of this committee that the laws would be more harmful than beneficial. The committee bases its conclusion upon the fact that there is definitely no evidence either of overproduction of oil or disruption of the price market and no immediate fear of either." [23] Professor Summers noted that at the time this committee report was made, Illinois had reached a new high of daily production, and the posted field price for oil had been reduced from $1.15 to $1.05 per barrel, and 54,200 barrels were sold daily to certain skimming plants at thirty-three cents under posted figures. The defined kinds of physical waste—unnecessary drilling, operation of wells at full flow, and the flaring of casinghead gas (which Illinois has always allowed)—were flourishing.

A third organization, the Centralia-based Illinois Producers Equity Association, came out strongly against regulatory legislation in 1939. This group operated in the Salem–Lake Centralia field which, according to the president of the Independent Oil Producers Association of Illinois, alone lost $10,000 a day in 1938 through wasteful production methods. This same spokesman claimed Illinois was losing $27,000,000 annually in its unregulated practices.

Despite continued support by Governor Henry Horner, and

nominal but favoring support voiced by the leading Republican contenders for the governorship in 1940, Dwight H. Green and Richard J. Lyons, no laws resulted. But with the new legislature in 1941, backed by Governor Green with an administration measure, the contending forces finally were able to reach a compromise which resulted in the first Illinois Oil and Gas Conservation Act,[24] but only after reaching total stalemate in the General Assembly which stimulated hurried consultation with Secretary Harold Ickes in Washington by Senator Charles F. Carpentier, a member of a subcommittee set up to work out a compromise. The threat of federal regulation for national defense purposes forced the matter through the legislature.

The law which Illinois enacted was amended slightly in 1945 but thereafter remained on the books until it was rather extensively altered in 1951 and again in 1964. The 1941 act did not define "waste" (either physical or economic), its provisions on spacing were prolix and somewhat ambiguous with a great many exceptions allowed, it gave no authority to the Department of Mines and Minerals to make rules and regulations on waste or wasteful methods, there were none of the recommended provisions on open flow of oil and gas wells, on prorationing, or on utilization of casinghead gas for production of carbon black (regarded as an uneconomic use), flaring of gas was allowed, and no qualifications were stipulated for the personnel administering the laws.

Summers wrote in 1948,

The Illinois oil and gas conservation law is not a true conservation measure within the generally accepted meaning of the term. It neither defines nor prohibits waste, the basic concept upon which state regulation of production of these natural resources must be grounded. It contains but a few of the many terms of other modern enactments through which physical and economic waste may be prevented and greater production achieved. The most important of these sections in the Illinois statute—spacing—is so fraught with exceptions and its enforceability so clouded with doubt, that it is in a large measure ineffectual as a conservation device, except through voluntary action.[25]

Improvements in the laws in 1945 and 1964[26] were designed to define physical waste (not economic), and to provide some of the more obvious controls lacking in the earlier law, but prorationing was and still is not required. In an extensive study of conservation laws in existence among compact member states in 1964, the compact commission recorded Illinois as responding "no" to the following questions:

1. Does your [state regulatory] agency have any requirements with respect to obtaining a permit to [plug and abandon] a well, prior to work?

2. Does your agency have administrative regulations for the use of equipment for automatically transferring custody of hydrocarbons?

3. Does your agency require the submission of reports indicating the bottom-hole pressure as recorded in a producing well?

4. Does your agency specify a set amount of casing for the drilling of a well?

5. Does the agency require the use of a form that, when executed, certifies that the operation of the wells involved and the production therefrom is in compliance with the rules and regulations of the regulatory body?

6. Does your agency have administrative regulations for authorization to commingle hydrocarbons from various leases or properties in common facilities?

7. Does your agency have a regulation of maximum gas-oil ratio per well?

8. [In regard to requirements for initial potential tests to be run on all drilling operations]: Are they witnessed?

9. Does your agency have regulations involving the use of meters for the measurement of oil or gas?

10. Are there requirements of your regulatory body making it necessary for the operators to submit periodically reports indicating that each well is capable of producing its assigned rate? [Since Illinois has no prorationing, it naturally has no "assigned rate" for each well.]

11. Does your agency have a requirement regarding the submission of periodic reports indicating the amount of hydrocarbons processed by particular plants? Particular leases or individual wells?

12. Does your agency require that a public hearing be held on all matters involving the following for particular pools: Spacing? Drilling? Production? Allowables?

13. Are transporters required to file periodic reports?

14. Does your agency have authority to establish tubing requirements? [27]

Although the terms of the compact assert its purpose to be conservation of oil and gas by the prevention of physical waste, the prevention of "economic waste" has been a result of its operation even though the compact specifically denies any authorization of practices by member states designed primarily or directly for that effect. Article V states,

It is not the purpose of this compact to authorize the states joining herein to limit the production of oil or gas for the purpose of stabilizing or fixing the price thereof, or create or perpetuate monopoly, or to promote regimentation, but is limited to the purpose of conserving oil and gas and preventing the avoidable waste thereof within reasonable limitations.

The compact commission's definition of waste is "the production of oil in excess of reasonable market demand." The Illinois definition is: " 'Waste' means 'physical waste' as that term is generally understood in the oil and gas industry," which includes seven specifically identified prohibited practices.[28] Various methods of controlling "physical waste," such as prorationing (the setting of production quotas in conformity with market demand), well-spacing, the unitization of all producers in a given field, are inextricably interwoven with economic questions of overriding importance, and from the compact's inception the commission has found it necessary to admonish representatives for reference to and concern with pricing, and to deny any concern of its own with this or other profits questions of industry economics which may arise through operation of the compact in the member states.

The compact came into existence, however, as a direct result of the industry chaos which developed from the discovery of the East Texas oil field in the late twenties, with the resultant glutting of the crude petroleum market which pushed the price of oil down during the Depression years to as low as ten cents a barrel.* From that time until now the industry's economic health has never been divorced from industry concern for "conservation for the avoidance of physical waste." Commission conference records contain references to industry economic matters, pricing is not totally ignored by spokesmen at commission meetings and in recent years a leading activity has been sponsorship and backing of legislative opposition to United States oil import policies on which industry members of the commission have openly lobbied, have adopted numerous resolutions that have been freely circulated and frequently transmitted to Congress and federal administrative agencies, and studied at length. While the wording of these resolutions has varied from time to time over the years, all have contained specific references to current happenings which certain segments of the industry view as alarming or threatening to the protections desired for the domestic industry. For instance, at the December 1968 annual meeting in Miami a resolution was adopted which urged denial by the Foreign-Trade Zones Board of any application "that might result in foreign oil products or foreign petroleum derived petrochemical plant products moving into the United States 'outside of' or 'in-addition to' the quantities of foreign petroleum and products permitted to be imported," in the Foreign-Trade Zones of Maine, Georgia, and Hawaii.[29]

For a considerable number of years commission conference proceedings have shown concern for natural gas regulatory policies of the Federal Power Commission; resolutions have consistently urged the transfer of gas regulatory activities to the states. The relationship of this proposed move to industry pricing activity is clearly shown in the wording of the December 1966 version:

---

* The discovery of the East Texas field with its frantic rush to exploit it, duplicated the earlier experience of the oil industry with the Tulsa pool. Distribution facilities were totally inadequate to carry the overproduced crude to market; the market was inadequate for its consumption; refineries could not keep pace with production. The danger of exhausting reserves, while inadequate storage resulted in burning and loss, led oilmen to demand strong curbs, and for a time military rule prevailed in Texas and Oklahoma oil fields.

[Be it resolved that] appropriate legislation be enacted by Congress so that the production and gathering of natural gas be only under the jurisdiction of State regulatory agencies, and that the price of this mineral resource reflect its market value in open competition with other fuels.[30]

"Market demand prorationing" discussions absorbed early petroleum conservation proponents. Not much is said in recent years by the compact commission, but critics of the oil industry have had a great deal to say about it, with prompt rebuttals from the industry against charges of price-determining, hammering oft-repeated facts and arguments designed to show the untruth of the charges of protectionism under the guise of conservation.[31]

Probably the most persistent question the Interstate Oil and Gas Compact Commission is required to answer is that of the relationship of "petroleum conservation" with "petroleum pricing." Since it is obvious to even the most elementary thinking on economics that "scarcity" and "controlled supply" under classic economic theory can be expected to equate with "higher demand," "competition to acquire," and therefore "higher prices," the oil conservationists' constant denial that petroleum conservation has any direct concern with prices troubles the questioners. The literature of petroleum economics is filled with this discussion. For years the late General Ernest O. Thompson of the Texas Railroad Commission (the leading regulatory agency in the nation for the determination of production quotas) was compelled to reiterate again and again the conservation definitions of "physical waste" and "economic waste." The definitions which the IOCC has always used are those which were early recognized by the old NRA Petroleum Code. As interpreted by one writer (using the modern-day view of conservation of natural resources as "the fullest, most efficient and most economic use of existing resources" rather than "hoarding" or "reservation of resources for future use and need"), he notes:

To conserve a natural resource . . . is not to hoard it. . . . True conservation . . . is a much more positive concept which means two very definite things: (1) the prevention of waste, and (2) the limitation of production to consumptive demand.

. . . .

The oil industry as a whole did not like governmental interference and cared little for conservation for its own sake. It nevertheless accepted both with good grace because it was convinced that stabilization was impossible without [it]. *Laissez-faire* had not only failed to curb but actually encouraged ruinous practices and the states had proved themselves incompetent in coping with the problem. Federally controlled production was the logical remedy.[32]

The key word is "stabilization." The oilmen of the thirties and forties accepted conservation for the control of "physical waste" because it offered "economic stabilization."

As noted by yet another early oil economist,

Stabilization today does not mean the control of prices. It does not mean the guarantee of profits to the marginal operators. Stabilization means the withholding of sufficient quantities of oil so that the total scarcity values of the goods which compose the costs employed by the industry as a whole to the total goods for which they are sold by the industry will leave a profit. Stabilization means the reduction of uncertainty to certainty.[33]

With this logic held by the industry, the Oil Compact Commission has proceeded with its assignment of finding, designing, and promoting interstate and interindustry adoption of the best physical waste control practices while carefully avoiding sponsorship of practices specifically designed to control supply to avoid the "economic waste" of instability. Obviously, such production and supply controls as spacing, pooling, unitization, and prorationing require sacrifices on the part of some, give a favored economic and profits position to some, and shut out still others, and all of these are difficult for Americans to accept as proper meanings for "conservation." It is also apparent that there is great difficulty, if not the impossibility, of separating the control of physical waste from control of or involvement with oil economics.

As additional evidence of the compact's difficulty in separating itself from oil economics is the fact that the compact has found its greatest support among many of its worst enemies—the "independents," those oil producers and refiners whose industry functions are limited to only one or two of the four main activities of the oil industry: production, distribution, refining, and marketing, or whose operations are on a considerably smaller capitalized scale than those of the great "major," or "integrated," companies.* While independ-

---

* There are twenty or more large, integrated companies which operate in all four areas of the industry; these, with some semiintegrated companies, total sixty-eight. An additional sixty-one domestic United States companies are devoted to marketing only.

ents were instrumental in the compact's beginnings, a great many other independents and nonintegrated producers first opposed, then flocked into, the ranks of the compact commission's supporters as one of a number of defenses in their competitive struggles with the major companies. Illinois IOCC representatives have been chosen from the ranks of the independents. It is therefore interesting that Illinois, which for many years was largely composed of independents (today, much less so), neither embraced wholeheartedly the conservation creed nor fervently waved the oil compact's banner. To a considerable extent, the state's oil producers have gone their independent way, only gradually permitting the state on a piecemeal adoption basis to enact the conservation controls the compact recommends. There is a reason for this.

Since the compact requires member states to surrender none of their police powers over conservation and oil production, but merely to agree to work for conservation of oil and gas and prevention of physical waste,[34] there is considerable variation among compacting member states in the extent and kind of conservation statutes they have adopted. Illinois, to date, has enjoyed an exceedingly favorable economic position within the oil industry, due to certain "short haul" advantages it holds in transporting crude oil from the field to the great refineries of the state—Texaco's near Lawrenceville on the Ohio River and at Lockport, the Clark refinery at Blue Island, and the huge Shell, Mobil Oil, American Oil (Standard), and other refineries in the Wood River-Roxana area on the Mississippi near St. Louis. This permits a lower production cost per barrel, and thus makes Illinois crude very much in demand. Also until quite recently Illinois producing wells have been relatively shallow, thus making the initial costs of exploration and drilling less than is the case in some of the other states. The favorable profits position Illinois operators enjoyed was one over which they determinedly fought to keep their own control.

The situation on drilling is rapidly changing, however, for some of the older, shallower wells of the state are abandoned and exhausted or are gradually playing out, and since 1964 quite a few wells have been drilled to productive depths of over 7,000 feet. In 1965, Texaco, Inc., (and others) drilled its No. 1 Cuppy Well in the Dale Consolidated Pool to a total depth of 13,051 feet, making it the deepest producing well in Illinois. The second deepest well was drilled in Wayne

County in 1967 by Union Oil Company of California, being completed at 11,614 feet. This well, No. 1 Cisne Community, also recovered ten feet of oil between 7,749 and 7,867 feet in the Knox Dolomite strata, the first Knox discovery in the central Illinois basin.[35] Production figures had not by December 1968 been released on this deep well, but it is fair to say that future production in Illinois will tend to increasingly deeper depths, thus making the independents, the wildcatters, and the lone operators who did not need great amounts of capital to engage in oil production a rarer breed of men in this state.

Due to the state's heretofore favorable position, Illinois legislators have therefore been generous in allowing relatively uncurbed production and tardy in adopting recommended conservation laws which have the effect of limiting production. As noted in the compact commission's 1964 questionnaire on conservation laws, Illinois has no laws on prorationing. But unitization (the integration of the interests of different owners in a field into a single drilling unit) is not only permitted but encouraged, and may be compelled by the Mining Board since it is deemed to be the interest of all producers to maintain an oil pool's pressure whether by early prevention of gas waste or by later secondary recovery activities, which include repressuring by gas injection. (Illinois today is one of the larger "secondary recovery" states and its repressuring is done by water injection.) A good many powers have been granted to the state to control secondary recovery practices; the drilling or deepening of a well; the engineering methods used in all operations; reporting on drilling, geologic, and production facts and statistics, and the like. All in all, authorities are of the opinion that Illinois conservation laws meet the state's general obligations under the Interstate Oil Compact today, if in some ways minimally or not at all.[36]

State Policy-Determination and the Compact

The very size of the Interstate Oil Compact's membership makes the compact considerably more than the interest of a single state. The American capitalistic system with its philosophy that mining and private exploitation of natural resources are legitimate practices of laissez-faire enterprise, within the rights of private property, also makes the compact's purposes a general rather than a single state's concern. Furthermore, the oil industry's nationwide character minimizes the importance and role of individual states in some of their activities as regulators of the commonweal's interest in this natural resource.

This means that although an oil-producing state such as Illinois adopts and endorses the oil compact, the state actually has little leeway once it is within it to do a great deal to alter the agreement's operations or adjust the organizational arrangements which are implicit in the compact's and compact commission's scheme of operations. While Illinois's own conservation laws can and do influence the kind of internal organization the state sets up for handling oil and gas conservation, these laws cannot ignore or eliminate the basic relationships which the compact establishes internally and externally. The state can, of course, withdraw from the compact if it wishes to do so, but this the oil industry of the state will not permit as long as its interests are favorably served by the agreement—regardless of whether the interests of all of the people of Illinois not connected with the oil industry actually are being properly served by it. The strength of the compact as a symbol of public responsibility in conservation of natural resources establishes an image that all is well in petroleum activities, which may be misleading. There is, in this writer's opinion, no question that oil conservation laws are necessary and desirable and that the IOCC's recommended practices are probably as good as can be drawn. The problem lies in the uses which the industry has made of the advantages these laws afford to some. The governmental deficiency is in the states' failure to remain disinterested and independent of the industry it is supposed to police.

A state's membership in such a compact becomes essentially a policy question and not solely one of administrative mechanics. As a policy problem, if the state acquiesces in the preestablished assumptions of the compact, it must necessarily acquiesce in the kind of governmental-private industry organizational relationships that almost automatically result. The state must become a party to certain industry assumptions and practices. It must, in a sense, become an instrument or party-in-interest to private interests, and an operating partner in private enterprise activities. It can and probably has become the captive of the oil-production philosophy it endorses which, without the challenge possible from some vigorous and disinterested policing agency alert to change, to research and new developments, takes on the unassailable qualities of immutable, final law which the state may find it is powerless to change even though change may be needed.

Insofar as administrative theory is involved in any analysis of Illinois compact organization and the mechanics of oil administration, virtually all well-established principles of proper administrative practice are observed by this and, presumably, the other states party to the compact. That is, the compact representative is the chief executive of the state or his appointed delegate, and the latter is removable at the chief executive's pleasure. Further, the governor himself has power to withdraw the state from the compact when in his judgment such action is warranted. (It goes without saying that it is extremely unlikely any governor will ever feel persuaded to do this on his own initiative.) The compact's representative has no moneys of the state in his control, and receives no compensation for his duties. Such state moneys as are involved in direct compact operations are not only small, they are also annually audited, and they are of the nature of membership dues, paid directly to the compact commission for its disposition. There are no other state employees devoted full-time to the Interstate Compact itself.

Within the state's bureaus and agencies charged with effectuating the compact's principles (as expressed in state conservation laws), all employees are covered by the state's personnel code, and their salaries and expenses are presumably properly budgeted and accounted for. Principles of proper (although sometimes minimal) reporting are observed through the publications of the Oil and Gas Compact Commission in Oklahoma City and the published reports of the Oil and Gas Division of the Illinois Department of Mines and Minerals. Lines of control are clear and definitive. The state's regulatory functions which result from adoption of conservation laws are not under the Illinois compact representative's control. Being outside that control and under designated agencies of the state, they appear to conform and adhere generally to all recommended principles of administrative law and practice.

What, then, can be concluded about this particular interstate compact and its effects on this particular state which can be said about it generally? Perhaps the only significant judgment one can make in terms of state governmental interests is that this interstate compact is an instrument for substantively shaping a major national economic policy question and it is not intended to be an administrative regulatory subsystem. Any view of its merits or efficacy as an interstate development in federalism must inevitably be concerned with the national compact's and compact commission's policies, economic philosophy, and their effects on a state's shaping of policy.

Were one to recommend to the State of Illinois what it might do to reestablish its right of control over the compacts it enters, one might say that periodic compact review is in order, and that in this compact's case the state might very well undertake a new and intensive legislative and executive appraisal of the principles implicit in the Interstate Oil Compact for their relevance in a changing world of technology and economic organization, to ascertain the validity of the compact's original assumptions, to the end of revising state oil and gas conservation law and production practices if such revision is indicated. Every compact member state might profitably do this. In brief, although periodic review of the compact by member states and the Congress is possible through the compact's need to be renewed periodically, intensive review—such as seemed likely in the wake of the 1967 United States attorney general's report—is never undertaken.*

Such a review not only could assist member states in their efforts to keep their own souls in policy-making and administration, but it might also reveal whether existing conservation methods have actually encouraged monopoly or "favored position" practices, neglected pollution of the states' air and waters, destroyed or discouraged their wildlife, ruined good land and recreational sites, created pricing arrangements directly or indirectly, exploited the states' oil and gas resources unduly, or had any appreciable effect on the oil industry's taxpaying and tax-bearing capabilities. All of these are matters of considerable interest to the states' citizens at large and, presumably, of interest to the states' governments.

The recommendation is one which would have been made in any event, but is doubly emphasized by recent challenges which have been

* Congress' action in 1967 of granting the oil compact only a two-year renewal was the direct result of the negative content of the Attorney General's Report for that year. It seemed to promise that Congress would give extra attention to the compact when it next came up for renewal, but as of this writing no such inquiry has been or promises to be undertaken. In fact, a "clean bill of health" has been given to the compact and the compact commission in living up to the prohibitions of the compact's article V, although the congressional committee has not proposed to return to the four-year renewal practice. See Senate Report 199, Committee on Interior and Insular Affairs, *Consenting to Extension of the Inter-State Oil and Gas Compact*, 91st Cong., 1st Sess., May, 1969.

made to the oil industry's long-held, solidified principles and practices of conservation, challenges which come from informed and respectable sources, and which cannot intelligently be ignored. Specifically, the oil industry has been criticized as one that has become static and, indeed, shows evidences of obsolescence through its failure to modernize itself, partially as a result of its unchallenged security behind the protections of the legal walls it has built for itself, including conservation law.

Not all such criticisms have come from outside the industry. Some have come from within it. For instance, the industry's tendencies to concentrate on the more profitable aspects of oil production have been at the cost of exploration and creation of new reserves. This was a function the wildcatter filled and was allowed to fill. High risks and uncertain profits always made exploration a gamble which the major companies to a considerable extent allowed the independents and small operators to carry. Today with the costs of drilling and exploration mounting, the wildcatter is disappearing, but the secure and established companies have not been filling the gap he is leaving behind. The industry itself knows this and confesses its own shortcomings. Harold M. McClure, Jr., president of both the Independent Petroleum Association of America and the McClure Oil Company, told the IOCC at its June 1968 meeting, "show me an oil industry or a segment thereof that is 'psyched out' of wildcatting, and I can point to an industry and a nation prematurely and artificially destined to find itself in a 'have-not' position as to essential petroleum supplies." [37]

The chief criticisms, however, have come from the economists, critics whom the oil industry refers to as consisting "mainly of the theoretical textbook economists and college professors who have the profits from their books or grants as an incentive for attacking the big companies in the oil industry," and whose observations are sources of "misguided authority." [38] Whether the academicians deserve such downgrading or not, their criticisms have been emerging in more volume and with greater frequency during the past decade. Robert Engler's *The Politics of Oil*, which appeared in 1955 as a series of articles in the *New Republic* and then was issued in book form in 1961, largely a journalistic account of oil production conditions in the United States, did much to spark the examination which today's more technical criticisms represent.

One such viewpoint has been expressed by Dr. Morris Adelman, of the Massachusetts Institute of Technology.[39] More recently, a considerable oil industry hubbub resulted from the nonacademic *Fortune* magazine's publication of an article by its staff member, Gilbert R. Burck, entitled, "A Giant Caught In Its Own Web." [40] *Fortune* itself responded editorially to the mass of protesting letters it received from members of the oil industry, "We believe that history has already moved forward, and that the U.S. oil industry should move with it." [41]

These writers question the validity of prorationing; of small, marginal independent operations; of limits set on federal import quotas (directly resulting from compact commission influences); of unitization as it is presently practiced; of indiscriminate and superfluous drilling; and of possible misuse of the highly criticized 27½ percent depletion allowance of the United States income tax.* The attack rests on a view of the industry as protected by its conservation laws, an economic empire that is self-serving and in a great many of its practices not altogether in the public interest.

A powerful reply to these challenges appeared in *Petroleum Management*, in February 1966,[42] defending the status quo in oil conservation practice and the existing modus operandi of the oil industry. Both the attacks and the responses contain much that is provocative, and raise important questions and doubts.

The attack continued on a more official level in 1967. At that time the attorney general of the United States issued the customary annual report on the workings of the oil industry under the compact. It hit a new record in brevity, consisting of only four pages. Attached to it, however, was an eighty-seven-page, unsigned staff memorandum containing much of the criticisms voiced by the economists. In the words of John M. Houchin, who responded to it before the Oil and Gas Compact Commission,

It is a frontal assault upon the responsibility and integrity of the integrated companies and not the conservation program as such.

To develop its thesis, the memorandum broadens the definition of the conservation program to include the Federal tax laws such as the resource depletion allowance, cost depreciation and capital gains tax, which it calls incentives; import controls; public lands administration;

---

* As of December, 1969, Congress passed and President Nixon signed a tax reform measure which reduced the depletion allowance to 22 percent.

the Connally Act; and even the gathering of statistics. This broad definition gives the staff the opportunity to voice the views of the critics on these subjects under the guise of reporting on the Compact.[43]

Mr. Houchin's shocked reaction to the inclusion of the above subjects in the Justice Department's examination is difficult to understand, when any superficial scrutiny of Oil Compact Commission publications and records reveal the members of the Interstate Oil and Gas Compact have repeatedly, year after year, considered and adopted at annual meetings public resolutions on oil imports policies; on United States land laws review and revision; and it is a matter of historical fact that the Connally Act was passed almost in the same breath as the law giving consent to the Oil Compact in 1935 and has always been regarded as part of a legislative package containing all the ingredients necessary to stabilize the petroleum industry. True, the commission's annual meetings have carefully skirted tax questions, yet the public does not. Depletion allowance, in the public's mind, means oil depletion allowance, whether or not other depletion allowances are granted in the laws of the country. Furthermore, when the attorney general was empowered and instructed to provide Congress with an annual report on the workings of the compact, it was done because of the possibility that industry operations under the compact and its conservation laws might work contrary to the antitrust laws of the nation and that the attorney general was the proper agent to keep informed on this, and to keep Congress informed on it.

The questioning of the industry in late 1967 was paralleled with the emergence of a Resources for the Future, Inc., study in November 1967, *Economic Aspects of Oil Conservation Regulation,* by Dr. Wallace F. Lovejoy of Southern Methodist University, and Dr. Paul T. Homan, a consultant with Resources for the Future and former Southern Methodist professor.[44] Their research paper was answered with the published monograph by Stanley Learned, *Petroleum Conservation—The Myths and Realities,* previously cited in this study. Conceding that the Lovejoy and Homan presentation "on the whole, is more responsible and less dogmatic than most previous presentations," and "the subject of oil conservation regulation should create discussion and clarification which, hopefully, will result in better understanding of the complexities of the subject," Learned yet attempted to refute the authors' premises that the oil industry is inefficient, that property rights are not necessarily immutable, that the oil industry opposes unitization, that conservation regulation has resulted in excess producing capacity, that prorationing has supported prices at high levels and that one of its primary purposes has been to stabilize prices, that stripper wells ought to be eliminated, and other related topics.

But, again, the present study's concern is interstate compacts and their effects on federalism, and the oil compact is only one of many such agreements. The fact that almost all current criticisms of the oil industry's economic practices inevitably come to focus on the compact and the conservation laws it promotes and protects underscores the previous judgment made in this study: that any consideration of this compact is intimately and paramountly a policy question. It is a question of whether such a compact, once joined, strips or neutralizes a state in a portion of its sovereignty, and this study concludes that to a degree this is true—if a state endorses all conservation recommendations or only part of them, as does Illinois.

At present, any official state review of oil production concepts is filtered through a bureaucracy that is largely oil industry-dominated. Regulatory personnel are themselves intimately associated with the industry and its interests. The highly technical nature of the facts and information surrounding the industry necessarily requires those who are best informed on oil matters to administer the public's oil concerns, and this means that industry personnel are the chief source of supply for the state agencies' personnel needs. Such a situation combined with the intimate links of the oil compact with the private industry's trade associations, is hardly the most objective structure for obtaining a clear and unbiased view of all the facts and truths about the nation's and the states' oil resources, or of what is needed in public policy to protect the interests of all the people and not those of the oil industry alone.

That there is a foreseeable change ahead for oil and gas production cannot be denied. Water and air pollution control laws have been strengthened nationally so that additional restraints are bound to result for oil producers who heretofore have not been compelled to do much about their water and air polluting activities. This is no small problem in Illinois. Improved and growing understanding of how to produce petroleum economically from the vast quantities of oil shale and lignite coal which cover so much of the West has approached a point where potential producers will be demanding the right to begin, if production is not obstructed by the existing protected industry interests. The capital necessary to create a processing plant for the production of synthetic gasoline from coal, a plan afoot in Illinois, means that the undertaking will of necessity be in the hands of one of the great major companies and the independents will suffer yet another blow to their precarious position. The use of nuclear energy for much of the nation's fuel and power requirements is no longer a remote possibility but at hand, a development of not too many years away.

All such facts point powerfully to the likelihood that industry critics are right when they say the existing industry conservation philosophy is obsolete. At the very least, review is needed, but there is scant evidence that such a review is being undertaken or is contemplated by the oil compacting states. It is difficult to avoid concluding that the industry decision-making features of the compact and its conservation laws create an arrangement which defeats state governmental initiative in the proper exercise of state police powers through such techniques as review. Illinois, no less than the other oil compact states, may not be wholly submissive to the "industry self-regulating" principle of the compact, but one cannot escape the view that it appears to be so.

7

Interstate Compacts

A Question of Federalism

CRITICAL EXAMINATION of even a few interstate compacts may tend to introduce a bias in regard to them which must be guarded against. In our federal system it is essential that states, like persons, have legal mechanisms through which mutual activities can be accomplished jointly under proper and binding terms. No state can always operate alone, nor is it desirable today that any should. Therefore, the contractual arrangement which the interstate compact represents is a constitutional imperative for certain intergovernmental purposes. It is, however, this qualifying element, "for certain intergovernmental purposes," to which this study has been led and about which questions have arisen in abundance.

Contracts, of whatever kind, cannot purposefully be drawn for just any kind of activity. Some contracts, although valid, are poorly conceived; some are the product of bad judgment; some, although entered by legally recognized equals, actually are between unequals with one party far better able to meet the terms of the obligation than the other. Some are resorted to inadvisedly, where perhaps another legal arrangement might more profitably be used to serve the sought ends. So it appears to be with some of today's interstate compacts, particularly those of the economic developmental type which have been described here.

It is also certain that the best contract is entered within a frame of broader considerations, purposes, and restraints than those of the interested parties alone. Social values must be upheld; realities of the existing economic system preserved; the state, which is the source and the ultimate guarantor of law, must be not only the strength of the contract but the arbiter and judge of its performance and must itself be protected.

In the light of all such considerations, it is not possible for one holding a concern for the future of American life and government to emerge from a close look at the four interstate compacts of this study with unqualified endorsement of them as exemplary designs for successful regional and interstate government in America. The enacted compacts, as vehicles to advance purposes and activities seen by their creators as desirable for the compacting members, are themselves faulty. The conception of one, the design of another, the agency practices of yet another, demonstrate the imperfect condition of political knowledge and experience existing in this vital area of American state and national government. As operating, at least three of these compacts appear relatively ineffectual in demonstrated performance and achievement as opposed to the projected expectations which went into their creation. Instead of instruments for positive, constructive state solution of today's compelling social and economic problems, they appear merely to provide new complexities in administrative organization and practice, and to erect additional power centers, often ineffective in accomplishing public ends but generally obstructive while officially establishing particularized vested interests in state-protected positions of individual advantage.

A fair appraisal of them, grounded on limited knowledge and observation, is possible only if it rests on the recognition that additional research of a far more intensive kind than has been possible here is needed before any conclusions can be adjudged as final and absolute. It is, however, clearly evident that what these compacts reveal is a state acknowledgment of need in a federal system, but a political response that appears to be little more than a state gesture along the lines of self-protection rather than toward responsible and constructive achievement to eradicate the problems that created the need.

Conclusions Reached On This Study's Four Compacts

In examining a few of one state's interstate compacts to determine what such compacts actually are in today's state governments, a definition, a general image, and an evaluation of a meaningful kind were sought, to the end of placing all compacts in proper perspective and in their proper place in today's American federalism. Certain assumptions underlay the approach: first, that interstate compacting activity is an important and, indeed, essential part of a contemporary trend in inter-governmental relations that is here to stay. It was also assumed that the growth of interstate compacts has been occasioned in part by state-recognized need, although it has been observed that the desires and blandishments of certain special interests have had a considerable influence in their multiplication, and the lure of federal funds has had an immeasureable stimulating effect. Whatever the need, it has arisen from the limitations of state and national governments under heretofore accepted constitutional construction. It was further assumed that this growth is taking place in a somewhat legally undefined and politically uncharted area of our constitutional system and that it therefore needs closer observation than appears to be given by students of American government and the public at large.

The four interstate compacts of this study to which Illinois is party are only a few of those to which the state presently belongs or is considering joining. (See appendix E for the 1969 list of interstate compacts to which Illinois is party, and the accompanying list of compacts being considered for adoption.) They were chosen for examination not because they are necessarily characteristic or representative of all contemporary interstate compacts, but because they are active ones, on which considerable effort has been expended by their pro-ponents, their party states, and their officials. Because they are operating, there is available to a researcher a record for detailed examination which if not abundant is sufficiently revealing.

Other considerations in choosing these four compacts for study lay in the purposes they are designed to serve which make them uniquely modern: one is an economic developmental compact, one is a combination economic developmental and advisory-recommendatory compact, and two are advisory-recommendatory. The governing board of only one has been fully implemented with the necessary attributes of an operating agency, but two others might be called economic and social developmental agencies in embryo—not yet proved ready for full investiture as operating agencies but serving an apprenticeship in some degree of expectation, barring bad political fortune in the years ahead, of graduating to full-fledged status when time and political climate are kindly.

It was further assumed that the merits or demerits of these compacts and their agencies might be sufficiently noteworthy to provide valid assumptions applicable to other interstate compacts, existent or yet to be. What conclusions could be drawn about them as compacts per se, and compacts as devices, arms, or mechanisms of American state government; what their future might be, and what they portend for the future of the state system, were questions underlying the examination. Some answers are possible.

A great many critical observations about these selected compacts have been made within this study. It is unnecessary to repeat unduly, but some recapitulation is indicated. To pull the outstanding characteristics into a meaningful catalog, it can first be definitively said about compacts per se that they are, (1) essential to any nonfederal interstate undertaking of a formal, binding nature, (2) they are a special commitment of a state to a permanent, or relatively long-range interstate undertaking, (3) they take precedence over ordinary state statutes, (4) they contain potentialities for greater state achievement in interstate problem-solving, while at the same time (5) they contain potentialities for diminished state autonomy in decisions on these same matters. Their use should be tempered with the understanding by their creators that, (6) they are essentially experimental in the American system, and, being so, they deserve the fullest state oversight and caution in their application, their uses, and their operations, and, (7) certain concomitant developments, arising from their operations, likewise deserve such full state oversight and caution.

On the merit side of the balance sheet it can be said that these four compacts represent, (1) positive efforts of responsible and forward-looking states to bridge the barriers of state boundaries, local jurisdictions, and centralized and decentralized governmental and private power in the solution of twentieth-century social and economic problems; (2) sincere efforts to utilize the full possibilities offered by the United States Constitution for strengthening and serving the American people in their lives, livelihoods, and governmental needs at the grass-roots level; (3) efforts sanctioned and encouraged by a national government urgently in need of states properly equipped and capable of dealing with the state and national problems of today's world; and (4) efforts to find a means to enlist in the service of the states the private interests whose goals at best are self-interested, at worst antisocial.

The catalog of demerits is longer and it is risky, for what appears to be a shortcoming general to all or most interstate compacts requires examination of all or most of them to prove or disprove its existence, and that has not been done. It is, for example, possible to say that Congress gives inadequate attention to the consent process, yet two of these Illinois compacts have had rather thoroughgoing congressional attention (the Great Lakes Basin Compact and the Interstate Oil Compact). Even here, however, congressional attention has not itself been general but confined to highly specialized subcommittee and committee scrutiny, with questioning and testimony from parties-in-interest rather than a wide spectrum of technical, professional, and public-at-large witnesses.

Therefore, certain negative attributes as listed here were discerned in one or more of these four compacts (indicated by letter, according to the designation below).* The list is not intended to be all-inclusive; certain other deficiencies may appear in other interstate compacts which did not appear in these or were regarded as unimportant to the purposes of these.

Under these qualifications it can be said, (1) compacts generally are proliferating without sufficient identification and definition of their inadequacies, or with full regard for the fact that they are evolutionarily developing and are yet to a high degree unproved for many of the purposes being assigned to them (B, C); (2) they are sometimes inadequately drafted and often inadequately weighed during enactment (A, C. B, also, in the sense that no redrafting of the amended compact was made by the states before Congress granted consent); (3) they are emphatically not being adequately evaluated by objective and impartial observers (A, B, C); † (4) they are occasionally being attempted in spheres which may be improper or not necessary for their use, as political expedients rather than as carefully designed solutions to problems demanding this kind of solution (B; possibly C; to a limited extent, D); and, (5) they are inadequately policed (i.e., reviewed, in a systematic and regular way by both their member states and the national government) (A, B, C, D). Once operative through compact commissions and "not-for-profit" corporations, (6) they appear to be separatistic, from the public at large and

---

* A The Bi-State Development Compact.

B The Great Lakes Basin Compact.

c The Wabash Valley Interstate Compact.

D The Interstate Oil Compact.

† The author recognizes the contributions of the Council of State Governments in this area but does not classify the council as wholly "objective" or "impartial," being itself an agency of the states' governments and not a general purpose research agency.

from the states which create them (A, D; to a degree, C); (7) they are to some degree undemocratic and unrepresentative (A, B, D); (8) they manifest tendencies to be somewhat unresponsive to the general populations they are designed to serve and highly responsive to select, specialized interests of an exceedingly narrow kind (A, B, C, D); (9) there is no gubernatorial veto (A); (such a veto is not seen as needed in strictly "advisory-recommendatory" compacts), or provision for regular, thorough state audit (A); (such an audit should be provided when any revenue-producing powers exist); and (10) with increasing tenure there comes decreasing control by their creators, and increasing control by the specialists and technicians who handle their day-by-day activities (A, D). This last judgment, however, can be made and is made of most of the specialized governmental bureaus of all levels of American government, and is not unique to interstate compact agencies alone. The fact that the latter are responsive to no single government under clear lines of authority, heightens the possibilities of independence.

It is recognized that there is room for debate on some of these classifications, but all have been made on the assumption that an interstate compact is a highly formal agreement of a highly responsible and obligatory nature, and if any omissions are detected which weaken the concept they are critical. Some of these deficiencies arise from shortcomings of the American governmental system itself. For example, no one has yet been able to resolve the power questions posed by special interests in American representative organizations. Modernization of legislatures for dealing with intergovernmental problems has been nonexistent or monumentally slow. Few have yet satisfied themselves that they have found a way to keep governmental bureaus consistently responsive to the public at large.

Furthermore, the faults of interstate compact agencies are sometimes faults of American governmental institutions generally: the failure to find an effective control substitute for the clumsy mechanism of the direct vote of the people, the generally unsatisfactory results in the search for means to administer regional affairs effectively on a level intermediate between states and nation, the incapacity of the national government itself effectively to deal with regional or local problems directly, thus requiring innovations for which the states and the people are not prepared or not equipped to handle, and do not understand.

But some are uniquely the faults of the states, and these emerge as defects in some of the examined compacts of this study: the failure of the states to draft compacts with adequate built-in controls, not for the purpose of protecting the federal system but to keep the people's control over their government secure; the failure to grant veto power to the governor, thus pinpointing at least one seat of authority and responsibility; the failure critically to review compacts in operation; the failure to mandate representation of a broad range of interests in appointments to compact commissions; the failure to provide for regular state audit where substantial monetary operations are involved, and to require adequate reports; the failure to provide full-time executive and legislative machinery through which all of a state's interstate compact matters can be examined for continuing critical oversight, information, and control;[1] the growing practice of using the "not-for-profit" corporation for purposes that are semipublic, semiprivate, without evaluation of the economic and social effects of this device in widespread use; and the failure to question the role played in state and local affairs today by private profit "specialist," "planning consultant," and "planning engineering" firms.

The Question of State Sovereignty and Popular Control

In any consideration of interstate compacts the question of what happens to state power is fundamental. The lawyers who deny that the state loses any of its sovereignty when it enters a bi- or multistate agreement refer to strictly worded constitutional and statutory provisions which supposedly guarantee to signatory states ultimate independence and retention of power. Such is the Illinois statute of the oil compact which allows the governor to withdraw the State of Illinois when in his judgment such withdrawal is warranted. All of these compacts have clauses which stipulate that particular provisions are not binding unless the states give their assent, and clauses which withhold taxing power, and the like. In this most ultimate sense no state loses any of its statehood by entering any interstate agreement which contains such provisions.

Likewise it is argued that in the case of local governments the voters lose none of their rights through a metropolitan area compact because they have no rights other than those of the United States Constitution and those the state chooses to grant them when it incorporates towns or creates counties. If the state chooses to inaugurate some new pattern of local government that is clearly not in conflict with the state's constitution it can do so, as long as the people lose none of their ultimate power to control the state itself.

But this strictly legalistic point of view ignores the political side of the matter. A compact entered is an obligation which, as long as it exists, diminishes the freedom of the state to act independently in a particular sphere of interest, and since it has no real control over the acts of its fellow compacting members, it is always bound to a degree by their sins of omission and commission. A proliferation of interstate obligations carries significant implications for a state: diversion of revenues from state to interstate purposes, preoccupation of governors and legislatures with interstate affairs, diminution of administrative jurisdictions and authority when matters are shifted to regional operations, imperfect or no control over local planning in a metropolitan area compact, etc. This listing is indicative. It could be much longer.

In practice, the State of Illinois has not withdrawn from the interstate compacts it has entered. It goes along with them. In practice, the state has generally complied with the terms of these agreements, naming representatives to commissions, paying their expenses, enacting commission-recommended statutes, appropriating moneys when asked, creating not-for-profit corporations to administer recommended programs. This can be, and is, adduced as evidence the state is satisfied with the operations of its compacts and compact agencies. Actually it is evidence only of a lack of positive dissatisfaction on the part of the state's elected officials. It cannot be assumed that it accurately reflects the feelings, opinions, or desires of other elements of the state: the people (transit users, for example, in the Belleville area of the Bi-State Development Compact; property owners whose land may be taxed or taken over for purposes they neither want nor understand), the legislatures (Illinois's Assembly actions in creating a bevy of port and planning agencies on the Illinois side of the Mississippi at St. Louis), the potential entrepreneurs who cannot enter a field of economic activity because of an economic policy defining "wastefulness" (such as landowners who cannot drill for oil or who are bound by an established and protected pattern which gives production advantages to the existing oil industry), taxpayers of the compacting states and the nation (who will have to pay the bill for building large inland waterway systems which may favor only a narrow roster of communities and heavy industrial shippers, or which may really not be needed at all for the nation's transportation system), the governor (who has no veto power whether he wants it or not or whether he sees a need for it or not).

When a compact has been adopted without requirements for regular review, none but the aggrieved will pose the challenge of whether it ought to be continued—in its present form, in some modified form, or not at all. (By regular review the author implies something more than mere rote handling. Illinois is one of only two states—Kansas is the other—requiring quadrennial renewal of the Interstate Oil Compact. Such periodic renewal has resulted in no thoroughgoing legislative review of the compact in Illinois.) And to this extent the state is bound, not free, and it has yielded up some of its sovereignty.

Furthermore, this strictly legal interpretation does not cover that nameless condition of the American political process which develops when a vested interest comes into being with governmental sanction. The adoption by a state of any new program or policy immediately establishes a set of interests. Such interests, once governmentally armed and implemented, cannot thereafter be ignored or easily abolished. The political realities of our system do not allow it. Any attempt to repeal compacts involving substantial interstate special interests will encounter formidable difficulties. In practice, a state will avoid such confrontations unless there is overwhelming demand and evidence that they are needed. And this is not sovereignty, in the sense that sovereignty implies freedom to act, to act responsibly, and in a manner superior to any other government or source of power.

The complex governmental system this nation has built for political democracy and economic and social freedom demands social stability as well as social flexibility. It imperatively demands that popular control over immediate political ends or ultimate social and philosophical goals not be lost or delegated away. It must include recognition of rights, powers, duties, and obligations of subdivisional governments, for it is not yet convincing that this country has abandoned its original national assumptions that self-government is possible only when local and personal participation in the policy-making process, with a relatively high degree of control over it, are possible. A shift of power to an agency removed from popular or local governmental control is a loss of power for the people and their local governments.

An interstate compact, by its very nature, shifts a part of a state's authority to another state or states, or to the agency the several states jointly create to run the compact. Such an agency under the control of special interests or gubernatorially appointed representatives is two or more steps removed from popular control, or even of control by a local government. Armed with "planning authority" and "advisory-recommendatory" (lobbying) power, such an agency has immeasureable potential power to influence the lives of the populations who live under it but who do not participate in the planning, the legislative, and the decision-making processes. Add to the agency the power to create and operate enterprises which carry plans to completion and the loss to the people of control may become virtually total.

Federal and state actions designed to relieve mayors and other locally elected officials of the intergovernmental dilemmas they face have tended toward shifting problems into some kind of regional pattern of administration or into the state's control. Almost universally, the mayors who testified in the "Creative Federalism" hearings protested against giving the state governments more authority in local affairs, complained about existing state powers and authority, and repeatedly stressed that their state governments were not yet equipped to deal effectively or sympathetically with local governmental problems.

Lawyers, theoreticians, and other designers of regional intergovernmental and interstate mechanisms cannot afford to ignore these protests and pleas. They are symptomatic, and what they are symptomatic of is the fear of, and to a degree, the actual loss of local self-government in the American system today, and the concomitant loss by the people of their power to decide. It is sovereignty partially given up, perhaps not irrecovably, but practically, and exceedingly difficult to regain once relinquished.

It must be emphasized, however, that because this study strongly urges precautions in the adoption of interstate compacts and places considerable stress on existing negative aspects found in these four agreements, it cannot be assumed that the study itself is anti-interstate compact in its orientation, or against interstate involvement. Rather, it is urged that compacts are useful and are needed in present-day state governments, but it is imperative for the future of the state system that a potentially useful device such as this not be abused, misapplied, or carelessly accepted without recognition of pitfalls, omissions, failures, or without some effort given to improving serious shortcomings, such as the diminution of popular control. It is a plea for more care on the part of the states if it is the will of the American people to retain the states and their traditional local self-governing system.

Questions which might well be asked by state legislatures and governors considering enactment of interstate compacts are:

1. Can the state perform its share of the compact's obligations? (Performance, here, means "with full faith and credit" and includes financial, administrative, and political considerations.)

2. Is the compact the proper means available to serve the purposes for which it is intended? Does it contain concealed or potential purposes not desired by those who are asked to enact it?

3. Does the compact support and uphold the total purposes of the nation and its sovereign powers?

4. Does the agreement through the sharing of state power actually diminish state power ("state," here, meaning the total polity)?

5. If state power is not diminished perceptibly, will any elements of the polity unjustly or unequally be placed in an advantageous or disadvantageous posture which cannot be defended as necessary to the broader public purposes of the state?

6. Have minimal, essential controls (definition of commissioners' qualifications, provision for representativeness, periodic and thorough audits, restraint in use of the "not-for-profit" corporation) been included?

7. Does the compact specifically require periodic review by all elements concerned with it, including the Congress of the United States?

No doubt most of these questions are asked at one time or another by some, during the enacting process. It is not convincing, at the present time, that they are asked by all who have a hand in creating today's interstate compacts.

The Question of "Consent in Advance"

The Council of State Governments, the American Bar Association, the National Association of Attorneys General, and the Advisory Commission on Intergovernmental Relations recommend more use of "consent in advance" practices to reduce congressional involvement in enactment of certain types of compacts, to "promote a more expeditious process" for review and consent.[2] A clear description and delineation of the exact types of compacts and their special attributes which may be suitable for "consent in advance" has not yet been made public by Congress if any such categorical proposal has been given to its committees by any interested group.

Although this study, in its insistence that the consenting role of Congress is an exceedingly important stage which cannot be abdicated, appears to take a position contrary to the recommendations of the above groups, actually it does not. But something further needs to be said about "consent in advance."

This study assuredly does not recommend less congressional attention than is now being given, but it does recognize that Congress's role is primarily to guarantee with consent that it and the states are not jeopardizing the ultimate sovereignty of the nation via a compact and its arrangements. This study concludes that while the four compacts here examined hold no such specific jeopardy, the Great Lakes Basin Compact as originally drawn obviously held a questionable potential. The two other compacts involving navigable waterways held a promise of state interference with if not usurpation of the federal government's prime role in water matters. In actual administration the Bi-State Development Agency still holds such a potential, although as long as the Wabash Valley Interstate Compact confines its commission to an "advisory-recommendatory" role it holds no threat of significance.

Congress shares its concern for the shape and form of federalism with the United States Supreme Court, the chief executive, the states, and the people. Concern for what may happen under interstate compacts is Congress's responsibility under the Constitution, and herein its position is first. But questions of joining or not joining an interstate compact, of creating one, renewing or not renewing it, of appropriating money for its support, of sanctioning and implementing activities, are uniquely the responsibilities of the states and their people, and it is the states and their people which should have an intense concern for what they may be gaining, losing, abandoning, delegating, harming, or benefitting through the path of interstate compacts, in the fullest legal, political, and philosophical sense.

The Advisory Commission on Intergovernmental Relations' recommendations to the states and local governments are generally directed toward a loosening and relaxing of restricting state laws which bind grass-roots governments and citizens' groups in multitudinous ways, while recognizing that the existing legal restraints were the outgrowth of the muckraking and earlier reform eras' revelations of corruption of a pervasive sort in state and local life.[3] What is difficult to reconcile in the current ACIR philosophy is why it seemingly believes broad relaxation of restraints today will not encourage or make possible some of the same kind of wheeling and dealing in developmental and planning matters involving public works and services as occurred around the turn of the century, but this time with large federal outlays of money as part of the plum. Obviously, the ACIR does recognize that popular control and a popular voice are still needed, for occasional recommendations refer to citizen control and citizen decision-making authority, popular referenda in taxing matters, and the like. But it is exceedingly cautious in placing any emphasis on widespread use of referenda, possibly because the popular referendum as a governmental decision-making device has operated negatively on many occasions when need for a favorable decision on public developmental proposals was great. It is, of course, a potential restraint of tremendous importance. But it is at the same time the most dependable guarantee of widespread citizen participation, to rouse a sense of identity of the citizen with local governmental problems as well as to educate him on the social needs which he creates and which he must pay for. The loss to American government will be incalculable if popular referenda come to be abandoned totally, with decision-making handed over completely to professional, technical, and other experts, as well as professional politicians. For expert knowledge, no matter how informed or well trained, will always be by appointment or by hire, requiring a professional ethic of sufficient strength to guarantee a certain nobility of performance, and an educational method of sufficient depth and certainty to guarantee objectivity, broad vision, and comprehensive grasp of all human problems in any given situation on all occasions, none of which have yet been developed.

Moreover, none will deny that treaties of the United States with foreign states have had tremendous impacts on the American people, nor that there have been treaties which the American people have not liked and some which have both at the time of enactment and in retrospect been deemed unwise. State governments, however, have not customarily in the past posed such burdens on their people through sweeping intergovernmental contracts and obligations. Obviously the question of an international treaty is no matter for popular referendum. But it is difficult to understand why some kind of popular referendum, either prior to enactment or on questions involving proposed activities of a compacting agency, cannot be used in some limited fashion in the operations of interstate compacts. The kind of relatively unrestrained autonomy that is essential for the national government in international decisions seems not to be necessary for state governments in their purely domestic role, a role that in most compacts is essentially administrative. But in "economic developmental" compacts requiring repeated legislative action, and allowing revenue-bonding power, eminent domain, possibly taxing power, without some single authority above the compact agencies to supervise and control their activities, there is most assuredly a possibility for significant loss by the people of autonomy and rights of various kinds through ill-considered, ill-managed, or even arrogant compacting actions.

It is argued that the customary "balanced" commission, with compacting states equally represented in the governing board, is sufficient ultimate control to protect the people of the several states. The matter is questionable, as witness the New York Port Authority case. The quorum possibilities in two of this study's compacts partially negate the argument. There are other factors which render the "equal balance" concept less than secure: unequal state needs, resources, populations, laws and constitutions, and taxing powers of the compacting states. In any event, it all depends upon the appointees to the governing board.

It is futile to deny that some interstate compacts have encountered and will continue to encounter a wary reception or active dislike from the populations most intimately affected by them. It is also futile to assert that full state legislative attention is given to appraising popular feeling before granting approval to proposed compacts, their renewal, their implementation. It is this area of today's interstate compacting activity which very much needs improving.

It would appear, therefore, that "consent in advance" is of limited suitability: for boundary settlements of a traditional kind, reciprocal arrangements to implement law enforcement activities, in certain limited areas which Congress "blankets under" in general law (such as the Federal Highway Safety Act of 1958), and compacts of the "advisory-recommendatory" type, written in some standardized form which does not include unqualified or undefined property-owning powers, revenue-bonding powers, taxing powers, metropolitan-area planning powers (the Advisory Commission on Intergovernmental Relations to the contrary), or other unqualified and ill-defined power of a sweeping or obscure kind. Compacts containing such powers, it would appear, require close and intensive congressional scrutiny prior to enactment.

Until the states and the Congress have perfected their processes for handling compacts, have perfected their legal structure surrounding them and their operations, have become sophisticated in their understandings of compact implications and probable effects of certain types, it would seem that congressional consent and review procedures are still very much needed. For the states do not convincingly show that they have yet reached a point where they can altogether be trusted to operate alone on such matters having vital implications for the federal system and to the people.

The Question of the Role of Private Consulting Agencies and Governmental Planning for Social and Economic Development

A question of considerable interest and importance which has arisen repeatedly in this study's researches is one without answers, it would appear, since to the author's knowledge no comprehensive study has been published giving thorough attention to it. This is the question of the political role being played today in nationwide governmental planning and decision-making at all levels of government by private profit consulting agencies of the planning and advisory type.

It takes little reflection to realize that huge outlays running into millions of dollars in public and private funds are being expended annually on surveys, studies, planning, consultation, and research for the guidance of elected officials in operating and improving American government and society. No city undertakes a change in transit operations without consulting a transit advisory concern on a fee basis. No community attempts to launch an extensive water supply and sewage disposal program without hiring a consulting firm to make a study. Airports, tunnels, roads and streets, lighting, fire protection, soil and wildlife conservation, waterway improvements, community facilities, parks and recreation—the list of major public works and utilities is impressive of matters which state and local governments seemingly regard as beyond their local capacities to plan for, to contract for, and to build properly and adequately, without first purchasing the specialized technical services of a private consulting group for substantial sums.

Two major questions emerge: How much worth in terms of dollars spent do these governments receive in advice and guidance in return for their money? How much influence on local decision-making do the recommendations of such private consulting firms actually have? There is a third group of questions which arise from the first two: Are "feasibility studies" and "economic appraisals" used to convince and persuade a reluctant community to move in a desired direction through the recommendations of such studies? How many and what kind of possibly competing interests do such private consulting groups work for at the same time? Is it possible for a private employing agency to receive any benefits from the terms of a study made for a public employing agency? At what stage of legislation is the consulting agency hired? What considerations enter into the selection of a particular consulting agency in preference to another? Do Americans believe today that amateurs in government, chosen by the people to govern for a time, cannot make competent public decisions entailing large expenditures without the acquiescence of technical advisors? Has their belief in the omniscience of such consultant firms reached the same level as their seeming faith in "science" and "scientists"? How stringent are state laws on the licensing and professional standards required for such consultant firms to do business on a contractual basis with public agencies and officials? Are any such consultant firms tied to manufacturers of equipment, materials, supplies of a necessary kind? Building contractors? Realtors and land development companies?

These are large questions which open up a potentially productive field of inquiry for the Advisory Commission on Intergovernmental Relations, the Council of State Governments, the National Association of Attorneys General, university researchers in political and economic science, and the committees of the United States Congress. No one denies there are many highly technical matters encountered by governing bodies requiring expert engineering knowledge, expert assistance in surveying all factors entering into a comprehensive plan of development, and knowledgeable advice in computing costs and kinds of expenditures. The choice, it would seem, lies between a government's maintaining a costly, full-time expert planning group or hiring private groups on a special project basis. Today, however, governments have created and staffed full-time planning agencies of their own and yet seem compelled to hire private planning groups to assist them. It is this area of the problem that needs exploration.

Three of the present interstate compacts provide illustrations of this phenomenon. The State of Illinois has a fully implemented state economic and developmental planning agency: the Illinois Department of Business and Economic Development. Yet few of the problems of concern to the Great Lakes Basin Compact, the Bi-State Development Compact, or the Wabash Valley Interstate Compact have been referred to the department. In fact, each of these three compacts represent specialized planning operations for specialized planning areas, and the paths of the one rarely if ever converge with those of the others.

Not only is the Department of Business and Economic Development not directly involved with the specialized compact agency planning, the compact agencies themselves (three of which are planning agencies) rely frequently on the planning assistance of other public and private consulting groups, or spend much of their time opposing the plans of these others. In the case of the Bi-State Development Agency, it has dealt not only with the Southwestern Metropolitan Area Planning Commission (SWIMPAC), the St. Louis Human Development Corporation, and the East-West Gateway Coordinating Council, but also regularly on a contractual basis with the private W. C. Gilman agency and the private Sverdrup, Parcel and

Associates. The East-West Gateway Coordinating Council has used the Governmental Research Institute of St. Louis. As for the Wabash Valley Interstate Compact Commission, in its "coordinating" activities it plans and at the same time utilizes university faculty planning and research and university planning facilities, the planning product of the Army Corps of Engineers, that of a half-dozen other federal agencies, a similar roster of state agencies, and the private firm of Marcou, O'Leary and Associates to appraise its own planning potential and to outline for it a plan for the Wabash Valley.

As noted in discussion of the Bi-State Development Agency, each major developmental project undertaken by the agency to date has been preceded by a hired, privately drafted feasibility study which has never yet denied the proposed project is anything but highly meritorious and needed. The original Harlan Bartholomew and Associates plan for the St. Louis metropolitan area was itself a plan for the bistate agency to develop but, as noted, was never really used and has generally been set aside in the passing years.

The nature of the governmental problem posed here needs not be belabored. Of most interest to this study would, of course, be the influence of such private planning agencies on the decisions of interstate agencies in their planning, an area even less easily understood than the strictly intrastate local governmental kind, and having vital implications for the future of the federal system.

This study has no answers to these questions. It can only pose them as having dramatically arisen from limited examination of a limited number of interstate compacts. It can, however, insist that we need to know more about the matter.

Some Final Observations

This chapter begins with the title, "Interstate Compacts: A Question of Federalism," and that is the way this study must end. What has most clearly emerged from the research is a conviction that increasing involvement by the states in interstate compacts heralds the beginning of a new shape for American federalism: a complex system being made even more complex, less clearly compartmentalized, more difficult to control by law and popular action because less easily seen and less easily organized for the placing of responsibility and authority.

In this new stage of federalism's evolution, the people of the United States appear to play a diminished role. Authority, planning, negotiation, decision-making, administration move into the realm of governors, special economic development interests, combinations of mayors and other locally elected officials, revenue bond purchasers, appointed technicians and specialists, and private planning consultants. In Robert Salisbury's terms, it is a "new convergence of power." State legislatures and the Congress assume the task and role once held in state government by the voters: the giving or withholding of consent. The one remaining role for the people is that of taxpaying, and it would seem that their consenting role in this is also diminishing.

It is possible to emerge from this examination in accord with the sentiments expressed in 1968 by the late veteran Congressman Barratt O'Hara, of Chicago, who opposed the Great Lakes Basin Compact in all efforts to obtain consent for it until 1968, when he finally consented because of a promise he made to his state's governor:

Nor am I as certain as are many others that regional rule and sovereignty should be substituted for State government. I appreciate as much as anyone that there are many serious problems . . . that are of common concern to States. . . . But whether these problems can reach the wisest and fairest of solutions by the withdrawal of the sovereignty of the individual States and the substitution by compact of a regional supergovernment has not as yet been conclusively demonstrated.

It may be that in time the wisdom of regional supergovernments will be demonstrated so conclusively that another generation will change our Constitution to do away with States altogether and in their stead substitute regional governments. I make no such prediction. . . .

The responsibility placed upon the Congress by the Constitution is not to be treated trivially or discharged lightly and in haste. The increasing number of compacts, and the apparently sound arguments in their behalf, would seem to argue that no new compacts should be approved without the most thorough-going . . . research.[4]

Since it is difficult if not impossible to take a position counter to a trend that seemingly is founded on genuine need simply to preserve the existing form of institutions which may have grown outmoded, one can only conclude that the growth of interstate compacts is an inevitable trend, that Congressman O'Hara's advice and plea are good and should be heeded, and that it is a matter for time and practice to resolve.

But one final admonition can be offered: if there is a serious concern herein for the future of state governments, one of the first areas of attack on the problem must be within the states themselves. Legislatures are imperatively in need of reorganization, the governors' offices need attention, the state departments and bureaus need realignment, reexamination, reconstitution, and restaffing. State laws and constitutions need overhauling. All of these needs have been stressed so many times it is redundant to repeat them again.

Yet this is where the future of the states and the federal system lies and here is where today's seeming need for interstate compacts arises. If the states were as strong and as competent as they ought to be the people would be certain of retaining control over them and there would be little to fear and much to welcome in a state's interstate operations. There would be scant reason to doubt the continuation of the federal system of government. It cannot be said that this is the case today.

APPENDIXES/NOTES/BIBLIOGRAPHY/INDEX

APPENDIX A: Remuneration of the Bi-State Transit System by Certain Illinois School Districts in Transporting School Children at Reduced Rates of Fare, June 1967

Bi-State transports students on all regular service lines in the Illinois area of operation (Madison, St. Clair, and Monroe Counties) at reduced rates of fare. Its 1967 contracts are as follows:

School District	Per Day	Avg. 180-day school term
* Belleville Dist. 118	$ 71.50	$ 12,870
* Belleville Dist. 201	296.10	53,298
Central Dist. 204	22.00	3,960
E. Alton-Wood River Dist. 13	17.65	3,177
* E. Alton-Wood River Dist. 14	89.00	16,020
E. Alton-Wood River Dist. 15	28.85	6,993
* E. St. Louis Dist. 189	47.80	8,604
Granite City Dist. 9	953.20	171,576
Madison Dist. 12	103.80	18,684
O'Fallon Dist. 90)		
O'Fallon Dist. 203)	197.65	35,577
Pontiac Holiday Dist. 105	54.60	9,828
Venice Dist. 3	88.40	15,912

* Only a portion of students in this district carried by Bi-State.
Source: Letter, Robert Granda, Illinois Legislative Council, from Leo A. White, Superintendent, Bi-State School Operation, June 2, 1967. (See p. 351 n 87).

APPENDIX B: *Great Lakes Basin Compact*

PUBLIC LAW 90–419; 82 STAT. 414

[S. 660]
AN ACT GRANTING THE CONSENT OF CONGRESS TO A GREAT
LAKES BASIN COMPACT, AND FOR OTHER PURPOSES.

*Be it enacted by the Senate and House of Representatives of the
United States of America in Congress assembled, That:*

The consent of Congress is hereby given, to the extent and subject
to the conditions hereinafter set forth, to the Great Lakes Basin Compact which has been entered into by the States of Illinois, Indiana,
Michigan, Minnesota, New York, Ohio, Pennsylvania and Wisconsin
in the form as follows:

GREAT LAKES BASIN COMPACT

The party states solemnly agree:

Article 1

The purposes of this compact are, through means of joint or
cooperative action:

1. To promote the orderly, integrated, and comprehensive development, use, and conservation of the water resources of the Great
Lakes Basin (hereinafter called the Basin).

2. To plan for the welfare and development of the water resources of the Basin as a whole as well as for those portions of the Basin
which may have problems of special concern.

3. To make it possible for the states of the Basin and their people
to derive the maximum benefit from utilization of public works, in the
form of navigational aids or otherwise, which may exist or which may
be constructed from time to time.

4. To advise in securing and maintaining a proper balance among industrial, commercial, agricultural, water supply, residential, recreational, and other legitimate uses of the water resources of the Basin.

5. To establish and maintain an intergovernmental agency to the end that the purposes of this compact may be accomplished more effectively.

Article II

A. This compact shall enter into force and become effective and binding when it has been enacted by the legislatures of any four of the States of Illinois, Indiana, Michigan, Minnesota, New York, Ohio, Pennsylvania, and Wisconsin and thereafter shall enter into force and become effective and binding as to any other of said states when enacted by the legislature thereof.

B. The Province of Ontario and the Province of Quebec, or either of them, may become states party to this compact by taking such action as their laws and the laws of the Government of Canada may prescribe for adherence thereto. For the purpose of this compact the word "state" shall be construed to include a Province of Canada.

Article III

The Great Lakes Commission created by Article IV of this compact shall exercise its powers and perform its functions in respect to the Basin which, for the purposes of this compact, shall consist of so much of the following as may be within the party states:

1. Lakes Erie, Huron, Michigan, Ontario, St. Clair, Superior, and the St. Lawrence River, together with any and all natural or man-made water interconnections between or among them.

2. All rivers, ponds, lakes, streams, and other watercourses which, in their natural state or in their prevailing conditions, are tributary to Lakes Erie, Huron, Michigan, Ontario, St. Clair, and Superior or any of them or which comprise part of any watershed draining into any of said lakes.

Article IV

A. There is hereby created an agency of the party states to be known as The Great Lakes Commission (hereinafter called the Commission). In that name the Commission may sue and be sued, acquire, hold and convey real and personal property and any interest therein. The Commission shall have a seal with the words "The Great Lakes Commission" and such other design as it may prescribe engraved thereon by which it shall authenticate its proceedings. Transactions involving real or personal property shall conform to the laws of the state in which the property is located, and the Commission may by by-laws provide for the execution and acknowledgement of all instruments in its behalf.

B. The Commission shall be composed of not less than three commissioners nor more than five commissioners from each party state designated or appointed in accordance with the law of the state which they represent and serving and subject to removal in accordance with such law.

C. Each state delegation shall be entitled to three votes in the Commission. The presence of commissioners from a majority of the party states shall constitute a quorum for the transaction of business at any meeting of the Commission. Actions of the Commission shall be by a majority of the votes cast except that any recommendations made pursuant to Article VI of this compact shall require an affirmative vote of not less than a majority of the votes cast from each of a majority of the states present and voting.

D. The commissioners of any two or more party states may meet separately to consider problems of particular interest to their states but no action taken at any such meeting shall be deemed an action of the Commission unless and until the Commission shall specifically approve the same.

E. In the absence of any commissioner, his vote may be cast by another representative or commissioner of his state provided that said commissioner or other representative casting said vote shall have a written proxy in proper form as may be required by the Commission.

F. The Commission shall elect annually from among its members a chairman and vice-chairman. The Commission shall appoint an Executive Director who shall also act as secretary-treasurer, and who shall be bonded in such amount as the Commission may require. The Executive Director shall serve at the pleasure of the Commission and at such compensation and under such terms and conditions as may be fixed by it. The Executive Director shall be custodian of the records of the Commission with authority to affix the Commission's official seal and to attest to and certify such records or copies thereof.

G. The Executive Director, subject to the approval of the Commission in such cases as its by-laws may provide, shall appoint and remove or discharge such personnel as may be necessary for the performance of the Commission's function. Subject to the aforesaid approval, the Executive Director may fix their compensation, define their duties, and require bonds of such of them as the Commission may designate.

H. The Executive Director, on behalf of, as trustee for, and with the approval of the Commission, may borrow, accept, or contract for the services of personnel from any state or government or any subdivision or agency thereof, from any inter-governmental agency, or from any institution, person, firm or corporation; and may accept for any of the Commission's purposes and functions under this compact any and all donations, gifts, and grants of money, equipment, supplies, materials, and services from any state or government or any subdivision or agency thereof or inter-governmental agency or from any institution, person, firm or corporation and may receive and utilize the same.

I. The Commission may establish and maintain one or more offices for the transacting of its business and for such purposes the Executive Director, on behalf of, as trustee for, and with the approval of the Commission, may acquire, hold and dispose of real and personal property necessary to the performance of its functions.

J. No tax levied or imposed by any party state or any political subdivision thereof shall be deemed to apply to property, transactions, or income of the Commission.

K. The Commission may adopt, amend and rescind by-laws, rules and regulations for the conduct of its business.

L. The organization meeting of the Commission shall be held within six months from the effective date of the compact.

M. The Commission and its Executive Director shall make available to the party states any information within its possession and shall always provide free access to its records by duly authorized representatives of such party states.

N. The Commission shall keep a written record of its meetings and proceedings and shall annually make a report thereof to be submitted to the duly designated official of each party state.

O. The Commission shall make and transmit annually to the legislature and Governor of each party state a report covering the activities of the Commission for the preceding year and embodying such recommendations as may have been adopted by the Commission. The Commission may issue such additional reports as it may deem desirable.

Article v

A. The members of the Commission shall serve without compensation, but the expenses of each commissioner shall be met by the state which he represents in accordance with the law of that state. All other expenses incurred by the Commission in the course of exercising the powers conferred upon it by this compact, unless met in some other manner specifically provided by this compact, shall be paid by the Commission out of its own funds.

B. The Commission shall submit to the executive head or designated officer of each party state a budget of its estimated expenditures for such period as may be required by the laws of that state for presentation to the legislature thereof.

C. Each of the Commission's budgets of estimated expenditures shall contain specific recommendations of the amount or amounts to be appropriated by each of the party states. Detailed commission budgets shall be recommended by a majority of the votes cast, and the costs shall be allocated equitably among the party states in accordance with their respective interests.

D. The Commission shall not pledge the credit of any party state. The Commission may meet any of its obligations in whole or in part with funds available to it under Article IV(H) of this compact, provided that the Commission takes specific action setting aside such funds prior to the incurring of any obligations to be met in whole or in part in this manner. Except where the Commission makes use of funds available to it under Article IV(H) hereof, the Commission shall not incur any obligations prior to the allotment of funds by the party states adequate to meet the same.

E. The Commission shall keep accurate accounts of all receipts and disbursements. The receipts and disbursements of the Commission shall be subject to the audit and accounting procedures established under the by-laws. However, all receipts and disbursements of funds handled by the Commission shall be audited yearly by a qualified public accountant and the report of the audit shall be included in and become a part of the annual report of the Commission.

F. The accounts of the Commission shall be open at any reasonable time for inspection by such agency, representative or representatives of the party states as may be duly constituted for that purpose and by others who may be authorized by the Commission.

Article VI

The Commission shall have power to:

A. Collect, correlate, interpret, and report on data relating to the water resources and the use thereof in the Basin or any portion thereof.

B. Recommend methods for the orderly, efficient, and balanced development, use and conservation of the water resources of the Basin or any portion thereof to the party states and to any other governments or agencies having interests in or jurisdiction over the Basin or any portion thereof.

C. Consider the need for and desirability of public works and improvements relating to the water resources in the Basin or any portion thereof.

D. Consider means of improving navigation and port facilities in the Basin or any portion thereof.

E. Consider means of improving and maintaining the fisheries of the Basin or any portion thereof.

F. Recommend policies relating to water resources including the institution and alteration of flood plain and other zoning laws, ordinances and regulations.

G. Recommend uniform or other laws, ordinances, or regulations relating to the development, use and conservation of the Basin's water resources to the party states or any of them and to other governments, political subdivisions, agencies, or inter-governmental bodies having interests in or jurisdiction sufficient to affect conditions in the Basin or any portion thereof.

H. Consider and recommend amendments or agreements supplementary to this compact to the party states or any of them, and assist in the formulation and drafting of such amendments or supplementary agreements.

I. Prepare and publish reports, bulletins, and publications appropriate to this work and fix reasonable sales prices therefor.

J. With respect to the water resources of the Basin or any portion thereof, recommend agreements between the governments of the United States and Canada.

K. Recommend mutual arrangements expressed by concurrent or reciprocal legislation on the part of Congress and the Parliament of Canada including but not limited to such agreements and mutual arrangements as are provided for by Article XIII of the Treaty of 1909 Relating to Boundary Waters and Questions Arising Between the United States and Canada. (Treaty Series, No. 548).

L. Cooperate with the governments of the United States and of Canada, the party states and any public or private agencies or bodies having interests in or jurisdiction sufficient to affect the Basin or any portion thereof.

M. At the request of the United States, or in the event that a Province shall be a party state, at the request of the Government of Canada, assist in the negotiation and formulation of any treaty or other mutual arrangement or agreement between the United States and Canada with reference to the Basin or any portion thereof.

N. Make any recommendation and do all things necessary and proper to carry out the powers conferred upon the Commission by this compact, provided that no action of the Commission shall have the force of law in, or be binding upon, any party state.

Article VII

Each party state agrees to consider the action the Commission recommends in respect to:

A. Stabilization of lake levels.

B. Measures for combating pollution, beach erosion, floods and shore inundation.

C. Uniformity in navigation regulations within the constitutional powers of the states.

D. Proposed navigation aids and improvements.

E. Uniformity or effective coordinating action in fishing laws and regulations and cooperative action to eradicate destructive and parasitical forces endangering the fisheries, wildlife, and other water resources.

F. Suitable hydroelectric power developments.

G. Cooperative programs for control of soil and bank erosion for the general improvement of the Basin.

H. Diversion of waters from and into the Basin.

1. Other measures the Commission may recommend to the states pursuant to Article VI of this compact.

Article VIII

This compact shall continue in force and remain binding upon each party state until renounced by the act of the legislature of such state, in such form and manner as it may choose and as may be valid and effective to repeal a statute of said state, provided that such renunciation shall not become effective until six months after notice of such action shall have been officially communicated in writing to the executive head of the other party states.

Article IX

It is intended that the provisions of this compact shall be reasonably and liberally construed to effectuate the purposes thereof. The provisions of this compact shall be severable and if any phrase, clause, sentence or provision of this compact is declared to be contrary to the constitution of any party state or of the United States, or in the case of a Province, to the British North America Act of 1867 as amended, or the applicability thereof to any state, agency, person or circumstance is held invalid, the constitutionality of the remainder of this compact and the applicability thereof to any state, agency, person or circumstance shall not be affected thereby, provided further that if this compact shall be held contrary to the constitution of the United States, or in the case of a Province, to the British North America Act of 1867 as amended, or of any party state, the compact shall remain in full force and effect as to the remaining states and in full force and effect as to the state affected as to all severable matters.

Sec. 2. The consent herein granted does not extend to paragraph B of article II or to paragraphs J, K, and M of article VI of the compact, or to other provisions of article VI of the compact which purport to authorize recommendations to, or cooperation with, any foreign or international governments, political subdivisions, agencies or bodies. In carrying out its functions under this Act the Commission shall be solely a consultative and recommendatory agency which will cooperate with the agencies of the United States. It shall furnish to the Congress and to the President, or to any official designated by the President, copies of its reports submitted to the party states pursuant to paragraph O of article IV of the compact.

Sec. 3. Nothing contained in this Act or in the compact consented to hereby shall be construed to affect the jurisdiction, powers, or prerogatives of any department, agency, or officer of the United States Government or of the Great Lakes Basin Committee established under title II of the Water Resources Planning Act, or of any international commission or agency over or in the Great Lakes Basin or any portion thereof, nor shall anything contained herein be construed to establish an international agency or to limit or affect in any way the exercise of the treatymaking power or any other power or right of the United States.

Sec. 4. The right to alter, amend, or repeal this Act is expressly reserved.

Approved July 24, 1968.

APPENDIX C: *Treaty—Great Britain:*
January 11, 1909

January 11, 1909

Treaty between the United States and Great Britain relating to
boundary waters between the United States and Canada. Signed at
Washington, January 11, 1909; ratification advised by the Senate,
March 3, 1909; ratified by the President, April 1, 1910; ratified by
Great Britain, March 31, 1910; ratifications exchanged at Washing-
ton, May 5, 1910; proclaimed, May 13, 1910.

BY THE PRESIDENT OF THE UNITED STATES OF AMERICA

A PROCLAMATION

Water Boundary With Canada. Preamble

Whereas a Treaty between the United States of America and His
Majesty the King of the United Kingdom of Great Britain and Ireland
and of the British Dominions beyond the Seas, Emperor of India, to
prevent disputes regarding the use of boundary waters and to settle all
questions which are now pending between the United States and the
Dominion of Canada involving the rights, obligations, or interests of
either in relation to the other or to the inhabitants of the other, along
their common frontier, and to make provision for the adjustment and
settlement of all such questions as may hereafter arise, was concluded
and signed by their respective Plenipotentiaries at Washington on the

eleventh day of January, one thousand nine hundred and nine, the original of which Treaty is word for word as follows:

Contracting Powers

The United States of America and His Majesty the King of the United Kingdom of Great Britain and Ireland and of the British Dominions beyond the Seas, Emperor of India, being equally desirous to prevent disputes regarding the use of boundary waters and to settle all questions which are now pending between the United States and the Dominion of Canada involving the rights, obligations, or interests of either in relation to the other or to the inhabitants of the other, along their common frontier, and to make provision for the adjustment and settlement of all such questions as may hereafter arise, have resolved to conclude a treaty in furtherance of these ends, and for that purpose have appointed as their respective plenipotentiaries:

Plenipotentiaries

The President of the United States of America, Elihu Root, Secretary of State of the United States; and

His Britannic Majesty, the Right Honorable James Bryce, O. M., his Ambassador Extraordinary and Plenipotentiary at Washington;

Who, after having communicated to one another their full powers, found in good and due form, have agreed upon the following articles:

Preliminary Article

Boundary Waters Defined

For the purposes of this treaty boundary waters are defined as the waters from main shore to main shore of the lakes and rivers and connecting waterways, or the portions thereof, along which the international boundary between the United States and the Dominion of Canada passes, including all bays, arms, and inlets thereof, but not including tributary waters which in their natural channels would flow into such lakes, rivers, and waterways, or waters flowing from such lakes, rivers, and waterways, or the waters of rivers flowing across the boundary.

Article I

Navigation Free to Both Countries

The High Contracting Parties agree that the navigation of all navigable boundary waters shall forever continue free and open for the purposes of commerce to the inhabitants and to the ships, vessels, and boats of both countries equally, subject, however, to any laws and regulations of either country, within its own territory, not inconsistent with such privilege of free navigation and applying equally and without discrimination to the inhabitants, ships, vessels, and boats of both countries.

Lake Michigan and All Connecting Canals Included

It is further agreed that so long as this treaty shall remain in force, this same right of navigation shall extend to the waters of Lake Michigan and to all canals connecting boundary waters, and now existing or which may hereafter be constructed on either side of the line. Either of the High Contracting Parties may adopt rules and regulations governing the use of such canals within its own territory and may charge tolls for the use thereof, but all such rules and regulations and all tolls charged shall apply alike to the subjects or citizens of the High Contracting Parties and the ships, vessels, and boats of both of the High Contracting Parties, and they shall be placed on terms of equality in the use thereof.

Article II

Control Over Waters Crossing Boundary, etc., Retained

Each of the High Contracting Parties reserves to itself or to the several State Governments on the one side and the Dominion or Provincial Governments on the other as the case may be, subject to any treaty provisions now existing with respect thereto, the exclusive jurisdiction and control over the use and diversion, whether temporary or permanent, of all waters on its own side of the line which in their natural channels would flow across the boundary or into boundary waters; but it is agreed that any interference with or diversion from their natural channel of such waters on either side of the boundary, resulting in any injury on the other side of the boundary, shall give rise to the same rights and entitle the injured parties to the same legal remedies as if such injury took place in the country where such diversion or interference occurs; but this provision shall not apply to cases already existing or to cases expressly covered by special agreement between the parties hereto.

Navigation Not to Be Injured

It is understood, however, that neither of the High Contracting Parties intends by the foregoing provision to surrender any right, which it may have, to object to any interference with or diversions of waters on the other side of the boundary the effect of which would be productive of material injury to the navigation interests on its own side of the boundary.

Article III

Further Diversions, etc., Subject to Special Agreement

It is agreed that, in addition to the uses, obstructions, and diversions heretofore permitted or hereafter provided for by special agreement between the Parties hereto, no further or other uses or obstructions or diversions, whether temporary or permanent, of boundary waters on either side of the line, affecting the natural level or flow of boundary waters on the other side of the line, shall be made except by authority of the United States or the Dominion of Canada within their respective jurisdictions and with the approval, as hereinafter provided, of a joint commission, to be known as the International Joint Commission.

Government Works for Harbor, etc.

The foregoing provisions are not intended to limit or interfere with the existing rights of the Government of the United States on the one side and the Government of the Dominion of Canada on the other, to undertake and carry on governmental works in boundary waters for the deepening of channels, the construction of breakwaters, the improvement of harbors, and other governmental works for the benefit of commerce and navigation, provided that such works are wholly on its own side of the line and do not materially affect the level or flow of the boundary waters on the other, nor are such provisions intended to interfere with the ordinary use of such waters for domestic and sanitary purposes.

Article IV

Consent for Dams, etc., Altering Water Levels

The High Contracting Parties agree that, except in cases provided for by special agreement between them, they will not permit the construction or maintenance on their respective sides of the boundary of any remedial or protective works or any dams or other obstructions in waters flowing from boundary waters or in waters at a lower level than the boundary in rivers flowing across the boundary, the effect of which is to raise the natural level of waters on the other side of the boundary unless the construction or maintenance thereof is approved by the aforesaid International Joint Commission.

Polluting Boundary Waters Forbidden

It is further agreed that the waters herein defined as boundary waters and waters flowing across the boundary shall not be polluted on either side to the injury of health or property on the other.

Article V

Niagara River. Diversion of Waters Limited

The High Contracting Parties agree that it is expedient to limit the diversion of waters from the Niagara River so that the level of Lake Erie and the flow of the stream shall not be appreciably affected. It is the desire of both Parties to accomplish this object with the least possible injury to investments which have already been made in the construction of power plants on the United States side of the river under grants of authority from the State of New York, and on the Canadian side of the river under licenses authorized by the Dominion of Canada and the Province of Ontario.

Use Above the Falls

So long as this treaty shall remain in force, no diversion of the waters of the Niagara River above the Falls from the natural course and stream thereof shall be permitted except for the purposes and to the extent hereinafter provided.

By United States

The United States may authorize and permit the diversion within the State of New York of the waters of said river above the Falls of Niagara, for power purposes, not exceeding in the aggregate a daily diversion at the rate of twenty thousand cubic feet of water per second.

By Canada

The United Kingdom, by the Dominion of Canada, or the Province of Ontario, may authorize and permit the diversion within the Province of Ontario of the waters of said river above the Falls of Niagara, for power purposes, not exceeding in the aggregate a daily diversion at the rate of thirty-six thousand cubic feet of water per second.

Use for Navigation, etc., Not Affected

The prohibitions of this article shall not apply to the diversion of water for sanitary or domestic purposes, or for the service of canals for the purposes of navigation.

Article VI

St. Mary and Milk Rivers
Apportionment of Waters for Irrigation
By United States   By Canada

The High Contracting Parties agree that the St. Mary and Milk Rivers and their tributaries (in the State of Montana and the Provinces of Alberta and Saskatchewan) are to be treated as one stream for the purposes of irrigation and power, and the waters thereof shall be apportioned equally between the two countries, but in making such equal apportionment more than half may be taken from one river and less than half from the other by either country so as to afford a more beneficial use to each. It is further agreed that in the division of such waters during the irrigation season, between the 1st of April and 31st of October, inclusive, annually, the United States is entitled to a prior appropriation of 500 cubic feet per second of the waters of the Milk River, or so much of such amount as constitutes three-fourths of its natural flow, and that Canada is entitled to a prior appropriation of 500 cubic feet per second of the flow of St. Mary River, or so much of such amount as constitutes three-fourths of its natural flow.

Diversion of St. Mary River

The channel of the Milk River in Canada may be used at the convenience of the United States for the conveyance, while passing through Canadian territory, of waters diverted from the St. Mary River. The provisions of Article II of this treaty shall apply to any injury resulting to property in Canada from the conveyance of such waters through the Milk River.

Measurement by Reclamation and Irrigation Officers

The measurement and apportionment of the water to be used by each country shall from time to time be made jointly by the properly constituted reclamation officers of the United States and the properly constituted irrigation officers of His Majesty under the direction of the International Joint Commission.

Article VII

International Joint Commission Established

The High Contracting Parties agree to establish and maintain an International Joint Commission of the United States and Canada composed of six commissioners, three on the part of the United States appointed by the President thereof, and three on the part of the United Kingdom appointed by His Majesty on the recommendation of the Governor in Council of the Dominion of Canada.

Article VIII

Jurisdiction, etc.
Principles Declared

This International Joint Commission shall have jurisdiction over and shall pass upon all cases involving the use or obstruction or diversion of the waters with respect to which under Articles III and IV of this treaty the approval of this Commission is required, and in passing upon such cases the Commission shall be governed by the following rules or principles which are adopted by the High Contracting Parties for this purpose:

Mutual Rights

The High Contracting Parties shall have, each on its own side of the boundary, equal and similar rights in the use of the waters hereinbefore defined as boundary waters.

Precedence of Uses

The following order of precedence shall be observed among the various uses enumerated hereinafter for these waters, and no use shall be permitted which tends materially to conflict with or restrain any other use which is given preference over it in this order of precedence:

(1) Uses for domestic and sanitary purposes;

(2) Uses for navigation, including the service of canals for the purposes of navigation;

(3) Uses for power and for irrigation purposes.

The foregoing provisions shall not apply to or disturb any existing uses of boundary waters on either side of the boundry.

Temporary Diversions

The requirement for an equal division may in the discretion of the Commission be suspended in cases of temporary diversions along boundary waters at points where such equal division can not be made advantageously on account of local conditions, and where such diversion does not diminish elsewhere the amount available for use on the other side.

Compensating Remedial Works

The Commission in its discretion may make its approval in any case conditional upon the construction of remedial or protective works to compensate so far as possible for the particular use or diversion proposed, and in such cases may require that suitable and adequate provision, approved by the Commission, be made for the protection and indemnity against injury of any interests on either side of the boundary.

Changes in Water Levels

In cases involving the elevation of the natural level of waters on either side of the line as a result of the construction or maintenance on the other side of remedial or protective works or dams or other obstructions in boundary waters or in waters flowing therefrom or in waters below the boundary in rivers flowing across the boundary, the Commission shall require, as a condition of its approval thereof, that suitable and adequate provision, approved by it, be made for the protection and indemnity of all interests on the other side of the line which may be injured thereby.

Decisions of Commission

The majority of the Commissioners shall have power to render a decision. In case the Commission is evenly divided upon any question or matter presented to it for decision, separate reports shall be made by the Commissioners on each side to their own Government. The High Contracting Parties shall thereupon endeavor to agree upon an adjustment of the question or matter of difference, and if an agreement is reached between them, it shall be reduced to writing in the form of a protocol, and shall be communicated to the Commissioners, who shall take such further proceedings as may be necessary to carry out such agreement.

Article IX

Reference of Future Questions

The High Contracting Parties further agree that any other questions or matters of difference arising between them involving the rights, obligations, or interests of either in relation to the other or to the inhabitants of the other, along the common frontier between the United States and the Dominion of Canada, shall be referred from time to time to the International Joint Commission for examination and report, whenever either the Government of the United States or the Government of the Dominion of Canada shall request that such questions or matters of difference be so referred.

Reports by Commission

The International Joint Commission is authorized in each case so referred to examine into and report upon the facts and circumstances of the particular questions and matters referred, together with such conclusions and recommendations as may be appropriate, subject, however, to any restrictions or exceptions which may be imposed with respect thereto by the terms of the reference.

Effect of Reports

Such reports of the Commission shall not be regarded as decisions of the questions or matters so submitted either on the facts or the law, and shall in no way have the character of an arbitral award.

Submission of Reports

The Commission shall make a joint report to both Governments in all cases in which all or a majority of the Commissioners agree, and in case of disagreement the minority may make a joint report to both Governments, or separate reports to their respective Governments.

Divided Decisions

In case the Commission is evenly divided upon any question or matter referred to it for report, separate reports shall be made by the Commissioners on each side to their own Government.

Article X

Submission of Disputes to Commission
Authority of Commission

Any questions or matters of difference arising between the High Contracting Parties involving the rights, obligations, or interests of the United States or of the Dominion of Canada either in relation to each other or to their respective inhabitants, may be referred for decision to the International Joint Commission by the consent of the two Parties, it being understood that on the part of the United States any such action will be by and with the advice and consent of the Senate, and on the part of His Majesty's Government with the consent of the Governor General in Council. In each case so referred, the said Commission is authorized to examine into and report upon the facts and circumstances of the particular questions and matters referred, together with such conclusions and recommendations as may be appropriate, subject, however, to any restrictions or exceptions which may be imposed with respect thereto by the terms of the reference.

Decisions

A majority of the said Commission shall have power to render a decision or finding upon any of the questions or matters so referred.

Reference to Umpire of Undecided Questions

If the said Commission is equally divided or otherwise unable to render a decision or finding as to any questions or matters so referred, it shall be the duty of the Commissioners to make a joint report to both Governments, or separate reports to their respective Governments, showing the different conclusions arrived at with regard to the matters or questions so referred, which questions or matters shall thereupon be referred for decision by the High Contracting Parties to an umpire chosen in accordance with the procedure prescribed in the fourth, fifth, and sixth paragraphs of Article XLV of The Hague Convention for the pacific settlement of international disputes, dated October 18, 1907. Such umpire shall have power to render a final decision with respect to those matters and questions so referred on which the Commission failed to agree.

Article XI

Transmission of Decisions and Reports

A duplicate original of all decisions rendered and joint reports made by the Commission shall be transmitted to and filed with the Secretary of State of the United States and the Governor General of the Dominion of Canada, and to them shall be addressed all communications of the Commission.

Article XII

Organization and Meetings of Commission

The International Joint Commission shall meet and organize at Washington promptly after the members thereof are appointed, and when organized the Commission may fix such times and places for its meetings as may be necessary, subject at all times to special call or direction by the two Governments. Each Commissioner, upon the first joint meeting of the Commission after his appointment, shall before proceeding with the work of the Commission, make and subscribe a solemn declaration in writing that he will faithfully and impartially perform the duties imposed upon him under this treaty, and such declaration shall be entered on the records of the proceedings of the Commission.

Personnel
Payment of Expenses

The United States and Canadian sections of the Commission may each appoint a secretary, and these shall act as joint secretaries of the Commission at its joint sessions, and the Commission may employ engineers and clerical assistants from time to time as it may deem advisable. The salaries and personal expenses of the Commission and of the secretaries shall be paid by their respective Governments, and all reasonable and necessary joint expenses of the Commission, incurred by it, shall be paid in equal moieties by the High Contracting Parties.

Extent of Authority

The Commission shall have power to administer oaths to witnesses, and to take evidence on oath whenever deemed necessary in any proceeding, or inquiry, or matter within its jurisdiction under this treaty, and all parties interested therein shall be given convenient opportunity to be heard, and the High Contracting Parties agree to adopt such legislation as may be appropriate and necessary to give the Commission the powers above mentioned on each side of the boundary, and to provide for the issue of subpoenas and for compelling the attendance of witnesses in proceedings before the Commission. The Commission may adopt such rules of procedure as shall be in accordance with justice and equity, and may make such examination in person and through agents or employees as may be deemed advisable.

Article XIII

Special Agreements Described

In all cases where special agreements between the High Contracting Parties hereto are referred to in the foregoing articles, such agreements are understood and intended to include not only direct agreements between the High Contracting Parties, but also any mutual arrangement between the United States and the Dominion of Canada expressed by concurrent or reciprocal legislation on the part of Congress and the Parliament of the Dominion.

Article XIV

Exchange of Ratifications
Duration

The present treaty shall be ratified by the President of the United States of America, by and with the advice and consent of the Senate thereof, and by His Britannic Majesty. The ratifications shall be exchanged at Washington as soon as possible and the treaty shall take effect on the date of the exchange of its ratifications. It shall remain in force for five years, dating from the day of exchange of ratifications, and thereafter until terminated by twelve months' written notice given by either High Contracting Party to the other.

Signatures

In faith whereof the respective plenipotentiaries have signed this treaty in duplicate and have hereunto affixed their seals.

Done at Washington the 11th day of January, in the year of our Lord one thousand nine hundred and nine.

ELIHU ROOT [SEAL]

JAMES BRYCE [SEAL]

Consent of United States Senate

And whereas the Senate of the United States by their resolution of March 3, 1909, (two-thirds of the Senators present concurring therein) did advise and consent to the ratification of the said Treaty with the following understanding, to wit:

Resolution

"Resolved further, as a part of this ratification, That the United States approves this treaty with the understanding that nothing in this treaty shall be construed as affecting, or changing, any existing territorial or riparian rights in the water, or rights of the owners of lands under water, on either side of the international boundary at the rapids of the St. Mary's river at Sault Ste. Marie, in the use of the waters flowing over such lands, subject to the requirements of navigation in boundary waters and of navigation canals, and without prejudice to the existing right of the United States and Canada, each to use the waters of the St. Mary's river, within its own territory, and further, that nothing in this treaty shall be construed to interfere with the drainage of wet swamp and overflowed lands into streams flowing into boundary waters, and that this interpretation will be mentioned in the ratification of this treaty as conveying the true meaning of the treaty, and will, in effect, form part of the treaty;"

Ratification

And whereas the said understanding has been accepted by the Government of Great Britain, and the ratifications of the two Governments of the said treaty were exchanged in the City of Washington, on the 5th day of May, one thousand nine hundred and ten;

Proclamation

Now, therefore, be it known that I, William Howard Taft, President of the United States of America, have caused the said treaty and the said understanding, as forming a part thereof, to be made public, to the end that the same and every article and clause thereof may be observed and fulfilled with good faith by the United States and the citizens thereof.

In testimony whereof, I have hereunto set my hand and caused the seal of the United States to be affixed.

Done at the City of Washington this thirteenth day of May in the year of our Lord one thousand nine hundred and ten,

[SEAL] and of the Independence of the United States of America the one hundred and thirty-fourth.

WM H TAFT

By the President:
P C KNOX
Secretary of State.

PROTOCOL OF EXCHANGE

Protocol of Exchange of Ratifications

On proceeding to the exchange of the ratifications of the treaty signed at Washington on January 11, 1909, between the United States and Great Britain, relating to boundary waters and questions arising along the boundary between the United States and the Dominion of Canada, the undersigned plenipotentiaries, duly authorized thereto by their respective Governments, hereby declare that nothing in this treaty shall be construed as affecting, or changing, any existing territorial, or riparian rights in the water, or rights of the owners of lands under water, on either side of the international boundary at the rapids of the St. Mary's River at Sault Ste. Marie, in the use of the waters flowing over such lands, subject to the requirements of navigation in boundary waters and of navigation canals, and without prejudice to the existing right of the United States and Canada, each to use the waters of the St. Mary's River, within its own territory; and further, that nothing in this treaty shall be construed to interfere with the drainage of wet, swamp, and overflowed lands into streams flowing into boundary waters, and also that this declaration shall be deemed to have equal force and effect as the treaty itself and to form an integral part thereto.

The exchange of ratifications then took place in the usual form.

IN WITNESS WHEREOF, they have signed the present Protocol of Exchange and have affixed their seals thereto.

DONE at Washington this 5th day of May, one thousand nine hundred and ten.

PHILANDER C KNOX [SEAL]

JAMES BRYCE [SEAL]

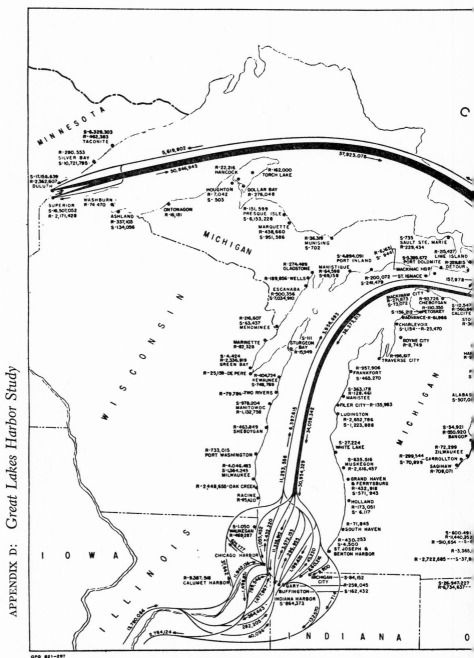

1964 domestic freight tonnage by direction of movements at major ports on the Great Lakes excluding local and intraport traffic.—

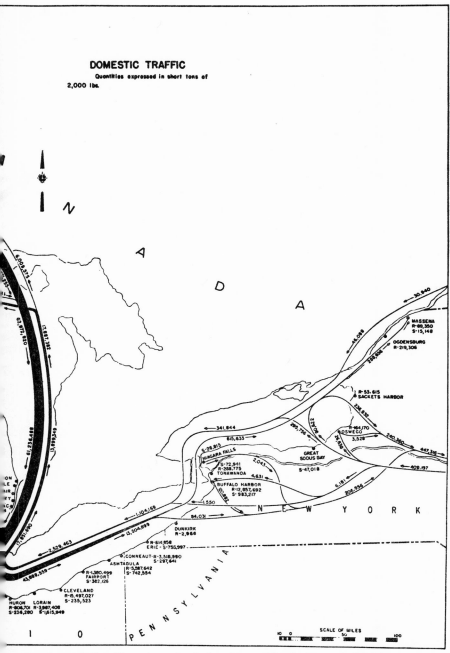

DOMESTIC TRAFFIC
Quantities expressed in short tons of
2,000 lbs.

Courtesy of the Department of the Army, North Central Division,
Corps of Engineers

APPENDIX E: *Interstate Compacts to Which Illinois Is Party or Which Are Under Consideration*

COMPACT AND DATE OF ENACTMENT

Driver License Compact (1963)
Great Lakes Basin Compact (1955)
Illinois–Indiana Air Pollution Control Compact (1965)
Illinois–Indiana Bridge Commission Compact (1965)
Illinois–Missouri Bridge Commission Compact (1965)
Interstate Civil Defense and Disaster Compact (1967)
Interstate Compact for Education (1967)
Interstate Compact on Juveniles (1961)
Interstate Compact for the Supervision of Parolees and Probationers (1935)
Interstate Compact on Library Services (1961)
Interstate Compact on Mental Health (1965)
Interstate Compact on Mentally Disordered Offenders (1967)
Interstate Oil and Gas Compact (1935)
Interstate Transfer of Sexually Dangerous Persons (1963)
Midwest Nuclear Compact (1967)
Missouri–Illinois Bi-State Development Compact (1949)
Missouri–Illinois–Jefferson–Monroe Bridge Commission (1965)
Multistate Tax Compact (1967)
Ohio River Valley Water Sanitation Compact (1939)
Pest Control Compact (1967)
Uniform Motor Vehicle Registration Proration and Reciprocity Agreement (1967)
Upper Mississippi Riverway Compact (1967)
Vehicle-Equipment Safety Compact (1963)
Wabash Valley Interstate Compact (1959)

UNDER CONSIDERATION
(1969)

National Guard Mutual Assistance Compact

Repeal of Multistate Tax Compact Advisory Committee, H.B. 1545, 76th Gen. Assembly, Introduced April 10, 1969.

1 Introduction: *Today's Federalism*

1. *Congressional Record*, vol. 112, Pt. 20, 89th Congress, 2d Sess., Oct. 13, 1966, p. 28524.

2. Ibid.

3. U.S., Congress, Senate, Committee on Government Operations, Subcommittee on Intergovernmental Relations, *Creative Federalism, Hearings, Parts I, IIA,* and *IIB.* 89th Cong., 2d Sess., 1966; and 90th Cong., 1st Sess., 1967.

4. Jo Bingham, "Save Our States." Summary of remarks of a staff member of the National Association of Manufacturers' government relations division, reprinted in the NAM *Intergovernmental Reporter,* vol. 1, no. 2, Dec. 1967.

5. Advisory Commission on Intergovernmental Relations, *The Advisory Commission on Intergovernmental Relations.* Brochure M–17. (Washington, D.C.: Government Printing Office, May 1, 1967), pp. 1–12.

6. New York, Alaska, Rhode Island, Tennessee, California, Pennsylvania, Colorado, Illinois, New Jersey, Washington, Missouri, Ohio, Wisconsin, Connecticut, Minnesota, Vermont.

7. "Summary of Information on Existing State Offices of Local Affairs," table prepared by the Advisory Commission on Intergovernmental Relations, *Congressional Record,* vol. 113, pt. 20, Sept. 26, 1967, pp. 26900–26901.

8. Illinois Department of Finance, *Appropriations,* 74th Gen. Assbly., p. 66; H.B. No. 2194, Approved July 17, 1965.

9. S. 698, H.R. 18826, 90th Cong., 1st Sess., 1967. *Pub. Law* 90–577, 82 *U.S. Stat.* 1098, approved Oct. 16, 1968.

10. *Creative Federalism Hearings, Part II-A,* p. 479.

11. See, particularly, the Committee for Economic Development, *Modernizing State Government,* July, 1967; and the Chamber of Commerce of the U.S., *Modernizing Local Government,* 1967.

12. Frederick L. Zimmermann and Mitchell Wendell, "Interstate Compacts," *The Book of the States,* 1966–67 volume (Chicago: Council of State Governments, 1966), pp. 236–37.

13. Ibid., p. 237.

2 Interstate Compacts: A Device of Federalism

1. Wabash Valley Interstate Compact (Illinois-Indiana); the Great Lakes Basin Compact; the New York Power Authority.

2. 7 Pet. 249, 8 L. Ed. 672 (1833).

3. 13 S. Ct. 728, 148 U.S. 518, 37 L. Ed. 537 (1893).

4. *Interior Airways, Inc.* v. *Wien Alaska Airlines, Inc.*, 188 F. Supp. 107 (1960).

5. *Dresden School Dist.* v. *Norwich Town School Dist.*, 203 A.2d 598; 124 Vt. 227 (1964).

6. *Green* v. *Biddle*, 8 Wheat. 85, 5 L. Ed. 547 (1823).

7. *Virginia* v. *West Virginia*, 11 Wall. 59, 20 L. Ed. 67 (1871).

8. *State* v. *Cunningham* 102 Miss. 237 (1912).

9. *State* v. *Joslin* 116 Kans. 615 (1924).

10. Frederick L. Zimmermann and Mitchell Wendell, "Interstate Compacts," *The Book of the States*, 1960–61 volume (Chicago: Council of State Governments, 1960), p. 239.

11. See U.S., Congress, Senate, Committee on Interior and Insular Affairs, *Extending the Interstate Oil Compact, Hearings*, 88th Cong., 1st Sess., 1963, pp. 3–6.

12. "Status of ACIR Recommendations to the Federal Goverment," *Congressional Record*, 90th Cong., 1st Sess., vol. 113, no. 54, Apr. 12, 1967. See Pub. Law 87–60.

13. *State* v. *Doe* 178 A.2d 271, 149 Conn. 216 (1962).

14. *Vernon's Annotated Missouri Statutes* §§ 454.010–454.200; *Ivey v. Ayers* 301 S.W.2d 790 (1957).

15. *Duncan* v. *Smith* 262 S.W.2d 373, 42 A.L.R.2d 754 (1953).

16. *U.S.* v. *Rauscher* 7 S. Ct. 234; 119 U.S. 407 (1886); *Holmes* v. *Jennison* 14 Pet. 572, 10 L. Ed. 579 (1840); *People* v. *Curtis* 50 N.Y. 330 (1872).

17. *Ex parte Tenner* 128 P. 2d 338; 20 Cal. 2d 670 (1942).

18. Zimmermann and Wendell, *Book of the States*, 1960–61, p. 239.

19. 306 F.2d 270; 113 U.S. App. D.C. 110; 83 S. Ct. 206; 371 U.S. 902.

20. *Congressional Record*, 86th Cong. 2d Sess., 1960, vol. 106, pt. 13, pp. 17284–85.

21. Ibid., p. 17285.

22. 42 *Stat.* 174–80; Joint Resolution, approved Aug. 23, 1921.

23. 42 *Stat.* 822–26; Joint Resolution, approved July 1, 1922.

24. *U.S.* v. *Tobin*, 195 F. Supp. 605 (1961).

25. "The Compact Clause of the Constitution—A Study in Interstate Adjustments," *Yale Law Journal*, vol. 34, May 1925, pp. 685–758.

26. *U.S.* v. *Tobin*, p. 606.

27. Ibid., pp. 595–96.

28. Ibid., pp. 595–96.

29. *Congressional Record*, 86th Cong., 2d Sess., 1960, vol. 106, pt. 13, p. 17289.

30. Ibid., pp. 17126–27.

31. Ibid., pp. 17281–82.

32. Ibid., pp. 17282–83.

33. U.S., Congress, House, Committee on the Judiciary, *Proceedings Against Austin J. Tobin*, 86th Cong., 2d Sess., Aug. 23, 1960, H. Rept. 2117. Reprinted in *Congressional Record*, vol. 106, pt. 13, pp. 17279–81.

34. *Congressional Record*, 87th Cong., 2d Sess., Vol. 108, p. 13483.

35. *Congressional Record*, vol. 106, Pt. 13, p. 17279.

36. Ibid., p. 17280.

37. *U.S.* v. *Tobin*, 611–12.

38. Ibid., p. 610.

39. Ibid., note 97 (p. 610).

40. *Tobin* v. *U.S.*, 306 F. 2d 270 (1962).

41. Ibid., pp. 272–73.

42. *U.S.* v. *Tobin*, 371 U.S. 902 (1962).

42. Leslie W. Dunbar, "Interstate Compacts and Congressional Consent," *Virginia Law Review*, vol. 36, 1950, p. 762.

44. The classification is that of the Council of State Governments. See Frederick L. Zimmermann and Mitchell Wendell, *The Book of the States*, 1966–67 vol. (Chicago: Council of State Governments, 1966), pp. 240–41.

45. James B. Conant, *Shaping Educational Policy*, ch. 5 (New York: McGraw-Hill Book Company, 1964), pp. 109–34.

46. Terry Sanford, *Storm Over the States* (New York: McGraw-Hill Book Company, 1967), pp. vii, xi.

47. Ibid., pp. 116–17.

48. Illinois Commission on Intergovernmental Cooperation, *Report on Five Interstate Compacts* (Springfield: March, 1967), pp. iii, 1–9.

49. Illinois 76th General Assembly, H.B. 2370, 1969. A $39,000 proposed appropriation to support the Compact is also before the legislature (May, 1969).

50. Zimmermann and Wendell, *Book of the States*, 1966–67 vol., p. 240.

51. Ibid., pp. 240–41.

52. *House Bill* No. 908, Ill. 75th Gen. Assembly, 1967, pp. 9–10.

53. *Report on Five Interstate Compacts*, p. 7.

54. Richard H. Leach, "The Status of Interstate Compacts Today," *State Government*, vol. 32, spring, 1959; pp. 134–39.

55. S. 3428, 85th Cong., 2d Sess., 1958.

3 The Missouri-Illinois Bi-State Development Compact

Part 1 — The Bi-State Development Agency

1. *Laws of the State of Illinois* (hereafter cited as *Laws*), 1949, p. 449; *Laws of Missouri*, 1949, p. 558; 64 *U.S. Stats.*, Part I, p. 568 et seq. See Compact, ART. III, *Illinois Rev. Stats.*, 127 § 63r 1–12 (1965).

2. *Ill. Rev. Stats.* (1965), 127 § 63s–9 through 12; *Laws of Missouri*, 1958, 2nd Extra Session, p. 150; *Laws of Missouri*, 1959, S.B. 25; *U.S. Stats.*, Pub. Law 86–303, 1959.

3. Compact, ART. III, SECS. 1–8, and *Ill. Rev. Stats.* 127 § 63–s, 9–11.

4. Compact, ART. III, SEC. 8; ART. V, SECS. 2 and 4; ART. VI, SEC. 1; ART. VII, SEC. 2; *Ill. Rev. Stats.* 127 § 1, 7, 8, 9(b), and 10.

5. Compact, ART. III, SEC. 8; ART. V; ART. VI.

6. 64 *U.S. Stats.*, Part I, p. 571; Compact, ART. VII (Pub. Law 743).

7. 73 *U.S. Stats.* 582, 583.

8. Ibid.

9. *Ill. Rev. Stats.* 1965, 127 § 63s–10, 437.

10. *Annual Report*, July 1, 1962–June 30, 1963, p. 12.

11. *Ill. Rev. Stats.* 19 § 284–317; *Laws*, 1959, 71.

12. *Ill. Rev. Stats.* 19 § 451; *Laws*, 1961, p. 2993.

13. *Ill. Rev. Stats.* 19 § 501–50; *Laws*, 1965, S.B. 737.

14. *Ill. Rev. Stats.* 34 § 3091.1; *Laws*, 1963, p. 1619.

15. *Ill. Rev. Stats.* 127 § 63s–21 et seq.; *Laws*, 1965, H.B. No. 391. Passed as an Emergency Measure.

16. Minutes, Jan. 14, 1952 and May 16, 1961.

17. Compact, ART. IV; *Ill. Rev. Stats.* 127 § 63s–2, 63s–3, 63s–4.

18. Compact, ART. V; *Ill. Rev. Stats.* 127 § 63s–2.

19. Compact, ART. V; Agency *By-Laws*, ART. II, SECS. 8–10.

20. "By-Laws," ART. II, SEC. 1.

21. Ibid., ART. III, SEC. 2.

22. Minutes, vols. 1–6.

23. "By-Laws," ART. III, SEC. 5.

24. Minutes, July 10, 1950, vol. 1, et passim.

25. Ibid., Feb. 23, 1951.

26. Ibid., Dec. 27, 1951.

27. Ibid., Oct. 20, 1954, vol. 2.

28. Ibid., June 22, 1959.

29. See Henry J. Schmandt, Paul G. Steinbicker, and George D. Wendel, "The Campaign for Metropolitan Government in St. Louis." In Michael N. Danielson, *Metropolitan Politics* (Boston: Little, Brown & Co., 1966), p. 194 et seq.

30. "By-Laws," ART. II, SEC. 4.

31. Minutes, Apr. 10, 1959, p. 254.

32. *East St. Louis Journal*, "Illinois Bi-State Group Wants Chairman Post," April 12, 1959.

33. Ibid.
34. Ibid.
35. *East St. Louis Journal,* "Roos Chairman of Bi-State," June 23, 1959.
36. Ibid.
37. *East St. Louis Evening Journal.* "Bi-State Agency to Re-organize," Nov. 16, 1961.
38. Minutes, Mar. 31, 1965.
39. "By-Laws," Art. II, Sec. 2; Art. III, Sec. 3.
40. Ibid., Art. II, Sec. 3.
41. The amendments were first adopted by Illinois in 1953; by Missouri in 1957 and 1959; by Congress in 1959: *Ill. Laws* 1953, p. 1656; *Laws* 1959, S.B. 97; *Laws of Missouri* 1957, second extra session, S.B. 11; *Laws of Missouri* 1959, S.B. 25; and 73 *U.S. Stats.* 582 (Pub. Law 86–303), 1959.
42. Minutes, Apr. 28, 1965, p. 822.
43. Letter from R. E. Smyser, Jr., to author, May 4, 1966.
44. *Laws,* 1947, p. 248.
45. *Ill. Rev. Stats.,* 127 § 63s–7.
46. Minutes, Mar. 7, 1960.
47. *Alton Evening Telegraph,* "To Study Bi-State Cooperation," July 28, 1959.
48. The other Illinois members of the Pilot Committee were: Curt E. Eckert, of Eckert Orchard Assn., Belleville; Robert Gauen, vice president, Gauen Lumber Co., Collinsville; William A. Hitchcock, vice president, State Savings and Loan Assn., of East St. Louis; Richard Judson, supervisor of training, Standard Oil Co., Wood River; Robert Maucker, plant manager, Alton Box Board Co., of Alton; Lloyd McBride, subdivision director, United Steelworkers of America, of Granite City; and Charles Schmidt, executive partner of Oscar Schmidt Agency, of Edwardsville.
49. *East St. Louis Journal,* "Area Distrusts Missouri, Bi-State Members Told," "Goals Listed in St. Louis," and "Golden Decade Goals," Jan. 26, 1960.
50. *East St. Louis Journal,* "Needs Solved by Human Action, Bi-State Leaders Cautioned," Feb. 28, 1960.
51. *East St. Louis Journal,* "Metropolitan Development: Bi-State Advisory Council Set Up," April 12, 1960.
52. *East St. Louis Evening Journal,* "Super Bi-State Unit Proposed," Nov. 20, 1961.
53. *East St. Louis Evening Journal,* "Metro Team Aim: New Industry," May 13, 1964. Members of this group were: Raymond R. Tucker, mayor of St. Louis; James Krause, planning and zoning chairman, St. Clair County Bd. of Supervisors; Harold Landolt, chairman, Madison County Bd. of Supervisors; H. A. Kluge, Superintendent of highways, Madison County; Herbert K. Moss, presiding judge, County Court, Jefferson County; Clem A. Burgess, presiding judge, County Court, St. Charles County; and D. Reid

Ross, director, business and industrial development commissioner, St. Louis County.

54. *Annual Report*, July 1, 1964–June 30, 1965, p. 11.

Part 2—Functions and Politics

55. John C. Bollens, ed., *Exploring the Metropolitan Community* (Berkeley and Los Angeles: University of California Press, 1961), p. 49.

56. Ibid., pp. 97–98.

57. Ibid., pp. 131–32.

58. *Annual Report*, 1962–63, p. 14; also, interview with Col. R. E. Smyser, Jr.

59. *Annual Report*, 1962–63, p. 14.

60. Ibid.

61. *Annual Report*, 1962–63, p. 16. Also Minutes, vol. 1.

62. Ibid., p. 16; Minutes, Vol. 1.

63. Minutes, Oct. 20, 1954, vol. 2.

64. *Annual Report*, 1962–63; p. 16.

65. Minutes, June 18, 1956.

66. Minutes, Jan. 25, 1962, p. 363.

67. *Annual Report*, 1964–65, p. 8. Also *Annual Reports*, 1965–66, 1966–67, 1967–68.

68. Minutes, Dec. 27, 1951 and Aug. 2, 1954.

69. Ibid., Nov. 25, 1955.

70. Ibid., Apr. 23, 1956, pp. 22–23.

71. Ibid., June 18, 1956.

72. Ibid., Oct. 15, 1958.

73. Bollens, *Exploring the Metropolitan Community*, p. 414.

74. *East St. Louis Evening Journal*, "Bi-State Transit Decision Near," Mar. 30, 1962.

75. Minutes, June 30, 1960.

76. Ibid., Sept. 27, 1962.

77. The acquired lines were: St. Louis Public Service Co., $19,450,000; St. Louis County Transit Co., $180,000; East St. Louis City Lines, $1,000,-000; Ferguson-Broadway Bus Line, Brown Motor Lines, Inc., Citizens Coach Co., $752,880; Belleville-St. Louis Coach Co., $648,150; County Coach Co., $5,570; Community Coach Co., $400,000; Vandalia Bus Lines, Caseyville Bus Lines, Industrial Bus Lines, O'Fallon-Belleville Coach Co., $723,460; Wood River-Alton Bus Lines, $22,500; and V-K Bus Lines, $12,000. *Annual Report*, 1962–63, p. 3.

78. Ibid., p. 3. The management and all personnel required for the operation of Bi-State Transit System are provided by fixed-fee contract with the Service Corporation, whose chief officers are (June, 1968): John C. Baine, chief executive officer; S. Carl Robinson, administrative officer; Guido Moss, operating manager; P. E. Lohoefner, controller; and R. E. Krupp, director of planning and assistant operating manager.

79. *Annual Report*, 1963–64, pp. 3–4.

80. Ibid., p. 4.

81. *Annual Report*, 1967–68, Bi-State Transit System financial statement, p. 6, note 3.

82. *St. Louis Post-Dispatch*, "Bi-State Bus Budget Anticipates Deficit," Feb. 29, 1968.

83. *St. Louis Post-Dispatch*, "Bi-State's Revenues Down, Costs Are Up," Mar. 1, 1969.

84. Richard Jacobs, "Five Firms Seek Publicity Job in Bus Subsidy." *St. Louis Post-Dispatch*, Dec. 17, 1967.

85. *St. Louis Post-Dispatch*, "Bi-State To Cut Night Service After Dec. 24," Dec. 21, 1967.

86. Aug. 31, 1967.

87. According to Bi-State's superintendent of school bus operations, Leo A. White, "Each district is handled under separate contract. Charges [in 1967] are based on time and miles involved, current rate being $3.25 per hour, with a two hour minimum, plus 33¢ per mile. Cost per student can vary considerably, as some school districts are able to get two or more trips per bus within the two hour minimum, while others are able to get only one trip. Wherever possible, Bi-State combined trips with two or more school districts to effect a saving for both districts." Letter, June 2, 1967, to Robert Granda, Illinois Legislative Council, Springfield.

88. *St. Louis Post-Dispatch*, "House Bills: Illinois Proposals for Transit Aid." Apr. 1, 1969.

89. Ibid.

90. *Annual Report*, 1964–65, p. 4.

91. *Annual Report*, 1967–68, p. 11.

92. Don R. Preston, *Preparing for the Future of Missouri*, report (Jefferson City, Mo.: Missouri Office of State and Regional Planning, 1967), passim.

93. *St. Louis Post-Dispatch*, "$30,000,000 Plan to Improve Transit," April 27, 1968, and "$25,560,000 in Aid For Pittsburgh Transit," Apr. 28, 1968.

94. *St. Louis Post-Dispatch*, "Rapid Transit Guides Adopted," May 8, 1969.

95. Bollens, *Exploring the Metropolitan Community*, p. 111.

90. *East St. Louis Evening Journal*, "First Area-wide Meeting Stirs Airport Interest," Nov. 3, 1960.

97. *Annual Report*, 1963–64, p. 9.

98. Ibid.

99. *Alton Evening Telegraph*, "Bi-State Signs Agreement to Acquire Parks Airport," Nov. 1, 1962.

100. *Annual Report*, 1962–63, p. 7.

101. *Annual Report*, 1963–64, p. 9.

102. Ibid.

103. *East St. Louis Evening Journal,* "Bi-State Awaits Action on Land Use, Road Plan," May 28, 1964.

104. *Annual Report,* 1964–65, pp. 9–10.

105. Ibid., p. 10.

106. *St. Louis Globe-Democrat,* "Gateway Panel Authorizes Airport Study," September 28, 1967.

107. *St. Louis Post-Dispatch,* "FAA Inquiry Into Bottoms Airport Site," Jan. 3, 1968.

108. *St. Louis Post-Dispatch,* "Airport Commission Worried Over Bills," January 18, 1968. Also, Governmental Research Institute, *Should a Metropolitan Airport Authority Be Established for the St. Louis Area? A Report for the East-West Gateway Coordinating Council* (St. Louis, 1968), p. 25.

109. *St. Louis Post-Dispatch,* "Committee Rejects Landing Strip Plan," Jan. 30, 1968; and "Airport Plan Backed By Gateway Council," Feb. 1, 1968.

110. Taylor Pensoneau, "Bi-State Review Urged To Solve Airport Jam." *St. Louis Post-Dispatch,* Feb. 1, 1968.

111. *St. Louis Post-Dispatch,* "Metropolitan Authority Urged for Handling Airport Problem," Apr. 25, 1968.

112. Governmental Research Institute, *Should a Metropolitan Airport Authority Be Established For the St. Louis Area?,* pp. 5, 60–72.

113. Ibid., pp. 6–7.

114. Ibid., p. 7.

115. Ibid., p. 67.

116. *St. Louis Post-Dispatch,* "Prospects for Airport Sale to Bi-State Called Dim," June 28, 1968.

117. Ibid.

118. *St. Louis Post-Dispatch,* "Baer Challenges Plan For Airport System," July 3, 1968.

119. Ibid.

120. *St. Louis Post-Dispatch,* "Opposes Tax for Airport Agency," July 16, 1968.

121. Illinois 75th General Assembly, July 16, 1968.

122. *St. Louis Post-Dispatch,* editorial, "Not the City's Job," July 19, 1968.

123. *St. Louis Post-Dispatch,* "Illinois Airport Requirement Cited," July 18, 1968.

124. *St. Louis Post-Dispatch,* "East Side Airport Bill Is Sent to Illinois Governor," July 25, 1968; Senator Simon was a cosponsor of this bill, along with Gilbert, Dixon, Donnewald, and Lyons.

125. Illinois 76th General Assembly, February, 1969.

126. *Annual Report,* 1965–66, p. 8.

127. Eugene Bryerton, "2 Agencies In Arch Job Far Apart," *St. Louis Post-Dispatch,* Jan. 18, 1968. Last of a series of stories.

128. *Annual Report*, 1967–68, pp. 8–9.

129. William H. Kester, "Gateway Arch Rides Exceed Estimate and Help Bi-State," *St. Louis Post-Dispatch*, July 18, 1968.

130. *Ill. Rev. Stats.*, 111½ § 240.31.

131. *St. Louis Post-Dispatch*, "Clean-Air Unit Fights For Adequate Funds," Mar. 30, 1969. Also, see continuing items, *Air & Water News*, vol. 2, 1968, et passim.

132. *Annual Report*, 1962–63, p. 7.

133. Ill. Rev. Stats. 1965, 127 § 63s–21, p. 438. *Laws*, 1965, H.B. 391; emergency measure, effective May 20, 1965.

134. *Annual Report*, 1963–64, p. 7.

135. Minutes, Nov. 10, 1960.

136. *Annual Report*, 1962–63, p. 14.

137. *Annual Report*, 1963–64, p. 11.

138. Minutes, July 30, 1963; pp. 612–13.

139. Minutes, Feb. 28, 1964; p. 674.

140. *Annual Report*, 1963–64; p. 11.

141. Minutes, June 18, 1964; pp. 696–98.

142. Minutes, Oct. 6, 1964, p. 704.

143. *East St. Louis Sunday Journal*, "Bi-State Defends Planning Role," June 28, 1964.

144. Bi-State Agency records, Memorandum, Gene Graves to Otto Kerner, June 18, 1964.

145. East-West Gateway Coordinating Committee, *Prospectus For Land Use and Transportation Planning Program* (St. Louis: Prepared by Alan Voorhees & Associates, Inc., May 26, 1965).

146. The fifteen-member E-WGCC consists of: the chairman, Board of Supervisors, Monroe County; presiding judge, St. Charles County; mayor, City of St. Louis; mayor, City of E. St. Louis; chairman, Board of Supervisors, St. Clair County; executive director, Department of Economic Development of Illinois; president, St. Louis County League of Municipalities; president, Southwestern Illinois Metropolitan Area Planning Commission; chairman, Board of Supervisors, Madison County; director, Illinois Department of Public Works and Buildings; director, Missouri State Division of Commerce and Industrial Development; president, Southwestern Illinois Council of Mayors; supervisor, St. Louis County; chairman, Missouri State Highway Commission; chairman, Bi-State Development Agency; and presiding judge, Jefferson County.

147. *Annual Report*, 1964–65, p. 11.

148. New York Port Authority, *Forbes or "Facts?"* Brochure. New York, 1967.

4   The Great Lakes Basin Compact

1. 75 *U.S. Stats.* 688–716; P.L. 37–328.

2. U.S. Army Corps of Engineers Report, *Effect of Additional Diver-*

sion of Water From Lake Michigan at Chicago, 85th Cong., 1st Sess., Jan. 1957, S. Doc. 28, p. 2.

3. U.S., Congress, House, Committee on Foreign Affairs, *Great Lakes Basin Compact, Hearings on H.R. 4314*, 85th Cong., 2d Sess., 1958, Great Lakes Commission, "Explanatory Statement Regarding Great Lakes Basin Compact," pp. 8–12. Also see U.S., Congress, Senate, Committee on the Judiciary, *Great Lakes Basin Compact, Hearings*, 85th Cong., 2d Sess., 1958, statement of Charles Schwan, Jr., of the Council of State Governments on Compact's origins, pp. 78–80.

4. House, Committee on Foreign Affairs, *Great Lakes Basin Compact, Hearings on H.R. 4314*, 85th Cong., 2d Sess., 1958, p. 9.

5. Ibid., p. 92.

6. Ibid., p. 64.

7. *Ill. Rev. Stats.* (1965), 127 § 192.1, ART. I, SECS. 1–5.

8. Ibid., ART. IV, SEC. A.

9. Ibid., ART. IV, SEC. J.

10. Ibid., ART. IV, SEC. H.

11. Ibid., ART. III, SECS. 1 and 2.

12. Ibid., ART. VI, SECS. A–N.

13. Ibid., ART. VII, SECS. A–I.

14. Ibid., ART. IV, SEC. b; ART. V, SECS. A–C.

15. Compact, ART. VIII.

16. House, Committee on Foreign Affairs, *Great Lakes Basin Compact, Hearings on H.R. 4314*, 85th Cong., 2d Sess., 1958, p. 30.

17. Ibid., p. 52.

18. Compact, ART. IX.

19. *Ill. Rev. Stats., Op. Cit.*, 127 § 192.3.

20. Compact, ART. IV, B and C.

21. House, Committee on Foreign Affairs, *Great Lakes Basin Compact, Hearings on H.R. 4314*, 85th Cong., 2d Sess., 1958, testimony of John R. Davison, consultant for Robert Moses, chairman, New York Power Authority, p. 74.

22. Great Lakes Commission, Report to the States, 1963–64 and 1965–66 volumes (Ann Arbor, Mich.), p. 3, both volumes.

23. Compact, ART. IV, SECS. H. J; ART. V, SECS. D–E; *Report to the States*, pp. 27–33.

24. Compact, ART. IV, SECS. A, H, I; and letter to the author, from Albert G. Ballert, director of research, Great Lakes Commission, June 5, 1968.

25. House, Committee on Foreign Affairs, *Great Lakes Basin Compact, Hearings on H.R. 4314*, 85th Cong., 2d Sess., 1958, "Supplemental Statement . . . of Marvin Fast," pp. 51–52.

26. Bernard Asbell, "The Great Chicago Water Steal," *Saturday Evening Post*, vol. 235, May 19, 1962; p. 33.

27. *A New Kind of Man for Illinois: John Henry Alterfer, Republican*

for Governor, campaign brochure (Carbondale: Printed by the *Southern Illinoisan,* June 9, 1968).

28. U.S. Congress, House, Committee on Public Works, *Lake Michigan Water Diversion, Hearings, on H.R. 3192,* 83d Cong., 1st Sess., 1953, pp. 65–66.

29. Ibid.

30. Ibid., p. 67.

31. Ibid., p. 3.

32. Ibid., pp. 68–72.

33. 63 *U.S. Stats.* 271.

34. 70 *U.S. Stats.* 701; 71 *U.S. Stats.* 367.

35. *S. 2476,* 89th Cong., 2d Sess., 1966.

36. 66 *U.S. Stats.* 71.

37. Letter from Douglas MacArthur II, assistant secretary of state for congressional relations, to Thomas E. Morgan, U.S., Congress, House Committee on Foreign Affairs, 89th Cong., 2d Sess., Oct. 4, 1966, in *Great Lakes Basin Compact, Hearings on H.R. 937, 12294, 12692, 13359, 14192, and 15042,* p. 111. (Hereafter referred to as *Hearings on H.R. 937.*)

38. Compact, Art. II, B.

39. House, Committee on Public Works, *Lake Michigan Water Diversion, Hearings on H.R. 3192,* 83d Cong., 1st Sess., 1953, p. 11.

40. *Pub. Law* 90–419; 82 *Stat.* 414; 90th Cong., 2d Sess., approved July 24, 1968.

41. Senate, Committee on the Judiciary, *Great Lakes Basin Compact, Report to Accompany S. 660,* 90th Cong., 2d Sess., June 10, 1968, S. Rept. 1178, pp. 9–10.

42. Ibid., p. 5.

43. House, Committee on Foreign Affairs, *Great Lakes Basin Compact, Hearings on H.R. 937,* 89th Cong., 2d Sess., 1966, pp. 10–13, particularly pp. 12–13.

44. House, Committee on Foreign Affairs, *Great Lakes Basin Compact, Hearings on H.R. 4314,* 85th Cong., 2d Sess., 1958, pp. 20–21.

45. House, Committee on Foreign Affairs, *Great Lakes Basin Compact, Hearings on H.R. 937,* 89th Cong., 2d Sess., 1966, p. 18.

46. Ibid., pp. 6–7.

47. Ibid., pp. 36–37.

48. *Congressional Record* (Daily edition), 90th Cong., 2d Sess., July 15, 1968, p. H6523.

49. Ibid., p. H6524.

50. House, Committee on Foreign Affairs, *Great Lakes Basin Compact, Hearings on H.R. 937,* 89th Cong., 2d Sess., 1966, p. 45.

51. Ibid., pp. 111–12.

52. U.S., Congress, House, Committee on Public Works, *Lake Michigan Water Diversion, Hearings on H.R. 1,* 86th Cong., 1st Sess., 1959, p. 305.

53. The facts for this discussion of the Chicago water diversion problem

are chiefly drawn from the U.S. Army Corps of Engineers Report, *Effects of Additional Diversion of Water From Lake Michigan at Chicago*, 85th Cong., 1st Sess., Jan. 1957, S. Doc. 28, except where otherwise noted.

54. 273 *U.S.* 642; Special Report, pp. 5–7.

55. 281 *U.S.* 696 (1930) Decisions per Curiam; Justice Holmes deciding.

56. U.S. Army Corps of Engineers Report, *Effects of Additional Diversion of Water From Lake Michigan at Chicago*, pp. 11–12. Also, 352 *U.S.* 945 (1956), Decisions Per Curiam.

57. House, Committee on Public Works, *Lake Michigan Water Diversion, Hearings on H.R. 3192*, 83rd Cong., 1st Sess., 1953, Testimony of Col. W. D. Milne, p. 2.

58. U.S., Congress, Senate, Committee on Public Works, *Diversion of Water From Lake Michigan, Hearings on S. 1123 and H.R. 2*, 85th Cong., 2d Sess., 1958, p. 13.

59. U.S. Army Corps of Engineers Report, *Effects of Additional Diversion of Water From Lake Michigan at Chicago*, p. 1.

60. Ibid., pp. v, vi.

61. Ibid., p. vi.

62. Ibid., p. vii.

63. Bernard Asbell, "The Great Chicago Water Steal," *Saturday Evening Post*, vol. 235, May 19, 1962, p. 32.

64. Ibid.

65. U.S., Congress, Senate, Committee on Interior and Insular Affairs, *Indiana Dunes National Lakeshore, Hearings on S. 360*, 89th Cong., 1st Sess., 1965, p. 25.

Most of the facts of this entire account are to be found in testimony and materials of these Hearings and in the following: U.S., Congress, Senate, Committee on Interior and Insular Affairs, *Indiana Dunes National Lakeshore, Hearings on S. 2249*, 88th Cong., 2d Sess., 1964; U.S., Congress, House, Committee on Interior and Insular Affairs, *Indiana Dunes National Lakeshore, Hearings on H.R. 51, H.R. 4412 and Related Bills, Part I*, 89th Cong., 1st Sess., 1965, held at Valparaiso, Ind.; and William Peeples, "The Indiana Dunes and Pressure Politics," *Atlantic Monthly*, vol. 211, Feb. 1963, pp. 84–88.

66. Secretary of the Army, *Report on the Great Lakes Harbors Study—Interim Report on Burns Waterway Harbor*, 1963; pp. 9, 11, 33. Also issued as *House Doc. 160*, 88th Cong., 1st Sess., 1963.

67. Statement of Sen. Paul Douglas, in Senate, Committee on Interior and Insular Affairs, *Indiana Dunes National Lakeshore, Hearings on S. 2249*, 88th Cong., 2d Sess., 1964, pp. 51 et seq.

68. Ibid., p. 32.

69. Secretary of the Army, *Report on the Great Lakes Harbors Study*, pp. 1–56.

70. Ibid., p. 2.

71. Ibid., p. 18.

72. Ibid., pp. x–xv.
73. Ibid., p. xx.
74. Ibid., p. xxiv.
75. A copy of the map appears in Senate, Commitee on Interior and Insular Affairs, *Indiana Dunes National Lakeshore, Hearings on S. 2249,* 88th Cong., 2d Sess., 1964.
76. Great Lakes Commission, *Great Lakes News Letter,* vol. 12, no. 4, Mar.–Apr., 1968; p. 2.
77. Ibid., p. 3.
78. House, Committee on Foreign Affairs, *Great Lakes Basin Compact, Hearings on H.R. 4314,* 85th Cong., 2d Sess., 1958, pp. 31–32.
79. Great Lakes Commission, brochure, *10th Anniversary, 1955–1965.* (Ann Arbor, Mich., 1965).
80. U.S., Congress, House, Committee on Foreign Affairs, *Great Lakes Basin Compact, Report to Accompany S. 660.* 90th Cong., 2d Sess., July 3, 1968, H. Rept. 1640, pp. 2–3.
81. Statement of Robert Moses, Chairman, Power Authority, State of New York, presented by John R. Davison, consultant for Robert Moses, in House, Committee on Foreign Affairs, *Great Lakes Basin Compact, Hearings on H.R. 4314,* 85th Cong., 2d Sess., 1958, pp. 69–73, also pp. 73–84.
82. Ibid.
83. Ibid., p. 79.
84. Senate, Committee on the Judiciary, *Great Lakes Basin Compact, Hearings,* 85th Cong., 2d Sess., 1958, p. 13.
85. Ibid., p. 132.

5 The Wabash Valley Interstate Compact: *A Bi-State Approach to Resource Development*

1. *Laws of the State of Illinois* (hereafter cited as Laws), 1959, p. 59; *Ill. Rev. Stats.* 1965, 127 § 63t–1 to 63t–3, pp. 441–43; *Laws of Indiana,* 1959, Ch. 3; *Ill. Sen. Bill* No. 78, 71st Genl. Assbly., (Sens. Lewis, Green, Zeigler, Broyles, Peters, Davis, Sprinkle, Meyer, and Friedrich), approved March 20, 1959. *Ind. House Enrolled Act* No. 22, approved Feb. 26, 1959.
2. 73 *U.S. Stats.* 694.
3. Wabash Valley Interstate Commission, *Annual Report,* Jan. 1962, Foreword. (Published at Terre Haute, Ind.), pages not numbered.
4. The Illinois Counties involved, in whole or in part, are: Iroquois, Ford, Champaign, Vermilion, Livingston, Douglas, Edgar, Shelby, Coles, Clark, Cumberland, Effingham, Jasper, Crawford, Marion, Clay, Richland, Lawrence, Jefferson, Wayne, Edwards, Wabash, Hamilton, White and Gallatin.
5. Some of the streams are: Big Creek, Little Raccoon Creek, Little Wabash River, Lost Creek, Patoka River, Skillet Fork, Mississinewa River, White River, Salt Fork Creek, Eagle Creek, Muscatatuck River, Little Walnut, Big Blue River, Indian Creek, Mill Creek, Flat Branch, Embarrass

River, Four Mile Creek, Crawfish Creek, Vermilion River, Little Vermilion, Bonpas, Big Walnut Creek.

6. Wabash Valley Interstate Commission, *A Bi-State Approach to Resource Development*, brochure (Terre Haute, Ind., 1966).

7. Ronald R. Boyce, *Regional Development and the Wabash Basin* (Urbana: University of Illinois Press, 1964), p. 11.

8. Ibid., p. 11.

9. *Ill. Rev. Stats.* 1965, 127 § 63t–2, p. 443.

10. Ibid., 127 § 63t–1; Compact, Art. III(a), p. 441. 1968 members the Commission are: *Illinois*—Dr. William I. Goodman, Urbana; Robert Lichtenberger, Fairfield; James R. Raibley, Mt. Carmel; John Rooney, Robinson; Robert Williams, Mill Shoals; Lyle Eversole, Hindsboro; Dr. D. W. Morris, Carbondale. *Indiana*—Frederick J. A. Beyer, Indianapolis; Dennis Heeke, Dubois; Wisher Myers, Veedersburg; Thomas Mumford, Griffin; D. C. Pfendler, West Lafayette; Louis E. Powell, Kokomo; Joseph Quinn, Jr., Terre Haute. *Federal Representative*—Ernest P. Howe, Bloomington, Indiana.

11. Compact, Art. III(b).

12. Compact, Art. III(d); the Commission's present executive director (the only person yet to serve in this position) is Byron K. Barton, appointed in June 1960, a former director of conservation education of the State of Illinois.

13. Compact, Art. VI A(1–6); *Ill. Rev. Stats.*, 1965, 127 § 63t–1, p. 442.

14. Compact, Art. VI B(1–6).

15. Ibid., Art. VI C(1–3).

16. Ibid., Art. VI D and E.

17. *Ill. Rev. Stats.* 1965, 127 § 63t–3, p. 443.

18. 73 *U.S. Stats.* 698, *Pub. Law* 86–375, Art. VIII, Sec. 2.

19. 73 *U.S. Stats.* 698, Art. VIII, Sec. 3.

20. Ibid., Art. VIII, Secs. 4–8.

21. Wabash Valley Interstate Commission, *By-Laws, 1966.* (Terre Haute, Ind., 1966), Art. I, Sec. B(I).

22. Ibid., Art. I, Sec. B 2(a).

23. Ibid., Art. I, Sec. B 2(b) and (c).

24. Ibid., Art. I, Sec. B 2(d); Art. I, Sec. B 3.

25. Ibid., Art. I, Sec. B 7(a).

26. Wabash Valley Interstate Commission Minutes, Jan. 25, 1960. Director Barton holds a Ph.D. degree from the University of Nebraska, is a former professor and head of the Department of Geography, Eastern Illinois University, and as noted previously in this study, has had experience in conservation work in Illinois government.

27. Letter from Thomas Mumford, WVIC chairman, to Blucher A. Poole, June 21, 1960, records of the commission.

28. *By-Laws*, Art. I, Sec. B 7(a) and (b).

29. Ibid., ART. I, SEC. B 4(b).
30. Ibid., ART. I, SEC. B 4(a).
31. Ibid., ART. I, SEC. B 5.
32. Compact, ART. V, SEC. (a).
33. *By-Laws*, ART. I, SEC. C 1.
34. Compact, ART. V, SEC. (b).
35. *Annual Report*, January 1963, p. 7.
36. Minutes of meeting in the office of the governor of Illinois, May 22, 1962. From *Annual Report*, Jan. 1963, pp. 12–13.
37. *Annual Report*, 1968, p. 29.
38. *Annual Report*, 1967, p. 22.
39. *By-Laws*, ART. I, SEC. C 1(b), and C 2(b).
40. Letter of Russell Imbler, Jr., Nov. 19, 1959; WVIC files, Southern Illinois University.
41. The 1960 Wabash Valley Association's list of officers included these members of the WVIC's Board of Commissioners: J. Roy Dee, President; Charles Hedde, Secretary; E. Earl Allen, Mrs. C. B. Baldwin, Rabb Emison, Thomas F. Mumford, Joseph L. Quinn, Jr., Directors. Also on the list as a director was Guy E. McGaughey, Jr., whose father, Guy E. McGaughey, Sr., was for a number of years the Illinois representative of the Interstate Oil and Gas Compact; Mr. McGaughey, Jr., is also a member of one of the working committees of the oil compact. Mumford and Quinn continued as members of all WVIC boards through December, 1968, the present writing.
42. Chamber of Commerce, Terre Haute, Ind., *Wabash Valley Compact*, pamphlet issued for Ceremonial Signing, Jan. 25, 1960, at Terre Haute, p. 1.
43. Ibid.
44. Miscellaneous records of the Wabash Valley Interstate Commission, Southern Illinois University.
45. Letter of transmittal to B. K. Barton, Dec. 22, 1964, in miscellaneous materials of the Wabash Valley Interstate Commission, Southern Illinois University, Carbondale.
46. Minutes, January 19, 1961.
47. *Annual Report*, Jan. 1961 (pages unnumbered).
48. Wabash Valley Interstate Commission, *ASCS Funds to Stabilize Farm Land and Protect City Water Supply*, "ACP Special Project, Rattlesnake Creek"; and *Who May Benefit From Small Watershed Projects?*, brochures (Terre Haute, Ind., 1966).
49. *Annual Report*, 1965, pp. 12–13.
50. *Annual Report*, 1967, pp. 19–20.
51. Ibid., p. 21.
52. Minutes, Jan. 19, 1960.
53. Ibid., July 21, 1960.
54. Wabash Valley Interstate Commission materials, 1961–63 Budget Request.

55. Wabash Valley Interstate Commission materials.

56. Wabash Valley Interstate Commission, *Regional Planning For the Wabash Valley* (Terre Haute, Ind., 1965), p. 1.

57. Ibid., p. 6.

58. Ibid., pp. 7–8.

59. Ibid., pp. 8–10.

60. Minutes, Oct. 18, 1961.

61. *Annual Report*, Jan. 1963, "The Chairman's Report" (page not numbered). Also, pp. 5–6, numbered report.

The reports of the commission for 1963 were unsystematically handled. Two reports were issued. The page-numbered 1963 *Annual Report* does not contain all data in the unnumbered version.

62. Carbondale, Ill., Wabash Valley Interstate Commission files, Southern Illinois University, "Air Industrial Park, Lawrenceville, Illinois" (Carbondale, Ill.: Report prepared by R. S. Henderson & Associates, Industrial Consultants, n.d.).

63. Vincennes, Indiana, Airport Board, "Lawrenceville-Vincennes Airport Report," Sept. 9, 1963 (Wabash Valley Interstate Commission Materials, Terre Haute, Indiana).

64. Minutes, Oct. 18, 1962.

65. *Annual Report*, Jan. 1963, "The Chairman's Report" (page not numbered).

66. Indiana Senate Enrolled Act No. 444, *An Act concerning the acquisition, maintenance, financing and operation of air terminals by governmental units located in more than one state; and the creation of airport authorities,* sponsored by R. V. Walsh, Glenn, Burgoon, Blades, Lewis, May 14, 1963, *Burns' Indiana Stats.* 14–805, 810.

Illinois House Bill No. 1258, 73rd Gen. Assbly., 1963. Laws, 1963. *Ill. Rev. Stats.* 1965, Ch. 15½, § 251, 257.

67. *The Terre Haute Star*, Jan. 25, 1963, "Interstate Body Suggests Steps to Aid Economy;" and *Annual Report*, Jan. 1963, page-numbered report.

68. As constituted in 1963, the members of the authority were: Michael Bonewitz, Vincennes; Reuel Buchanan, Lawrenceville; William Downes, Chicago (appointed by Gov. Kerner as Illinois state representative); Rabb Emison, Vincennes; James Funk, Vincennes (appointed by Gov. Welsh as Indiana representative); Richard Kixmiller, Vincennes; Ivan Mayfield, Lawrenceville (Chairman); and Kenneth Wherry, Lawrenceville.

69. Members of the Industrial Corporation Board were: Charles W. Cullison, president (physician); Lyman H. Bell, vice-President (Hoosier Gas Corporation); John H. McCaughey, treasurer (McGaughey Insurance); John A. Ward, secretary (sales manager, Knox County Sand Co.); L. T. Wampler, director (Wampler Agency); G. Wendell Farrington, director (Central Illinois Public Service Company); Edward Benecki, director (attorney); and Norbert Welch, director (physician).

70. *Annual Report*, 1967, pp. 10–12.

71. Minutes, April 20, 1961.

72. Paul Day Cribbins, *A Proposed Navigable Waterway for the Wabash and Maumee Rivers* (Lafayette, Ind.: Purdue University, 1959), p. 295.

73. Ibid., p. 191.

74. *Annual Report*, Jan. 1963, page 9 of unnumbered pages.

75. Ibid., p. 10, unnumbered pages.

76. Ibid., p. 25, unnumbered pages.

77. *Annual Report*, 1965, p. 8.

78. Armin K. Ludwig, *The Transportation Structure of the Lower Wabash Valley* (Terre Haute, Ind.: Wabash Valley Interstate Commission, 1963).

79. *Annual Report*, 1965, pp. 8–9.

80. Wabash Valley Interstate Commission, "Economic Impact of a Navigable Waterway on the Wabash Basin," mimeographed report, n.d. (In files of WVIC, Terre Haute, Ind.).

81. *Annual Report*, 1965, p. 30.

82. *Annual Report*, 1966, p. 7.

83. Wabash Valley Interstate Commission, *Cross-Wabash Valley Waterway: Summary Report*, n.d. (Terre Haute, Ind.: issued 1967).

84. Ibid., p. 3.

85. Ibid.

86. *Annual Report*, 1967, pp. 5–6.

87. *Annual Report*, 1968, p. 3.

88. Upper Ohio Valley Association, *Lake Erie-Ohio River Canal; Comments of the Upper Valley Association on Review of Reports on Lake Erie-Ohio River Canal*, 3 vols. (Cleveland, 1965).

89. Illinois, 75th Gen. Assbly., *Sen. J. Res.* 19, 1967; Indiana, 95th Gen. Assbly., *H. Concur. Res.* 39, 1967; Resolution adopted Mar. 6, 1967, U.S. Sen. Comm. on Public Works; adopted October 19, 1967, U.S. House Comm. on Public Works, 90th Cong., 1st Sess.

90. *Annual Report*, 1964 (misnumbered, 1963), pp. 6–8.

91. *Terre Haute Star*, "Letters to the Editor," January 23, 1964.

92. *Terre Haute Star*, "Huge Refuge for Wildlife Approved," June 9, 1966.

93. *Annual Report*, 1966, pp. 1–2.

94. *Annual Report*, 1963 (page-numbered edition), pp. ii through 2.

95. Marcou, O'Leary and Associates, *A Planning Program for the Wabash Valley* (Washington, 1967), 25 pp. See also, Wabash Valley Interstate Commission, *Annual Report*, "Progress Through Planning," 1968, pp. 26–28.

96. Marcou, O'Leary and Associates, *A Planning Program for the Wabash Valley*, p. 4.

97. *Annual Report*, 1968, pp. 35–37.

6   The Interstate Oil Compact

1. Six interstate compacts have larger memberships: the Civil Defense and Disaster, Education, Mental Health, Parolees and Probationers, Vehicle Equipment Safety, and Compact on Juveniles. Council of State Governments, *Interstate Compacts, 1783–1966: A Compilation,* 1966 (Chicago, 1966).

2. *Laws of the State of Illinois* (hereafter cited as Laws), 1935, p. 1418.

3. 49 *Ill. Stats.* 939, 1935.

4. 77 *U.S. Stats.* 145; Pub. Law 88–115; Pub. Law 90–185 (81 *U.S. Stats.* 560); *Compact Comments,* newsletter of the Interstate Oil Compact Commission, vol. 24, no. 3, March 1969, p. 1; S.J. Res. 54, 91st Cong., 1st Sess., 1969.

5. *Ill. Rev. Stats.* 1965, 104 § 21.

6. Ibid., 104 § 22.

7. Ibid., 104 § 24.

8. Ibid., 104 § 19: Interstate Oil Compact, Art. II.

9. Compact, Art. VI, Par. 2.

10. Ibid., Par. 1.

11. Interstate Oil Compact Commission, *A Study of Conservation of Oil and Gas in the United States* (Oklahoma City, 1964), p. 9. Also, Compact, Art. VII.

12. The associate representative is George R. Lane, chief engineer of the Illinois Oil and Gas Division of the Department of Mines and Minerals.

13. *Ill. Rev. Stats.* 1965, 104 § 64; Act of July 29, 1941.

14. Ibid., Sec. 67 (2). See also, *Illinois Blue Book,* 1967–68 volume, pp. 759–64.

15. Interview by writer with Commissioner McGaughey, Apr. 27, 1966.

16. 49 *U.S. Stats.* 30, 15 *U.S. C.A.* § 715 et seq. (1940); the Act was made permanent in 56 *U.S. Stats.* 381 (1942).

17. Blakely M. Murphy, ed., *Conservation of Oil and Gas: A Legal History,* ch. 10, "Illinois, 1889–1948" (Chicago: American Bar Association, 1949), pp. 90–122.

18. Ibid., pp. 95–96.

19. *Compact Comments,* vol. 21, no. 11, Nov. 1966, p. 3.

20. *Centralia Evening Sentinel,* "Illinois Must Not Have State Proration," May 8, 1938.

21. Murphy, *Conservation of Oil and Gas,* p. 96, and note 14, pp. 96–97.

22. Ibid., p. 98.

23. Ibid., p. 100.

24. *Laws,* 1941, p. 934, as amended by *Laws,* 1945, p. 1091.

25. Murphy, *Conservation of Oil and Gas,* pp. 113–22.

26. *Ill. Rev. Stats.* 1965, 104 § 62–86.

27. Interstate Oil Compact Commission, Governors' Special Study

Commission, *A Study of Conservation of Oil and Gas in the United States,* 1964; pp. 278–307.

28. *Ill. Rev. Stats.* 1965, Ibid., Note 26.

29. The Interstate Oil Compact Commission, *The Oil and Gas Compact Bulletin,* vol. 27, no. 2, Dec., 1968; p. 51.

30. Ibid., Vol. 25, No. 2, Dec. 1966; p. 52.

31. Stanley Learned, *Petroleum Conservation—The Myths and Realities,* Eighth Annual Institute on Exploration and Economics of the Petroleum Industry, at Dallas, Tex., Mar. 7, 1968 (New York: Matthew Bender and Company, 1968), pp. 20–23.

32. René de Visme Williamson, *The Politics of Planning in the Oil Industry Under the Code* (New York: Harper & Brothers, 1936), pp. 26, 32.

33. L. M. Logan, *Stabilization of the Petroleum Industry* (Norman: University of Oklahoma Press, 1930), p. 7.

34. Compact, ARTS. III and IV.

35. *The Oil and Gas Compact Bulletin,* vol. 24, no. 2, Dec. 1965, p. 44; also, Ibid., vol. 27, no. 1, June 1968, p. 37.

36. *Ill. Rev. Stats.* 1965, 104 § 62–86, "Conservation of Oil and Gas"; also, "Some Aspects of Oil Conservation and Taxation in Illinois," Research Memorandum Prepared Pursuant to Proposal 327, Illinois Legislative Council, Research Memorandum File 1–535, Oct. 1951 (Springfield).

37. Harold M. McClure, Jr., "First You Must Find Petroleum—Then You Can Practice Conservation," *Oil and Gas Compact Bulletin,* vol. 27, no. 1, June 1968, pp. 5–9.

38. John M. Houchin, "The Attorney General's 1967 Interstate Oil Compact Report—An Industry Viewpoint From 35 Years' Experience," *Oil and Gas Compact Bulletin,* vol. 26, no. 2, Dec. 1967, pp. 18–19. Houchin is chairman of the Executive Committee of the Phillips Petroleum Company. This address is also in *Congressional Record* (Daily Edition), 90th Cong., 2d Sess., Mar. 13, 1968, pp. H1930–33, introduced into the *Record* by Representative Edmondson of Oklahoma.

39. Morris Adelman, "Efficiency of Resource Use in Crude Petroleum," *Southern Economic Journal,* vol. 31, no. 2, Oct. 1964, pp. 101–22.

40. Gilbert R. Burck, "A Giant Caught In Its Own Web," *Fortune,* vol. 71, no. 4, April 1965, pp. 113–19, 200, 202, 207.

41. "A Whiff of Crude," editorial, *Fortune,* vol. 71, no. 6, June 1965, p. 130.

42. Stanley Learned, "A Letter to *Fortune,*" *Petroleum Management,* Feb. 1966.

43. Houchin, "The Attorney General's 1967 Interstate Oil Compact Report," p. 19. See also U.S., Congress, Senate, Committee on Interior and Insular Affairs, *Interstate Oil Compact, Hearings on S.J. Res. 35,* 90th Cong., 1st Sess., 1967.

44. Wallace F. Lovejoy and Paul T. Homan, *Economic Aspects of Oil Conservation Regulation* (Baltimore: Resources for the Future, 1967).

7 Interstate Compacts: A Question of Federalism

1. Illinois, in 1969, through S.B. 74, 76th General Assembly, was considering amending its act creating its Commission on Intergovernment Cooperation to make it an information center for the General Assembly (no final action as of this writing). As introduced the measure would seemingly provide the kind of review powers the author has in mind.

2. Advisory Commission on Intergovernmental Relations, "Status of ACIR Recommendations to the Federal Government," *Congressional Record*, 90th Cong., 1st Sess., vol. 113, no. 54, Apr. 12, 1967. See also, Richard H. Leach, "The Status of Interstate Compacts Today," *State Government*, vol. 32, spring, 1959, pp. 134–39; and Senator Alan Bible's remarks, "Method For Obtaining Consent of Congress to Interstate Compacts," *Congressional Record*, 85th Cong., 2d Sess., vol. 104, Mar. 10, 1958, pp. 3677–78. Bible stated that his proposal was offered "at the request of the National Association of Attorneys General."

3. U.S., Congress, House, Committee on Government Operations, *Unshackling Local Government: A Survey of Proposals by the Advisory Commission on Intergovernmental Regulations*, 90th Cong., 2d Sess., Apr. 2, 1968, 24th report of the Committee, H. Rept. 1270.

4. *Congressional Record* (Daily Edition), 90th Cong., 2d Sess., July 15, 1968, pp. H6523–24.

Books

Altschuler, Alan A. *The City Planning Process*. Ithaca, N.Y.: Cornell University Press, 1965. Especially chapter 5, "The Goals of Comprehensive Planning," and chapter 8, "Opportunism vs. Professionalism in Planning."

Banfield, Edward C. "St. Louis: Better Than She Should Be." In *Big City Politics*. New York: Random House, 1966.

Banfield, Edward C., and Grodzins, Morton. "The Limitations of Metropolitan Reorganization." In *Democracy in Urban America*, edited by Oliver P. Williams and Charles Press. Chicago: Rand McNally and Company, 1961.

Berle, Adolf A. "Evolving Capitalism and Political Federalism." In *Federalism, Mature and Emergent*, edited by Arthur W. MacMahon. New York: Doubleday and Company, 1958.

Bollens, John C. *Exploring the Metropolitan Community*. Berkeley and Los Angeles: University of California Press, 1961.

Boyce, Ronald R. *Regional Development and the Wabash Basin*. Urbana: University of Illinois Press, 1964.

Buckley, Stuart E. *Petroleum Conservation*. New York: American Institute of Mining, Metallurgical & Petroleum Engineers, 1951.

Cribbins, Paul Day. *A Proposed Navigable Waterway for the Wabash and Maumee Rivers*. Lafayette, Ind.: Purdue University, 1959.

DeGolyer, E., ed. *Elements of the Petroleum Industry*. New York: American Institute of Mining and Metallurgical Engineers, 1940.

Elazar, Daniel J. *American Federalism: A View From the States*. New York: Thomas Y. Crowell Company, 1966.

Ely, Northcutt. *Oil Conservation Through Interstate Agreement*. Washington, D.C.: U.S. Federal Oil Conservation Board, 1933.

Handler, Milton. "Patterns of Trade Regulation in a Federal System." In *Federalism: Mature and Emergent*, edited by Arthur W. MacMahon. Garden City, N.Y.: Doubleday & Company, 1958.

Interstate Oil Compact Commission. *A Study of Conservation of Oil and Gas in the United States*. Oklahoma City, 1964.

———. *The Compact's Formative Years, 1931–35*. Oklahoma City, 1954.

Ise, John. *The United States Oil Policy*. New Haven: Yale University Press, 1926.

Jones, Victor. "Metropolitan Authorities." In *The Future of Cities and Urban Redevelopment*, edited by Coleman Woodbury. Chicago: University of Chicago Press, 1953. Also in *Metropolitan Politics*, edited by Michael N. Danielson. Boston: Little, Brown & Company, 1966.

Key, V. O., Jr. *American State Politics: An Introduction*. New York: Alfred A. Knopf, 1956.

Leach, Richard H., and Sugg, Redding S., Jr. *The Administration of Interstate Compacts*. Baton Rouge: Louisiana State University Press, 1959.

Logan, L. M. *Stabilization of the Petroleum Industry*. Norman: University of Oklahoma Press, 1930.

Lovejoy, Wallace F., and Homan, Paul T. *Economic Aspects of Oil Conservation Regulation*. Baltimore: Resources for the Future, 1967.

Mann, Seymour Z. "Across the Wide Missouri." In *Cases in American National Government and Politics*, edited by Rocco J. Tresolini and Richard T. Frost. Englewood Cliffs, N.J.: Prentice-Hall, 1965.

Merton, Robert K. "Bureaucratic Structure and Personality." In *Reader in Bureaucracy*, edited by Robert K. Merton, Ailsa P. Gray, Barbara Hockey, and Hanan C. Silvin. Glencoe, Ill.: Free Press, 1952.

Murphy, Blakely M., ed. *Conservation of Oil and Gas: A Legal History*. Chicago: American Bar Association, 1949.

Rourke, Francis E. *Bureaucracy, Politics, and Public Policy*. Boston: Little, Brown and Company, 1969. Especially chapter 6, "New Designs For Policy-Making," and chapter 7, "Bureaucracy As a Power Elite."

Sanford, Terry. *Storm Over the States*. New York: McGraw-Hill Book Company, 1967.

Schmandt, Henry J., Stinebicker, Paul G., and Wendel, George D. "The Campaign for Metropolitan Government in St. Louis." In *Metropolitan Politics*, edited by Michael N. Danielson. Boston: Little, Brown and Company, 1966.

Upper Ohio Valley Association. *Lake Erie-Ohio River Canal: Comments of the Upper Valley Association on Review of Reports on Lake Erie-Ohio River Canal*. 3 vols. Cleveland, 1965.

Wilbern, York. "Administrative Control of Petroleum Production in Texas." In *Public Administration and Policy Formation*, edited by Emmette S. Redford. Austin: University of Texas Press, 1956.

Williamson, René de Visme. *The Politics of Planning in the Oil Industry Under the Code*. New York: Harper & Brothers, 1936.

Woodbury, Coleman, ed. *The Future of Cities and Urban Development*. Chicago: University of Chicago Press, 1953.

Zimmermann, Erich W. *Conservation in the Production of Petroleum*. New Haven: Yale University Press, 1957.

Zimmermann, Frederick L., and Wendell, Mitchell. "Interstate Compacts." *The Book of the States*, 1960–61 vol., 1964–65 vol., 1966–67 vol., and

1968–69 vol. Chicago: Council of State Governments, 1960, 1964, 1966, and 1968.

————. *The Interstate Compact Since 1925*. Chicago: Council of State Governments, 1951.

Nongovernmental Reports, Brochures

A New Kind of Man for Illinois: John Henry Alterfer, Republican for Governor. Campaign brochure. Carbondale: Printed by the *Southern Illinoisan*, June 9, 1968.

Carbondale, Ill., Wabash Valley Interstate Commission files, Southern Illinois University. "Air Industrial Park, Lawrenceville, Illinois." Carbondale, Ill.: Report prepared by R. S. Henderson & Associates, Industrial Consultants, n.d.

Chamber of Commerce of the United States. *Modernizing Local Government*. Washington, D.C., 1967.

Chamber of Commerce, Terre Haute, Ind. *Wabash Valley Compact*. Pamphlet issued for Ceremonial Signing, Jan. 25, 1960, at Terre Haute.

Committee for Economic Development. *Modernizing State Government*. New York, 1967.

Council of State Governments. *Interstate Compacts, 1783–1966: A Compilation, 1966*. Chicago, 1966. *1966–67 Supplement*. Chicago, 1969.

Governmental Research Institute. *Should a Metropolitan Airport Authority Be Established for the St. Louis Area? A Report for the East-West Gate way Coordinating Council*. St. Louis, 1968.

Harlan Bartholomew and Associates. *Development of the Missouri-Illinois District*. St. Louis, 1950.

Learned, Stanley. *Petroleum Conservation—The Myths and Realities*. New York: Matthew Bender and Company, 1968.

Marcou, O'Leary and Associates. *A Planning Program for the Wabash Valley*. Washington, 1967.

Memorandum of Understanding. Resolution adopted by Madison-St. Clair Counties (Illinois) mayors and county officials, with the Southwestern Illinois Metropolitan Planning Commission and Illinois Department of Public Works and Buildings (in connection with creation of the East-West Gateway Coordinating Council). Granite City, Illinois: Sept. 29, 1964.

Oklahoma City, Okla. Records of the Interstate Oil and Gas Compact Commission. "Transcript of Proceedings." Conference of Oil State Governors. Dallas, Tex.: Feb. 15–16, 1935.

Tri-Cities (Ill.) Chamber of Commerce. "East-West Gateway Coordinating Council." Mimeographed report. Granite City, Ill., Feb. 3, 1967.

Articles

"A Better Atmosphere For Oil Regulation." Editorial. *The Oil and Gas Journal*, vol. 61, no. 50, Dec. 16, 1963, p. 43.

Adelman, Morris. "Efficiency of Resource Use in Crude Petroleum." *Southern Economic Journal*, vol. 31, no. 2, Oct. 1964, pp. 101–22.

Asbell, Bernard. "The Great Chicago Water Steal." *Saturday Evening Post*, vol. 235, May 19, 1962, pp. 30–33.

Ascoli, Max. "As Texas Goes. . ." Editorial. *Reporter Magazine*, vol. 16, no. 6, Mar. 21, 1957, p. 10.

"A Whiff of Crude." Editorial. *Fortune*, vol. 71, no. 6, June 1965, p. 130.

Banfield, Edward C. "The Politics of Metropolitan Area Organization." *Midwest Journal of Political Science*, vol. 1, no. 1, May 1957, pp. 77–91.

Bingham, Jo. "Save Our States." National Association of Manufacturers, *Intergovernmental Reporter*, vol. 1, no. 2, Dec. 1967.

Burck, Gilbert R. "A Giant Caught in Its Own Web," *Fortune*, vol. 71, no. 4, Apr. 1965, pp. 113–19.

Carey, William D. "Intergovernmental Relations: Guides to Development." *Public Administration Review*, vol. 28, no. 1, Jan.–Feb. 1968, pp. 22–25.

Cater, Douglass. "The General and the Umbrella." *Reporter Magazine*, vol. 16, no. 6, Mar. 21, 1957, pp. 11–15.

Compact Comments. Newsletter of the Interstate Oil Compact Commission. Many issues, 1957–present.

Derge, David R. "Metropolitan and Outstate Alignments in Illinois and Missouri Legislative Delegations." *American Political Science Review*, vol. 52, Dec. 1958, pp. 1051–65.

Dodd, Alice Mary. "Interstate Compacts." *U.S. Law Review*, vol. 70, Oct. 1936, p. 557–78.

Dunbar, Leslie W. "Interstate Compacts and Congressional Consent." *Virginia Law Review*, vol. 36, Oct. 1950, pp. 753–63.

"East St. Louis Confronts Its Problems." *Illinois Business Review*, vol. 24, no. 6, June 1967, p. 3.

Engler, Robert. "How To Influence People." *New Republic*, vol. 133, no. 13, Sept. 26, 1955, pp. 21–25.

———. "Just So They Vote Right." *New Republic*, vol. 133, no. 10, Sept. 5, 1955, pp. 11–15.

———. "Oil and Politics." *New Republic*, vol. 133, no. 9, Aug. 29, 1955, pp. 11–15.

———. "The Operators Move In." *New Republic*, vol. 133, no. 11, Sept. 12, 1955, pp. 10–15.

———. "The Sweet Smell of Oil." *New Republic*, vol. 133, no. 12, Sept. 19, 1955, pp. 12–15.

———. "Where Politicians Fear to Tread." *New Republic*, vol. 133, no. 14, Oct. 3, 1955, pp. 14–17.

Frankfurter, Felix, and Landis, James M. "The Compact Clause of the Constitution—A Study in Interstate Adjustments." *Yale Law Journal*, vol. 34, May 1925, pp. 685–758.

Hamilton, Randy. "The Regional Commissions: A Restrained View." *Public Administration Review*, vol. 28, no. 1, Jan.–Feb. 1968, pp. 19–22.

BIBLIOGRAPHY

Houchin, John M. "The Attorney General's 1967 Interstate Oil Compact Report—An Industry Viewpoint From 35 Years' Experience." *Oil and Gas Compact Bulletin*, vol. 26, no. 2, Dec. 1967, pp. 18–19.

Interstate Oil Compact Commission. "Illinois Report." *Oil and Gas Compact Bulletin*, vol. 24, no. 2, Dec. 1965, p. 44.

———. "Illinois Report." *Oil and Gas Compact Bulletin*, vol. 27, no. 1, June 1968, pp. 37–38.

———. "Resolution Adopted on Federal Regulation of Natural Gas Production." *Oil and Gas Compact Bulletin*, vol. 25, no. 2, Dec. 1966, pp. 51–52.

———. "Resolution Adopted on Oil Imports Policies." *Oil and Gas Compact Bulletin*, vol. 27, no. 2, Dec. 1968, pp. 50–51.

LaMotte, Clyde. "Kennedy Does Have An Oil Policy." *Oil and Gas Journal*, vol. 61, no. 14, Apr. 8, 1963, pp. 44–46; 163.

———. "Under Lyndon Johnson: Less Squabbling, More Action, No Basic Changes Affecting Oil." *Oil and Gas Journal*, vol. 61, no. 48, Dec. 2, 1963, pp. 101–3.

Leach, Richard H. "Interstate Agencies and Effective Administration." *State Government*, vol. 34, no. 3, summer 1961, pp. 199–204.

———. "The Status of Interstate Compacts Today." *State Government*, vol. 32, no. 2, spring 1959, pp. 134–39.

Learned, Stanley. "A Letter to *Fortune*." *Petroleum Management*, Feb., 1966.

Levin, Melvin R. "Planners and Metropolitan Planning." *Journal of American Institute of Planners*, vol. 33, no. 2, Mar. 1967, pp. 78–90.

Logan, L. J. "Interstate Compact Proving Valuable Aid to Industry." *Oil Weekly*, vol. 90, Aug. 8, 1938, p. 15.

McClure, Harold M., Jr. "First You Must Find Petroleum—Then You can Practice Conservation." *Oil and Gas Compact Bulletin*, vol. 27, no. 1, June 1968, pp. 5–14.

Peeples, William. "The Indiana Dunes and Pressure Politics." *Atlantic Monthly*, vol. 211, Feb. 1963, pp. 84–88.

Rockwell, Matthew L. "Interlocal Cooperation: The State's Role." In *The State and Its Cities*, Urbana: Institute of Government and Public Affairs, University of Illinois Bulletin, vol. 64, no. 108, Apr. 28, 1967, pp. 71–79.

Routt, Garland C. "Interstate Compacts and Administrative Cooperation." *Annals of the American Academy of Political and Social Sciences*, Jan. 1940, pp. 93–102.

Salisbury, Robert H. "St. Louis Politics: Relationships Among Interests, Parties, and Government Structure." *Western Political Quarterly*, vol. 13, June 1960, pp. 498–507.

———. "Urban Politics: The New Convergence of Power." *Journal of Politics*, vol. 26, Nov. 1964, pp. 775–97.

Schaller, Lyle E. "Is the Citizen Advisory Committee a Threat to Representative Government?" *Public Administration Review*, vol. 24, Sept. 1964, pp. 175–79.

Spengler, Joseph J. "The Economic Limitations to Certain Uses of Interstate Compacts." *American Political Science Review,* vol. 31, no. 1, Feb. 1937, pp. 41–51.

Newspapers

Air and Water News. Vol. 2, et passim.

Alton (Ill.) *Evening Telegraph.* "Bi-State Signs Agreement to Acquire Parks Airport." Nov. 1, 1962.

————. "To Study Bi-State Cooperation." July 28, 1959.

Belleville (Ill.) *News-Democrat.* "Typical Bi-State Service." Editorial. Aug. 31, 1967.

Bryerton, Eugene. "2 Agencies In Arch Job Far Apart." *St. Louis* (Mo.) *Post-Dispatch,* Jan. 18, 1968.

Centralia (Ill.) *Evening Sentinel.* "Illinois Must Not Have State Proration." May 8, 1938.

East St. Louis (Ill.) *Journal.* "Area Distrusts Missouri, Bi-State Members Told." Jan. 26, 1960.

————. "Illinois Bi-State Group Wants Chairman Post." Apr. 12, 1959.

————. "Goals Listed in St. Louis." Jan. 26, 1960.

————. "Golden Decade Goals." Jan. 26, 1960.

————. "Metropolitan Development: Bi-State Advisory Council Set Up." Apr. 12, 1960.

————. "Needs Solved by Human Action, Bi-State Leaders Cautioned." Feb. 28, 1960.

————. "Roos Chairman of Bi-State." June 23, 1959.

————. "The Logical View." Editorial. Apr. 12, 1959.

East St. Louis (Ill.) *Evening Journal.* "Bi-State Agency to Re-organize." Nov. 16, 1961.

————. "Bi-State Awaits Action on Land Use, Road Plan." May 28, 1964.

————. "Bi-State Transit Decision Near." Mar. 30, 1962.

————. "First Area-Wide Meeting Stirs Airport Interest." Nov. 3, 1960.

————. "Metro Team Aim: New Industry." May 13, 1964.

————. "Super Bi-State Unit Proposed." Nov. 20, 1961.

East St. Louis (Ill.) *Sunday Journal.* "Bi-State Defends Planning Role." June 28, 1964.

Haas, Paul. "Letter to The Editor." *Terre Haute* (Ind.) *Star,* Jan. 23, 1964.

Jacobs, Richard. "Five Firms Seek Publicity Job in Bus Subsidy." *St. Louis* (Mo.) *Post-Dispatch,* Dec. 17, 1967.

Kester, William H. "Gateway Arch Rides Exceeds Estimate and Help Bi-State." *St. Louis* (Mo.) *Post-Dispatch,* July 18, 1968.

Pensoneau, Taylor. "Bi-State Review Urged To Solve Airport Jam." *St. Louis* (Mo.) *Post-Dispatch,* Apr. 21, 1968.

St. Louis (Mo.) *Globe-Democrat.* "Gateway Panel Authorizes Airport Study." Sept. 28, 1967.

St. Louis (Mo.) *Post-Dispatch.* "Airport Commission Worried Over Bills." Jan. 18, 1968.

————. "Airport Plan Backed by Gateway Council." Feb. 1, 1968.
————. "Baer Challenges Plan For Airport System." July 3, 1968.
————. "Bi-State Bus Budget Anticipates Deficit." Feb. 29, 1968.
————. "Bi-State's Revenues Down, Costs Are Up." Mar. 1, 1969.
————. "Bi-State To Cut Night Service After Dec. 24." Dec. 21, 1967.
————. "Clean-Air Unit Fights For Adequate Funds." Mar. 30, 1969.
————. "Committee Rejects Landing Strip Plan." Jan. 30, 1968.
————. "East Side Airport Bill Is Sent To Illinois Governor." July 25, 1968.
————. "FAA Inquiry Into Bottoms Airport Site." Jan. 3, 1968.
————. "House Bills: Illinois Proposals for Transit Aid." Apr. 1, 1969.
————. "Illinois Airport Requirement Cited." July 18, 1968.
————. "Metropolitan Authority Urged For Handling Airport Problem."
Apr. 25, 1968.
————. "Not The City's Job." Editorial. July 19, 1968.
————. "Opposes Tax for Airport Agency." July 16, 1968.
————. "Prospects for Airport Sale to Bi-State Called Dim." June 28, 1968.
————. "Rapid Transit Guides Adopted." May 8, 1969.
————. "$30,000,000 Plan to Improve Transit." Apr. 27, 1968.
————. "$25,560,000 in Aid For Pittsburgh Transit." Apr. 28, 1968.
Terre Haute (Ind.) *Star.* "Huge Refuge for Wildlife Approved." June 9,
1966.
————. "Interstate Body Suggests Steps to Aid Economy." Jan. 25, 1963.

Government Agency, Department Documents

Advisory Commission on Intergovernmental Relations. *Eighth Annual Report.* Washington, D.C.: Government Printing Office, Jan. 31, 1967.
————. *Governmental Structure, Organization, and Planning in Metropolitan Areas.* Report A-5. Washington, D.C.: Government Printing Office, July 1961.
————. *Metropolitan America: Challenge to Federalism.* Report M-31, to U.S. Congress, House Committee on Government Operations. Washington, D.C.: Government Printing Office, Aug. 1966.
————. *Metropolitan Councils of Governments.* Report M-32. Washington, D.C.: Government Printing Office, Aug. 1966.
————. *The Advisory Commission on Intergovernmental Relations.* Brochure M-17. Washington, D.C.: Government Printing Office, May 1, 1967.
————. *Unshackling Local Government—A Survey of Proposals by the Advisory Commission on Intergovernmental Relations.* U.S. Congress, House Report No. 1643, June 22, 1966.
Attorney General, State of Michigan. *A Report to the Governor on the Gasoline Price Investigation, 1955–56.* Lansing: 1956.
East-West Gateway Coordinating Council. St. Louis Metropolitan Area. *By-Laws, Approved December 8, 1965.* St. Louis: 1965.
————. *Interim Progress Report.* E. St. Louis, Ill.: May 31, 1967.
————. *Land Use and Transportation Planning Program for the St. Louis*

Metropolitan Area, Summary Report. E. St. Louis, Ill.: July 1965.

East-West Gateway Coordinating Committee. *Prospectus for Land Use and Transportation Planning Program.* St. Louis: Prepared by Alan Voorhees & Associates, Inc., May 26, 1965.

Great Lakes Commission. *Great Lakes Newsletter,* vol. 12, no. 4, Mar.–Apr. 1968; no. 6, July–Aug. 1968; vol. 13, nos. 1–3, Sept.–Oct., Nov.–Dec. 1968; and no. 4, Mar.–Apr. 1969.

————. *Report to the States.* 1963–64; 1965–66, Ann Arbor, Michigan.

————. *10th Anniversary, 1955–1965.* Brochure. Ann Arbor, Mich., 1965.

Illinois Commission on Intergovernmental Cooperation. *Report and Recommendations to Governor Kerner and the 74th General Assembly.* Springfield: Mar. 1965.

————. *Report and Recommendations to Governer Kerner and the 73rd General Assembly.* Springfield: Mar. 1963.

————. *Report on Five Interstate Compacts With Recommendations to the 75th General Assembly.* Springfield: Mar. 1967.

Illinois Department of Finance. *Appropriations: 74th General Assembly.* Springfield, 1965.

Illinois Department of Mines and Minerals. *Annual Report.* Springfield, 1964.

Illinois Legislative Council. "Illinois Adherence to Interstate Compacts." Memorandum to the Commission on Intergovernmental Cooperation. File 4–497. July 9, 1962. Springfield.

————. "Some Aspects of Oil Conservation and Taxation in Illinois." Research Memorandum Prepared Pursuant to Proposal 327. Research Memorandum File 1–535. Oct. 1951. Springfield.

Interstate Oil Compact Commission. Minutes of the Commission, Sept. 12, 1935–Dec. 3, 1955. Oklahoma City.

————. Minutes of the Executive Committee, Jan. 21, 1942–1955. Oklahoma City.

————. "Transcript of Proceedings of Quarterly Meetings." Unpublished records of the commission, Oklahoma City.

Ludwig, Armin K. *The Transportation Structure of the Lower Wabash Valley.* Terre Haute, Ind.: Wabash Valley Interstate Commission, 1963.

Missouri-Illinois Bi-State Development Agency. *Annual Reports,* 1961–62; 1962–63; 1963–64; 1964–65; 1965–66; 1966–67; 1967–68. Published at St. Louis.

————. "By-Laws." (As of 1966.) Mimeographed. St. Louis.

————. Materials. Southern Illinois University files of the agency, Carbondale.

————. Minutes, 1949–67. Unpublished records of the commission, St. Louis.

New York Port Authority. *Forbes or "Facts?"* Brochure. New York, 1967.

Preston, Don R. *Preparing for the Future of Missouri.* Report. Jefferson City, Mo.: Missouri Office of State and Regional Planning, 1967.

Schad, Theodore M., and Boswell, Elizabeth. *Congressional Handling of*

Water Resources, Washington D.C.: Library of Congress, Legislative Reference Service, Dec. 15, 1967.

"Status of ACIR Recommendations to the Federal Government." *Congressional Record,* 90th Cong., 1st. sess., vol. 113, no. 54, Apr. 12, 1967.

U.S. Department of Health, Education and Welfare. "Pollution of Interstate Waters, Mississippi River, St. Louis Metropolitan Area." Transcript of conference, St. Louis, Mar. 4, 1958.

U.S. Department of Justice. *Report of the Attorney General, Pursuant to Sec. 2 of Joint Resolution of July 28, 1955: Consenting to an Interstate Compact to Conserve Oil and Gas.* Washington, D.C., Sept. 1, 1956.

Vincennes, Indiana, Airport Board. "Lawrenceville-Vincennes Airport Report," Sept. 9, 1963. Wabash Valley Interstate Commission Materials, Terre Haute, Indiana.

Wabash Valley Interstate Commission. *A Bi-State Approach to Resource Development.* Brochure. Terre Haute, Ind., 1966.

――――. *Annual Reports.* Jan. 1962; Jan. 1963; Jan. 1965; Jan. 1967; and Jan. 1968. Published at Terre Haute, Ind.

――――. *ASCS Funds to Stabilize Farm Land and Protect City Water Supply* and *Who May Benefit From Small Watershed Projects?* Brochures. Terre Haute, Ind., 1966.

――――. *By-Laws, 1966.* Terre Haute, Ind.

――――. *Cross-Wabash Valley Waterway: Summary Report,* n.d. Terre Haute, Ind., issued 1967.

――――. "Economic Impact of a Navigable Waterway on the Wabash Basin." Mimeographed report, n.d. In files of WVIC, Terre Haute, Ind.

――――. Minutes of the Commission, 1960–68, Terre Haute, Ind.

――――. Miscellaneous Records. Southern Illinois University files of unpublished commission materials, Carbondale, Illinois.

――――. *Regional Planning For the Wabash Valley.* Terre Haute, Ind., 1965.

United States Congressional Hearings, Reports

House, Committee on Foreign Affairs. *Great Lakes Basin Compact, Hearings on H.R. 937, 12294, 12692, 13359, 14192, and 15042.* 89th Cong., 2d Sess., 1966.

――――. *Great Lakes Basin Compact, Hearings on H.R. 4314.* 85th Cong., 2d Sess., 1958.

――――. *Great Lakes Basin Compact. Report to Accompany S. 660.* 90th Cong., 2d Sess., July 3, 1968, H. Rept. 1640.

House, Committee on Government Operations. *Unshackling Local Government: A Survey of Proposals by the Advisory Commission on Intergovernmental Regulations.* 90th Cong., 2d Sess., Apr. 2, 1968, H. Rept. 1270.

House, Committee on Interior and Insular Affairs. *Indiana Dunes National Lakeshore, Hearings on H.R. 51, H.R. 4412 and Related Bills Part I.* Valparaiso, Indiana. 89th Cong., 1st Sess., 1965.

House, Committee on Interstate and Foreign Commerce. *Consenting to an*

Interstate Compact to Conserve Oil and Gas. Report to Accompany S.J. Res. 38. 84th Cong., 1st Sess., June 27, 1955, H. Rept. 917.

House, Committee on the Judiciary. *Interstate Compact Creating Bi-State Development Agency and Metropolitan District Between Missouri and Illinois.* 81st Cong., 2d Sess., Aug. 9, 1950, H. Rept. 2839.

————. *Proceedings Against Austin J. Tobin.* 86th Cong., 2d Sess., Aug. 23, 1960, H. Rept. 2117.

House, Committee on Public Works. *Lake Michigan Water Diversion, Hearings on H.R. 3192.* 83d Cong., 1st Sess., 1953.

————. *Lake Michigan Water Diversion, Hearings on H.R. 1.* 86th Cong., 1st Sess., 1959.

Secretary of the Army. *Report on the Great Lakes Harbor Study—Interim Report on Burns Waterway Harbor.* 88th Cong., 1st Sess., 1963, H. Doc. 160.

Senate, Committee on Government Operations, Subcommittee on Intergovernmental Relations. *Creative Federalism, Hearings, Parts I, IIA,* and *IIB.* 89th Cong., 2d Sess., and 90th Cong., 1st Sess., 1966 and 1967.

Senate, Committee on Interior and Insular Affairs. *Consenting to an Interstate Compact to Conserve Oil and Gas.* 86th Cong., 1st Sess., July 23, 1959, S. Rept. 564.

————. *Consenting to an Interstate Compact to Conserve Oil and Gas. Report to Accompany S.J. Res. 38.* 84th Cong., 1st Sess., May 3, 1955, S. Rept. 266.

————. *Consenting to the Extension of the Interstate Oil and Gas Compact.* 91st Cong., 1st Sess., May 1969, S. Rept. 199.

————. *Extending the Interstate Oil Compact, Hearings.* 88th Cong., 1st Sess., 1963.

————. *Indiana Dunes National Lakeshore, Hearings on S. 2249* 88th Cong., 2d Sess., 1964.

————. *Indiana Dunes National Lakeshore, Hearings on S. 360.* 89th Cong., 1st Sess., 1965.

————. *Interstate Oil Compact, Hearings on S.J. Res. 35.* 90th Cong., 1st Sess., 1967.

Senate, Committee on the Judiciary. *Great Lakes Basin Compact, Hearings on S. 1416.* 85th Cong., 2d Sess., 1958.

————. *Great Lakes Basin Compact. Report to Accompany S. 660.* 90th Cong., 2d Sess., June 10, 1968, S. Rept. 1178.

————. *Interstate Compact Creating Bi-State Development Agency and Metropolitan District Between Missouri and Illinois.* 81st Cong., 2d Sess., July 13, 1950, S. Rept. 2041.

Senate. Committee on Public Works. *Diversion of Water From Lake Michigan, Hearings on S. 1123 and H.R. 2.* 85th Cong., 2d Sess., 1958.

U.S. Army Corps of Engineers. *Great Lakes Harbor Study—Final Report.* 90th Cong., 1st Sess., 1967, H. Doc. 1512.

U.S. Army Corps of Engineers Report. *Effects of Additional Diversion of*

BIBLIOGRAPHY

Water From Lake Michigan at Chicago. 85th Cong., 1st Sess., Jan. 1957, S. Doc. 28.

Court Decisions

Barron v. Baltimore, 7 Pet. 249, 8 L. Ed. 672 (1833).
Dresden School District v. Norwich Town School District, 203 A.2d 598, 124 Vt. 227 (1964).
Duncan v. Smith, 262 S.W.2d 373, 42 A.L.R.2d 754 (1953).
Ex parte Tenner, 128 P.2d 338, 20 Cal. 2d 670 (1942).
Green v. Biddle, 8 Wheat. 85, 5 L. Ed. 547 (1823).
Holmes v. Jennison, 14 Pet. 572, 10 L. Ed. 579 (1840).
Interior Airways, Inc. v. Wien Alaska Airlines, Inc., 188 F. Supp. 107 (1960).
Ivey v. Ayers, 301 S.W.2d 790 (1957).
Pennsylvania v. Wheeling & Belmont Bridge Co., 18 How. 421, 433 (U.S. 1856).
People v. Curtis, 50 N.Y. 330 (1872).
State v. Cunningham, 102 Miss. 237 (1912).
State v. Doe, 178 A.2d 271, 149 Conn. 216 (1962).
State v. Joslin, 116 Kans. 615 (1924).
Tobin v. U.S., 306 F.2d 270; 113 U.S. App. D.C. 110; 83 S. Ct. 206; 371 U.S. 902 (1962).
U.S. v. Rauscher, 7 S. Ct. 234, 119 U.S. 407 (1886).
U.S. v. Tobin, 195 F. Supp. 605 (1961).
Virginia v. Tennessee, 13 S. Ct. 728, 148 U.S. 518, 37 L. Ed. 537 (1893).
Virginia v. W. Virginia, 11 Wall. 59, 20 L. Ed. 67 (1871).
Virginia v. W. Virginia, 246 U.S. 565 (1918).
Wisconsin, Michigan and New York v. City of Chicago and State of Illinois, Decisions per Curiam, 273 U.S. 642 (1926).
Wisconsin, Michigan and New York v. Chicago & State of Illinois, Decisions per Curiam, 281 U.S. 696 (1930).
Wisconsin, Michigan and New York v. Chicago & State of Illinois, Decisions per Curiam, 352 U.S. 945 (1956).

Laws

Articles of Incorporation, East-West Gateway Coordinating Council. Under the Missouri General Not-for-Profit Corporation Act, Adopted December 8, 1965.
"Conservation of Oil and Gas." *Laws of the State of Illinois,* 1965, (Hereafter cited as *Laws*) Ill. Rev. Stats., 104 § 62–86.
The Great Lakes Basin Compact. *Ill. Rev. Stats.,* 1965, 127 § 192.1; *Pub. Law* 90–419; 82 *U.S. Stat.* 414, 90th Cong., 2d Sess., Approved July 24, 1968.
Housing Act of 1961. *Pub. Law* 87–60.
Illinois Little Egypt Regional Port District Act. *Laws,* 1965, S.B. 737; *Ill. Rev. Stats.,* 19 § 501–50.

Illinois-Missouri Bridge Commission Compact. *Laws,* 1965, H.B. 391; *Ill. Rev. Stats.,* 127 § 63s–21 et seq.
Illinois Southwest Regional Port District Act. *Laws* 1961, p. 2993; *Ill. Rev. Stats.,* 19 § 451.
Illinois Tri-City Regional Port District Act. *Laws* 1959, p. 71; *Ill. Rev. Stats.,* 19 § 284–317, 1967.
Intergovernmental Cooperation Act. *Pub. Law* 90–577; 82 *U.S. Stat.* 1098, 1968.
The Interstate Oil and Gas Compact. 77 *U.S. Stat.* 145, *Pub. Law* 88–115; *Ill. Rev. Stats.* 49 § 939, 1935.
Missouri-Illinois Bi-State Development Compact. 64 *U.S. Stat.,* Part I, 568 et seq.; *Laws of Missouri.* 1949, p. 558; *Ill. Rev. Stats.,* 127 § 63r 1–12, 1967.
Missouri-Illinois Bi-State Development Compact, Amended. *Pub. Law* 86–303, 73 *U.S. Stat.* 582, 1959.
Missouri-Illinois-Jefferson-Monroe Bridge Compact. *Ill. Rev. Stats.,* 1965, 127 § 63s–31 et seq.
New York Port Authority Act. 42 *U.S. Stat.* 174–80, 1922; 42 *U.S. Stat.* 822–26, 1922.
Southwestern Illinois Metropolitan Area Planning Commission Act. *Laws,* 1963, p. 1619; *Ill. Rev. Stats.,* 34 § 3091–1.
Treaty—Great Britain: January 11, 1909. 36 *Stat.* 2448, *T.S.* No. 548.
U.S. Constitution Annotated, Art I, sec. 10, cl. 3.
The Wabash Valley Interstate Compact. *Ill. Rev. Stats.,* 1965; 127 § 63t–1 to 63t–3; *Pub. Law* 86–375; 73 *U.S. Stat.* 694, 1959.

INDEX